THE GLOBALIZATION
OF
THEOLOGICAL EDUCATION

THE GLOBALIZATION
OF
THEOLOGICAL EDUCATION

Alice Frazer Evans
Robert A. Evans
David A. Roozen
Editors

ORBIS BOOKS

Maryknoll, New York 10545

The Catholic Foreign Mission Society of America (Maryknoll) recruits and trains people for overseas missionary service. Through Orbis Books, Maryknoll aims to foster the international dialogue that is essential to mission. The books published, however, reflect the opinions of their authors and are not meant to represent the official position of the society.

Library of Congress Cataloging-in-Publication Data

The Globalization of theological education / Alice Frazer Evans,
    Robert A. Evans, David A. Roozen, editors.
        p. cm.
    Includes bibliographical references and index.
    ISBN 0-88344-918-8
    1. Theology—Study and teaching. 2. Christianity and culture.
3. Missions—Theory. 4. Christian union. I. Evans, Alice F.,
1939- . II. Evans, Robert A., 1937- . III. Roozen, David A.
BV4022.G57   1993
207—dc20   93-24374
                                                    CIP

This book is dedicated to
partners throughout God's creation
who have shared with us
their hospitality, their courage, their vulnerability,
their wisdom, and their faith

CONTENTS

CASE AUTHORS

Erskine Clarke, Columbia Theological Seminary
Gordon Dicker, United Theological Seminary, Australia

Alice Frazer Evans, Plowshares Institute
Robert A. Evans, Plowshares Institute
Liso Jafta, Rhodes University, South Africa
G. Douglass Lewis, Wesley Theological Seminary
James N. Pankratz, Concord College, Canada
Anne Reissner, Maryknoll School of Theology
Robert L. Stivers, Pacific Lutheran University
Richard F. Vieth, Lancaster Theological Seminary
Ronald C. White, Huntington Library and University of Southern California

FOREWORDS

I

WALTER BRUEGGEMANN

It is because Christian faith and Christian ministry are inescapably linked to real life that globalization presses upon us. As is often the case, the defining pressures of theological education are not initiated by theological schools or generated by the church. They are rather emergents in the life of culture where the church and its theological schools find their rightful habitat.

So it is with globalization. The emerging accent is nothing that churches or seminaries have decided about (beyond a pervasive and enduring horizon for mission) or even voted upon. The theme is rather a deep and massive redefinition of larger patterns of social relations, a theme that is complex in its origin and mind-boggling in its consequences. This redefinition of social relationships, which touches every phase of public reality and which therefore intrudes into our most intimate sense of self, will inevitably be viewed as a mix of promise and threat. It will therefore be variously understood as God's gift, God's judgment, or not at all work pertaining to God.

Regardless of how globalization is experienced and construed, it is a great new fact of our thinking, believing, knowing context. The process of globalization as it concerns critical theological thought is much like the process whereby we emerge from our tribal realities, peek over the top of the hill, and discover in the next valley people who are also "doing it" ("it" being theology.) They do it partly the way we do, partly differently from us. We notice at a glance that we are not the only ones doing it, that others who do it differently may be doing it effectively and faithfully, and that our way of doing it is not the only way and may not be the best way. As we watch the people in the next valley do their theological work, we may over time modify our ways of doing it in light of what we see over there.

It is no wonder, given the stunning experience of peeking over the hill into the next valley, that we have great and unsettled questions about what all of this means and how we should respond, what we should appropriate of the new reality, and how much we should be open to change. These essays reflect not only our bewilderment, but also a rich offer of bold and inventive responses to the challenge that is globalization. Given the great new fact of globalization, we will live with uncertainty and a multiplicity of definitions and strategies for a long time to come. These essays, however, not only reflect some bewilderment. h ;y are also evidence of a deep and common resolve that fidelity to the theological task entails a serious, sustained, and intentional response to the new situation in which God has placed us.

Given that bewilderment and that resolve, one can only express profound gratitude for the largeness of spirit and the care of thought that are here mustered to our common benefit. I am especially impressed that these essays in their candor do not stay at the level of intellectual generalization, but regularly focus on concrete practice where matters are never as clean, settled, or unambiguous as our generalizations had seemed. In these several concrete practices, albeit done with some misgiving, we are witnesses to a major revision of categories for theological education.

Most of us who teach in theological schools seek to be bilingual as we live in both church and academy. It will no doubt be the case that globalization stretches the horizon of the church to see how we are a part of a large ecumenical enterprise, that the "household" is not limited to our smaller national or denominational horizon. Specifically, the church in this context will learn in fresh ways that the faithful church in other contexts reads the text of the Bible very differently than we do, congenial as we have become to our undetected and unacknowledged vested interests. Seminarians who engage in these projects will inevitably be different kinds of pastors, perhaps more at home in a variegated theological milieu, no doubt more intentional about the larger shape of the church.

In like manner, the reality of globalization means an exploding diversity in critical study of the Bible. There can already be seen in the Society of Biblical Literature the emergence of modes of scripture study that stand alongside (and not always dependent upon) historical criticism which has long been our preferred approach. Our several cultural contexts teach us that there is more than one way to read a text responsibly. And as the monopoly of our normative ways of reading is challenged or rivalled, we witness changed power relationships even in critical study because new readings and methods come along when readers in the next valley are taken seriously. We are learning, even in the guild, that our accepted ways of reading, so trusted in our valley, are not everywhere else regnant.

In both church and academy there is a prospect of transformation, not a grudging act of repentance, but a welcome change that lets us in the church be more faithful and in the academy invites us to more effective readings. We do not know the outcome of these changes, but they are, without our seeing the outcome, powerfully underway.

I welcome these essays as materials for a new conversation, and I imagine an emerging baseline for a new consensus for our future work. As we anticipate that through "immersions" students will have a loop of critical feedback on their own preferred ideological commitments, so also faculties and theological schools are thereby invited to a fresh self-discernment which may in turn produce fresh missional energy. Even if we do not yet see the future shapes of our work in theological education, these essays make clear that there will be no more "business as usual." No more "business as usual" is not the same as "all things new." No more "business as usual" nonetheless may be a marker on the way to a more faithful enactment of our vocation in theological education.

II

DANIEL J. HARRINGTON

I have been associated with *New Testament Abstracts* since 1963 and have been its general editor since 1972. We summarize about 1700 articles and 750 books a year. Every day I see biblical and theological journals from all over the world and written in many languages. In addition to my professional interest in biblical interpretation, I maintain an amateur fascination with religious sociology. I have long been interested in the social location of the biblical interpreter.

My participation in the Pilot Immersion Project's travel seminar in the Philippines, China, and Hong Kong in May-June 1991 enabled me to meet professors of Scripture and other religious people in societies that had been quite distant from me. I regularly see a few journalists from the Philippines and Hong Kong, but on our trip I experienced first-hand the great love for the Bible that unites Christians all over the world. I heard (to my delight) that a chief complaint of Chinese Protestant ministers and church workers was that they had not taken enough Bible courses during their seminary studies. A Filipino Catholic professor of Old Testament showed me how he uses his biblical training to help theological students insert themselves among the poor and share in developing the theology of struggle. I learned from Chinese professors of New Testament how the Scriptures sustained them during the sufferings of the Cultural Revolution, how they are trying to develop an indigenous Chinese Christianity with John's Gospel as a focus, and how the "household codes" of the New Testament fit with traditional Chinese social values.

From these and other conversations I came away with a fresh perspective on what I knew from my reading. The social location of the biblical interpreter is an essential element in hermeneutics. The Scriptures are basically the same for all Christians, but what may seem most important in them differs for Filipinos (in an overwhelmingly Christian country in constant political turmoil, with a shaky cultural identity) and Chinese (one per cent Christian, under tight political control, with a strong national identity).

The context of the interpreter does affect how a biblical text is read. Affirmation of this principle has made me more explicitly and unashamedly pastoral in teaching. Having seen how Scripture looks different in different social settings, I feel more obliged to show my students how to actualize Scripture in a North American context. I hope also to make students more sympathetic to the minority status of early Christians in the Greco-Roman world in light of the experiences of Chinese Christians today. Exposure to the terrible poverty in the Philippines brought alive for me (and my congregations, I hope) the letter of James in a series of sermons shortly after my return.

The essays and case studies in this volume demonstrate that globalization is an important perspective in theology today. A global perspective can help all Christians and other people recognize the wonderful vitality and richness of the move-ment begun when "the Word became flesh and lived among us" (John 1:14).

III

GARTH M. ROSELL

As we joined in worship, the sounds of Calcutta's streets drifted noisily through open windows to mingle with the quiet prayers of those who had gathered. Against the far wall, surrounded by her beloved Missionaries of Charity, sat Mother Teresa, a woman whose very name has become synonymous with Christian compassion and service. The India Immersion Team, of which I was privileged to be a part, had seen firsthand some of the remarkable ministries to which these dedicated missionaries had given their lives. It was not until we worshipped together, how-ever, that I came to appreciate fully the profoundly spiritual base of their joyful service. "Our work," as Mother Teresa has said, "is only the expression of the love we have for God. In the slums we are the light of God's kindness to the poor."

Mother Teresa's life and work, like those of many who have preceded her, stand as eloquent reminders of the urgency of reaching out (sometimes across traditional boundaries) to a broken world. Such reminders, I am convinced, are especially needed within the theological seminaries of North America. In an age of privatization and institutional insularity, it seems especially important that we learn how to move beyond our relatively isolated, homogeneous, and parochial structures in order to engage the global realities beyond our gates. If we are to be faithful to the commission which Christ gave us, we must discover how to build bridges more effectively to distant shores and how to join hands with unfamiliar partners. Insularity, by its very nature, seems to be inimical to the Gospel. Perhaps what we need is something similar to the Apostle Peter's vision in Acts 10 — the sort of paradigm shift which enabled the early Christian communities to recognize that the Good News which they proclaimed was intended to bless people of every nation, race, gender, and class. For me, such a shift became more clearly visible in India. Since I returned home, the experience has continued to transform many of the ways in which I think, teach, and live.

My experience is not unique. During the past decade, an interest in globali-zation has been growing within many of the member institutions of the Association of Theological Schools in the United States and Canada. A number of articles on the subject appeared in *Theological Education*, and a special committee has been established to help give impetus and direction to this increasingly important area. Furthermore, during the past five years twelve of our schools have been involved in the Pilot Immersion Project for the Globalization of Theological Education. Participation in the project has begun to reshape both individuals and institutions. While it is still too early for a full assessment, the Pilot Immersion Project may represent one of those rare moments in theological education when fundamental change actually takes place.

Whether or not this change occurs, there can be little question that these important initiatives, along with others, are helping theological educators to rethink how and why they are doing their work. These initiatives are also helping to remind us that genuine excellence in theological education seems to require that theological schools seek to overcome the kind of cultural captivity which can effectively cut them off from major segments of the world. As one who has served both as an academic dean and as a member of a teaching faculty, I am grateful for the practical encouragement which globalization programs have provided to help me develop a more genuinely global perspective. As a church historian, I have long been aware of my tendency to focus almost exclusive attention upon Western traditions. Now, however, I find that the scope of my reading, the shape of my courses, and even the listings in my bibliographies have expanded to become increasingly global.

Much, of course, remains to be done—both individually and institutionally. Concerns about what effect the adoption of a more global vision might have on already beleaguered institutional faculties and budgets should be addressed. Questions about the nature and meaning of globalization itself must be answered. Discussions about how such interests might affect the mission of individual schools should be held. Given this ongoing agenda, I am grateful that our editors have given us this new volume, written from diverse perspectives and focusing on a variety of themes, to help us in our important task. The book has been designed not so much to offer conclusions as to encourage fresh discussion and discovery.

IV

BARBARA BROWN ZIKMUND

When I moved from Chicago to California in 1980 it was a new adventure. I told my friends that I was moving to the West Coast. As the years passed and I embraced the challenges of theological education in California, I realized that I had not moved to the West Coast; I had moved to the eastern shore of the Pacific ocean. This shift in my consciousness reflects several things.

First of all, it witnesses to the diversity of California. California is, as one historian puts it, a place where the world rushed in. From its beginnings diverse peoples made California a remarkable mixture of humanity and ideas. Today the dominance of persons from the Pacific region in California forces all scholars schooled in the legacies of Western civilization to wake up to the fact that 55 percent of the world's population lives in Asia.

Second, it highlights the fact that during the past few decades all of us involved in theological education have gone through a "consciousness raising" cycle, moving into and out of various types of self-awareness. Faculty, students, administrators, trustees, alumni/ae and supporters of theological seminaries have been pushed to define themselves against a broader and more diffuse landscape. For example, in the 1960s I defined myself as a Congregationalist, rather than a Methodist or a

Presbyterian. In the 1970s I spoke of myself as a Protestant, someone to be distinguished from a Roman Catholic. In the 1980s I often identified myself as a liberal, contrasting my stance with more conservative and evangelical interpretations of theology and education. And now as we move into the 1990s, I am coming to a new awareness of myself as a Christian, in a world of increasing religious diversity and in a world which challenges the viability of religious commitment itself.

In the early 1980s I travelled to Asia, meeting with church leaders and visiting theological schools in Hong Kong, Taiwan, Japan and the Philippines. In those contexts I became increasingly aware of the fact that global forces affect everyone in the world, calling us to find our own voice against the overpowering force of global media. In those contexts I also found resistance to my sometimes naive enthusiasm about globalization. Why?

The power of global communications and economies is overwhelming, impinging uncomfortably upon local values and traditions. It is not surprising that leaders of theological education in many settings are more concerned about contextualization than globalization. They are aware that faith development and effective spiritual leadership must be rooted in the personal and the humane traditions of local cultures, not in global images promoted by the media borrowed from American and European societies. Globalization raises appreciation for the local context, even as it stretches traditions to change and expand.

I have been president of Hartford Seminary since 1990. Earlier in this century the Kennedy School of Missions at Hartford Seminary was a leader in mission education, training missionaries who spread out around the world sponsored by the large Protestant mission boards. Dozens of our graduates are still working in ministry settings outside of North America.

Today, however, the Seminary no longer offers a degree leading to ordination. Its programs seek to maintain a crucial balance between the local and the global, and between the traditional and the intensive. Our Doctor of Ministry program focuses upon the congregation, the local community of faith where people find basic support for their religious commitment. Our Master of Arts program in Islam and Christian-Muslim relations stretches students beyond their Christian roots to appreciate the rich insights of Islam. We have traditional courses meeting once a week, and we teach in intensive modules five times a semester or during summer session.

We have responded to the globalization with a new purpose statement which begins: "Hartford Seminary is an educational institution seeking to serve God by supporting faithful living in a multi-faith and pluralistic world." We are committed to the importance of faithfulness. We are convinced that faith finds its meaning in living. And we are keenly aware that we do all that we do in a multi-faith and pluralistic world. In programs and research we seek to support faithful living, without sacrificing or compromising our faith.

Not all theological schools choose to embrace the globalization agenda so broadly. All of theological education, however, is being shaped and reshaped by the issues highlighted in this book. I find this an exciting collection of materials for two reasons.

First, there is an effort to sustain a healthy tension between the global and the local. All faithful living is grounded in a particular context, shaped by language and culture. Quality education must cultivate a global consciousness, without ignoring the power of tradition.

Second, there is an openness to diverse methodological approaches. The decision to explore such a variety of themes through essays, cases and commentary highlights the journey, rather than the destination. Quality theological education needs to explore diverse methods suitable to diverse contexts.

Over the past decade I have been involved with global theological education through the World Council of Churches. At present I serve as the Association of Theological Schools (ATS) representative to the World Conference of Associations of Theological Institutions (WOCATI). I have learned a great deal from my colleagues in these organizations.

Recently I participated in a week-long Outward Bound experience in Colorado. In new environments, whether they are cultural or physical, our capacity to see ourselves in a new way and our receptivity to new ideas and tasks expands. This happens for several reasons. We become more self-conscious about our own strengths and weaknesses. I had never done any serious hiking or rock climbing. I felt like a fool. And yet when the day was over and I had actually climbed to the top of a 100 foot cliff, I *knew* more. I knew more about myself and my colleagues in the class. In these situations we discover that we depend upon others, that we are inter-dependent. In fact it is impossible to climb the rock without supportive help from those holding the ropes at the top. We discover that we are vulnerable.

I know that when I have new experiences which stretch my mind, my habits and my body, I change. As an educator I am convinced that North American theological education is discovering new implications for biblical and theological traditions in its encounter with the global "other." Globalization is not far away. It comes near when people are stretched as individuals and in institutions to look at things differently and to live with new realities, even for a very short intensive time. God does not require great trees to make a difference; consider the mustard seed.

INTRODUCTION

DAVID A. ROOZEN, ALICE FRAZER EVANS, and ROBERT A. EVANS

When the day of Pentecost had come, they were all together in one place. And suddenly from heaven there came a sound like the rush of a violent wind, and it filled the entire house where they were sitting. Divided tongues, as of fire, appeared among them, and a tongue rested on each of them. . . . And at this sound the crowd gathered and was bewildered, because each one heard them speaking in the native language of each. Amazed and astonished, they asked, "Are not all these who are speaking Galileans? And how is it that we hear, each of us, in our own native language? Parthians, Medes, Elamites, and residents of Mesopotamia, Judea and Cappadocia, Pontus and Asia, Phrygia and Pamphylia, Egypt and the parts of Libya belonging to Cyrene, and visitors from Rome, both Jews and proselytes. Cretans and Arabs — in our own languages we hear them speaking about God's deeds of power." All were amazed and perplexed, saying to one another, "What does this mean?"

Acts 2: 1-12, NRSV

For the Christian church "globalization" is the late twentieth-century equivalent of Pentecost. To be self-conscious about globalization is to be amazed and perplexed by the growing interdependence of the world's diversity and disparity. To open oneself to globalization is to be confronted with a new reality and to ask, what does this mean?

Globalization is a definitive feature of the modern world. Engaging the challenges and opportunities of globalization, therefore, is not an option for those seeking to live faithfully. We face globalization's challenges and opportunities every day. The only questions are: What do they mean? and What does the Gospel demand in response?

What does it mean when the face of the parish changes?

Father Peter Kravitz leaned forward as the volume of the conversation increased. Sue Johnson asked, "Why should we change when everything has been going well in our parish?" Before she could finish, Ben Riley interjected, "But everything is changing. Like it or not, the neighborhood near the church where I am living is quite different today than even five years ago." Pam Riverton spoke up, "Yes, everything around us is changing, Ben, but I believe the church should be one place where there is some stability."

1

"Father Peter," Ben continued, "you seem to understand the Hispanic culture. What are your thoughts about the proposal to start a Spanish Mass in the fall?"

What does it mean when a seminary student wonders if she can ever go home again?

The question for Dalton DuBose—it was enough to trouble her sleep—was what was she going to do when she graduated from seminary. Her question about life after seminary was complicated by her life before seminary as a child of affluence and by a three-week January immersion course/experience in Central America, required by her seminary of all M.Div. students. Was she to push away from Central America to home, to forget what she had heard and seen in Central America, to repress the questions that had been raised, and continue to live a life marked by kindness and acceptance of civic responsibilities? Or was she to abandon the road that led smoothly from her past, from her home and place, give up the assumptions about the nature of the U.S. and her place in it, and adopt some radical—God knows what—ministry in solidarity with the poor? Or was there some middle way, some way to avoid extremes? The closer she came to graduation, the more she wondered why the seminary had put her in such a situation. Was it fair or right to require such a course of her? Was the course intended to do anything more than produce "liberal guilt" in her? Or did the seminary, with its growing endowment, really expect her to make radical changes and become alienated from her family and the congregation that had nurtured her? She didn't see any of her professors doing that. So, at night she had trouble sleeping.

What does it mean when Western education sets an international student apart from his or her people?

Rev. Aimes was noticeably upset about a conversation he had just had with Anthony—a young pastor thinking about leaving the ministry. "George, if I've said it once," he asserted to the president of a major Protestant denomination in Jamaica, "I've said it a thousand times. It's a mistake to allow our young seminarians to go overseas with our support and blessings. Needless to say, I appreciate the kind of academic education they receive there. But once they have been exposed to the stimulation of a highly technical culture and the creature comforts that our churches simply can't afford, then we've lost them for an effective ministry here on the island. . . . They can no longer relate to the needs of their own people. I think we ought seriously to consider not letting any more of our young people study abroad."

What does it mean to let the world teach us a passion for justice?

How would Joe Seramane teach this course? What would he say? Where would he begin? Mike Reardon sat with his class notes before him as he prepared to teach the fundamental moral theology course, a course that he had taught many times in his nine years on the faculty. Once again he found himself reflecting on the story of Joe Seramane. It was a story that had haunted him since his return from South Africa. The man, the story and the questions were as present to him on this cold snowy evening in Minneapolis as they had been that August evening in Johannesburg. Mike knew that he could not teach any of his courses in the same way as he had taught them before South Africa. As he began to rethink the fundamentals course, he struggled to name just how it would be different. In the past he had taught that good moral action is grounded in community and not in an individualistic misuse of human freedom. That was still fundamental. But he suspected that in the past he had taught the course in a disembodied way. He began to recognize that he, himself, had moved from being aware of justice to having passion for justice. But, how do you teach this? How would Joe Seramane or the people of Soweto teach this course? What would they say to us?

What does it mean to honor differences in making globalization integral to a theological curriculum?

"The problem," Bill Jones said, his voice rising in anger, "is you want the tail to wag the dog. Biblical studies, not a globalization program, is the heart of a theological curriculum." Joel Simons listened to his friend and colleague and could feel his own face begin to flush with anger. For Joel, Bill represented a primary challenge to globalization, for he had a conservative counter-vision that was deeply rooted in theological education in the United States. At the heart of this counter-vision was a defense of the West and an insistence on the universal validity of Western theological traditions. Bill had stated on more than one occasion that Joel had developed an ideological agenda and that the globalization program was an expression of that agenda. The agenda, as Bill interpreted it, was to subvert the theological traditions and through them the cultural assumptions of the West. Joel tried once again to explain, but he and Bill seemed to have ex-communicated one another. Each seemed to be speaking a language the other could not understand.

What does it mean for a seminary to make choices in a world of options?

President Robert Lyman sat in his office wondering about globalization and its ramification for Fort Worth Seminary. In moments like this, he felt as though globalization had gone wild! Everyone at the seminary talked about globalization but meant different things by it. Each group that returned from an immersion trip had a new project or issue to push. President Lyman wondered: "Is there no end to globalization? Will its continuing demands and its potentially divisive character sink the ship or at least divide the crew so that it tries to sail off in all directions at once?"

An Invitation to Engagement and Transformation

Globalization is the escalating reality of a growing and increasingly interdependent global population. It is also, as evident in the above excerpts from several of the case studies in this volume, the escalating reality of polarization by ideology, nationalism and the skewed distribution of global resources in which the extremes of affluence and poverty coexist. Globalization discloses a world in which alienation from God, neighbor and self can no longer be masked by consumption or ideology. Globalization reveals an international community in which oppression, loss of freedom (sometimes in the name of freedom) and exploitation weaken any pretense of the commonality of humankind. Nevertheless, globalization is also, although all too infrequently acknowledged, the occasion of amazing transformation and reconciliation.

Globalization of theological education — as the phrase is used in this book — is the church's response in the training and nurture of its leadership to the challenges and opportunities of globalization. In the context of North American theological education — the primary focus of this book — globalization shapes an emerging response: an awareness moving toward embodiment in new forms of preparation for ministry; a crest of circling issues and questions in search of defining paths; and a diverse array of experimental and pilot programs and projects. It is an urgent process of engagement and discovery to which this book is an invitation to all those concerned with the educational ministry of the church. *What does it mean to minister faithfully and effectively within the new reality of global interdependence and polarization? How does one prepare leaders for building up a Church able and willing to respond to the challenge of global witness and service?*

The invitation to engage such questions is also an invitation to transformation. There is a consensus among the contributors to this book that the intensity and pace of social, technological, economic, geo-political and ideological developments and confrontations, and the empowered and impassioned voices of marginalized Christians and other peoples around the world demand of the North American church radically new ways of discerning and responding to the Spirit. Indeed, there is a consensus among contributors to this book that the new understanding demanded by the new global context requires nothing short of a conversion in the thinking of most who minister in North America, including theological educators, and calls for a transformation of the ethos and structure of the institutions through which they minister, including seminaries. And, there appears to be agreement among the contributors to this book that the conversion/transformation requires, as a point of departure, the confession of nearly 2,000 years of accelerating ethnocentrism within the dominant (and dominating) ecclesiastical, intellectual and educational perspectives and structures of Christendom, an ethnocentrism fueled by an uncritical alliance with the hegemonic proclivities of Western culture.

Voices and movements of protest against the captivity of Christendom's dominant ecclesiastical structures to Western culture are not, of course, a new phenomenon. However, the new global reality of the late twentieth century makes the concern unavoidably urgent. The call for a biblically-based global vision is evident in declarations from such broadly representative Christian assemblies, as Geneva, Lausanne and Rome.

We are deeply stirred by what God is doing in our day, moved to penitence by our failures. . . . We believe the gospel is God's good news for the whole world. . . .

The message of the Bible is addressed to all. . . . [The Holy Spirit] illuminates the minds of God's people in every culture to perceive its truth freshly through their own eyes and thus discloses to the whole church ever more of the many-colored wisdom of God.

We need to break out of our ecclesiastical ghettos. . . . World evangelization requires the whole church to take the whole gospel to the whole world. . . . The church is the community of God's people rather than an institution, and must not be identified with any particular culture, social or political system or human ideology.

Lausanne Covenant
International Congress on World Evangelization
Lausanne, Switzerland, 1974

Within the Association of Theological Schools (ATS) in North America, awareness of the new global context crystallized under the banner of globalization during the early 1980s. The Association's Committee on Global Theological Education responded with appropriate boldness:

> The leadership of the Association is convinced that globalization represents a highly significant issue that must be seriously addressed. Globalization is a complex concept involving content and structure, "a prismatic combination of human relationships, ways of thinking, ways of learning, and ways of Christian living." Minimally it involves escaping from ignorance and provincialism; in its most serious consideration it involves us in questions regarding the church's mission to the entire inhabited world.[1]

Through a series of discussions and votes at biennial meetings in the late 1980s, the entire Association endorsed the Committee's urging by designating the 1990s as a priority decade for the globalization of theological education, and by adopting a globalization standard for the accreditation of all member institutions. Neither the accreditation standard nor the designation of priority, however, specified in any detail what globalization was or what a globalized theological education would entail. Rather, in respect for the emergent nature of responses to globalization the priority and standard were set forth as mandates to the Association's member schools to engage in a process of individual and mutual discovery. *How can a seminary change the way it teaches in light of the ultimate goal of enabling the Church to be more faithful in an increasingly interdependent world?*

Theological faculties, administrations and boards of trustees must come to terms with the ATS charge. They have over a decade of theological reflection, personal struggle and programmatic experimentation to draw upon. Nevertheless, there has been no prior attempt to pull together these diverse efforts, experiences and questions into a single, comprehensive introductory reference. That is the purpose of this book. As such it is both reflective of and deeply indebted to those growing numbers of scholars, schools, projects, parishes and students which have already invested themselves in the process of discovery. Many projects were in concert with the work of the ATS Committee on Global Theological Education and its successor, the Task Force on Globalization.

Contributing authors to this volume were selected on the basis of their sustained involvement in the globalization efforts of the past decade — as leaders either in their disciplines or individual schools, or as international dialogue partners with North American colleagues. Invitations were extended not only to cover a wide spectrum of substantive and programmatic themes, but also to represent a broad matrix of diverse constituents including, in particular, theological orientation, gender, race and relationship to and within North American seminaries. Given our personal commitments to the inclusion of all of God's people, we regret and confess that while a broad range of voices are indeed present in the book, we and all of North American theological education remain challenged to give more prominence to those we have historically marginalized.

On first thought, this book might appear to be written exclusively for seminary faculties, leaders and students. It is not. It is for all who grapple with faithful living in the modern world in service of church institutions — whether seminaries, colleges, parochial schools, denominations, ecumenical organizations or congregations. We especially hope it will be useful to pastors and laity concerned about the educational ministry of their congregations. Many laity have greater exposure to the everyday realities of globalization than do theological faculties. And, while much of the book focuses on seminaries as educational institutions, the principles which underlie the issues and proposals are also applicable to the renewal of the educational ministry of congregations. Since a major task of seminaries is the preparation of parish leaders, congregational and denominational leaders are a necessary dialogue partner with seminaries regarding the content and structure of that preparation.

Although reflective of past work on the globalization of theological education, the book is not a historical summary of it or a report on any specific or series of globalization projects. Rather, the book is organized thematically, drawing broadly on the issues and insights, questions and dilemmas, and successes and failures encountered in the previous work. Nevertheless, many of the contributions use the Pilot Immersion Project for the Globalization of Theological Education in North America (PIP/GTE) as a primary experiential point of reference. A brief description of this project at the outset, therefore, will be helpful background for the reader. A more detailed description of the structure of the project is contained in the Roozen essay in Chapter 11.

The PIP/GTE is a five-year effort on the part of twelve geographically and theologically diverse seminaries to test a model for making the institutional changes necessary for the global context to become integral to the program and ethos of each institution.[2] The model being tested uses a series of external catalysts to stimulate each participating institution's reflection and action, out of its own distinctive history. The intent of the project is for each participating seminary to articulate its own understanding of globalization and to set forth and begin implementation of an internal strategy of institutional change appropriate to the embodiment of this understanding.

The principal external interventions include: a series of short-term, international, cross-cultural immersion experiences for faculty, administrators, trustees and students; an external consultant with special experience in globalization and institutional change; and seed money to support student global experiences and faculty research. The twelve participating seminaries are grouped into three clusters, with intra-cluster sharing providing an additional source of mutual exchange.

The intentionality and intensity of cluster sharing varies considerably according to the geographic proximity of the clustered institutions.

The international immersion experiences incorporate transformative approaches to education described in, for example, *Pedagogies for the Non-Poor*.[3] Immersions give priority, but are not limited, to a justice perspective on global interdependence. Immersions are mutually designed by local hosts in the international settings visited and are typically three weeks in duration. Host designs for sharing their local reality invariably involve encounters with representatives of diverse perspectives on the principal issues in the host society. These voices range from those of senior government and church officials to dissidents to analysts from the religious, business, academic and government sectors of society. Home visits in rural and urban areas are important components as are regular sessions of reflection and worship with the local hosts.

Each school participates with its cluster partners in three international immersions during the project—one each to Africa, Asia and Latin America. A different team of six to eight faculty, administrators, trustees and students from each school goes on each immersion, such that by the conclusion of the third international immersion as many as twenty-four persons from each seminary will have participated. Each participant agrees to a covenant of preparation which includes readings and orientation meetings, and a covenant of participation to live simply under local conditions as arranged by the local hosts. Individuals and institutional teams also agree to a third covenant of application. This is a declaration of how learnings from the experience will be applied upon participants' return home. Participants respond in terms of their roles as individuals, as members of their institution and as citizens. Covenant partners are selected to support and hold one another accountable for individual and institutional covenants of application.

A seminary's immersions are spaced at roughly one-year intervals, and coordinated with a similar, iterative cycle of institutional assessment and planning concerning the articulation and embodiment of changes in the seminary's program and structure. The "at home" work is coordinated by an internal steering committee, chaired by a coordinator who is a faculty member or administrator ordinarily provided release time from normal responsibilities.[4] In addition to institutional planning, the steering committee has the responsibility for "at home" preparation for and debriefing of the international immersions, building linkages between immersion teams, mutual exchange with cluster partners, supporting individual and team research and experimentation, and developing expressions of mutuality with international hosts to the school's international immersion experiences.

A seminary's internal project steering committee also has responsibility for designing and implementing a cross-cultural, local (i.e., North American) immersion for the school's faculty, administration, trustees and students. The intent of the local immersion is three-fold: first, to develop relationships with ministries to/ of marginalized urban and rural communities in North America; second, to provide each seminary with the opportunity to employ and adapt the transformative pedagogy modeled in the international immersions; and third, to expand the number of persons from the seminary who shared the common experience of a project immersion.

The work of a seminary's project steering committee is assisted by an external consultant, assigned to the school by the national project staff. The Plowshares Institute, staffed by Alice and Robert Evans and Hugh McLean, serves as the national coordinating body for the project. Plowshares staff worked in cooperation with a variety of international hosts to design and direct the international immersions. Major funding for the project has been provided by the PEW Charitable Trusts. PEW funding is supplemented by an annual contribution from each school, a contribution from each international immersion participant, and a grant from the Lilly Endowment, Inc. to support formative and summative evaluation of the project. David Roozen is coordinator of the Lilly Endowment funded evaluation and research.[5] William Kennedy serves as coordinator of the national team of consultants.[6]

The PIP/GTE confirms the experience of other sustained efforts toward the globalization of theological education in North America.[7] Intentionally opening oneself to the "other" within the diversity and disparity of the whole inhabited world is unsettling, to say the least. When oriented toward fundamental institutional change, opening oneself to the "other" typically moves through deepening cycles of resistance and enthusiasm as a program's heightening visibility draws more voices into the discussion and the implications of the transformation required become more clear. There are many good reasons to be skeptical about the possibility of a seminary (or a congregation or a denomination) changing itself. Nevertheless, the Gospel and the new global context demand it. The experience of the PIP/GTE and others suggests that while institutional transformation is difficult, and while change is costly in terms of resources, time and commitment, change is possible. Few if any of the seminaries currently engaged in the process of globalizing their vision and program would claim that they have been transformed. But many are confident that they are in the midst of transformation. This book is an invitation to share in their experience.

Structure of the Book

Globalization is a complex process involving, as the ATS Committee on Global Theological Education correctly perceived, both content and structure, both understanding and embodiment. Correspondingly, this book is divided into two major sections. The first deals with the diversity of emergent meanings given to globalization in the context of theological education. The second section deals with the implications for embodying the emergent understandings in our theological disciplines, educational pedagogy, and institutional planning and change.

Each of the two major sections contains six chapters, each dealing with a different dimension or theme. Each chapter includes three components: a foundational orientation (essay), a problem-posing case study, and a commentary on the case study. The essays are basic intellectual fare for theological educators. They provide an overview of past thinking and emerging perspectives related to their respective themes, filtered through each author's critical point of view.

The case studies present a very different, but complementary, approach to learning and reflection. They are descriptions of actual situations as seen by a writer through the eyes of a participant. The situations focus on a decision to be made which is left sufficiently open in the case to allow the reader to enter the process of decision making. The cases provide vicarious experiences that expose the reader to the conflicts, questions and genuine dilemmas of the situations, which, in turn, invite the creative application and testing of the insights and resources of tradition and theory (e.g., of the material in the essay) and the reader's own past experience.

Cases can be extremely useful for inducing reflection by an individual reader. A commentary follows each case in this book to further such reflection. While the cases are intentionally open-ended, the commentaries represent the specific points of view of experienced scholars and practitioners in the creative application of tradition, theory, and personal experience. Cases also work well for group discussion. The open-ended nature of the case situations call on group participants to listen to one another, to challenge their own and others' perceptions, and to build on one another's insights. There is tremendous potential in a good case discussion for developing skills of mutuality and building trust in a group of colearners. A "teaching note" is appended to each case to facilitate group discussion.[8]

The case studies are all true, although persons and places are disguised to protect their privacy. We extend special thanks and appreciation to those who offered their stories through the cases as an invitation to others to share in and learn from their experience.

We also extend our gratitude to the many contributors to this book, both named and unnamed. A complete list of essayists, case writers and commentators, including institutional affiliation, can be found at the conclusion of the book. A broad sampling of the growing numbers of church and community leaders, scholars, schools, projects and parishes which have already invested themselves in the process of discovery represented in the globalization of theological education can be found in the endnotes to essays and commentaries.

But even this represents only a small portion of those to whom we and readers owe thanks for their persistence in facing the amazement and perplexity, the opportunities and challenges of the globalization of theological educators. We especially include here all those who have shared with us personally in the Pilot Immersion Project—international immersion hosts and dialogue partners; local immersion coordinators, hosts and dialogue partners; seminary steering committee coordinators, faculty, administrators, trustees and students; consultants; theological reflectors; advisory committee members; church leaders; ATS staff; and foundation program officers.

And finally, for their own amazing persistence, patience and steadfastness in working with three at times perplexing and at times perplexed editors, our deepest thanks to Maralyn R. Lipner, program administrator, Plowshares Institute, and Mary Jane Ross, administrative assistant, Hartford Seminary Center for Social and Religious Research.

Notes

1. David S. Schuller, "Editorial Introduction," *Theological Education*, Volume XXII, Number 2 (Spring, 1986), p. 5.

2. The twelve participating institutions include: Cluster A—Denver Baptist Seminary, University of Dubuque Theological Seminary, Wartburg Theological Seminary and Wesley Theological Seminary; Cluster B—Catholic Theological Union, Lutheran School of Theology at Chicago, Chicago Theological Seminary and McCormick The-

ological Seminary; and, Cluster C—Gordon-Conwell Theological Seminary, Union Theological Seminary (New York), United Theological College (Montreal) and Weston School of Theology.

3. Alice Frazer Evans, Robert A. Evans and William Bean Kennedy (eds.), *Pedagogies For the Non-Poor* (Maryknoll, NY: Orbis Books, 1987). See especially, Chapter 7: "Traveling for Transformation," Chapter 10: "The Ideological Captivity of the Non-Poor," and Chapter 11: "Education for Emancipation: Movement Toward Transformation."

4. School coordinators for the Pilot Immersion Project included: Gary Bekker, Pierre Goldberger, David Hopkins, Robert Hubbard, Yoshira Ishida, Theodore Jennings, Wi Jo Kang, John Kaserow, Richard Lints, Brian McDermott, Heidi Hadsell do Nascimento, Edward O'Flaherty, Larry Rasmussen, Robert Schreiter, David Seotchmer, Graydon Snyder, Walter Smith, Douglas Strong, Susan Thistlethwaite, Janet Walton, Timothy Weber.

5. The program of evaluation and research includes a team of three theological reflectors, which includes Mortimer Arias, M. Shawn Copeland and M. Douglas Meeks.

6. The team of consultants includes Erskine Clarke, Toinette M. Eugene, Heidi Hadsell do Nascimento, Maryann Hedaa, Will L. Herzfeld, Paul G. Hiebert, Joseph Hough, Eleanor Scott Meyers, Garth M. Rosell and Arthur Van Seters.

7. For a description of other seminary-based globalization projects see, for example, *Theological Education*, Spring, 1986 and Spring, 1991. For a description of several non-seminary experiments in globalized, transformative education see, for example, *Pedagogies for the Non-Poor.*

8. These notes are intended to be suggestive, not to imply a best or only way to approach a particular case. General discussions of styles and techniques of case teaching can be found in many casebooks of potential interest to theological educators, including "Practical Hints for Teaching and Learning," pp. 34-42 in Louis and Carolyn Weeks, Robert A. and Alice F. Evans (eds.), *Casebook for Christian Living* (Atlanta: John Knox Press, 1977); "Choosing and Using Case Studies," pp. 145-154 in William R. Cromer (ed.), *Casebook for Youth Ministry* (Nashville: Broadman Press, 1991); "Introduction: Christian Ethics and the Case Method," pp. 1-12 in Robert L. Stivers, et al. (eds.), *Christian Ethics* (Maryknoll, NY: Orbis Books, 1989); "Writing and Teaching Cases," *Journal for the Association for Case Teaching*, Volume 1, Fall 1989, pp. 7-15; and "Models in Case Form," pp. 13-20 in *Pedagogies for the Non-Poor.* Additional information on case teaching workshops and case material is also available through The Association for Case Teaching, P.O. Box 243, Simsbury, CT 06070, (203) 651-4304.

PART ONE

EMERGING MEANINGS
OF GLOBALIZATION

[1]

AN HISTORICAL SURVEY

ESSAY

JUSTO L. GONZÁLEZ and CATHERINE G. GONZÁLEZ

According to the book of Acts, the very first action of the Spirit upon the nascent Christian community was to globalize theology. The account of Pentecost is "interrupted" by a catalogue of nations which the author of Acts has probably borrowed from some ancient list,[1] but whose presence becomes central to the account itself. Indeed, the great "miracle of Pentecost" is that all these people who are gathered from a variety of places, all hear of the "mighty acts of God" in their own tongue. It is the presence of these people that provides the occasion for the miracle, and it is on their behalf that the Spirit intervenes, so that they may hear the message in their own tongues.

Contrary to what is often claimed, the story of Pentecost is not the undoing of the multiplicity of languages stemming from Babel, but rather a demonstration that multiplicity of languages and cultures does not necessarily lead to division and confusion. In Pentecost the multiplicity of human languages is not denied, but rather affirmed. Furthermore, at Pentecost the Holy Spirit shows that all human languages are equally valid for the communication of God's revelation.[2]

According to the witness of the New Testament, the process of globalization begun at Pentecost was not easy. In fact, at least part of the process had begun well before Pentecost, since the Jews who were gathered in Jerusalem from the places listed in the catalogue of nations represented a form of incipient globalization that the earlier exiles had created. That was a beginning the church would build upon, for the wider issue of admission of the Gentiles still lay ahead. Indeed, a major part of the New Testament consists of letters and other documents dealing with the difficult issues arising out of this fuller globalization. How are Jew and Gentile to relate in the church? Under what conditions may Gentiles be added to the people of God? Must male converts be circumcised? Must all keep the dietary laws? What about meat from animals sacrificed to idols?

The answers given to these questions, and to many others like them, varied from time to time and from place to place. Yet one thing was clear: in the church born at Pentecost there must be room for Jew and Gentile, male and female, slave and free.

This was the original meaning of the word "catholic." Although "catholic" is often translated as "universal," there are nuances which such a translation does not reflect. While *universal* underlines unity and singleness, "catholic," which etymologically means "according to the whole" (or "according to all," from *kata* and *holon*) underscores the multiplicity of perspectives on which the totality is based.

In this sense, the formation of the canon of the New Testament was typically "catholic." Over against a number of "heresies," each of which stressed its particular perspective on the Gospel, and many claiming the authority of a single apostle, the church at large decided to put together a collection of four Gospels which, while agreeing on the essential, clearly differed and even contradicted each other. This was not done out of a naive failure to grasp the differences among these various witnesses to the Gospel. On the contrary, it was done out of a keen awareness that these various books looked at the single event of Jesus Christ from four different perspectives, and that it was the multiplicity of these perspectives that made the church "catholic." Together, the Gospel *kata* (according to) Matthew, the Gospel *kata* Mark, the Gospel *kata* Luke, and the Gospel *kata* John made the "catholic" (*kata* [according to] all) Gospel of Jesus Christ.[3]

Significantly, in this entire process, as the early church sought to combat doctrinal error, it did this not so much by seeking uniformity as by seeking a comprehensive multiplicity of perspectives. To the single Gospel of Truth of Valentinus, and to the single expurgated Gospel According to Luke of Marcion, the church at large opposed the fourfold witness to the Gospel of Matthew, Mark, Luke, and John. To the claim on the part of several gnostic teachers that their doctrines were derived from the secret teaching of some apostle, the church at large opposed a doctrine of apostolic succession that, in its original form, emphasized the multiple witness of various apostles. In their earliest forms, both the canon of the New Testament and the doctrine of apostolic succession, rather than signs of closure and exclusivity as they later became, were claims of openness and a multiplicity of perspectives and authorities.

The very existence of the canon of the New Testament, with its differing witnesses to the Gospel and to its meaning, should have sufficed to prevent the church from falling into the trap of confusing catholicity with universal uniformity.

At the same time, there was a clear limit to the sort of diversity that could be offered. The attack upon the various heresies was based upon the fact that they contradicted the "rule of faith" which listed the essentials of the Gospel. Granted there could be great variety in interpreting these statements,[4] but having more than one God, believing that material creation was evil, or denying that Jesus was crucified or raised from the dead were clearly among the items that were out of bounds for "catholic" churches.

Augustine, in his debates with the Donatists in North Africa, constantly draws upon the understanding of the church's catholicity as a necessary characteristic. The Donatists had not only rejected the Roman Catholics in North Africa, but they had also rejected as false churches all those others that recognized the Roman Catholic Bishop of Carthage. This included the Bishop of Rome, but also the churches in the East—in Antioch and Ephesus—who knew nothing about the situation in Africa. Augustine points to the Donatists' rejection of all of these churches, and therefore their claim that they—the Donatists—in this one area of the world, are the only true church. Augustine points to the promises to Abraham, that he would be the father of many nations, that through him all the nations of the earth should be blessed, as proof that the true church must extend through the whole world. The fact that the Donatists have thus cut themselves off from the rest of the church shows that they are not part of the church catholic.[5]

In the midst of the debate about the nature of grace in the Western church that originated in the conflict between Augustine and the followers of Pelagius, Vincent of Lerins wrote his "Commonitory: For the Antiquity and Universality of the Catholic Faith Against the Profane Novelties of all Heresies." This was written about 434, near the time of the death of Augustine. His issue was to show how the catholic faith can be distinguished from heresy. The famous "Vincentian canon" is contained in this essay. It has significance for our current discussion, though it was written to establish that Augustine's reaction to Pelagius contained novel interpretations, and ought not to be considered simply a defense of the church's traditional teaching. Furthermore, those who disagreed with Augustine on the issues of predestination ought not to be considered Pelagian heretics.

In chapter II Vincent gives the "rule" as to what should be held as the tradition: it is "that which has been believed everywhere, always, and by all. For that is truly and in the strictest sense 'Catholic,' which, as the name itself and the reason of the thing declare, comprehends all universally."[6] His intention is to show that what has recently been taught by Augustine (whom he does not mention by name) in North Africa is not "Catholic." What is interesting is that geographical universality is given the first place. The health of the whole is to be preferred to the novelty of one location. After this comes the argument from tradition, that can overcome heresy that has spread throughout a great portion of the current church.

Vincent holds to a certain uniformity in his understanding of catholicity—at least novel doctrines find no sympathy—but at the same time, he has a strong sense that no one portion of the church should be determinative of the theology of the whole. Antiquity is important, but that is not the first source of our evaluation of contemporary opinion.

In terms of globalization, Vincent is an interesting figure. He assumes that there is a core of doctrine that must be uniform, and at the same time, his concern is that new interpretations ought not to be imposed on the whole church by one portion of it. He holds that when we look at the tradition, decisions of councils are to be preferred to the writings of one, precisely because they represent the geographical spread that is essential to the meaning of catholicity. For him, "global," though a term he did not use, would need to take account of the essentials of the faith as expressed in the rule of faith and universal council decrees. New interpretations of but one sector of the church ought not to be made mandatory for the whole. There is a delicate balance between the need for universality and the rights of the particular. The medieval period would see increasing stress on the universal, but with one particular area—Rome in the West and Constantinople in the East, in different ways—imposing what was in reality the interpretation of one region upon the whole church to the extent that its power would permit.

The pressures in the direction of imposed uniformity were many. The very challenge of the "heresies" slowly led the church at large to try to define its faith in terms of uniformity. By the early Middle Ages, the church in Western Europe had also become the guardian of what was left of ancient Roman civilization,[7] and of the unity of an empire that no longer existed. *Romanitas*, which was taken to be the equivalent of civilization, must be preserved, and the church was the main instrument for that preservation. For such a church it was important that there be a single source of authority, a single language, and uniform practices in worship. From this perspective to be "catholic" meant not to have room for a variety of witnesses to a single gospel, but rather to have the sole authorized interpretation of that gospel. Whereas at Pentecost the Spirit had made it possible for people from different lands and cultures to hear of the mighty acts of God in their own tongues, the medieval Western church, faced by invasions from "barbarians," insisted that all must hear and worship God in the same language—the Latin of the empire whose remnants the church now sought to conserve.

This, however, was not the total picture, for there were still those who believed that the church needed the presence and witness of a variety of people, even at a cost to *Romanitas*. Outstanding among them was Paulus Orosius, who expressed his understanding of "globalization" as he commented on the "barbarian" invasions:

> If only to this end have the barbarians been sent within Roman borders, that throughout the East and the West the church of Christ might be filled with Huns and Suevi, with Vandals and Burgundians, with diverse and innumerable peoples of believers, then let God's mercy be praised ... even if this has taken place through our own destruction.[8]

Meanwhile in the East, although there was openness to a variety of languages, and although there was the understanding that in each culture and nation the church should develop its own autocephalic hierarchy, there was a similar insistence that all must believe and worship in exactly the same way and all must express the faith in the same formulae.[9]

There were many factors contributing to this emphasis on uniformity. One was the degree to which the church came to see itself as the preserver and transmitter of ancient culture. This view left very little room for conscious openness to other cultural perspectives. Another factor was the close connection between orthodoxy and social and political acceptability. But behind the emphasis on uniformity lay also an understanding of truth which the church had inherited from ancient philosophy and which saw truth as static, given, unaffected by human circumstances. From that perspective, truth is one, no matter where spoken or by whom, and therefore all must speak with a single voice, or truth itself suffers. Furthermore, since every bit of truth is just as important as any other bit, uniformity must be carried to the last detail of doctrine. Witness for instance the stercoranist controversy,[10] the debate over whether in God essence and attributes are the same,[11] and the bitter polemic in the thirteenth century over the hylomorphic composition of angels.[12]

From this perspective, what makes the church and its doctrine "catholic" is not that it is "according to the whole," not that it reflects the multiplicity of perspectives of the various people whom God has called, but rather that it preserves the one, universally valid truth given in every detail once and for all. (And, if it just so happens that this truth is best expressed in terms that the dominant culture finds most acceptable and comprehensible, this simply proves that said dominant culture has been selected by God as the ideal vehicle for the communication of universal truth.)

The Reformation of the sixteenth century signified little change. True, there was a greater variety of expressions of the faith as the church broke up into various bodies, each expressing the concerns and the culture of a particular region of Europe. There is positive value in this, for finally the German people were able to worship in their own language and with their own music, as did also the Swiss, the English, and the Scots. Yet these various expressions of the faith retained the notion that the faith cannot have different expressions, and therefore felt compelled to reject the others. Thus, although at first there was a sense that all Protestants were united in opposition against "Popery," it soon became evident that the divisions and enmities among Protestants were equally bitter and insidious.

Even without theological battles, the stage was set for national divisions among Protestant churches. Protestantism had developed in a time of clear national identity and bore the marks of that period even as the Roman Catholic Church bore the marks of coming to birth in the midst of the Roman Empire. Protestant churches were generally organized by nations, with national borders being the extent of the organizational structure of the church—a pattern that still holds true today. There could be strong and positive relationships across these borders, particularly within confessional groups such as Lutheran or Calvinist, but the churches were organized nationally. This national division grew less ecumenical and more national as theological study was increasingly in the national language rather than in Latin. This move occurred gradually over several centuries but led to the tendency to limit theological conversation to one's own language.

The breakdown of institutional Catholicism thus resulted in the further abandonment of "catholicity" in the ancient sense. Now each group had *the* truth, and the tendency was to define that truth in ever narrower terms, so that there were ever fewer people who could lay a claim on it. Among Lutherans, there were those who condemned as heretics not only all Catholics and Calvinists, but also any who dared assert that John 6 has anything to do with the eucharist. Among Calvinists, one had to be strictly orthodox, not only with regard to the doctrine of predestination itself, but also with regard to the order of God's decrees of predestination. In England, Protestantism splintered into dozens of groups, each claiming sole ownership of truth. Among Roman Catholics, the pope made a judgment on how "God" was to be translated into Chinese, a language of which he knew nothing.

Significantly, it was during this period that most major churches took steps to determine and supervise the sort of theological education that was to be required for ordination. In earlier times there had been attempts to determine what could and could not be taught at universities, for example, when the teaching of Aristotle was forbidden in Paris.[13] But the Reformation brought the university and its curriculum to the foreground of theological debate. The University of Prague had been the cradle of the Hussite movement. The Wittenberg faculty were the early leaders of Lutheranism. The University of Paris soon became the bulwark of Roman Catholicism. Eventually various brands of Lutheran theology coalesced around the universities of Wittenberg, Jena, Königsberg, and others. Thus the teaching of theology, rather than global, became more and more provincial, and each province claimed that it was the entire oikoumene. On more than one occasion, the various provinces went to war with each other—war that was often justified as a defense of the "universal" or "catholic" truth of the Gospel.

Partly as a result of this situation, new rationalist tendencies gained ground. In a way, these tendencies were a reaction to the endless debates among various theological factions. If it could be proven, as indeed it could be, that much of the debate had to do with matters on which there could be no absolute rational certainty, a more rational order might ensue—an order in which people did not go to war over the manner in which Christ is present in the eucharist, or over whether churches should have bishops or not.

Perhaps, by applying purely rational methods, it might be possible to reach a religious consensus. Such a consensus would be built around a "natural religion" to which all could agree and would leave aside matters that could only be proven by a resort to authority. Instead of arguing about the interpretation of an obscure text of Scripture, so it was hoped, people would come together around the clear dictates of reason.

In this respect, the rationalist program did achieve a measure of success. The sources of authority on which much of the earlier debate was founded were undercut, and as a result many came to the conclusion that the debates themselves were groundless. The debate about the meaning of Jesus' words in John 6, for instance, became irrelevant if after all Jesus never did speak such words.

Rationalism, however, shared a common assumption with the earlier theologies that it sought to discredit and to replace: it too believed that truth and rationality could be determined in purely objective terms, without regard to the social and cultural context of the thinker. Just as Abraham Calov, the fiery proponent of the strictest Lutheran orthodoxy, claimed that his truth was universally valid, so did the rationalists claim that through their methods they could arrive at universally valid truths. And, just as Calov was in fact a proponent of a very particular point of view, so were the Rationalists proponents of a particular point of view—mostly that of the growing European bourgeoisie and of males within that bourgeoisie. There was little or no awareness of how culturally bound such theology really was.

This would change, theoretically more than practically, with the work of Friedrich Schleiermacher. As a reaction to Rationalism and influenced by Romanticism, his theology had a strong stress on the actual living communities of faith that are the means of transmission of any religious orientation from one generation to another. Culture obviously plays a great role in religious orientation. Religious communities are embedded in their culture. One cannot speak of religious teachings without speaking of the historical communities that communicate these teachings. Nor can one equate religion with doctrine alone, but one must include all the nuances and non-rational elements that are communicated by these communities.[14]

One might anticipate from this cultural awareness some attempt at trying to separate European culture from the Gospel. However, that was not the case. Schleiermacher assumed the superiority of Christianity over other world religions, but he also assumed the connectedness of religion to the culture in which it arises. Therefore he connected the superiority of Christianity and the superiority of Western European culture, especially the culture of the Protestant north of Europe.

Schleiermacher displayed the reverse of the Rationalist tendency to ignore the connection of theology and culture. He was quite aware of the relationship, but rather than leading to globalization, his awareness served to strengthen the Europeanization of theology.

Within Europe, he urged the unification of Lutherans and Calvinists on the grounds of their great similarity over against Catholicism, which he viewed as almost a separate religion. One might assume that he probably believed that southern European culture, which was more closely tied to Roman Catholicism, also was distinct and inferior to that of the north. He viewed Judaism as completely separate from Christianity, and the Hebrew Scriptures as an introduction to what is really the Christian Bible—the New Testament. Here, too, he probably believed that Judaism formed a separate and inferior culture.

Schleiermacher was a strong proponent of missions, which he saw as the expansion of both Protestant Christianity and northern European culture. Since both that religion and that culture were superior, their expansion was a service and a duty to the rest of humankind. In other words, Schleiermacher's understanding of missions generally agreed with the "white man's burden" which became the driving force for much of the Protestant missionary enterprise. In that enterprise, the superiority of Western Protestant culture would play the role which miracles had played in the earlier expansion of Christianity:

Christ transmitted to them [the Apostles] the power of working miracles only as a sign to accompany the earliest preaching. Even if it cannot be strictly proved that the Church's power of working miracles has died out (and this the Roman Church denies), yet in general it is undeniable that, in view of the great advantage in power and civilization which the Christian peoples possess over the non-Christian, almost without exception, the preachers of to-day do not need such signs.[15]

It is significant to remember at this juncture that Schleiermacher also proposed a classification of the theological disciplines, and that the influence of his classification may be seen in theological curricula to this day.

While all this was taking place, Christianity was becoming for the first time a truly "universal" religion, at least in the geographic sense. As is well known, both the great Catholic expansion of the sixteenth century and the Protestant expansion of the nineteenth were closely tied with the colonial expansion of European powers. In our post-colonial age we are critical of that connection. Yet it is important to remember that most European Christian leaders, Protestant as well as Catholic, saw that connection as beneficial, not only to missions, but also to the colonized. Both Melanchthon and Calvin, for instance, believed that the work of taking Christianity to foreign lands was the responsibility of civil, rather than ecclesiastical, authorities.

The immediate result of the vast geographical expansions of the sixteenth and nineteenth centuries—the first mostly Catholic, and the second mostly Protestant—was the "universalization" of the church in its various branches, rather than its "globalization." Carbon copies of European Catholicism and of North Atlantic Protestantism appeared throughout the globe. In the Spanish and Portuguese colonies an ecclesiastical hierarchy was established, and converts were given

"Christian" names. In British, Dutch, and German colonies, as well as in places where the economic colonialism of the United States prevailed, Anglican, Methodist, Reformed, and Baptist churches were founded. Eventually, practically every *particular* church in the West became *universal*—witness the existence of a World Reformed Alliance and a World Methodist Council.

Although the best missionary theory declared that the purpose of the missionary enterprise was to found indigenous churches throughout the world, actual practice was far removed from theory. In the best cases, the "younger" churches were expected to become indigenous in what eventually came to be known as the "three selfs": self-support, self-government, and self-propagation. Even the development of those three "selfs" was thwarted by policies that fostered dependence. But, more important, a fourth "self" was hardly ever considered: "self-interpretation," or "self-theologizing." In theory, the "younger" churches were expected to reach a point of maturity where they would be able to govern themselves. But the possibility that they might develop their own theology was hardly ever considered. Western theology was expected to become universal theology.

There were many attempts in the "mission field" to develop an indigenous theology. Among Roman Catholics in Latin America, what is now known as "popular religiosity" combined elements of European Catholicism with traditional native cultures and traditions. For generations such "popular religiosity" was permitted to exist alongside official Catholicism and was even exploited by the hierarchy, but was seldom allowed to make an impact on the official doctrine and statements of the church. Also in Latin America, but now among Protestants, various Pentecostal groups were expelled from the "historic" denominations and were thus free to achieve a greater degree of indigenization—and growth—than their "mother" denominations. In Africa, several indigenous Christian communities arose. For the most part the Western churches refused to recognize them. In China, the early success of the Taiping rebellion, whose origins were deeply influenced by Christianity, did not sit well with Western diplomats and missionaries. Opposition led to extremism, and eventually the entire movement was crushed with the support of Western powers and churches and some twenty million deaths. Significantly, episodes such as the Taiping rebellion are not usually considered part of their discipline by Western historians of the church.

The first point at which it became obvious that the "younger" churches should not be a mere copy or reflection of the old was the ecumenical movement. Denominational divisions which the West took for granted, for they were part of its history, were clearly out of place in Asia or Africa. The Western Protestant missionary leaders themselves saw this, and therefore a series of regional and eventually world conferences were organized. The purpose of these conferences was to promote collaboration, avoid competition, and exchange experiences. Very soon, however, the "younger" churches took the lead in this nascent ecumenical movement and determined to carry it much further than mere collaboration and exchange of ideas and experiences. In the Edinburgh conference in 1910, out of more than a thousand participants, seventeen came from the "younger" churches; by 1928, at the Jerusalem Assembly of the International Missionary Council, more than a quarter of those present came from such churches. The change, however, went far beyond the matter of proportions in representation. The "younger" churches soon took the lead in pointing out the scandal of denominationalism and in taking concrete steps against it. In this regard, they still have the lead. If "globalization" is understood in terms of "catholicity" as discussed above, this means that the "younger" churches are far more "globalized" and "catholic" than their parent bodies. It also means that attempts at "globalization" on the part of schools that take denominationalism as a given and unchangeable premise will necessarily miss much of the value of such attempts.

If the most significant development in the history of Christianity in the nineteenth century was that it became for the first time a truly universal faith, the most significant development of the late twentieth century is that it is rapidly becoming a non-Western faith. "While, in 1900, 49.9 percent of all Christians lived in Europe, by 1985 that number is estimated to be 27.2 percent. And, while in 1900 81.1 percent of all Christians were white, projections are that by the year 2000 that number will be reduced to 39.8 percent."[16] In other words, the center of Christianity has moved away from the North Atlantic and toward the South—what was traditionally called "the mission field."

The shift in numbers of adherents was accompanied by a similar shift in the centers of creative theological activity and innovative pastoral practice. Beginning with the papacy of Pius XI (1922-1939) the number of native bishops from Asia, Africa, and Latin America increased rapidly. Obviously, such bishops were expected to hold the same views as those held in Rome. But the very fact that they labored under very different circumstances tended to nuance their concerns and their theology in different ways. At the Second Vatican Council only 46 percent of all prelates present came from Europe, the United States, and Canada while 42 percent came from Asia, Africa, and Latin America. There is no doubt that the presence of these bishops made a significant impact on the Council and especially on its most creative document, *Gaudium et Spes.*

Meanwhile, similar shifts have taken place among Protestants. Whereas a generation ago it was taken for granted that the most interesting and creative theological work would take place in the universities of the North Atlantic, that is no longer the case. Latin Americans who wish to pursue advanced theological studies are as likely to consider a school in Asia as one in Europe, and the number of Africans and Asians studying theology in Latin America is also increasing rapidly.

The "younger" churches, which took the lead in the Protestant ecumenical movement, and Roman Catholics in Asia, Africa, and Latin America are rapidly taking the lead in dealing with a number of theological issues which will be crucial in the next generation: the relationship between Christianity and culture(s); the social and economic implications of the gospel; the relationship between Christianity and various religious traditions; the role of the church in a post-Constantinian world; and so on. Out of the "younger" churches are coming theological works which the church at large can no longer ignore. The development of these new churches after the Second World War paralleled the end of colonialism, and the rejection of colonialism has an impact on the search for a theological identity. Development occurred also in the context of seeking to address the particular issues that were paramount in these new nations, rather than having the theological agenda set by the North Atlantic churches.

The widening of the dialogue as to the essential issues with which the Christian faith should deal in our time is in itself an increase in catholicity and therefore a decrease in the Europeanization of theology. Such a movement was not limited to the world outside the North Atlantic, however. Paralleling the rise of the new voices in the south and east was the demand to be heard within the North Atlantic area by those who had hitherto not been part of the dominant theology—women and minority ethnic groups, particularly in North America. Beginning in the 1960s, spurred on by the civil rights movement, the African-American churches moved to center stage. Their traditions and their leaders became known to the wider public. The issues which were central to their concerns became increasingly part of the agenda of the churches of the dominant culture. Hispanics also became increasingly vocal, especially as civil wars in Central America led to greater migration to the United States and the churches faced the issues of United States foreign policy regarding Central America. African-American and Latino voices also raised to a more visible level the concerns of the poor in the United States. Native American voices were added to the conversation, with the particular concerns that they represented.

The women's movement, beginning in the 1960s, also raised new elements in the discussion. Since women cut across all classes and groups, there was the potential for a wide variety of new agenda items. The intersections of gender, race, and class have not been easy, however, and there are frequent conflicts as to the central issues the churches should address.

Within the ecumenical movement itself, as well as in theological studies, the different agendas brought by those who have not traditionally been part of the discussion—whether on the basis of culture, race, class, or gender—have meant that the whole matter of what is a legitimate theological issue has itself been questioned. In the traditional world of theological study, the topics were fairly clearly outlined, even when there was great disagreement as to content: the doctrines of God, the Trinity, Christology, sin, redemption, the church, the sacraments, eschatology. These were clearly theological topics. Other issues, such as the situation of the poor, economic and political concerns, oppression on the basis of race or gender, concerns about hunger and child abuse were not really theological concerns per se but rather social concerns that Christians should address. There was a fairly neat division between what were traditionally "faith and order" agendas and what were "church and society" concerns. The new partners in the discussion did not recognize such a division and proposed as significant theological issues areas that were traditionally social ethics topics. The new voices were often dismissed as not really theological or as representing special interests rather than theology. The result has been a major conflict within the seminary and other theological academies.[17]

Though conflicts remain, a theological dialogue has developed which is "catholic" ("according to the whole") to an unprecedented degree. If the great achievement of the nineteenth century was the development of a truly universal church, the great challenge of the twenty-first will be the development of a truly catholic theology. The globalization of theological education is a means to equip students for this unavoidable theological task of their generation.

CASE STUDY[18]

Winning Over the Faculty

"The problem," Bill Jones said, his voice rising in anger, "is you want the tail to wag the dog. Biblical studies, not a globalization program, is the heart of a theological curriculum."

Joel Simons listened to his friend and colleague and could feel his own face begin to flush with anger. The argument—it had been going on for a decade— had been growing in intensity since the faculty of Seabrook Theological Seminary began discussions on a new curriculum. For Joel, who was a professor of ethics, the question was not one of biblical studies versus a globalization program but rather how one understands both the church catholic and the relationship of a theological tradition to its social and cultural context. He tried once again to explain what he understood the program to be about, but he and Bill seemed to have ex-communicated one another. Each seemed to be speaking a language the other could not understand.

Ten years earlier Joel had been asked to oversee the globalization program at Seabrook. A special grant had been awarded the seminary to expand its modest international program that involved bringing a few internationals to the campus each year. Relieved of one teaching course a year in order to administer the program, Joel had become increasingly intrigued by the program's possibilities and its implications for theological education at Seabrook. He had become convinced that a theological community, preparing students in a responsible manner for ministry into the twenty-first century, must seek to integrate into its total life new international perspectives and multicultural experiences. As a result, Joel had begun to work hard to develop a coherent strategy for making globalization something more than an interesting but peripheral concern at the seminary.

At the heart of his strategy was an attempt to nurture, in cooperation with certain key colleagues, a guiding vision of what Seabrook might be with a strong, integrated globalization program. Ed Darby, a former college dean and now dean of faculty at Seabrook, had given Joel some good advice when they talked about such a vision: "If you want the program to fly, the faculty has to be convinced that it is important and that it has academic integrity. If you don't win over the faculty, forget it."

Joel knew that he didn't need to "win over" some faculty members—they were already committed to the idea of such a program, if not to its particulars. Indeed, some of them saw from the beginning implications of globalization for Seabrook that Joel only slowly perceived. Anne Harrison, for example, professor of Old Testament, had spent a sabbatical in Nigeria and had long been an influential voice in the faculty for articulating perspectives and concerns that were informed by that experience. Robert Chastain, a senior member of the faculty and professor of pastoral care, had traveled extensively in Africa and Asia, holding workshops and working with missionaries. He had listened carefully to what African and

Asian church leaders had said to him, and he knew the power of such experiences in his own life and for his understanding of the contextual issues surrounding pastoral care.

But there were other faculty members who were not so much hostile to the concerns of globalization, at least not in the early years of the program, as they were indifferent. They saw no connection between globalization and their own disciplines and did not perceive, at least at first, any challenge to their established perspectives and familiar methods of teaching. Bill was one of these, only he had become increasingly hostile toward both Joel and the program as its hermeneutical and curricular implications became clearer.

For Joel, Bill represented a primary challenge to globalization, for he had a conservative counter-vision that was deeply rooted in theological education in the United States. At the heart of this counter-vision was a defense of the West and an insistence on the universal validity of Western theological traditions. Bill had stated on more than one occasion that Joel had developed an ideological agenda and that the globalization program was an expression of that agenda. The agenda, as Bill interpreted it, was to subvert the theological traditions and through them the cultural assumptions of the West. Globalization was intended to further that agenda by relativizing and contextualizing theological education. "You have become merely ideological," was a frequent complaint Bill made to Joel. Bill had stated more than once that it was possible to have a theology rooted in the Scripture that, while always needing to be corrected by Scripture, was not merely a reflection of a particular social and cultural context but had a transcendent, transcultural quality.

In spite of the growing hostility of Bill and a few others on the faculty, the globalization program had received from its earliest days strong support from the seminary's administration. The president, who had served as a local pastor, had a long history of supporting mission programs. He had worked hard to secure the special grant that got the globalization program off the ground; he believed that theological education ought to "open a window to the world" for students. The dean of faculty saw the program as having the potential to become an important new element in the seminary's life. He had spent a semester in Asia and a term in the Middle East. While Joel experienced the support of the administration from the beginning of the program, he believed such support needed to be solidified. In regard to the trustees, Joel believed they would support the program if the president supported it. But they needed to be a part of developing a vision of a Seabrook with a vigorous globalization program. Moreover, some trustees were suspicious of the term "globalization." What, one trustee asked, did the term mean? He was evidently uncomfortable with its possible political and economic implications.

Joel was convinced that if the faculty was going to enter into serious dialogue about globalization and theological education, as many members of the faculty as possible needed to participate in an intense immersion experience. This became one of Joel's primary objectives. As various opportunities arose for international travel and immersions sponsored by Seabrook, Joel worked hard to see that as many faculty members as possible participated. Through informal conversations and direct invitations by Joel, during the past decade 60 percent of the faculty had participated in a variety of international immersion experiences. Most experiences were in two to three week seminars with Seabrook students. Another 20 percent of the faculty, including many of those who had gone abroad, had also participated in a parallel program of "local immersions" in a nearby inner city area or in a rural setting.

Encouraging the faculty's participation were the enthusiastic reports of students who consistently spoke of their international experiences as being among the most important experiences of their seminary careers. Joel also discovered that reluctant faculty members could be more easily persuaded to go to the Mideast than to a so-called third-world region of Africa, Asia, or Latin America. The results, however, were similar at least in regard to faculty support of the program on return to Seabrook. Joel believed that an immersion experience was one of the most effective ways to develop enthusiasm for the program and to draw faculty members into a constructive conversation about the nature, purposes, and possibilities of globalization. Bill and a few others, however, were never available to participate.

From the beginning of the program, conversations with overseas partners had been critical for developing the program's conceptual framework. Key ingredients in that framework were a recognition of the increasingly interdependent nature of the modern world, the need for serious cross-cultural dialogue between theological communities, a commitment to mutuality, and a recognition that the program needed to be integrated into the total curriculum of theological education. Overseas partners, demonstrating the importance of mutuality, had insisted that a globalization program must not be a diversion from pressing local agendas. Rather, globalization should become a means to encourage serious attention to critical issues before the church's life and mission. Bill had picked up on that theme and often argued that going abroad was exotic travel, while going into the inner city a few miles from Seabrook raised the difficult "at home" issues.

The idea of mutuality played a major role in Joel's strategy for nurturing a new ethos at Seabrook. The seminary had long provided scholarships for five or six international students each year. Joel began talking to colleagues abroad about the meaning of mutuality. "You have told us," he said to John Kuchemi of Ghana, "that we can be of help to your pastors with our Th.M. program. But you can also help us. Our students need to come to grips with third-world realities and with the vitality of the church in your country. Will you provide opportunities for our students to spend time studying the life of your church, living with your pastors, and being the guests of your Conference?" The response had been positive and enthusiastic. In a similar manner, exchanges were developed with theological institutions in Asia, Europe, and Latin America. Seabrook provided each year a full scholarship for a student named by these partner institutions, and they in turn provided full scholarships for students from Seabrook.

In addition to his role with international students, Joel also began, in cooperation with the dean of faculty, to issue invitations to faculty members from these partner institutions to spend their sabbatical leaves on the Seabrook campus. The seminary provided a guest suite, board, and a modest stipend. Visiting faculty members were invited to participate in classes, and each year one or two were asked not only to teach an elective but also to be part of a teaching team for one or two required classes. Special attention was given to recruiting distinguished theological educators and church leaders from partner institutions.

When the seminary's trustees met each year, arrangements were made to have one of the visiting professors or church leaders lead an opening devotional and meet with the board. Other internationals often participated in a meal with the board. Joel was convinced that these contacts were extremely important and, together with student reports to the trustees about the importance of student international experiences, were influencing the development of a strong and positive image of the program among the trustees. Some members of the board, however, continued to be suspicious of the program. Was it too expensive? Did it represent an ideological perspective hostile to those who provided the considerable funds used to support the program?

During the first five years of the program, the number of internationals on the campus grew from five to an average of twenty. Their impact on the campus was significantly increased through the use of international students as resource persons in certain required classes. They brought to discussions on issues before the church catholic, especially peace and justice questions, not only valuable and often persuasive insights, but also a provocative variety of perspectives. The need for a special class for internationals was soon felt. A faculty team developed a course to raise contextual issues and introduce internationals to the culture and traditions that shaped theological education in the U.S.

While Joel had provided administrative leadership to these developments, they had been guided and supported by a number of faculty members, especially by those who served on the Globalization Committee and those who came back from immersion experiences convinced of the importance of the globalization of theological education. During the early years of the program the Globalization Committee prepared the ground for the introduction of a required course: "The Church in an Interdependent World." The course drew on learnings from previous years of immersion experiences, a senior course in supervised ministry, and the changes in world-view and institutional ethos which had been nurtured by the program. The course included a local and an international immersion experience. The local immersion was in an inner-city context. The international immersion was in Africa, Latin America, or the Mideast. Joel served, with Ron Carter, the director of Congregational Studies, as the lead teacher for the course and provided administrative oversight to its international component. Critical to the course's acceptance by the faculty was a strong analytical component that made clear the course was far from a simple travel seminar to interesting places.

With the establishment of "The Church in an Interdependent World," the basic elements in the globalization project were in place. Others would be added to strengthen the program: a joint continuing education program with a partner institution abroad; a Hispanic program for the increasing number of Hispanics in Seabrook's constituency; and a program on the church in Africa funded through a special grant from a national foundation.

Behind these specific programs lay significant financial commitments and fund-raising activities. The original five year grant provided "start-up" money. By the end of the grant, the program had become firmly established. Moreover, the financial situation of the seminary was secure and the additional cost of the program was absorbed into the seminary's budget. Joel was clear that the support of the administration had been critical to this move. Globalization was made a part of a new capital fund campaign, with a million dollar endowment the goal for the program. Joel was confident, based on conversations with the president, that the funds would be raised.

What Joel was not sure about was whether he, Bill, and other faculty members who shared Bill's concerns, would ever come to any agreement about the purpose and place of globalization at Seabrook. Joel knew that Bill had legitimate concerns: that globalization was merely "trendy," that it distracted from the serious work of traditional disciplines, and most important, that it emphasized social and cultural factors as determinative of theological commitments. But Joel also knew that Seabrook, whether it liked it or not, was living in an increasingly interdependent world. This social reality had in fact brought to the fore Joel's own theological commitment to globalization. Joel was convinced that the changing context of Seabrook demanded that elements of its own theological tradition, especially international ecumenicity, receive at the end of the twentieth century special attention and nurture.

Joel hoped that Bill, through an international immersion experience, would be drawn into serious discussions about the issues of globalization and would not simply be dismissive of them. He also had hopes for himself, knowing how his perspectives had been shaped by his commitments to globalization and how his own self-interests had gradually become wrapped up in the success of globalization at Seabrook. Joel hoped that he could listen to Bill, learn from him, and that through their dialogue, and through conversations with international partners, Seabrook would be strengthened in its tasks of preparing persons for ministry in the twenty-first century. But given the difficulties he and Bill were having in conducting a serious conversation, and given what increasingly appeared a clash of self-interests, Joel was not sure that he and his old friend would be able to transcend the barriers that had been raised by globalization.

TEACHING NOTE

Winning Over the Faculty

I. Objectives

A. To explore the dynamics connected with the development of a globalization program in a North American theological seminary.

B. To probe these dynamics by focusing on the task of gaining faculty support for a comprehensive globalization program.

C. To provide an opportunity for theological faculties to name and clarify for themselves fundamental issues connected with the globalization of theological education.

II. Opening

Have the group imagine a meeting of the faculty of Seabrook Theological Seminary. The debate between Bill Jones and Joel Simons has become a pressing issue as the faculty focuses on the development of a new curriculum. The faculty has heard a proposal for the new curriculum and is in the midst of a heated debate about the place of the globalization program in the curriculum.

A. What are Bill and Joel feeling?

B. Are there particular anxieties in the room that need to be identified in order to understand the debate?

C. Are there specific frustrations that need to be noted in order to understand the debate?

III. Identifying the Issues

A. Have the entire group identify the issues for Bill Jones. Put on newsprint under "Issues for Bill Jones."

B. Follow the same procedure under "Issues for Joel Simons."

C. Have the entire group reflect on the phrase "winning over the faculty." What important issues are behind such a phrase? What problems lurk in its assumptions?

IV. Analysis of Issues

A. A young African-American faculty member has been listening to the debate in the faculty meeting. She gives an analysis of what she has heard. Have the entire group imagine what she might say. Record on newsprint.

B. A visiting professor of Mission and Ecumenics from Brazil has also been listening to the debate and now gives his analysis of the issues and what he has heard. Have the entire group imagine what he might say. Record on newsprint.

V. Developing Strategies for Globalization

A. Have the entire group break into smaller groups. Ask each group to

1. Identify strengths and weaknesses of strategies developed at Seabrook for "winning over the faculty." Record on newsprint to report later to larger group.

2. Identify, on basis of earlier analysis, issues that now must be faced by Seabrook in regard to globalization as it faces the development of a new curriculum. Are there hard choices that have to be made? Record on newsprint to report to larger group.

B. Post newsprint and allow small groups time to study the findings of other groups.

C. With the entire group gathered again, ask participants to

1. Identify common themes from the small groups.

2. Reflect on the importance of "winning over the faculty."

3. Strategize about ways to meet the issues raised and move toward a new curriculum.

COMMENTARY

Winning Over the Faculty

SUSAN BROOKS THISTLETHWAITE

What is at stake in the globalization of theological education is not the adoption of one curricular approach over another. A much deeper struggle is going on, as this case so aptly describes. Two visions are in direct conflict. One is of a multi-faceted world where human knowledge of how God works is constituted through various cultural forms. The other is a "counter-vision" which is "a defense of the West and an insistence on the universal validity of its theological traditions."

Globalization in theological education is the "un-centering" of the intellectual hegemony of the West. The project of Western thought since the time of Plato has been to find the one, true, universal form behind the changing shapes of human culture. Early in its history, in its contact with Greco-Roman civilization, Christianity in the West adopted this penchant for the universal in its philosophical theology. This tendency to ignore the particular in favor of abstract universals made Christianity a full partner in the colonializing (and now neo-colonializing) efforts of Euro-Atlantic culture, since it was an ideal (pun intended) legitimator for the suppression of indigenous cultures and their religions.

Many faculty members and their institutions have begun their participation in the globalization of theological education without a recognition of the more profound epistemological implications of the project. For many individuals and schools, globalization has appeared to be one more dish on the intellectual potluck table of modern culture. Sampling from various cultural options is a formative ethos for many higher educational institutions in American religion.

The mainline Protestant seminaries and the more liberal Catholic institutions were largely formed by the late nineteenth century and early twentieth century modernist movement in religion in the United States. For much of the twentieth century, a rapprochement to modern culture via particularly psychology, though in some cases also sociology and anthropology, was deemed the way to bring religion into "dialogue" with the modern age. The *modus operandus* of this dialogical method was to find a common ground between the disciples of theology and those of modernity. A key condition of this intellectual endeavor was the assertion of a mode of "free inquiry." More conservative theological seminaries, both Catholic and Protestant, have come more recently to this rapprochement. But the increased interest in pastoral psychology in more conservative seminaries, for example, witnesses to this enduring shift.

The presumption that intellectual inquiry can be "freed" from particular class, gender, race, national, or other social and political contexts in order for this rapprochement to go on is the direct heir of the penchant for the universal in the West. Whether the field is pastoral care or biblical studies, the theological correlate of Plato is that there is a "God's-eye view" that the inquirer can adopt, whether by rational inquiry or by direct divine revelation.

Many individuals and even whole schools have become involved in the globalization project under the assumption that it would be conducted in the usual "God's-eye view" manner. When the universal legitimacy of their particular intellectual approach has been challenged, the cry of "ideology" has been heard throughout the halls of the seminary. Used pejoratively, the term "ideology" when applied to globalization in theological education connotes ideas captive to particular political agendas.

While the term "ideology" as a description of the social and political origins of ideas is not wholly inappropriate to describe globalization, a better term is "critical consciousness." The aim of the globalization of theological education is the development of a critical consciousness of the social location of the theological priorities of the West (and their social and political fallout) and a *critique* of those priorities in light of the different priorities of people around the globe.

Some individuals and schools who began their participation in the globalization project under the assumption that it would be one other among a range of interesting cultural options cry foul when they come to see more fully the implications of critical consciousness. Marie Augusta Neal aptly titled her book on liberation perspectives for first-world people *A Socio-theology of Letting Go*. The development of critical consciousness in theological education means *letting go* of the assumption of the universal validity and priority of the intellectual traditions of the West.

This is not to say, as some critics have, that Western intellectual ideas now have *no* validity. But the ground for testing their validity has now shifted. Where once the ground for testing the validity of an idea was its universal applicability, today it is the extent to which a thought is cognizant of its own shared social location and contributes to the elaboration of more complex ways of, as Robert Schreiter phrases it, "constructing local theologies."

The authors of the case are correct when they describe the response of some faculty to this more profound understanding of globalization as "growing hostility." As the shift taking place becomes clearer, faculty who were merely uninterested in globalization become more entrenched in their resistance to it. I want to lift up what the case implies: their *growing hostility is a more accurate response to globalization than their earlier indifference.*

Many academic Americans, socialized to unanimity in university life, fear conflict. But conflict can be a means for change when the conflict becomes overt rather than covert. Naming the conflict accurately is critical, however; otherwise, it will degenerate into personal or side issues. One of the jobs of the Globalization Committee is to allot sufficient time for all involved to describe the situation as they see it and be sure that adequate time is given for faculty members with different views to have their perspectives clearly heard. No early push to resolution for the sake of harmony in the faculty is helpful; in fact, premature resolution only pushes conflict to peripheral and personal issues and makes real conflict resolution even more difficult.

Finally, I want to lift up a profound source of conflict for faculty in the globalization of theological education that does not surface in the case. Some racial/ethnic minority faculty who are male and some women faculty of both racial/ethnic and dominant race origins object to globalization because they perceive it as an attempt to take attention away from the struggles for racial and gender justice in the midst of the particular faculty of which they are a part and in the United States, and to project these struggles thousands of miles away. They perceive the willingness of some dominant race males to embrace globalization as a move to dilute the struggles for racial and gender justice at home. Yet, since women faculty of all races and racial/ethnic minority males are usually more junior, untenured members of the faculty, they are expected to do the lion's share of the administrative work that globalization efforts entail.

These conflicts are rarely articulated overtly; many peripheral conversations, however, witness to the resentment non-dominant faculty members feel for globalization concerns articulated by senior faculty and administrators.

Globalization efforts scarcely come to an institution as to a *tabula rasa*. Institutions, as individuals, are formed by the power distributions of the larger society; and despite even well-meaning efforts to address power inequalities, they continue to exist.

Furthermore, and this source of the conflict must also be named, globalization is "in" right now in theological education. Money is available for study, for immersion tours, for publication. Funds for any kind of work in theological education have been shrinking since the end of World War II. Certainly administrators will adopt priorities for their schools that will make them eligible for funds so desperately needed. No wonder non-dominant faculty question the abiding commitment of their schools to global issues when they see these connections.

There is absolutely no way around these conflicts for faculty. "Winning over the faculty" means simply this: engagement in a long process of naming the sources of these conflicts in theological education and sustained efforts to change them at their roots. Adding a few immersions to the curriculum, setting up a faculty exchange or two with partner schools in other countries, increasing the number of foreign students—these all risk becoming window dressing without attention to the profound power struggle that globalization is really about. I have been part of the globalization effort at Chicago Theological Seminary since its inception. But I tell you this truly: I am not "won over," and I never will be until these more profound struggles over globalization are routinely on the table for individual faculties and for the globalization movement as a whole.

References

Katie Cannon, *Black Womanist Ethics*, Chico, CA: Scholars Press, 1988.

Paulo Freire, *Education for Critical Consciousness*, New York: Seabury, 1973.

Marie Augusta Neal, *A Socio-theology of Letting Go*, Mahwah, NJ: Paulist Press, 1977.

Robert Schreiter, *Constructing Local Theologies*, Maryknoll, NY: Orbis Books, 1985.

Susan Thistlethwaite and Mary Potter Engle, eds., *Lift Every Voice: Constructing Christian Theologies from the Underside*, San Francisco: Harper and Row, 1990.

Sharon Welch, *Communities of Resistance and Solidarity*, Maryknoll, NY: Orbis Books, 1985.

Notes

1. See S. Weinstock, "The Geographical Catalogue in Acts 2:9-11," *The Journal of Roman Studies*, 38 (1948), pp. 43-46; J. Brinkman, "The Literary Background of

the 'Catalogue of Nations'," *Catholic Biblical Quarterly*, 25 (1963), pp. 418-27.

2. On the direct implications of this understanding of Pentecost for multicultural education, see I. G. Malcolm, "The Christian Teacher in the Multicultural Classroom," *Journal of Christian Education*, 74 (1982), especially p. 53.

3. For more on this subject and on the implications of this understanding of catholicity for globalization as well as for theology, see J. L. González, *Out of Every Tribe and Nation: Christian Theology at the Ethnic Roundtable* (Nashville: Abingdon, 1992), pp. 18-37.

4. There were local variations in the rule of faith itself. For instance, Irenaeus included the doctrine of "recapitulation" in his summary of the rule, Tertullian included his own emphasis on the "new Law," and Origen believed that the typically Alexandrine theory of the various levels of meaning in Scripture was part of the rule of faith. See R.P.C. Hanson, *Tradition in the Early Church* (London: S.C.M. Press, 1962), pp. 91-92.

5. See Augustine, Letter 87.5. Also Letter 43.9.25.

6. *Comm.* 2 (Nicene and Post-Nicene Fathers, Series two, 11:132).

7. On how this affected the church's understanding of its mission, see A. Mandouze, "The Church and the Collapse of Roman Civilization," in *History's Lessons for Tomorrow's Mission* (Geneva: W.S.C.F., n.d.), pp. 39-50.

8. *Historia*, 7.41 (P.L. 31:1168).

9. This insistence was one of the reasons why the Chalcedonian orthodox found little of value in the views of those whom historians call the "verbal monophysites," whose differences with the Chalcedonians had to do more with formulae than with content.

10. See J. L. González, *A History of Christian Thought*, revised edition (Nashville: Abingdon, 1987), 2:213.

11. *Ibid.*, 2:182.

12. *Ibid.*, 2:245-46.

13. See T. de Andrés Hernansanz, "Un problema de hoy hace setecientos años: En torno a los acontecimientos de París de 1277," *Cuadernos Salmantinos de Filosofía*, 4 (1977), 5-16; J. Châtillon, *L'exercise du pouvoir doctrinal dans la chrétienté du XIIIᵉ siècle: Le cas d'Étienne Tempier* (Paris: Beauchesne, 1978).

14. Though this emphasis underlies much of Schleiermacher's writings, it is seen most clearly in the Fourth Speech and Fifth Speech in *On Religion: Speeches to its Cultured Despisers*. Source trans. John Oman (NY: Frederick Ungar, 1955).

15. Schleiermacher, *The Christian Faith*, 2nd ed., trans. H. R. Mackintosh and J. S. Steward (Edinburgh: T. & T. Clark, 1928), p. 450.

16. J. L. González, *The Story of Christianity*, vol. 2 (San Francisco, Harper & Row, 1984), pp. 396-97, based on data from D. K. Barrett, ed., *World Christian Encyclopedia* (Nairobi: Oxford University Press, 1982), global tables 18 and 29.

17. One of the best discussions and refutations of the view that what these new voices represent is not really theology is in Juan Luis Segundo, *The Liberation of Theology*, trans. John Drury (Maryknoll, NY: Orbis Books, 1976).

18. Copyright © 1993 by the Case Study Institute. The names of persons and places in this case have been disguised to protect the privacy of those involved in the situation.

[2]

MEANINGS OF GLOBALIZATION

ESSAY

*Living the Faith under the Conditions
of the Modern World*

WILLIAM E. LESHER

The title and subtitle accurately state the thesis of this essay. Globalization is a way to understand the response of faith to life in the modern world. What other possibility is there? In virtually every aspect of our daily lives we encounter the phenomenon of globalization, from the array of foods at the supermarket that literally makes every meal we eat a global repast to investment decisions we make, or that our pension fund counselors make for us, in selecting a portfolio from a worldwide collection of investment possibilities. Actually, globalization is not an option for those of us who live in North America. It is an unavoidable reality. Yet, as is often the case, our thought world, our religious world, and our theological world can and still do lag behind this world of daily reality.

The purpose of this essay, as described by the editors of this volume, is "to provide a critical approach to the emerging themes, issues, resources, and challenges related to the meanings of globalization, of which any theological educator dealing with globalization should be aware."

I welcome this assignment, not because I come to the task with a wealth of scholarly information to convey, but rather because I want to share some of my experience as a seminary president who has for nearly twenty years been engaged in some phase of globalization and theological education. There is an urgency about this task for me. Globalization as the forced, intimate encounter with all the states and conditions of human life on the planet is the overarching reality of our time. Relating that reality to our religious faith, which is the interwoven infrastructure of our daily lives, is an essential task and surely an urgent assignment for theological education. So this essay is not likely to be a cool, studied medium. It is more likely to be personal, opinionated, and, I hope, helpful to others who are engaged in the tasks of globalizing theological education.

What are we talking about? The first and most persistent issue of globalization is, What does the word mean? Is it another way to talk about world missions? No. Is it a new discipline? Not exactly. Is it just the latest fad in theological education? I don't think so. But globalization is hard to talk about and hard to describe, at least initially. This difficulty, of course, makes it easier for those faculty who tend to be defensive about the precision of the theological disciplines and those church members and leaders who are persuaded that there is really "nothing new under the sun" to write off globalization as another unwelcome diversion from the basic tasks of theological education.

But I have concluded that the difficulty in defining globalization is becoming a substantial advantage. The lack of a single succinct definition means that any inquirer who is really intent on knowing will need to explore various aspects of religious thought, experience, and activities that relate to the meaning of globalization, as the term is being used in theological circles today.

Here I will point to three ways to discuss the term "globalization."

The first is globalization as a basic personal perception or stance. Some people are global by nature. Others may never be. Most of us have a tendency one way or another that is cultivated as we are exposed to the options. The way a person responds to D. H. Lawrence's poem, "Song of a Man Who Has Come Through," may show with some accuracy the degree to which he/she is or could be globalized.

> Not I, not I, but the wind that blows through me!
> A fine wind is blowing a new direction of Time.
> If only I let it bear me, carry me, if only it carry me!
> If only I am sensitive, subtle, oh, delicate, a winged gift!
> If only, most lovely of all, I yield myself and am borrowed
> By the fine, fine wind that takes its course through the chaos of the
>   world
> Like a fine exquisite chisel, a wedge blade inserted;
> If only I am keen and hard like the sheer tip of a wedge
> Driven by invisible blows,
> The Rock will split, we shall come at the wonders, we shall find the
>   Hesperides.
> Oh, for the wonder that bubbles in my soul,
> I would be a good fountain, a good well-head,
> Would blur no whisper, spoil no expression.
> What is the knocking?
> What is the knocking at the door in the night?
> It is somebody wants to do us harm.
> No, no, it is three strange angels.
> Admit them, admit them.[1]

This famous poem evokes a number of basic human emotions that are characteristic of people (and institutions) who are likely to lead or take an active role in the movement toward globalization. They are people who sense that "a fine wind is blowing a new direction of Time." Not everyone perceives that this claim is true, in spite of the evidence that supports it. And many who perceive it shy away from it for it is personally frightening and institutionally threatening. The world is known by all of us to be chaotic, but many will take their chances on what is rather than yielding to the fine new wind. Some people, however, are inclined to yield. The more they are exposed to the vision, to the new possibilities, to the promise of a new way for the world to be, the more determined they become. The more the new potential reality permeates their thought, theology, and world vision, the more confident they are that the "Rock will split," which is to say, be rolled away.

There is always the question: what really is this knocking? And there are always the ready answers: the knocking is the dreadful future that is bound to do us harm, dilute our tradition, and throw us off course. But those likely to lead in the globalization of theological education see the divine at work in the future and understand globalization to be no less than the response of faith to the modern world.

The term "globalization" does have more concrete references, however, and is most commonly described as four faith responses to the conditions of life today. This typology of globalization was first articulated by Don S. Browning in an address to the Association of Theological Schools in 1986 and has become the common way to discuss the meaning of globalization in the seminary community today. One passage from Browning's address outlines the four-fold typology that has become a standard way of describing, if not defining, what is meant by globalization in religious circles.

> The word globalization has at least four rather distinct meanings. . . . For some, globalization means the church's universal mission to evangelize the world, i.e., to take the message of the gospel to all people, all nations, all cultures and all religious faiths. Second, there is the idea of globalization as ecumenical cooperation between the various manifestations of the Christian church throughout the world. This includes a growing mutuality and equality between churches in First and Third World countries. It involves a new openness to and respect for the great variety of local concrete situations. Third, globalization sometimes refers to dialogue between Christianity and other religions. Finally, globalization refers to the mission of the church to the world, not only to convert and to evangelize, but to improve and develop the lives of the millions of poor, starving and politically disadvantaged people.[2]

What this description, if not definition, lacks in precision, it gains in inclusiveness. This way of talking about globalization has made it possible, for example, for virtually all the member schools of the Association of Theological Schools in the United States and Canada to embrace the idea of globalization as a priority theme of the Association for the decade of the 1990s. Browning explained at the outset of his address that the word "globalization" was not familiar to him when he received the invitation to address the topic. So, as one who is playing a key role in lifting up and redefining the role of practical theology, Browning set out to do what good practical theologians are supposed to do: He studied the situation, immersing himself, as he put it, "among the indigenous population who use the term." At this point in the discussion of the globalization of theological education, the typology works well, precisely because it is grounded in the current pastoral experience of individuals and institutions. Indeed, at the same biennial meeting where Browning delivered his important address, the keynote was given by Francis Cardinal Arinze, President of the Vatican Secretariat for Non-Christians. Not surprisingly, Cardinal Arinze clearly described his priority for globalization in terms of world evangelization, though in his full and helpful discussion of globalization of theological education he broadened his definition of globalization to include ecumenism, dialogue, and social action as accompanying activities under the major theme of globalization as evangelization.[3]

In his address Browning shared his own experience in a congregational study group in which globalization was the theme and the participants were wholly focussed on concerns for social, economic, and political justice. He concluded his address, however, by saying, "Even though we have mainly concentrated on globalization as human development, we should remember that this [definition] can only find its proper place in our commitments if we place the meaning of this concept firmly within the context of the other three meanings of the word as well in spite of the tension that will inevitably emerge between them."

A major issue in globalization continues to be the meaning of the term itself. Browning has clearly advanced the discussion by making it plain that we must talk about several meanings that, as he says, "are distinguishable without being necessarily contradictory." Here is where the issue lies today. Whenever we enter the globalization discussion out of our personal or institutional pasts, we are challenged by the current discussion to see a larger framework. The common element among all theological traditions and educators today is the awareness that the context for theological education is the entire world. Our fundamental response to this new contextual awareness will probably be included in one or more of the four meanings of globalization described by Browning. But the way this four-fold description is functioning in theological circles today is to challenge our historically conditioned responses by considering how and why other colleagues in the faith motivated by the same gospel, albeit through different traditions, are responding in different ways.

I believe the globalization of theological education is paving the way for the various Christian traditions to broaden their characteristic approach to the mission of the church. This broader approach could result in a revisitation to the ecumenical discussion of this central theological theme in a way that characteristic positions from the past can be differentiated and seen as complementary rather than conflictual. Such discussions would open the way for an expansion of the concept of globalization in the various faith traditions. If this expansion is to take place, most likely theological seminaries will have to lead the way. A broader approach to the mission of the church is indeed one of the most promising aspects of the globalization of theological education.

The third way to talk about globalization is to relate the term to the concept of transformation, or to its more religious synonym, conversion. In 1988, I participated in the first travel seminar our school engaged in through the Pilot Immersion Project of Plowshares. The trip to Asia included representatives of four theological schools in Hyde Park, Chicago. On the plane returning from Taiwan and for several weeks after the trip, several members of our group tried to express a sense of what globalization meant to us in the light of the vivid impressions and experiences we had so recently encountered. The following statement is the result of this effort.

To become "global" in theological education is to be transformed by:
- the interdependence of the unique peoples and cultures of the world;
- the all-pervasive presence of poverty and injustice as fundamental evils that must be addressed by Christian and other groups of goodwill locally and globally;
- the need to inform our ministries and service with an understanding of economic realities; human rights issues; oppressive structures of gender, race, class, and violence; and the global environmental crisis;
- the universal significance of the reign of God as the call to discipleship and servanthood and the substance of hope for the future.

This transformation of individuals will cultivate in the theological community a new ethos of awareness of the worldwide human community and of the value of human relationships across cultural crises and will enable us to be a fuller expression of the whole people of God.

In some ways, this statement speaks more powerfully to me today than it did when it was first written. Globalization is merely words and ideas that can take up much time and energy, but signify very little unless there is a fundamental change in the consciousness of people and institutions. In time, this basic change in consciousness will modify the way we live the faith in the modern world.

Transformation/conversion is a difficult phenomenon to account for. Sometimes it is a sharp, clear break between the past and a new future, but often it is not. Paul Tillich described grace in his famous sermon on this subject in this way: "You are accepted. After such an experience we may not be better than before, and we may not believe more than before. But everything is transformed."[4]

As twenty-four experienced theological educators traveling to the Philippines, Hong Kong, and Taiwan and meeting with political power brokers and dissident leaders alike, we were not encountering circumstances or ideas that were altogether new to us. But to engage these people in the flesh, to have another life context be at the center rather than our own, to become listeners and learners, and to sense in a highly personal way our own vulnerability, to depend on strangers becoming new friends, was to experience some of the indispensable ingredients that make for the passage of transformation in globalization.

The problem is that transformation experiences of any kind are so ephemeral that they are easy to dismiss. We can pass them off, believing that such experiences do not apply to us or that we have already made the changes called for and integrated them in our life and thought and therefore that further exposures are unnecessary for us. If we are subjected to them, we tend to interpret their meaning wholly on the basis of conclusions previously reached.

These difficulties are especially applicable among academics of all disciplines, and theological faculties are no exception. It was a revelation for me, on the trip referred to above, to note that those traveling companions who were among the best at their craft, who had the ability to analyze and synthesize with alacrity and clarity, and who were the first to draw learned summary conclusions about an aspect or event of the trip, were the least transformed by the experience. In a real sense, they had never left home. Their own North American context remained the center of the experience, and from this center they interpreted the new and challenging life realities that only appeared at their periphery.

This reflection is not so much a judgment as it is an observation. Transformation is difficult in theological circles because, while it is a skill, it is not a skill of intellect. It is a right brain proficiency that readily engages all the faculties, but it begins with the skill of *kenosis*, with the ability to empty ourselves, so we can take into ourselves as fully as possible a new reality. Philippians 2:7, in a powerful way, describes the components of a transformative/conversion experience when it recounts the great *kenosis* of Christ, his own self-emptying of the God-head, being born in human likeness, and in that new reality taking the form of a servant. Something of this radical emptying of self and opening to a new reality, letting that new reality be the center for a while and only slowly testing to see if our tools of analysis, former conclusions, and faith commitments make contact or make sense in this new center, captures the deepest meaning of transformation. "Slowly" is the key word here. Transformation may be triggered by an all-encompassing event or a longer series of experiences, but in either case the transforming process takes time and patience.

Recently I was told about an incident that occurred on our campus during a summer session for missionary orientation. The group visited both Muslim and Buddhist communities, which are represented in surprising strength in the Chicago metropolitan area. Members of the group heard firsthand from believers about Islam and Buddhism, and they engaged adherents of these two great faith traditions in conversation and questions. For most participants, who had never met a Muslim or a Buddhist face to face, it was an important part of their orientation. One person complained, however, because no opportunity was provided for those participating to make a witness to Jesus Christ and an invitation to believe in him. This same impatience that readily translates into insensitivity and arrogance is apparent in theologians who either criticize inter-faith dialogue as a sell-out to religious pluralism or who participate with only the motive to tell their dialogue partners the truth in Christianity. Transformation precedes dialogue. Patience is required. Mutual respect needs to be established. Listening needs to take place. We need to meet one another in our common creation, in the spirit of the first article of the Apostles' Creed—for those with a Confessional heritage. Then, in the fullness of time, when human links have been established and we have let a different reality in, it is time to speak of Christ, and the chances are we will be heard.

Transformation is (and leads to) many things. It can be described in many ways. One seminary president with whom I talked in preparation for this article said, "Globalization is to be converted to a larger world than I grew up in and to learn how to let that larger world influence my local concerns." But whatever particular words are used to describe it, a transformation/conversion is fundamental to globalization.

We will have opportunity to discuss the transformative aspects of globalization when we take up specific implications of this process. But before we leave this opening section on the various meanings of globalization, we should note that the very skills, aptitudes, or personality characteristics we are describing here under the category of transformation are the same characteristics we expect from a good pastoral leader. Whether our model for ministry is a practical theologian, a pastoral director, or a priestly leader, we are generally describing individuals who are skilled at entering fully into a reality other than their own, who have honed the gift of active listening, who form bonds of common humanity and mutuality, and who then can contribute their own rich gifts that can transform a circumstance by which the pastor has already been transformed. This is to say that when we deal with the meaning of globalization in theological education, we are not dealing with a foreign ingredient but only with a bigger stage. The lessons learned and the transformation that may occur in a theological education that understands the entire world as the context contribute to the preparation of faithful pastoral leaders for local congregations in the modern world.

So far we have addressed the meaning of globalization from three perspectives. I have shown my bias as well as my experience by suggesting that there are some people who are global by nature and some who may never be; and I have, somewhat playfully, used D. H. Lawrence's whimsical poem as a way to measure the globalization potential of various people. More substantially, I have recounted the four-fold description of globalization that has differentiated without contradicting the major meanings of globalization held by different faith traditions. Finally, I have lifted up the transformation/conversion experience that lies at the heart of the meaning of globalization.

I will now turn to a discussion of issues and emerging themes that rise out of these meanings under five headings:

1. The Priority of the Biblical Message and Mandate
2. Global Reaction to Globalization in North American Seminaries
3. Globalization as Context and Content in the Theological Curriculum
4. Forms of International Contact
5. Outcomes of Globalization

I. The Priority of the Biblical Message and Mandate

When Cardinal Arinze addressed the Association of Theological Schools at the 1986 Biennial Meeting on the subject "Globalization in Theological Education," he began by telling "The Story."

"God so loved the world," he said, "that he gave his only son so that everyone who believes in him may not be lost, but may have eternal life." He went on to tell about the fall of Adam and Eve from paradise, about how they offended God and how humanity became a fallen race, about God's faithfulness, the promise of a Savior, the eventual coming of Christ, his ministry of calling, teaching and miracle-working, his bitter passion and death, his glorious resurrection, and the sending of the Spirit. He told of the founding of the Church, a new people of God, an extension of Christ's ministry as his mystical Body, as a community of Jesus present today in his disciples. He told that God meant for the Church to be for all humankind, that Jesus Christ really is the Savior of the world. There is no other savior, no one else is expected, for of all the names in the world this is the only one by which we can be saved.

The cardinal went on to talk about the universal nature of the Gospel, clearly forecast in the Old Testament and culminating in the Great Commission of Jesus to go and make disciples of all nations. He spoke of the global nature of the Church and the miracle of reconciliation that happens in Christ when he is our peace and the barriers are broken down that at one time kept us apart.

He told about St. Peter's transformation/conversion that resulted from his experiences with Cornelius the Greek and led Peter to declare boldly that God does not have favorites, but that anybody of any nationality who fears God and does what is right is acceptable to God. When Peter got home to Jerusalem, there were, as there always are, the objectors who were distressed that he was dealing with Greeks and had short-circuited the traditions of the Jews. But after hearing Peter's report, they grudgingly admitted the universal character of the call to the gospel. The Cardinal then recounted what he called a major landmark. When the Council of Jerusalem sanctioned that Greeks converted to the religion of Jesus Christ were not bound by Jewish customs, the way was opened for the spread of the Gospel to all the nations.[5]

One does not often hear "The Story" told at an ATS Biennium. Too often globalization in theological education is discussed only in terms of methods, issues, and problems. The message is muted, probably because it is assumed, possibly because the message itself can create conflict, or perhaps because for some it is even an embarrassment.

Whatever the cause, we must engage in a renewed study of the biblical message and the biblical mandate which are the basis and motive for the globalization of theological education.

If the literature is mute on this subject, it is because it is assumed we can no longer make the assumption. There is strong biblical incentive to embrace globalization as evangelization, ecumenism, dialogue, and development. We need to make our motivation explicit rather than implicit. Theological students do not necessarily come to seminary with either the biblical knowledge or the assumptions to motivate them in a commitment to globalization in their theological education. At the same time, the methods for teaching the biblical message in seminaries today do not readily result in transformation/conversion, which is what must happen if students are to be religiously motivated for globalization. When discussing this assignment with several seminary presidents whose schools are engaged in various stages of globalization, the assertion was made that globalization means "making the Bible central again." This issue is important in the developing discussion on globalization. It is filled with problems and possibilities. It will take a revolution in many faculties to teach the Bible for transformation. Faculties themselves will need to catch the spirit and work at length and in depth before change will occur in the classroom.

If the methods of globalization as they are discussed and debated by theological educators are not undergirded and infused with the mandate and the motivation of the biblical message, they will be written off by many in the seminary and surely in the Church as intrusions that have social and political intentions rather than religious motives. Indeed, globalization is neither the product nor the property of religion. It has its counterparts in business and politics that are in some cases antithetical to the meaning of globalization for the religious community. To be clear we must be explicit about the biblical message and mandate that inform and inspire all the forms globalization takes among us. If we break the biblical silence in the field of globalization, it is possible that theological faculties could find cause to rethink the whole presentation of biblical material in the curriculum. While the various forms of criticism currently applied to the biblical text would remain important components of instruction, the urgency to communicate the message of scripture and its mandate for ministry in the modern world would take higher priority. In this case again, globalization in theological education becomes an occasion, not to introduce a new theme, but vigorously to reinforce a standard theme in the preparation of pastoral leaders.

When Cardinal Arinze told "The Story" as the introduction to his keynote address, "Globalization of Theological Education," to the Association of Theological Schools, the assembly was rapt in its attention. The biblical message is the rock from which we are hewn. In this time of new adventures and possibilities in the faith communities, we must tell each other with greater frequency "The Story" whence we have come.

II. Global Reactions to Globalization in North American Seminaries

The first time I attempted to explain what globalization in theological education in North American seminaries is all about to a group of about thirty African theological educators at Makumira Seminary in Usa River, Tanzania, the reaction was sharp and plaintive. The first speaker shouted angrily that globalization was another perhaps even more devastating act of North American imperialism. The second speaker was less emphatic, but more pathetic. He said, "Just as we are beginning to get our own agenda moving, you are coming to usurp our efforts again." We talked further. I tried to say that globalization rose out of our need in North America and was not an effort to impose an agenda on colleagues in other parts of the world. If anything, globalization meant listening to what other agendas were being developed, perhaps building some agendas together, and inviting others to share in our theological efforts as critics and commentators. There were a few questions. Some said they could not believe that North American theologians were interested in what Africans thought and especially what they thought about the theological work of North Americans. Then the generators gave out, the lights went off, and we made our way through the darkness to our beds. I stayed at the meeting for another two days, and in that period nearly all of the participants engaged me in a further discussion about globalization of theological education in North America, what it could mean in Africa, and what it could mean for us all in the future.

Anyone who engages in globalization must be ready for this kind of response — not always from colleagues from the Two Thirds World. Often it comes from critics of globalization here among us. The criticism should not put us off. The fact is that the term "globalization," as it is used among us, is quite the opposite of imperialism. People who level that charge are not listening or have listened but have not heard. Globalization in theological education and in the Church is, as we have said, a means of living the faith under the conditions of the modern world. When we say this and add substance to these skeletal statements, when globalization is described as transformation/conversion, and when the types of globalization are conveyed, it becomes clear to most critics, especially those from abroad, that globalization is the opposite of the imperialism that they fear. It is a group of strange angels, indeed. It is a spirit they have not met before from most North American theologians, and this, alone, is a reason to admit these strange angels. Still the initial reaction is often negative and is only modified with contact and conversation.

At the 1992 ATS Biennium Meeting, the Association hosted the first Congress of the World Conference of Associations of Theological Schools (WOCATI). As a part of the welcome, the ATS Task Force on Globalization held a reception for the WOCATI delegates to ask their reactions to globalization in North American seminaries and their advice in charting future directions. In one small group globalization in North America was associated with "contextualization" in theological education in the Two Thirds World. As one delegate put it, "We are over-globalized to the point that we have no identity of our own. We have been taught to borrow everything because what we borrow is better than what we create ourselves. Contextualization is a defense against globalization that seeks to define us."

Reaction to our efforts at globalization from the Two Thirds World will be a constant issue as we progress in this direction. The term itself carries baggage with it, particularly from business circles, that is altogether different from the content we give the term in theological circles. Interpretation and definition are important, therefore, at every point. When our global colleagues grasp that we are expressing a new and welcome spirit of openness and mutuality, they respond most often with relief and cautious expectation.

Those who would advance the globalization of theological education must be highly sensitive to this initial reaction from abroad and practice ways to interpret globalization that demonstrate that we are speaking about a wind that blows a new direction. Again, we are talking about a process that will take a long time and that must be accompanied by actions as well as words that give evidence of the fine new wind. But given time and patience, this rock, too, will split.

It is clear that globalization is a North American need that rises out of our global isolation. Our theological colleagues from around the world know more about us than we know about them. They have been our students, they read our books, and until recently they have patterned their programs of theological education largely after ours. Now they are making some changes. Globalization means it is time to learn some things from them.

III. Globalization as Context and Content in the Theological Curriculum

A host of issues jump to the fore whenever curriculum in theological education is mentioned, for whatever reason. Globalization is no exception.

Some things, however, do seem to be agreed upon. One is that globalization is not a content to add on, but rather is the context in which the whole program is carried out. Again, this means a kind of transformation in the thinking of most people who minister through the tasks of theological education. It certainly means a change in mind set for the schools we serve. If there is general agreement on the idea, however, there are only emerging suggestions about the methods to in fact make globalization the context of our curricula. The notion of a global context raises the question of our current contextual assumptions. Many of us in denominational schools would likely need to say that the Church, we hope the whole Church, as it is expressed through our particular traditions is the primary context to which and for which we teach. Some schools might have a firmer sense than others that their context is the Church in this place and in this nation, and that all the pains and potential of being Christian in North America today are the content of classroom exploration. It is an almost unimaginable leap to contemplate what it would mean to have the entire world as the context for our curricula. It might mean that the historic photograph taken by the astronauts of the earth hanging in space would replace or at least stand alongside the church steeple as a symbol of the mission of our schools. It might mean that every subject is taught with a global twist so that both teachers and students are obliged to ask of every interpretation, doctrine, or ethical position how would this be received in Cairo, Kinshasa, Kyoto, or Guayaquil.

Ideas are flowing in this area. In 1985, Joseph Hough and John Cobb pressed forward the discussion of globalization in theological education in a significant way with their important book, *Christian Identity and Theological Education*. Education for global awareness is the heart of their proposals for theological education and constitutes the core of their theological curriculum. Their thesis is that the task of the Church and theological education is to keep alive the message of God's concern for the entire world as this is revealed in scripture. A key section reads: "The growing interconnectedness of all aspects of the biosphere and human involvement in it necessitates recognizing the importance of the global context to Christian self-understanding. In this sense, all Christian theology today should be global theology."[6]

Others are following in the path of Hough and Cobb. It is interesting to note that many professors who have participated in the Pilot Immersion Project of Plowshares report on changes they have made in the content and context of their own teaching. In the fall of 1992 the ATS Task Force on Globalization published a special supplement to the ATS journal, *Theological Education*, which contains a collection of papers by scholars in the foundational disciplines detailing how they have introduced globalization as the context of their classroom teaching.[7]

A number of institutions now have a critical mass of teachers who are thinking globally about their classroom and their institution and who are ready to act to effect local change. We are, I suspect, at the threshold of major developments in this area in the decade ahead.

This brings us to another aspect of the globalization discussion upon which experience is working a substantial consensus. Much of what we need to know and experience in order to effect a global context is available to us in our local settings.

The description of globalization as transformation (quoted above), which was developed with my colleagues on our return from Asia, was done with the intent of identifying what we had experienced on a very expensive, three-week sojourn to the other side of the world. We were attempting to develop some criteria by which global and local immersion experiences could be measured and evaluated. It seemed important to capture what we were feeling at the conclusion of that experience as a way to begin to shape criteria for the transformative process of globalization.

In that effort we identified at least four characteristics that contribute to the criteria for a transformative experience in globalization. First is the personal realization that in a profound way we are interdependent with all the peoples and cultures of the world. Internalizing that bond of common humanity is perhaps the heart of the transformative experience in globalization. Second for me, but fourth on the listing above, is the affirmation that the Gospel of Jesus Christ which reveals the universal reign of God is applicable and significant to all humanity, both as remarkable hope for those who embrace it and as a call to discipleship to all peoples. Third is the enormity of human suffering in the world and the biblical mandate to struggle with how we in the modern world bear each other's burdens. Fourth is a listing of some of the contextual areas that need to inform our theological education and our ministries.

What is currently being explored through the Pilot Immersion Project of Plowshares and by a number of theological schools independently is the extent to which personal transformation can be achieved locally.

My own sense is that the results will bring a mixed yes/no answer to this quest. There is no question that the poverty and injustice that must be experienced firsthand as part of the transformative process is available to us often within the very communities where we live and serve. As on the global scene, yet not to the same extent in all places, local poverty can be invisible to those in the dominant culture. Social structures are designed, in fact, to keep the fundamental human realities of the various cultures within our own nation separate and distinct. Globalization is about crossing these boundaries and discovering the realities that lie on the other side. This we are learning to do. We are also learning that we need the same kinds of guides, the same kind of intentionality, and the same kind of reflection that is needed when we go half a world away.

I believe we will find that transformation can and will happen in more local immersion experiences and that they will create a new context for a theological education that intends to prepare leaders for local churches that are struggling to live the faith in the modern world. But the many students involved in local immersions will, I suspect, need to be mixed with the few who are involved in global immersions. Transformation will become global as participants in both immersions work out the meaning of these experiences together.

Several years ago, I read the mission statement of the Ford Foundation. I was impressed to find that it was the Foundation's declared intention to find projects in the U.S. and in other parts of the world where there could be a transfer of learning. The assumption seemed to be that human need in the world has common components that can benefit from an international exchange of conditions, ideas, and solutions. Poverty among the black majority in South Africa can be distinguished in many ways from poverty in the African American community in the U.S. But the development of community organization in the U.S. and in African American communities has been an important export to the South African situation that the Ford Foundation has promoted. In a somewhat similar way as the Church becomes more globalized, interrelated, and interdependent we may find increasing points of exchange. In the area of ministry, for example, as some North American churches struggle with providing pastoral services to congregations that cannot afford full time ministry, the long experience of some churches in the Two Thirds World with catechists, evangelists, and diaconal ministries could possibly form a fruitful exchange of patterns and pitfalls as well as possibilities.

The point is that as local immersions develop in the theological curriculum as a way to globalize the context of theological education, as I am suggesting they will, attention should be given to maintaining specific international immersions and developing the ways to build in common reflection from these two sources of transformation.

A third area of consensus about the context and the content of globalization has to do with the growing pluralism of the student bodies and in some places the faculties of many of our theological schools. Truly, in some seminaries globalization begins at home. The many diverse groups who make up some theological communities make the global context an unavoidable reality.

One seminary president with whom I spoke in preparation for this chapter said that globalization on his campus had become increasingly stress-filled and complex. He went on to say that many students experienced the pluralism in the student body as an "assault on their cultural assumptions as well as on their belief structure." Indeed, the more pluralistic the school has become, the more complex and confusing the whole notion of globalization has become. There are, in fact, a myriad of global contexts on the same campus, and it is increasingly difficult and frustrating to discover any framework of commonality.

This may be the description of an extreme situation, but it has echoes on many seminary campuses. In these places, training in multiculturality will be an essential aspect of the globalization process. The transformation that we have discussed at length in the sections of this paper will become an indispensable part of campus life. The challenge is no longer to reach out beyond the present context for a global one, but to appropriate for educational and theological purposes the context that has so recently become a campus reality. This is no easy task. It has come upon some schools quickly and requires urgent attention. The most hopeful possibility is that seminaries in these circumstances will self-consciously accept the new contextual circumstance as their mission, that they will find ways to appropriate the skills of multiculturality as the way to live in this specific pluralistic theological community, and that in this process globalization in its variety of meanings will occur.

As in all aspects of the process of globalization, but here especially, these tasks must be approached with great patience. Globalization is creating a revolution in every area of human life and thought. It will not be accomplished in the religious community with less strain or without considerable pain. Indeed, these may be the most telling signs that the revolution is happening even to us.

IV. Forms of International Contact

Globalization means international contact. Indeed, it has been the revolution in the means of travel and communication that has brought about this new phenomenon of modern life to which we are attempting to respond faithfully and effectively. In this section we will note, encourage, and urge caution regarding some of the ways contact is and will be carried on in the globalization process in theological education.

Travel is indispensable to globalization. It is not all there is, to be sure. We have made a strong case above for local immersions as the basic way to achieve the transformation necessary to globalization. But we have also made it clear that a combination of experiences on the same campus, most local but some global, while debriefing and interpreting these experiences together, is needed to effect the goals of transformation. Travel plans, therefore, need to be built into the schedules of schools involved in globalization. Traveling for the purpose of globalization, however, should have several marked differences from other forms of international contact. I will mention three differences as examples.

Travelers for the purpose of globalization will want to be especially sensitive to the fragile infrastructure that exists in many if not most of the churches and theological institutions in the Two Thirds World. While hospitality in many places is generous and even effusive, resources are often extremely limited. It is not unheard of for host communities to go without their normal allotment of food to save up for international visitors. Travelers should be aware of these sacrifices, limit the size of groups traveling so as not to create undue burdens, accept humble and even uncomfortable accommodations graciously and gratefully, plan to assist hosts by covering added expenses that are incurred, and/or returning their favors with gifts of thanks and appreciation.

Time has a different meaning in many of the places we are likely to go. Running through areas of the world where people live more isolated, cyclical lives is easily interpreted as a sign of first-world arrogance and insensitivity. An even more pressing reason, however, for extending travel time is that the treasures of global travel are not usually revealed on first contact. Again, as with all aspects of globalization, patience is required. In spite of the expense to travel abroad, more time in one place is in the long run a better use of time for the purposes of globalization than shorter periods in many places. For the sake of building relations and a sense of continuity, concern, and seriousness, seminaries might be well advised to establish relations with one or more locations which are visited regularly by different small groups that can build on the experiences and the trust developed by previous travelers.

The limitation on the amount of money one spends is a small but significant part of travel for globalization purposes. It is a discipline that makes the traveler always conscious of the uniqueness of this trip compared to others. It is also a conspicuous signal to those who are visited that this person or group is traveling with a difference and has a seriousness of purpose that is far more important than the comforts they can purchase or the souvenirs they gather.

Travel by students from the Two Thirds World to North America is most likely to come as a result of international scholarship grants. As globalization has become a theme in North American theological education, seminaries have generally attempted to expand the number of their international students. While this early phase of expansion has helped North American schools get a better sense of the global context for theological education, questions should be raised about the value of these experiences for theological students from the Two Thirds World. One proposition worthy of discussion among theological educators in North America and with overseas colleagues in theological education and in the churches is the degree to which a North American M.Div. degree is a preparation for ministry in the Two Thirds World. My own sense is that whenever possible the first degree in ministry that leads to ordination in the pastoral office should be taken as close to home as possible, within the cultural context where ministry is to be done. For the most part, international students should be enrolled in M.Div. degree programs in North American seminaries only when the M.Div. represents an advanced theological degree not available in the student's region and only after the student has practiced ministry for several years.

The hazards of luring students, especially those from non-industrialized areas of the world, to spend long periods of time in North American seminaries are more clearly identified with Th.D. and Ph.D. studies. At the first International

Congress (WOCATI) referred to above, participants reflected on graduate theological education in North America. Their reflections were filled with the same ambiguities that mark many of the discussions on this topic by North American educators. How valuable is a North American research degree to a person on a small faculty with sparse resources who is likely to be teaching many subjects to students who have a very different context for ministry? What damage is done to a family that spends four to seven years in a North American context and then returns, sometimes to a social and political climate where children and spouses have severe difficulties readjusting? Should North American graduate faculties give serious attention to the content of doctoral programs for people preparing for leadership in theological education in the Two Thirds World? As a part of our own commitment to globalization should North American seminaries work strategically in the future to build up seminaries and religion departments in other areas of the world and to complement their resources where needed for doctoral education?

Without doubt, as the process of globalization in North American theological education moves forward, we will have to address these and many other related questions.

Exchange of theology professors is a major form of global contact that promises to increase in volume in the future. For the last decade, grants to professors to subsidize sabbatical leaves and academic study have increasingly emphasized travel and projects that engage North American scholars in issues in Asia, Africa, and Latin America. Recent events in Eastern Europe have begun to restore scholarly contact with some more traditional centers of exchange. Many theological educators have taught in seminaries around the world, and while this experience is often an importation of North American theological wisdom rather than a real exchange, it has been a component in the globalization of North American theological education.

Tight budgets challenge this flow of scholars to other parts of the world, but careful planning is needed to ensure that these contacts continue. As stated above, the strategic building up of global educational centers, partly with the planned use of exchange professors, is an agenda to be taken up in the process of globalization in the future.

Of equal consequence is the movement of faculty members from Africa, Asia, and Latin America to North America. Just as many schools have provided for a greater number of international students in recent years, so schools have sought the brightest and the best from the international pool of theological educators. This effort has resulted in some scholars from the Two Thirds World spending extended periods of time on exchange and research projects in North America and in some accepting full time appointments. This transfer of scholars could in the future work a considerable hardship on the development of theological education in other parts of the world and would surely give globalization the character of a new form of North American imperialism in theological education.

On the other hand, exchange and permanent appointment among the theological educators of the world is one of the most effective ways to stimulate globalization in theological education everywhere. There will be no simple or single solution to this issue. North American seminaries that are searching for the best available scholar in a particular discipline should not paternalistically rule out scholars from the Two Thirds World. These professors should have the opportunity to assess their own ministry and decide on God's call for themselves. At the same time, a global brain drain to more affluent centers of theological education will in no way work for the good of global theological education.

Sensitivity and discussion of this and related issues are important agenda items for all who are involved in the globalization process. A group that could become an ally in this discussion is the recently formed WOCATI. While the organization is new and without a solid, assured future, it is worth speculating on how a group of this kind might develop guidelines for strategic international exchange in theological education together with a coordinating mechanism that could bring the global resources of theological education to places of need and assist in the exchanges that are and will continue to be essential to global theological education.

Perhaps the most potential for international contact is in what is happening and could happen to a greater degree among theological educators as they pursue their personal studies and writing projects. Max Stackhouse provided an example of this when he included in the appendix of his book, *Apologia: Contextualization, Globalization, and Mission in Theological Education*,[8] reactions from three international scholars. The ATS Task Force on Globalization has regularly invited theological students and professors from other parts of the world to its seminars, and the result has been a series of essays in the general area of globalization. Written reflection is by far the least expensive and could become the most consequential way to further global thinking in theology. One can only speculate on how developments in theology would change if an active network of scholars were established in all parts of the world, if theological articles and books routinely included critical responses from theologians in other parts of the world, and if research projects in theology increasingly included international teams of theologians. Encouraging development in this direction is a means and a method most accessible to us all. Efforts in this area could be stimulated by a new generation of grant programs that have international collaboration in theological study as their focus. The newly formed WOCATI might also find a role to play in this promising area of global theological exchange.

V. Outcomes of Globalization

This could be termed the "so what" question. What difference will globalization in theological education make? to whom? and toward what end? Precise answers to such pointed questions are hard to come by at this stage, and lack of precision adds to the difficulty of advocating change to those who are resistant by nature or by vocation. Still, the direction of the answers is clear.

Krister Stendahl, in a commencement address at Harvard Divinity School, put it succinctly: "Unless it has happened in the churches, it has not been done."[9] The sub-title of this essay is "Living the Faith under the Conditions of the Modern World." We began by describing globalization in theological education, not as an idea that has developed out of the world of thought, but as the response of faith to a new historical condition of global interaction brought on by successful advances in the twentieth century in communication and travel. I am completing this essay during the Summer Olympics, 1992, held in Barcelona, Spain. One could hardly conceive of a better example of the phenomenon of globalization as we know it and live it today. Athletes from around the world march together in regal procession at the outset of the games. They live together in a single global Olympic Village. They compete vigorously as national representatives but under an agreed upon set of international rules that are interpreted and applied by an international court of judges. Commentators rehearse the personal stories of leading contestants, bringing North American audiences into intimate touch with world athletic heroes, their struggles, courage, and determination. Even commercial advertisers get into the global spirit by showing how their products are used around the world because, as they put it, while customs change, essentially we are alike. Globalization in theological education is a religious response to this already established reality.

In these initial years, our response to globalization has focussed largely on what goes on within seminaries. This essay attempts to mark some of the accomplishments and to point to the next range of challenges. I believe one of the next challenges is the need to focus greater attention on globalization in the local parish.

In 1988 the ATS Task Force on Globalization prepared a vision statement as a part of its Biennial Report. The statement describes what a globalized seminary would look like in the year 2000. Efforts of this kind seem at times to be adventures into science fiction. But like futuristic fiction of all kinds, some such efforts do become the imaginative catalysts that more practical practitioners shape into actual blueprints for change. We now need a well-crafted vision statement for a globalized local parish.

Some things we can already identify. A globalized parish:

- will need a pastoral leader who has been transformed to see the entire world as the context for his/her parish ministry and the arena of the gospel message;
- will be a place where members struggle with the biblical message and mandates that call for a multidimensional response to conditions in the modern world which include evangelization, ecumenism, dialogue, and development;
- will renew its missional efforts in each of the above categories and consciously attempt to relate its local and its global actions;
- will celebrate the whole of God's creation by including in its regular worship liturgical elements, prayers, and hymns from Christian communities in other parts of the world;
- will establish and maintain an ongoing relationship (alone or in a group of congregations) with a parish or parishes in other parts of the world as a means of experiencing firsthand the reality of the global Christian fellowship and as a basis upon which to develop a variety of relationships in the future; and
- will remain open to God to determine step by step what faithfulness means in the new age of globalization.

I close with this thought. We confess that the Church is a holy mystery, called, redeemed, and sent by God through the power of the Holy Spirit to be the Body of Christ in the world in every age. In a very concrete way, globalization in theological education and in the Church is the attempt to use the unique resources of this age to further the ongoing mission of Christ's Body in the world. Where will it lead? No one really knows. Already though, more professors, students, church leaders, pastors, and members of congregations are experiencing the global dimension of the Church than ever before. In a time when unity and fragmentation, increased mutuality and mounting violence compete for dominance on the global stage, globalization in religious circles is a way of clearly casting the Church's lot with the things that make for peace. As always, the Church will play this role out of weakness not strength. It is no match for the movements of the principalities and the powers. But its strength is evidenced in its weakness. The Church has symbolic powers far beyond its own realization; which is to say God might yet use a renewed, globally aware, compassionate, inter-dependent Church in a dramatic way to further God's mission in the world.

CASE STUDY[10]

Why Globalization?

Professor Oscar Lopez was really looking forward to this segment of the faculty retreat. "We need to get clearer," the chairperson had instructed them, "why we want globalization of Midwestern's curriculum and what we expect seminarians to gain from it." Earlier in the retreat, the Globalization Committee had reported on its one-year pilot project, including an evaluation of the seminarians' cross-cultural experiences in Ghana and Mexico. Now the faculty was dividing into subgroups to engage each other in discussion of globalization's rationale, in the hope of arriving at a more focussed statement of purpose for the Globalization Project. Several faculty had indicated that before they could vote on the future of the pilot, a clearer statement of its theological rationale was needed. Lopez, Midwestern's professor of world missions, expected that this discussion might prove crucial in the decision whether or not to incorporate the pilot into the regular curriculum.

Midwestern Theological Seminary

Midwestern was a century-old seminary located in the farm belt on the outskirts of a large city that was increasingly becoming a center of international commerce. Closely related to a major Protestant denomination, Midwestern's mission historically had been to train young men from the area to serve as pastors in what was colloquially referred to as Farmdale. Earlier in the century the school had also sent missionaries to Asia and Africa, not so much to plant new churches as to support the young churches already existing there. After World War II the preparation of missionaries had virtually ceased at Midwestern, but a trickle of traffic began flowing the other way, as students from the young churches sought a Western education culminating in a more prestigious degree. There were also frequent visitors from the overseas churches to which Midwestern was historically related. In addition, many of the faculty had at some time in their career studied abroad, mostly in Europe.

In recent years the range of students had broadened to include women and men of many denominations and all ages. Culturally the seminary community had become more diverse. African Americans and Hispanics began coming in increasing numbers, although they still constituted small minorities within the student population. In the decade of the 1980s Midwestern had also put greater emphasis on experiential learning, placing students in field sites with competent supervision and required reflection time. All this provided the backdrop for the Globalization Pilot Project, launched in the late 1980s at a time when the Association of Theological Schools in the United States and Canada (ATS) was placing major emphasis on the globalization of theological education.

Kairos

Before coming to Midwestern Theological Seminary five years earlier, Oscar Lopez had been a missionary in Latin America for two decades, after which he taught world religions in a liberal-arts college for several years. He had written numerous articles in his areas of expertise and had served on the Faith and Order Commission of the World Council of Churches.

Lopez viewed the current emphasis on globalization as a *kairos* — a "critical moment" — in the short history of missiology. In a published article Lopez had identified three such *kairoi*. The first was the historic 1910 World Missionary Conference in Edinburgh, which had given powerful impetus to the teaching of missions in North American seminaries. The second was the landmark "Study of Theological Education in the United States and Canada" in 1956, which advocated "clear understanding of the nature and mission of the Church" as the centerpiece of a sound theological education. The "mission" that this study moved to the center, however, was that of the local church. *World* missions was consequently shunted to the margin.

Lopez's third *kairos* was the 1988 report of the ATS Committee on Global Theological Education. Recognizing the profound connectedness of human life worldwide, the committee recommended that globalization become a major program emphasis for North American seminaries in the 1990s, permeating every field of study. At about the same time as the ATS report, Joe Hough and John Cobb were arguing that "all Christian theology today should be global theology," recognizing God's concern for the whole world and Christ's redemption of all peoples. "The world consciousness that is today Christian consciousness," they wrote, "should permeate the entire curriculum and not be relegated to only one of its parts." To accomplish this they advocated interdisciplinary team-teaching of such core courses as "The global context of our lives," "What is the church's mission today?" and "What does the reality of Buddhism say to us about our faith and our mission?" Lopez regarded this new global vision as the third *kairos* because missiology offered exactly the kind of holistic and interdisciplinary approach that globalization required.

Given the background that Lopez brought to Midwestern, it was only natural that he would be appointed to the Globalization Committee by the dean, himself a strong advocate of globalization. Lopez soon persuaded the committee to propose a pilot project, the core of which was a three-week overseas "immersion" experience for seminarians. If this year-long pilot proved successful, the proposal called for its incorporation into the curriculum as a standard requirement for the M.Div. degree.

Within the faculty there had been little vocal opposition to the pilot project before it was adopted unanimously. There also had been little discussion of its rationale. "If we had waited for a consensus on theological rationale," the dean quipped afterward, "we'd still be debating it!" Hence Lopez was eager to see what direction the current faculty discussion would take.

In Search of a Rationale

Lopez filled his cup at the coffeemaker and joined his subgroup of four. There was Mary Carmody, professor of systematic theology and an "institution" at Midwestern. Lopez had learned that one needed her support to accomplish anything significant at Midwestern. At the other end of the age spectrum was Werner Hildebrandt, associate professor of hermeneutics, appointed the previous year. Despite his youth, Hildebrandt already had an established reputation as a biblical scholar. He had been raised Lutheran in the Midwest and continued to be an active participant in the Lutheran Church on the local and synodical levels. And there was James Jackson, professor of worship and preaching. With degrees in music and theology as well as a D.Min. from Princeton, he had joined the faculty after serving for a decade as pastor of a large AME church. Obviously bursting to talk about a recent class session in which several seminarians had shared some learnings from their immersion experience, Jackson had already begun.

"We were working on Luke 6:20, 'Blessed are you poor.' They began telling how the word 'poor' now has so many more ramifications than the economic definition they brought to Mexico. Contrary to their expectations, in the midst of incredible misery they found joy and spiritual depth that put them to shame. One said she left Mexico wondering who in fact was rich and who was poor. The experience compelled them to wrestle with what poverty really means. These are different people than those who left for Mexico. I've seen seminarians change over the years, but never like this in just three weeks. It's astounding! Think what it's going to mean for them to open up the scriptures and preach in the light of this experience."

On the heels of Jackson's story Werner Hildebrandt sounded a more skeptical note. "It's an interdependent world. Business knows this, and so do we as faculty," said Hildebrandt, recalling his recent post-graduate study in Tübingen. "But that's not the world of our students. How does globalization play out in Farmdale? For that matter, how does it play out in my own field? I'm not clear what the theological justification is for globalization. It sounds a lot like old time liberalism."

"It's not liberalism but *liberation*, Werner, that's at the heart of globalization," Lopez shot back. "I don't have to tell you that in Hebrew Scripture God consistently takes the side of the oppressed, and that in the New Testament Jesus' mission is 'to bring good news to the poor.' Globalization means getting involved in that liberating activity of God, being in solidarity with the marginated — globally and locally."

"That rhetoric may play well in San Salvador," replied Hildebrandt, "but I don't think people in Farmdale would know what you're talking about, let alone recognize it as 'Good News.' "

"I share Werner's perplexity concerning the rationale," said Mary Carmody. "We've made up our minds to have a Globalization Project — that issue's settled and I support it. But we've had little discussion of its theological underpinnings. The economic and political reasons are obvious, but what's the *theological* rationale? Sometimes I suspect that our real reason is aesthetic: we think it's intrinsically good for people to have the most intense and varied experience possible."

Agreeing that "experience for its own sake" wasn't a good enough reason, Lopez tried to put it in broader perspective. "An immersion experience in a culture significantly different from our own is an important way of overcoming our parochialism. As a kid I was afflicted with acute myopia. Today we live and minister among persons suffering from myopia, whose vision may not extend beyond their own family or church or country. We marvel that shirts cost so little without ever questioning the sweatshops in Mexico that make that price possible. Our sympathy is aroused by seeing starving Ethiopian children on TV but not enough to make us change our lifestyles. What *does* change us is direct contact with persons whose life-experience is different from our own—and that's a change that cannot be achieved in a classroom."

"Overcoming parochialism is a worthy objective," acknowledged Carmody, "but it's more sociological than theological. I've heard many theological reasons for globalization, but each runs in a different direction. A goal I often hear is to enter into dialogue with world religions, which, of course, means holding in abeyance the question of Christ's uniqueness. Another is liberal humanitarianism, usually fueled by guilt for our national and religious imperialism. At the opposite extreme is a postmodern version of nineteenth-century evangelism—you know, 'Win the world for Christ.' "

"Actually, it's evangelism in reverse," suggested Lopez. "Contrast the spiritual malaise in mainline U.S. churches with the spiritual energy in the Two Thirds World. From Brazil to Korea, from South Africa to China, a vitality of faith is emerging among the poor. There's newfound joy in the Lord, active witnessing for Christ, and involvement in issues of justice and humanization. Some see globalization as our eagerness to tap into that spiritual energy found in the churches of Africa, Asia, and Latin America."

"We're looking for something out there that can save us," Carmody commented.

Hildebrandt didn't see that spiritual energy as something U.S. churches could tap into. "Wherever I look in other cultures, I see energy in highly defined, homogeneous groups. Here, however, we are committed to pluralism and inclusivity. You can't just take the energy that comes from cultural homogeneity and transfer it to our pluralistic situation."

Carmody cited her sabbatical experience in support of that. "All my life I've prized pluralism, but in Japan it is no virtue at all. Japan is a successful culture because it is absolutely homogeneous. Every Japanese church I saw was like that, and there was a theological rationale for it."

"Homogeneity is stressed in the church growth movement," observed Jackson. "All the members of a congregation are similar, you pander to that sameness, and the church grows."

"A gospel that gives a clear Christian identity is exactly what the churches here in Farmdale need," agreed Hildebrandt, "but you can't import identity from abroad. Cross-cultural experience doesn't enable a pastor to shape congregational identity—it could actually create confusion instead."

Lopez exploded. "I disagree *profoundly*. Most of our students are upwardly mobile and want to fit into a middle-class congregation where everyone mirrors everyone else. That's a problem, because for a church to serve the community, it has to reach out to those who are different. Experiencing cultural differences and acquiring the social analytical tools to bridge those differences are *exactly* what our students need."

"I don't disagree," Hildebrandt replied. "In fact, it's the lack of those skills that troubles me. Fifteen years ago seminarians came right out of college and lacked experience. Today they are rich in experience but lack analytical skills. I have students who can't construct a theology beyond a few biblical quotes! It's not more experience they need, but concentrated academic work to develop the necessary analytical skills."

"They have no hooks on which to hang these new experiences," Carmody added. "A cross-cultural experience is like stepping out of one framework of interpretation and into another, and afterward trying to translate everything back into your original framework. Parochialism is the failure to recognize this plurality of frameworks. But I wonder if it's even possible to step from one framework into another."

"It's hard," Hildebrandt agreed. "But now you're suggesting that the goal of education is not to maximize experience, but to learn how to compare and analyze experiences."

"Which is very *Western!*" Carmody chuckled.

Hildebrandt pressed home his point. "What we need, then, is a whole department of anthropology—as if we don't have enough to teach already! Do we really want to add to the curriculum another whole layer that has little to do with the work of the parish?"

"But wouldn't it be true," Jackson queried, "that in biblical studies you're already working at understanding another culture? Aren't the tools needed to interpret a biblical text a lot like those needed to understand another culture?"

"I would agree with that," Hildebrandt replied.

"Then we really don't need that additional layer of courses. We could build on what's already in the curriculum."

"Sure, but if we want seminarians to have those analytical and hermeneutical tools, we should concentrate on that during their seminary career instead of placing them in churches or other field settings before they've acquired the skills needed to analyze and interpret those experiences."

"Does analysis precede experience," Jackson asked Hildebrandt, "or does experience precede analysis? I don't think it's an either/or. In my Afro-American music course I require students to make four visits to black churches, then return to reflect on their learnings in class. Some have the analytical skills to process those experiences. Others need help, for which I'm there and available. And some aren't ever going to get it."

"That points to another concern I have," added Carmody. "If a transcultural experience remains superficial, then it's a nice, harmless diversion—a contemporary version of 'The Grand Tour.' But if our students really engage people from other religions and cultures—if they become genuinely *immersed*, which is what we say we want for them—then there's a vulnerability and a threat. The ground could be cut out from under them by the clash of cultures and religions. It can be shattering! That's what happened to me. I wish I had never gone to Japan. Then I could go on with my naive belief in the value of pluralism."

"Well, yes," acknowledged Jackson, "but some of our students come back from black churches with that vertigo, too. Something bothers them, and they come back with their heads spinning. So there's a conflict, Mary, and you're saying it's uncomfortable. But isn't that what it's all about?"

New Biblical Perspective

Even as he protested that he could see no relevance of globalization for his own field, Hildebrandt did acknowledge that one of his students had surprised him with a direct application of a transcultural experience to biblical interpretation. The student had been in Hildebrandt's course in Ephesians a number of years earlier at another school. Hildebrandt had interpreted the epistle as a triumphalist document and therefore cautioned against direct application to the contemporary world, which, he believed, needed no more Christian triumphalism.

Shortly after the conclusion of the course, the student visited South Africa for two weeks. On his return he came straight to Hildebrandt's office. "You won't believe this," he told his professor, "but in that culture one of the most important documents is Ephesians! Where people are genuinely downtrodden and oppressed, Ephesians isn't read in a triumphalist way, but as a cause of great hope. It's read with a futuristic, not a present cast — not triumphalist at all!"

Reflecting on that event, Hildebrandt commented: "If only everyone could go and see that the culture frames the religious tradition, and that there's a meaning of that tradition in relation to the culture. That student learned something very important."

At that point Lopez's subgroup was interrupted by the call to reconvene. As the faculty gradually reassembled, Lopez marvelled at the diversity of opinion expressed in the previous hour. He began to wonder if the faculty could ever come to agreement on a statement of theological rationale, and whether the difficulty of that task might not impede or even prevent incorporation of the pilot into the regular curriculum.

TEACHING NOTE

Why Globalization?

In this case Midwest Theological Seminary has arrived at a turning point in its globalization project. After completing a one-year pilot (preceded by years of planning led by the Globalization Committee), the faculty must decide whether or not to incorporate the project into the regular M.Div. curriculum. Several of the faculty want a clearer statement of the project's theological rationale before making this decision. This situation makes the case a useful tool for theological schools that are (a) contemplating the initiation of a globalization program, (b) writing the rationale for a program already adopted, or (c) evaluating a program that is in place.

I. Objectives
Possible objectives for the case discussion are:

A. to identify the reasons for incorporating globalization into the curriculum, especially the various theological reasons for such a program;

B. to identify the theological and pedagogical issues that must be addressed in developing such a program;

C. to draft a theological rationale for a globalization project.

II. Issues
Discussion might well open with a listing of the issues found in the case. Fol-

lowing such a listing, the group should decide which issue(s) it wishes to pursue. Here are some of the issues that have been identified by readers:

A. What are the possible theological justifications for globalization of the curriculum? Which ones do we consider appropriate and which ones inappropriate?

B. Are the faculty members solidly behind the project, as they say they are, or does the dispute over rationale indicate an underlying lack of support?

C. Is a consensus on theological rationale necessary, or is it better avoided, as the dean implies?

D. What pedagogical issues must be faced regarding immersion experiences (e.g., value of experiential learning, acquiring the necessary analytic tools, adequate debriefing)?

E. How will local congregations benefit from globalization of the theological curriculum?

III. Persons

If it is known in advance that the case discussion is to focus on issue #1, then skip the listing of issues and begin with the four characters in the case: Lopez, Jackson, Hildebrandt, and Carmody. Identify and record the theological justifications and objections enunciated by each. Note also what personal experiences have shaped the stance of each and what is personally at stake for each in the outcome. This could be done by the whole group, or by four subgroups, one to develop the profile of each character.

IV. Analysis

Optionally, these four positions can be further analyzed in terms of Don Browning's four definitions of globalization: 1) evangelization, 2) ecumenical cooperation, 3) interreligious dialogue, 4) liberation and justice (see "Resources").

V. Ownership

Ask participants to indicate by vote which of the four characters best represents their own position. Possible resistance to such a forced choice can be overcome by allowing time after the vote for individuals to qualify their choice.

VI. Brainstorming

Pose to the group this question: "If we were to mount a globalization project, how would we state its theological rationale?" Divide into groups of three or four to draft statements. Have each group record its draft on newsprint for sharing with the whole group.

ADDITIONAL RESOURCES:

Browning, Don S. "Globalization and the Task of Theological Education in North America." *Theological Education*, Vol. XXII, No. 1, pp. 43-59.

Hough, Joseph C., Jr., and John B. Cobb, Jr. *Christian Identity and Theological Education*. Chico, Calif.: Scholars Press, 1985.

COMMENTARY

Why Globalization?

M. SHAWN COPELAND

The faculty of Midwestern Theological Seminary has endorsed a program of globalization but is not precisely sure why. We might conjecture that this interest is either an unconscious paean to the school's history of training young men for the missions in Asia and Africa or a way of maintaining contact with the churches of those continents with which Midwestern has had an historic relationship. Students from various countries and cultures of Asia and Africa regularly matriculate at Midwestern; perhaps engagement in globalization is a way of upholding the U.S. side of the exchange. Or, perhaps, acceptance of a program of globalization helps the faculty to feel less isolated, more a part of the current trends in theological education. There have been changes in the demography and cultural diversity of the school's student body with increased numbers of second or third career students, women, African Americans, and Hispanic Americans. Paradoxically, globalization may be a way of deflecting attention away from the concerns of these "non-traditional" students; Midwestern's faculty may be suffering from a case of what Professor Jamie T. Phelps calls "global vision and domestic blindness."[11]

The stances of faculty members participating in the subgroup range from the cautiously tentative to the enthusiastic. Close attention to the discussion reveals genuine if heretofore unarticulated questions which challenge the dean's galloping commitment to the project ("If we had waited for a consensus on theological rationale, we'd still be debating it!"). Some of these implicit and explicit questions include: How is theological education to be *reconceived* in relation to globalization? Can the model of theological education to which we are accustomed be reconciled with the demands globalization makes of faculty and students? What will globalization mean for the entire seminary curriculum? What are the expected outcomes for administration, faculty, and students of a globalization program? What pedagogical methods and learning experiences are best suited to a program of globalization? What is the desired effect of globalization on the church? What is the mission and ministry of the church today? What is the relation of globalization to ministry in local parishes in the United States? What skills are needed for effective gospel ministry in a world considered a global village? What is meant by interdependence and dependence, by development, underdevelopment, and overdevelopment? What is liberation? What is relativism? What is pluralism? What is theology? What are the theological underpinnings of globalization? How do we teach seminary students to do theology? What is the relation between theology and social analysis? What is the relation between theology and cultural studies? What is contextual theology? What does it mean to say that "all Christian theology today should be global theology"? What is the relation of globalization to missiology? How is Christian theology seriously and authentically to engage world religions?

Certainly, there are many other questions to be raised; still, these questions afford some appreciation of the wide-ranging effects of a school's decision to participate in a globalization program. None, however, is more important than those which concern experimentation in theological education and a clear and explicit theological rationale for globalization with its accent on social analysis. In any such endeavor, pedagogy and theory are intimately intertwined; to speak explicitly about one is to speak implicitly about the other. Indeed, these issues are quite in the thick of the Midwestern faculty's discussion. In what follows, I will comment briefly on these issues relating them to the case of Midwestern and to the wider instance it represents.

Pedagogy and Theories of Knowing

While pedagogy can never be isolated from theories of knowing, uncritical theories of knowing breed bias. I use the term "bias" in the technical sense in which Bernard Lonergan employs it.[12] Bias denotes aberrations of human under-standing or affect which exclude and repress insights and the further questions which they generate. Bias stems from the more or less conscious and deliberate refusal to think, to understand, to act, and to live attentively, intelligently, ration-ally, and responsibly. Narrow and limited intellectual, moral, and religious horizons are not only the *products* of bias; they *reproduce* bias. I begin with bias because one of the most obvious and general objectives of any program of globalization of theological education in the United States is increased and critical openness, regard, and appreciation for social and cultural experiences which differ from those we hold in common. How do we as theological educators go about fostering such critical openness, regard, and appreciation? How do we facilitate and support our students' discovery and appreciation of difference without reinforcing bias? How do we assist our students in becoming conscious of their own bias? Indeed, how do *we* become conscious of our *own* capitulation to bias when that bias springs from a communal flight from understanding and is embedded in and supported by the whole fabric and texture of our civilization and culture?[13]

We begin to respond to these questions and our biased situation, I think, by attending to the human mind. If the teacher's most basic and sacred task is to nurture the mind, it is necessary to know just what mind is, to have a concrete and precise grasp of the mind's natural desires and spontaneity, its dynamic struc-ture and operational mode of development, its value. As theological educators we are forced to meet prior and crucial questions: What does it mean to know? "What am I doing when I am knowing? Why is doing that knowing? What do I know when I do it?"[14] The common ocular metaphor of "knowing as looking" is a source of misunderstanding; it fosters a kind of picture-thinking that relies dangerously and uncritically on visual images. All too easily and all too often, visual images have been used to buttress racist, sexist, imperialist definition and delimitation. As a foundation for knowing, visual images (sense experiences) are incapable of mediating the normative and critical exigencies of intelligence and reasonableness.

Critical realism affords a proper and adequate foundation for knowing, for the thorough-going social and personal transformation that globalization programs advocate. Critical realism grounds human knowing in the intellectual operations through which truths are discovered, verified, and revised. On a critical realist account, knowing is a dynamic, self-assembling structure involving distinct and irreducible activities: seeing, hearing, smelling, touching, tasting, inquiring, imagining, understanding, conceiving, reflecting, marshalling and weighing the evidence, judging. No single one of these activities alone may be named knowing; each is but a component in human knowing and is not to be confused with knowing itself.[15] Critical realism offers a "radical cognitive therapy aimed at a basic liberation of all human subjects through a heightening of their awareness whereby they appropriate the imperatives of human freedom as dynamic orientations to be attentive, to be intelligent, to be reasonable, and to be loving."[16] This stance apprehends racism, sexism, and classism not simply as topics or problems to be solved, as something already-out-there-now and brutally real, but as the alienation of human intelligence, as the biased and iniquitous ways of living that they are. Consideration of cognitional theory is a central step in experiential education because, while the implementation of a program of globalization calls for a radical shift in pedagogical methods, the *mind* (of students and faculty) is still the *primary site* of learning, of knowing, and of deciding and acting for practical and intelligent change.

The pivotal step for Midwestern's globalization program is faculty participation in an immersion experience; this step insinuates an important shift in pedagogical method in theological education. To speak about the globalization of theological education is not mere talk of adding some novel feature or textbooks or courses to the seminary curriculum. The globalization of theological education is to grasp a new way of reconceiving the meaning of education as well as the substance and function of the entire seminary curriculum. Certainly globalization programs challenge faculty to reevaluate the banking mode of education as *the* singular and legitimate pedagogical approach. Or to put it bluntly: with globalization, those of us who are theological educators face the loss of personal power and control in the learning process. Faculty no longer function as highly specialized experts. Rather, they become *co-learners*; "the flow is in both directions."[17] Faculty are propelled headlong into the process of learning and unlearning, researching data, questioning authorities, reflecting on new and different social and cultural experiences, revising former positions, marshalling and weighing new evidence against the old, reaching different and probable judgments, making new choices and decisions. Yet, the role of teacher is in no way diminished; faculty are invited to model education as dialogical, as critical dialectical thinking, as questioning, as morally and intellectually responsible to the Christian mission, as "the practice of freedom."[18] The globalization of theological education asks of us what it and we ask of our students: humility and reverence before the minds and hearts of others; rigorous self-examination; integrity; openness to the conversion of our intellectual, moral, and religious orientations; commitment to the practical and intelligent social transformation for justice in history and society.

Midwestern Seminary

After two years, the faculty of Midwestern Theological Seminary is still unable to articulate a coherent and substantive theological rationale for its decision to engage in a program of globalization. In a certain sense, this inability is not all that surprising. It is widely acknowledged that the Christian church in general and the Christian mission in particular have been wrestling for some time now with multiple grave, staggering, and complex crises. Quite unimaginable in the nineteenth century, this situation stems from several factors including the waning hegemony of the West, the home of Christianity for more than a millennium, coupled with the emergence of other political, economic, and cultural spheres of power; the rise of peoples' struggles which contest the structured biases of racism, sexism, class exploitation, and imperialism; in the West, a loss of confidence in the promises of the Enlightenment; the proliferation of weapons of mass destruction; the historical tragedies of Auschwitz, Hiroshima and Nagasaki, war and gulag, and chronic mass starvation in the Third World.[19] This situation of crisis makes us even more conscious of the impossibility of merely fabricating idealistic theological constructions.[20] At the same time, we have not shifted fully and competently into the new paradigmatic way of understanding and articulating theology. We are caught in the gap. It is not surprising that the faculty of Midwestern Theological Seminary has not yet developed a theological rationale for the globalization program. Yet the current state of theology teaches us that all theology is tentative and contextual; that all theologies take their data, problems and questions, metaphors, and analogies from the various cultural contexts or matrices (i.e., political, economic) from within which they arise. Globalization recognizes fruitful possibilities for theology even in this time of transition.

The elements of a full and coherent theological rationale surface in the faculty conversation. An outline of such a rationale can be put forward. *First,* the faculty recognizes that it has a distinctive contribution to make to the mission and ministry of the church—the preparation of the next generation of Christian ministers, preachers, pastors, and religious educators. A significant dimension of their task as theological educators is helping students to learn to think theologically *with* and *on behalf of* the church. *Second,* the faculty grasps that human living is not only inter-dependent, but that inter-dependence has inescapable moral and ethical (as well as aesthetic) consequences. The technological, economic, political, and cultural overdevelopment of some sectors of the world depends upon and requires the technological, economic, political, and cultural underdevelopment of other sectors. *Third,* the group recognizes that humanity, richly and disconcertingly diverse as it is, is more than some aggregate of autonomous isolated monads; human beings are intrinsically and metaphysically connected. Moreover, God's concern is for the whole and all the world; Christ's redemption is for all peoples and makes the whole world and all the world new. *Fourth,* some method of social analysis provides a way of apprehending, organizing, understanding, and judging social (technological, economic, and political) patterns and their meanings. Social critique takes a rigorous and concrete form with verifiable content, thus obviating simplistic moral idealism. Moreover, the social facts have moral, ethical, and religious consequences. *Fifth,* the group recognizes that culture frames the creation and reception of religious traditions; culture also extracts symbols, meanings, and values from that tradition. Christian theology in mission has the intellectual and moral responsibility to attend seriously, that is, concretely and experientially, to the voices of various peoples of various cultures in the proclamation of the Gospel of Christ.

These elements converge in a theological rationale which suggests that a globalization program offers an approach to theological education that grasps the mission and ministry of the church as humble response to the life and ministry, passion and death, and resurrection of Jesus of Nazareth, the Christ of God. More than most approaches, globalization advances the *end* of theological education as its motive: preparing for the coming Reign of God. Globalization offers an approach to theological education that requires learners (faculty and student) to grapple with the social incongruities uncovered in various cultural matrices and with the relationship between redemption and the concrete social transformation of human persons.

Notes

1. D. H. Lawrence, *Selected Poems* (New York: Viking Press, 1959), p. 74.

2. Don S. Browning, "Globalization and the Task of Theological Education," *Theological Education* (Autumn 1986) (Vandalia, Ohio: Association of Theological Schools, 1986), pp. 43-59.

3. Francis Cardinal Arinze, "Globalization of Theological Education," *Theological Education* (Autumn 1986) (Vandalia, Ohio: Association of Theological Schools, 1986), pp. 7-31.

4. Paul Tillich, *The Shaking of the Foundations* (New York: C. Scribner's Sons, 1948).

5. Arinze, pp. 8-11.

6. Joseph C. Hough, Jr., and John B. Cobb, Jr., *Christian Identity and Theological Education* (Chico, California: Scholars Press, 1985).

7. *Theological Education Supplement* (Pittsburgh, Pennsylvania: Association of Theological Schools, 1992).

8. Max L. Stackhouse with Natawan Boonprasat-Lewis, et al, *Apologia: Contextualization, Globalization, and Mission in Theological Education* (Grand Rapids, Michigan: W. B. Eerdmans, 1988).

9. Krister Stendahl, Commencement Address, Harvard Divinity School, n.d.

10. Copyright © 1993 by the Case Study Institute. The names of persons and places in this case have been disguised to protect the privacy of those involved in the situation.

11. Professor Jamie T. Phelps, O.P., is assistant professor of doctrinal theology at Catholic Theological Union (Chicago) where she teaches courses in systematic theology and missiology. Professor Phelps is a participant in the Pilot Immersion Project (PIP).

12. The term "bias" in its technical sense as developed by philosopher-theologian Bernard Lonergan departs completely from the notion of bias as personal preference or inclination of personal temperament. Lonergan identifies four principal manners in which bias or distortion may occur. There is the dramatic bias which appears as the denial of painful effects in the day-to-day living out of our lives; this bias is brought to light by psychology. There is the individual bias of egoism. There is the group bias of ethnocentricism or social class or racial conflict between groups and the gender-based societal conflict between men and women. And finally, there is the general bias of common sense by which common sense smugly deems itself omni-competent and pits itself against theory or science or philosophy. This last form of bias plays a distinctive role in constricting and distorting insights for the practical, intelligent, imaginative ordering of the human good in society and in history. See *Insight, A Study of*

Human Understanding (1957; New York: Philosophical Library, 1973), pp. 191-206, 218-42.

13. Lonergan, *Insight,* pp. xiv-xv.

14. Lonergan, *Method in Theology* (New York: Herder and Herder, 1972), p. 25.

15. See Bernard Lonergan, "Cognitional Structure," in *Collection: Papers by Bernard Lonergan, S.J.,* ed. Frederick Crowe (Montreal: Palm Publishers, 1967), pp. 221-39. For a detailed account of a cognitional theory see *Insight, A Study of Human Understanding.*

16. Matthew L. Lamb, *Solidarity with Victims: Toward a Theology of Social Transformation* (New York: Crossroad Publishing, 1982), p. 85.

17. Paulo Freire, *Education for Critical Consciousness* (1969; New York: The Seabury Press, 1974), p. 125.

18. *Ibid.,* pp. 1-58.

19. David J. Bosch, *Transforming Mission: Paradigm Shifts in Theology of Mission* (Maryknoll, New York: Orbis Books, 1991), pp. 181-89; Hans Küng, "A New Basic Model for Theology: Divergences and Convergence," in Hans Küng and David Tracy, eds., *Paradigm Change in Theology: A Symposium for the Future,* trans. Margaret Köhl (New York: The Crossroad Publishing Company, 1989), pp. 439-52.

20. *Ibid.,* p. 447.

[3]

GLOBALIZATION AS EVANGELISM

ESSAY

PAUL G. HIEBERT

Globalization has surfaced in our western consciousness in the past decade, but its reality has been emerging over the past four centuries. Exploration, trade, colonialism and modernity have engulfed relatively autonomous societies and drawn them inexorably into worldwide economic and sociopolitical systems.

Christian missions have played an important role in this globalization of the world. Missionaries from the west went around the world preaching the Gospel of Jesus Christ, and planting congregations. The church is one of the first truly global bodies to emerge. Today it is among the first to raise the question about the nature of globalization and its implications for us as human beings.

Before we define evangelism in a global era, we must examine how it was viewed in the eras leading up to the present.

I. Evangelism in the Modern Era

We are all people of our times. This is true whether we accept the worldview of our age or resist it. In both cases our agenda is determined largely by the assumptions and questions of the world around us. It is important, therefore, for us to examine the assumptions of modernity to see how these shaped our definition of evangelism for the last two centuries.

A. The Worldview of Modernity

Modernity is the grandchild of the Renaissance and the child of the Enlightenment. It has profoundly shaped western thought, and now the world, providing them with a model of globalization. It is a model seeking a unified world built on a single global culture and interlocking economic, political and social systems.

One of the characteristics of modernity is a shift from a God to a human centered world. In the Medieval west God ruled God's creation. In the Enlightenment nature was divorced from the supernatural and seen as an autonomous

64

reality operating by mechanistic principles. God may rule the heavens, but humans are the rulers of the earth.[1] They do so by reason, by discovering the laws of nature that enable them to engineer the world around them (Locke), by fitting into nature (Rousseau), or by a strong leader (Nietzsche).

A second characteristic of modernity is the separation between *rex cogitans* (the realm of objective, scientific knowledge) and *rex extensa* (the material realm of nature). The former is made up of "facts" and "natural laws" that can be discovered by the empiricism of Bacon and the rationalism of Descartes. The human goal is to integrate these into one grand unified theory of reality that will enable us to rule nature. In this public realm of positive knowledge there is no room for the subjectivism of feelings or values. These are relegated to the private world of personal opinion. For many modern people, religions belong to this private sphere of life.[2]

A third element of modernity is a stress on the emancipated, autonomous individual. As Allen Bloom points out, this is seen in the shift from the word "soul" with its religious connotations of divine origin and eternal destiny, to Locke's term "self" with its notions of the autonomous person.[3] People learned to see themselves as free beings capable of making their own choices and creating themselves. As Peter Berger points out, we came to believe in the self-made person who can become what she or he wants to be through self-engineering.[4] Self-fulfillment and freedom became unquestioned "goods."

A fourth characteristic of modernity relevant to our analysis is its emphasis on progress. A deep faith emerged that positive knowledge based on reason and facts would create a better world. In principle, all problems came to be seen as solvable, given enough research and human effort.

One of the fruits of modernity was the rise of western technology and political power, and the theory of evolution that validated its superiority. Another fruit was colonialism in which the western countries sought first to exploit, and then to "civilize" the non-western world.

B. Evangelism Defined in the Modern Era

Western Christians in the nineteenth and early twentieth centuries were largely children of the Enlightenment. At points they resisted elements of modernity, but most did not see the worldview of which they were a part. It should not surprise us that their views of evangelism were shaped in response to the Enlightenment paradigm.

In the first place, the church accepted the separation of reality into supernatural and natural realms. Christianity dealt with spiritual matters, science with the material world. Evangelism was to call people to a spiritual salvation and to eternal life in heaven.

The division between evangelism and social concern did not come easily. Early in the eighteenth century Christians were also leaders in social reform. Evangelism for Jonathan Edwards, the Wesleys and William Carey was a call to repentance from sin and lives transformed by the power of God. They stressed "service to the soul" and "service to the body."

By the end of the nineteenth century, however, the dualism of the Enlightenment won out, and most Christians left the care for human needs to the state and to science. For example, the Student Volunteer Movement, founded in 1886, had as its watchword, "the evangelization of the world in this generation." Evangelism for the movement meant leading people to a personal, saving faith in God through Christ that would lead to eternal salvation.

Those in the church more influenced by the inherent secularism of modernity sought to reinterpret Christianity in human terms. They defined sin as social evil, and salvation as freedom from want and the achievement of full human potential by all. David Bosch notes,

> Gradually, mainline theologians began to abandon the dramatically super-natural aspects of the traditional postmillennial view of history. The idea of history as a cosmic struggle between God and Satan was discarded, as was belief in the physical return of Christ. The kingdom was not future or other-worldly, but "here and now"; it was, in fact, already taking place in the dramatic technical advances of North America.[5]

The key ideas of the new mood were continuity and social progress. Postmil-lennialism was now wedded to the theory of evolution. Building God's Kingdom was now as much a matter of technique and program as religious piety and depend-ence on the leading of God. Jesus the Savior became Jesus the benevolent and wise teacher, the spiritual genius in whom the religious capacities of humankind were fully developed.[6] This led to the Social Gospel Movement with its permeative rather than conversionist view of Christian influence. Adherents to other faiths were not seen as eternally lost but as needing the fulfillment they could find in Christ.

Much of the church accepted the Enlightenment belief that truth is equated with objective, propositional knowledge. Evangelism was defined as the presen-tation of that truth and conversion as the mental affirmation of it. Subjective responses to objective truth, both personal experiences with God and moral obe-dience, were seen as fruits of conversion, not essential parts of it.

The church also bought into the notion of the autonomous individual. This influenced the definition of evangelism in different ways. In evangelical circles, it led to a stress on personal salvation based on the decision of each individual. People were held responsible for their own destinies and capable of making their own decisions.[7] Evangelists, therefore, invited people to make personal decisions for Christ. They also felt personally responsible for the salvation of the lost. In liberal circles, the focus on the individual took another track. Salvation was increas-ingly defined in terms of self-fulfillment here on earth.

Individualism influenced both evangelicals and liberals in yet another way, namely the rise of voluntarism. With notable exceptions evangelism and missions became the activity not so much of denominations and churches, but of individuals with personal callings, and voluntary societies of like-minded people.

Finally, the church, for the most part, accepted uncritically the modern belief in human progress. Wilbert Shenk writes,

> The seventeenth-century New England Puritan missionaries largely set the course for modern missions. They defined their task as preaching the gospel so that Native Americans would be converted and receive personal salvation.

But early in their missionary experience these New Englanders concluded that Indian converts could only be Christians if they were "civilized." The model by which they measured their converts was English Puritan civilization. The missionaries ... gathered these new Christians into churches for nurture and discipline, and set up programs to transform Christian Indians into English Puritans.[8]

Similarly in 1890, Rev. T. W. Pearce pointed out that merely introducing Christianity to China was not enough. Western civilization, in its entirety, had to "overcome" Chinese civilization.[9] Evangelism, therefore, was to make a person a Christian and a modern human.

This equation of progress with Christianity and modernity reinforced the old notion of Christendom, namely that the west and its cultures were Christian, and the rest of the world and its cultures were pagan. This led to a differentiation between evangelism and missions. Missions was carried out in the pagan world and included training converts in western Christian ways.

A second consequence of linking the gospel with western culture was the close association Christian missions came to have with colonialism. At the beginning of the eighteenth century European trading corporations were hostile to missionary efforts. As colonialism matured and became the purview of national governments, a rapprochement took place. Bosch notes,

As it became customary for British missionaries to labor in British colonies, French missionaries in French colonies, and German missionaries in German colonies, it was only natural for these missionaries to be regarded as both vanguard and rearguard for the colonial powers. Whether they liked it or not, the missionaries became pioneers of Western imperialistic expansion.[10]

In a similar vein John Philip, superintendent of the London Mission Society at the Cape of Good Hope after 1819 and a strong champion for the oppressed peoples in the colonies, wrote,

While our missionaries ... are everywhere scattering the seeds of civilization, social order, happiness, they are, by the most unexceptionable means, extending British interests, British influence, and the British empire. Wherever the missionary places his standard among the savage tribe, their prejudices against the colonial government give way.[11]

In the United States, missions were equated not with direct colonial expansion but with the American belief in Manifest Destiny. Many Christians believed that God had uniquely chosen and blessed America, and America, therefore, had an obligation to Christianize and civilize the world.

C. Assessment

The evangelistic efforts in North America during this era were remarkably successful. At the time of American Independence only about five percent of the population were church members.[12] As a result of two Great Awakenings the percentage doubled by 1800. It reached a peak of about sixty percent in 1970 as a result of the extensive evangelistic and revival programs of the Methodist, Baptist and Presbyterian churches, and, more recently, the birth of new evangelistically oriented denominations.

The results of western mission efforts were equally impressive. By the middle of the twentieth century the church was to be found in most countries of the world. In 1900 ninety-five percent of the church was in the west and white. By 2000 only an estimated sixty percent of the world's Christians will be in western lands – a testimony to God who works despite the faults of God's messengers and the flaws of their methods.

Among these flaws was the divorce of spiritual salvation from social transformation. Mainline missions increasingly equated salvation with social development, and lost the wholeness of the gospel. Conservatives, shaped by the nineteenth-century traditions of revivalism, pietism, evangelicalism and, more recently, pentecostalism, preached a spiritual gospel that did not address the deeper social realities around them.

A second flaw had to do with defining faith as a mental affirmation of rational truth. This was countered by the Pentecostal and Charismatic movements which defined faith in terms of personal experience. Neither moved beyond these to see faith ultimately as an ethical response to truth and experience, as obedience to Christ's call to a life of radical discipleship. Consequently, the churches that were planted often did not manifest the transforming power of the Spirit in the lives of the people, in the life of the church as a community or in the world around them. The influences of pietism and holiness were felt from time to time, but these stressed primarily personal holiness defined in spiritual terms.

A third fault in modern evangelism was its extreme individualism. On the one level this led to defining sin in personal terms and ignoring corporate sin that manifests itself in social structures and cultural ideologies. Even the Social Gospel Movement sought mainly to help people improve their conditions within the existing social systems rather than calling for a radical transformation of those systems. Development, not revolution, was its answer to poverty, illiteracy and oppression.

At a deeper level the emphasis on individualism often led to a weak ecclesiology. The church often resembled a club, a voluntary gathering of similar people with shared interests, rather than a covenant community in which Christians of different classes and ethnic groups care for one another because they belong to the same body.

At the deepest level, individualism was itself an expression of the human-centered view of the Enlightenment. Across the board Christians came to see evangelism and missions as the task they were called to do for God. Less emphasis was placed on seeking the guidance of God and more on planning, organization and human effort. "The building of the kingdom of God had become as much a matter of technique and program as it was of conversion and religious piety."[13]

Finally, evangelism in the modern era suffered from the tie of Christianity to western culture, colonialism and notions of progress. Christianity came to be identified with western culture. Mission converts became cultural aliens in their own lands, and the church a colonial outpost. Culture, not the gospel, was often the greatest offense that kept people from becoming Christians.

The idea of western superiority often produced in missionaries an arrogance and a triumphalism that was not befitting the gospel. It also led to the mission control of young churches long after they were able to lead themselves.

II. Evangelism in the Postmodern Era

The vision of establishing one modern world led by the west crumbled following two world wars and the collapse of colonialism. Empires that had taken two centuries to build were dismantled in a decade. The collapse was not as complete as it may seem. On the one hand, neocolonialisms of many kinds persist. On the other, new nation states emerged out of the colonial empires. These states now challenge traditional tribal and ethnic groupings, seeking to appropriate the benefits of modernity for themselves. In the two-thirds world modernity has not died. Now everyone wants a share in it.

A more profound challenge to modernity has come from the loss of faith in progress as a cure to human ills. The failure of development to improve conditions around the world and the growing social and ecological crises in the west are raising the question whether science can engineer a utopian world. Despite years and billions of dollars spent on development the rich countries are richer and the poor are poorer. In poor countries the powerful benefit most from the programs. The results are often disastrous.[14] Out of this disillusionment with modernity has emerged the challenge of postmodernity.

A. The Postmodern Context

Postmodernism is a reaction to colonialism and a response to the growing cultural and religious pluralism in the west. It declares that all human knowledge is subjective because it is determined by its sociocultural and historical contexts. It rejects the search for a unified theory of truth and the creation of one global culture to unify the world. Linda Hutcheon writes,

> Willfully contradictory, then, post modern culture uses and abuses the conventions of discourse. It knows it cannot escape the implications of the . . . domains of its time. There is no outside. All it can do is question from within.[15]

Jean-Francois Lyotard adds, "Let us wage war on totality; let us be witness to the unpresentable; let us activate the differences . . ."[16] In postmodernism, pluralism is not a description of human realities, but a philosophical dogma that affirms the integrity of every religion and condemns all attempts to convert people as a moral violation.[17] Thomas Kuhn levels a similar attack on objective knowledge.[18] He concludes that there is no objective way to show that one theory is more true than another. We can only make decisions based on personal preference and usefulness. The result is subjectivism and pragmatism. Frederic Burnham writes, "The fundamental characteristic of the new postmodern era is epistemological relativism."[19]

Rather than unity, postmodernism celebrates diversity. It calls for an appreciation of other systems of belief and the affirmation of cultural and religious differences. Its cardinal sin is ethnocentrism, the claim that our beliefs are more true than those of others.

One consequence of this subjectivism is that postmodernity is a denial of a universal *humanum*. Donald Shriver writes, "By what right does anybody speak of the human—especially in a time when we are discovering the alienations and the destructive potentials of universal principles, including the principle of humanity?"[20] The focus now is on the group and the self. All knowledge is determined from the perspective of the culture and the person, all knowers are participants in that which is known. The focus is on an experientialism that emphasizes "a deeper interest in expanded experience and realization of the self; a heightened sensitivity to vulnerable personal relations, and increased social perceptiveness."[21]

Finally, postmodernism rejects a mechanistic view of the world and has lost faith in human engineering and technique. The existing human systems are perceived as intrinsically evil, and in need of radical transformation.

B. Evangelism Defined in the Postmodernism Era

Postmodernism is beginning to affect the church and its definition of evangelism. First, if all knowledge is subjective and all points of view are valid, other religions can no longer be seen as false. There is truth in all of them. Christ is no longer seen as one who alone can save fallen humankind. John Hick, for example, argues that the Christian belief in Jesus as divine has produced in it a religious exclusivism and triumphalism. He calls Christians to remove Christ from his position in the Trinity so that Christians can truly enter into dialogue with people of other religions. Of twelve recent books on Christ and other religions, only one out of the twelve affirms the uniqueness of Christ.[22]

In this setting evangelism can no longer be defined as winning people to a saving faith in Christ, for that is ethnocentric and arrogant. In evangelism we must dialogue with people of other faiths to find common grounds for our understanding of the human dilemma and to join efforts to achieve the full humanization of all people.

Second, because all knowledge is seen as context bound, it is important to define the gospel from within each human setting. It is the cultural and historical contexts that define the existential questions we must answer, and answers must be sought within that context. We must affirm, therefore, all local theologies as valid expressions of the gospel.

Third, postmodernity views humans as intrinsically good, at least those who are poor and oppressed. Evil resides in structures of human power that exploit the powerless. In this setting evangelism as a call to personal faith is replaced by evangelism as social transformation. It is to make the poor and oppressed aware of their social realities (conscientization), and to join with them in their struggle for liberation and justice (solidarity).

C. Assessment

The postmodern critique of modernity is a necessary corrective to the arrogance of modernity. Postmodernity challenges us to think more profoundly about power and pluralism and what the gospel has to say about them. We must reject the ethnocentrism and arrogance of the west. This does not mean, however, that we must sacrifice truth to do so. To say that all solutions to the human dilemma are right is to say that none is right. The result is a relativism that closes the door to a serious search for truth or to divine salvation.

In contrast to modernity, which views science and theology as acultural and ahistorical systems of knowledge, postmodernity rightly reminds us of the contextual nature of all knowledge and of the need to contextualize the gospel. In reaction, it goes too far and is in danger of absolutizing the context. Bosch writes,

> This approach ends up having a low view of the importance of *text*, as coming from outside the context. The very idea that texts can judge contexts is, in fact, methodologically doubted. The message of the gospel is not viewed as something that we bring *to* contexts, but as something that we derive *from* contexts. "You cannot incarnate good news into a situation, good news arises out of the situation," writes Nolan.[23]

Postmodern theology rejects the central affirmation of orthodox Christianity that God has indeed broken into history and culture to reveal to us truth and to make a way of salvation. Owen Thomas notes,

> In its view of nature postmodern theology rejects mechanism and affirms panexperientialism in which feeling and intrinsic value are attributed to all individuals comprising nature. This is the ontological basis for its naturalistic theism or affirmation of a cosmic soul as natural reality interacting with the world as part of the natural process.[24]

This no longer is Christianity. It is closer to Hinduism in which everyone is god, and all roads lead to enlightenment.

Postmodernism not only denies us salvation from without, it also rejects true communication among us as humans. Kuhn concludes that paradigms of human knowledge are incommensurable. We cannot truly understand another paradigm until we convert to it. We are left stranded, therefore, on our cultural and personal islands. Peters notes,

> Without commitment to a universal *humanum* in some form, radical pluralism fails philosophically to give any good reason why we should honor someone else's opinion or conviction when it differs from our own.[25]

In the end, postmodernity is a reactionary movement with little agenda of its own except to destroy colonialism. It offers few real solutions to the human dilemmas of sin, oppression, poverty, violence and ecological exploitation. Max Stackhouse points out that compassion and commitment are no guarantee that we will not produce bad sociology, practice poor politics and pursue debatable historical analysis.[26]

This lack of a clear agenda of its own is seen in its view of sin. By attributing evil to human systems, postmodernity overlooks the fact that the poor and oppressed sometimes prey upon one another. Sin is not the preserve of a privileged few. We are all sinners, and given the opportunity we sin freely without regret.

III. Evangelism in a Global Era

Modernity and postmodernity are very much alive, competing for our allegiances. But other forces are now at work challenging the assumptions of both. Globalization is drawing individuals, peoples and nations into worldwide economic, political and social networks, and the celebration of diversity is giving way to a search for the common unity underlying humankind.

The implications of this globalization for humanity are not yet clear. Some, like Berger, argue that postmodernity is one of the periodic reactions to modernity and that globalization is modernity reemerging on a world scale.[27] Others, like Huston Smith, argue that "post-post-modernity" will be a new order, building on the past, but different from it in significant ways.[28] We can only suggest here some of the continuities and discontinuities of globalism and their implications for the church and evangelism.

A. The Global Context

On the surface, globalism is the growing interconnectedness of peoples and nations. International travel, communications, banking, business and government are linking together people of the world in complex ways. The revival of ethnic and national loyalties and religious fundamentalisms are resisting these global forces, but it remains to be seen whether they can effectively stop the move toward global systems.

The church itself is both a contributor to and benefactor of this globalism. During the modern mission movement the church became a world body. Today, an estimated 914 million of the world's 1,512 million Christians are found in the vital young churches of the two-thirds world.[29] Increasingly, these churches and the churches in the west are joining in common cause through the ecumenical movement in the mainline churches, and global networks of cooperation among evangelicals.

Globalism also means that the dominance of the west is decreasing as young Asian, African and Latin American nations enter the global arena. We see this in Christianity where liberation, African and Asian theologies have captured the center stage in theological debate. In missions, the number of missionaries sent out by churches in the two-thirds world will soon exceed those sent out by the west.

Despite the resurgence and affirmation of pluralism, there is a growing unity in the world and in the church. It is based not on the uniformity of modernity, nor the isolationism of postmodernity, but on networking and common endeavor. We see this in global banking, communications and trade. We see it in the church where there is a growing willingness to work together for the cause of Christ.

Beneath these social realities there is emerging in philosophy and the social sciences a search for the unity of the human race which runs deeper than the surface differences of culture, language, race and gender. As Christians we must begin with the affirmation that all humans are created in the image of God and are part of one biological family.

There is also a growing pessimism about our human abilities to save ourselves.

Poverty, oppression, wars, crime, social chaos and ecological disasters have assumed unheard-of proportions. People in many countries are locked in the grip of social and cultural systems from which they cannot possibly wrench themselves free. Regarding North America Richard Halverson, chaplain of the United States Senate, says,

> Nothing is clearer than that God alone is able to rescue our decaying society; nothing is clearer than that he waits for his people to reject materialism as a way of life; and that the crisis requires repentance from worldly wayward-ness and devotion to prayer.[30]

In the church there is a growing awareness that the final "salvation will not be wrought by human hands, not even by *Christian* hands."[31]

From this pessimism is emerging an awareness of the depth of human sin. We are not good people beguiled into evil. We are all sinners at heart, rebels against God and against other humans. We bring about poverty, exploitation, wars, deceit and evil. We cannot save ourselves.

In the global world the cognitive objectivism of modernity and experiential subjectivism of postmodernity are both challenged. Knowledge is seen as both objective and subjective. It connects the external world to our apprehension of it. But knowledge alone is no solution to our human predicament. Nor are inner experiences. What we need are transformed lives and transformed sociocultural structures.

B. Defining Evangelism in a Global World

What is evangelism in a global world? We are in danger of western arrogance if we discuss this question without consulting our Christian sisters and brothers around the world. Samuel Escobar reminds us that,

> Internationalization of Christian mission means acknowledging that God has now raised up large and thriving churches in nations where sometimes the Bible was not even translated a hundred years ago. In these churches of the Southern Hemisphere, churches of the poor, churches of the Third World, God is raising up a new missionary force.[32]

Many of these churches have not gone through modernity and postmodernity to reach globalization. They are now developing their own understandings of evan-gelism. Most follow the evangelical or charismatic definitions of evangelism, calling people to faith in Jesus Christ, but with less of a separation between spiritual salvation and social transformation. Here we will limit our discussion of global evangelism to what it means for the church in the west.

Several themes are emerging in the global paradigm of evangelism in the west. The first is a focus on evangelism as first and foremost the work of God (*missio dei*). In contrast to the human-centeredness of modernity and postmodernity, the church is rediscovering the fact that evangelism is derived from the very nature and work of God. It is God who reaches out to save humans. As Jürgen Moltmann notes, "It is not the church that has a mission of salvation to fulfill in the world;

it is the mission of the Son and the Spirit through the Father that includes the church."[33] This should make us hold lightly our human planning and efforts, and cause us to depend more on prayer, the guidance of the Holy Spirit and the work God is already doing in the world.

Second, the center of the message is the coming Kingdom of God. Bosch notes,

> Evangelism is announcing that God, Creator and Lord of the universe, has personally intervened in human history and has done so supremely through the person and ministry of Jesus of Nazareth who is the Lord of history, Savior and Liberator. In this Jesus, incarnate, crucified and risen, the reign of God has been inaugurated.[34]

The kingdom Christ will establish is one of righteousness and peace, and at his coming every knee shall bow before him as Lord (Phil. 2:10-11).

Righteousness and sin are defined by the Kingdom, not by the best world we can build. Salvation is not bettering our human conditions. It is the restoration of humans and creation to the perfection they had before the fall. By these standards the awfulness of sin in the world, and the need for and greatness of God's salvation are manifest.

Salvation, too, must be defined in terms of the Kingdom. It is true that God offers people salvation as a present gift and with it the assurance of eternal bliss. As important as this is, the central theme of salvation is not personal enjoyment of salvation. It is the glory of God. The goal of evangelism is not individual salvation, or even the planting of churches, but the irrupting reign of Christ on earth and the glory of God.[35] We invite people to make Christ the Lord of their whole lives. He, in turn, makes them citizens of his Kingdom, now and in eternity, and he transforms their lives into his likeness. The focus on Christ the King and on the Kingdom he brings eliminates the dualism that hurt evangelism in the past.

Third, we must reject the extreme individualism of the past that defines salvation only in personal terms. Christ does call individuals to repent and believe, but their conversion does not pertain only to their personal act of conviction and change. It also involves a commitment to the community of faith.

This community of believers, the church, is where Christ is Lord. It is a manifestation of the Kingdom of God already invading the earth and a sign of the fullness of that Kingdom yet to come. In the midst of a "crooked and perverse generation," the Christians are to be "without blemish," shining "as lights in the world" (Phil. 2:15). They are to be communities characterized by holiness, love and truth.

But the church does not live for itself. It is called to be a witness to the world of the King and Kingdom. It is a resident alien community on earth whose very existence calls people from their old lives into the light of Christ's transforming power, and assures the world that God can change our human realities and that justice will come and peace will reign. Stanley Hauerwas and William Willimon note,

> Christianity is more than a matter of a new understanding. Christianity is an invitation to be part of an alien people who make a difference because they see something that cannot otherwise be seen without Christ.[36]

By its very challenge of sin, the church, like Christ, elicits opposition and per-secution. These are central to its growth (Acts 9:16, 4:27-30). But in a world that uses violence, the church is called to the nonviolent resistance of evil. It seeks to break down the walls of hatred between individuals, sexes, ethnic groups, classes and nations through its life and witness.

Fourth, we must contextualize the message and the methods of evangelism, for people must hear the gospel in ways they understand. But we must go beyond contextualization to inculturation. Hearing the gospel in our own contexts is not enough. The gospel calls us to respond and be transformed by God into new creatures and new societies. Lesslie Newbigin writes,

> There can never be a culture-free gospel, yet the gospel, which is from the beginning to the end embodied in culturally conditioned forms, calls into question all cultures, including the one in which it was originally embodied.[37]

Too often the church has been converted to the predominant culture, not to the Christ of the gospels.

Fifth, we must reject faith in our human ability to build a better world by our efforts. If there is to be salvation on earth, it must be the work of God through God's people. We wait with anticipation for the coming Kingdom, even as we labor in obedience to the Lord to manifest the Kingdom in the lives of God's church and people.

The process is the work of the Holy Spirit in the Christian community. It must begin in the local community, including the laity, but it must also include the larger community of Christians around the world. Its theological reflection here must be Christological. Just as Christ became fully human, while remaining fully God, the gospel must be fully expressed in human cultures, while it remains fully God's revelation to us and power within us. The reflection must also be ecclesiological. It is the church that provides the hermeneutical community in which the Word of God must be heard, understood and obeyed.

Lastly, we must avoid arrogance, manipulation and coercion in evangelism (II Cor. 4:2). We do not bring salvation; God already has done so. We are witnesses of God's acts, inviting people to follow Christ and enter the Kingdom. We do not stand in judgment over them, because it is only by the grace of God in Christ "that we know the terrible abyss of darkness into which we must fall if we put our trust anywhere but in that grace."[38] We are not to dispute, but to share the Good News with love and respect, joy and anticipation. We dare not equate the message with ourselves or our cultures. Rather, we point beyond ourselves and our cultures to Christ. We and churches should be radiant manifestations of the Kingdom because the life of the believing community prepares the way for the gospel.

C. Training for Evangelism in a Global World

What implications does all this have for seminary training, particularly in the area of evangelism? These will obviously vary from school to school. Nevertheless, certain general principles emerge.

1. New Conceptual Frameworks

First, the seminaries must take the lead in helping the church develop new conceptual frameworks to respond to the growing pluralism inherent in globalism. This must take place on several levels.

One central task of the seminary is to integrate theology with the social sciences, biblical exegesis with human exegesis, in a way faithful to biblical truth. To do so, its theology must move below current discussions that deal with explicit beliefs to the categories and assumptions that underlie the conversion. In other words, it must develop a biblical worldview in which both theology and Christian under-standings of the social sciences are embedded. Only then will both fields be com-plementary, not rivals in the definition of truth.

Integration requires us to deal with the question of epistemology. It is here that we lay the foundations for dealing with others and "otherness."[39] We must reject an old positivism with its intellectual arrogance and an instrumentalism with its narcissistic relativism. We must develop a critical realism that reaffirms the place of truth in the life of the seminary but acknowledges the limits of our knowledge of that truth.

Another central task of the seminary is to move beyond a purely cognitive approach to knowledge to recognize the need for experiential and evaluative understandings of reality. It is here that the Pilot Immersion Project, for example, broke new ground. Through carefully planned and repeated immersions in other cultures, not only individuals but whole schools came to grips with the reality of the human dilemma around the world. Even in schools like Denver Seminary, which have long traditions of involvement in missions, the immediacy of the Pilot Immersion Project immersion experiences created a profound awareness of pov-erty, oppression, systemic evil and the lostness of humans apart from the Kingdom of God.[40]

In the Pilot Immersion Project learning experiences went far beyond cognitive reflection. Emotional involvement and moral response were integral parts of a learning experience that brought a whole person into identification with and response to humans in their contexts. It is this incarnational "knowing of the whole by the whole" that must become an integral part of all seminary training if we are to be Christian witnesses in the world.

2. New Organizational Patterns

It is clear that global thinking is not something that we simply add to seminary training. We must move beyond being sensitive to other cultures to issues of struc-ture and power.

Parsons and Shils suggest a model that helps us understand the changes that need to take place if seminaries want to minister effectively in a pluralistic world.[41] They note that humans are part of three interacting sub-systems: individuals, soci-eties and cultures. For any change to endure it must affect all three of these. If we change individuals but not their social systems, cultural beliefs and values, the change will not last. Or if we change a community's worldview but not its social organization, we create tensions in the seminary that sap its energies.

On the level of individuals, globalization in a seminary requires new attitudes on the part of faculty, administration, staff and students toward people of other cultures, ethnic communities and classes. This personal growth can be facilitated by well-planned immersion experiences in other societies.

On the level of social organization globalization includes adding faculty from other cultures and exchanging faculty and students with schools in other parts of the world. It also requires a reallocation of resources and redistribution of power so that no one group controls the institution. Here immersion experiences can provide initial contacts for exchange. More significantly, involving trustees and top administrators in such experiences helps those with the responsibilities of leadership and power to understand the issues involved and to make institutional changes.

On the level of culture, globalization begins with fundamental changes in curricula and syllabi. Such changes must include non-western churches and theologies, and must test how our western worldview has shaped the way we read the Scriptures. It also means developing a new institutional culture that celebrates human diversity while affirming the underlying unity of the gospel and the church. Here we need to draw upon one of the greatest resources in North American seminaries, namely, the growing ethnic and cultural diversity of North American cities and the growing number of international students attending the seminaries.

Evangelism is not an option for the church. It is of the very nature of God and God's people to reach out to a lost and broken world with a message of hope and salvation. Evangelism is not the only task of the church, but is the task the church can do best on earth.

CASE STUDY[42]

Changing the Face of the Parish

Father Peter Kravitz leaned forward as the volume of the conversation increased. Sue Johnson asked, "Why should we change when everything has been going well in our parish?" Before she could finish, Ben Riley interjected, "But everything is changing. Like it or not, the neighborhood near the church where I am living is quite different today than even five years ago." Pam Riverton spoke up, "Yes, everything around us is changing, Ben, but I believe the church should be one place where there is some stability." "Father Peter," Ben continued, "you seem to understand the Hispanic culture. What are your thoughts about the proposal to start a Spanish Mass in the fall?"

Now the ball was in Peter Kravitz's court. This was the first of twenty district meetings within the parish called to discuss the proposal. As a recent seminary graduate, Peter had been a parish priest for only fourteen months. But as he arrived for the house meeting, old timers told him that attendance was unusually high. Peter knew that as the first priest at Christ the King parish able to preach in Spanish, his parishioners would want to know his response to the proposal. He knew that what they were talking about was much more than beginning a Mass in Spanish. Currently the leadership of the parish was completely Anglo, but both new leadership and new ministries would be needed for the growing number of Hispanic parishioners. Peter knew, more than most in the room, that the changes being discussed would change forever the face of the parish.

In coming to the district meeting Peter knew that someone would ask Ben's question. He had heard these and other questions in a number of settings in recent years. "Why don't immigrants learn English?" "Why should we, the long-standing members of the church, be forced to change our ways?" Sitting quietly in his study earlier in the day, Peter pondered all of the facets of his theological education that had brought him to this moment. Because of the emphasis on multicultural education at St. Luke's Seminary, he had changed so much in the last six years. What could he say, therefore, to the people of his parish as they faced the prospect of change?

Readiness for Ordination

A native of Texas, Peter attended mostly white Catholic schools through the eighth grade. What a change it was to begin a public high school in the ninth grade. For the first time Peter attended classes with many Hispanics. He found himself confronted daily with the presence of multicultural tension.

After high school Peter worked for three years. In 1981 he began his studies at St. Michael's College, a school of the Diocese of San Antonio. In the fall of 1985 Peter entered St. Luke's Seminary. His aim was to become a parish priest.

Along with their theological studies students were invited to study Spanish. But the encouragement was not too strong, and Peter joined the rather general rebellion against the Spanish classes. He and his fellow students asked why Americans living in Texas should learn another language. The good news was that there was not much pressure to do so. The students knew that they could be ordained without knowing Spanish well.

After a year away from St. Luke's, Peter returned to find a new situation. A new bishop, George Kennedy, had been installed in the Diocese of San Antonio. In 1987 Bishop Kennedy appointed Keith Murchison as the new rector of the seminary. The bishop came to the seminary to meet with the faculty. He encouraged the seminary to marshall its resources for "globalization." He suggested that central to a curriculum sensitive to globalization could be immersion experiences in their neighbor to the South, Mexico. The bishop said that this new curriculum was vital in the training of priests for a new day in the church. He told the faculty that the changing face of the church in the Southwest called for the need of a second language. In a dialogue with the faculty, several professors raised the question: "But what if a student is ready for ordination and does not have a second language?" The bishop replied: "I question the readiness for ordination."

Dr. Cecelia Gonzalez was hired as the director of a newly expanded language and cultural studies program. Spanish classes were shifted to 8 A.M. each weekday, a time period when no other classes were scheduled. Peter was impressed that Rector Murchison started attending the Spanish classes. The other students took notice that the head of the seminary was studying Spanish alongside them. On Mondays all of the services were in Spanish, including the homily. But in the midst of these changes grumbling among both faculty and students continued.

The Importance of Immersion

A central aspect of the globalization program was an immersion project. All students were expected to participate at the end of their second year. Peter was a part of the first group that traveled to Mexico in the summer of 1988. He and three other students went to Cuernavaca, a cultural center south of Mexico City. Peter lived with the Sanchez family. For two months the four seminarians studied Spanish daily.

But much more happened than studying a language. As recorded in his journal, Peter "saw more clearly the Mexican people. Growing up in Texas I had a very prejudiced view of Mexico." Being forced to speak Spanish daily meant "rubbing shoulders with Mexican people in a whole new way." His eyes were opened to the values of their culture. He fell in love with the city of Cuernavaca, which was particularly proud of its cultural heritage and various arts.

He also saw the church in a different light. The immersion experience "gave me a vision of the church in Mexico very different than my previous conceptions back home in San Antonio." He was impressed with the popular devotion of Mexican Christians. Peter found a chief value of encountering the Mexican church to be his growing concern to meet people where they are and not impose forms of ministry alien to their culture.

Upon his return to St. Luke's, Peter was eager to compare notes with other seminarians. He was dumbfounded by the attitude of Carl. Carl had fought against the Spanish classes at the seminary. He had not been shy in saying he did not like

Hispanics. He did not want to participate in the immersion experience. Now he returned from Mexico filled with enthusiasm. "The immersion experience was the catalyst for seeing both my studies and my ministry in a whole new light." Carl asked for his third year internship to be in a parish with a high percentage of Hispanics. He encouraged others to appreciate the Hispanic culture.

Not everyone affirmed Carl's and Peter's new insights. An old friend asked him if it was necessary to go all the way to Cuernavaca when there were Hispanics all around him in Texas? Peter answered: "You can hide from Hispanics here. You can go home at night. Whenever something is difficult, you don't do it." The immersion experience had been difficult, but now Peter entered into his theological education with new energy.

Looking back on Mexico and forward to opportunities in Texas, Peter and many of the others returning from the immersion experience had a new commitment to be "diligent in trying to understand their faith experiences." This was not always easy. Grateful for St. Luke's efforts in the language and cultural studies program, a few of the students now felt that some of their professors were starting too much from their graduate school training in theology rather than the real conditions of ministry. A few months after his return from Mexico Peter participated in a student-faculty colloquium called to talk about the direction of the language and cultural studies program at the seminary. James Evans, professor of moral theology, expressed appreciation for the new emphasis on language study but questioned the time given to this endeavor. He asked about the implications of all this for the maintenance of the excellence in theological scholarship which was part of the seminary's identity. Several faculty members questioned what they perceived to be the shift to experience-based education as symbolized in the emphasis on the immersion experience. Joseph Blinco, professor of biblical studies, interjected: "A seminary cannot do everything. As for me, I want to argue for a classical theological education." John Rexford, the chaplain of the seminary, who guided the faculty in the program of spiritual direction with students, shared that his own understanding of spirituality had been deeply influenced by his participation in immersion experiences in both Mexico and Guatemala. Father Ernesto Cardoza, professor of New Testament, spoke up to say that his understanding of the content of the Gospel of Luke "was challenged by my student's reading of Luke in the context of two months in Mexico." Finally, Paul Martinez, professor of practical theology, tried to summarize the debate by saying it was "a matter of priorities." How did the seminary balance serving the changing needs and patterns of church ministry and the need for excellent scholarship?

The Face of the Parish

Peter graduated from St. Luke's in June, 1990, and was called to Christ the King parish. The parish of over 2200 families is 70 percent Anglo, 20 percent Hispanic, and 10 percent Asian. The majority of those who attend regularly are over fifty.

Although the diocese had encouraged new possibilities at Christ the King parish, Peter felt a tension between diocesan and parish guidelines and the needs of the people. In his fourteen months at Christ the King Peter discovered that his new parish was much more structured than comparable parishes in Mexico. For example, newcomers could not participate in the sacraments until they were registered in a parish. For immigrants, some of whom were illegal aliens entering Texas, this guideline amounted to an insurmountable obstacle. Mexican parishes did not have this guideline. Peter found himself sympathetic to the immigrants. He became aware again that a commitment to globalization sometimes produces unsettling questions and tensions.

Peter saw the face of the parish changing. Like so many communities in Texas, San Antonio was experiencing an influx of Hispanics. The majority were first generation, with most coming from Mexico and Central America. Projections were that the percentage of Hispanics in the parish would rise steadily.

Peter saw his education at St. Luke's as responsible for shaping his attitudes about ministry in the changing neighborhoods that made up the parish. Despite his concerns that the curriculum was not changing enough to reflect the new realities of ministry in a multicultural setting, he was grateful for the training he received at St. Luke's. "I feel much more at home when I call in an Hispanic home because of my experience in Mexico. I am aware of the culture." Peter was convinced that speaking Spanish was the entrée into the Hispanic culture.

Peter believed the senior priest, Father John, was also open to the changes in the parish. At age fifty-two he was taking Spanish classes. But at age thirty-two Peter was bringing to his ministry much more facility in both language and culture. He was clear that his arrival at Christ the King helped lay the concrete plans for the proposal to greatly increased ministry to the Latinos within the parish. Because of his knowledge of the culture, Peter was aware that many new services would need to be available. These would range from Spanish baptisms, to celebrations indigenous to Hispanic culture, to educational programs. Part of the proposal would be the hiring of a Spanish ministry coordinator.

Facing Change

More than almost anyone in the room Peter recognized what was at stake as parishioners debated the proposal. Thinking back over the past six years, he was grateful for a seminary education that prepared him for ministry in a changing parish. But he was also in touch with the fears and questions of persons who had been faithful members of Christ the King for years. Not long ago these were some of his questions. It was time to answer Ben's question.

TEACHING NOTE

Changing the Face of the Parish

I. Goals

A. To explore the changing face of American society in terms of ethnic diversity.

B. To identify the fears and questions of members of Christ the King parish.

C. To describe and analyze the multicultural education at St. Luke's Seminary which helped prepare Father Peter for this ministry.

D. To help parishes see both the problems and possibilities in globalization.

II. Establishing the Context

A. Ask participants to consider what sociological changes have occurred in their own communities in the past ten years. Drawing on the Commentary by Harold J. Recinos (which follows), discuss the national statistics on population change. How have these changes affected ministries in participants' local congregations? If there are no changes, why not?

B. Identify the changes in the community which will affect the ministry of Christ the King parish.

C. What are the signs of acceptance and of resistance to change in Christ the King? What signs of acceptance and of resistance do participants see in their own congregations?

III. Issues in the Parish

What factors influence the questions of the members of Christ the King parish as they discuss initiating a Spanish Mass? (Possible responses: challenge to the dominant Anglo culture and language; threat to the current leadership of the parish; anxiety about the traditions and stability of the parish; additional demands on the staff and programs to respond to the newcomers; growing attendance at Mass with the assignment of a Spanish-speaking priest, etc.)

IV. Role of Theological Education

A. Father Peter acknowledges that he is much more open to expanding the ministry of Christ the King parish to the Hispanic community because of his seminary education. Identify the strengths and limitations of the new curriculum at St. Luke's Seminary that prepared Peter for his first assignment.

Strengths

Possible responses: required language skill; intensive exposure to another culture; experience-based education, etc.

Limitations

Possible responses: Less time for scholarship given demands of language and cultural studies; difficulty of paradigm shift from a more classical model of theological education; demanding shift for students and faculty to different models of teaching and learning, etc.

B. What changes were made in the seminary in response to the new bishop's insistence on globalization? Would participants suggest other changes to meet the bishop's goals?

C. If the case discussion is focused on theological education, consider setting up a role play between Dr. Cecelia Gonzales and Prof. Joseph Blinco, discussing how the current curriculum should be changed to better prepare students to meet the needs of parishes in Texas.

V. Response to the Parish

What problems and what possibilities are in the future for Christ the King parish? What concrete advice would participants give Father Peter about introducing a Spanish Mass and applying his learnings from St. Luke's language and cultural studies program? How can the present parishioners be involved in the decisions about and implementation of new programs?

VI. Resources for Change

Beyond the parishioners themselves, on what resources can Father Peter and Father John call to adapt to the changes in the parish? Consider Scripture, church traditions, the community, etc.

COMMENTARY

Changing the Face of the Parish

HAROLD J. RECINOS

Latino Presence

Twenty million Latinos live in the United States making it the sixth largest Spanish-speaking nation in the world. By the next century Latinos will be the largest racial/ethnic group in the country. Latinos live mostly in urban areas scattered over nine states — California, Texas, New York, Florida, Illinois, New Jersey, New Mexico, Arizona and Colorado. The Mexican, Puerto Rican and Cuban populations are three of the earliest and largest Latino groups. However, the Central and South American populations are growing subdivisions of the Latino presence. Who are the Latinos? Latinos have unique historical factors that have brought them into contact with the United States as well as different national cultures among them.[43]

By 1987, poverty in the Latino community increased by 90 percent or from 2.9 million to 5.5 million people. In contrast, poverty rates had declined for the black and white population.[44] Latino school drop out rates are double that of the black and white community. Of one hundred Latinos beginning kindergarten only two will finish graduate school.[45] Intravenous drug abuse is widespread, producing high levels of HIV infection. Latin Americans constitute about 6 to 8 percent of the total population of the United States, but they account for 14 percent of AIDS cases in the nation. Moreover, Latino children under fifteen represent 22 percent of all children with AIDS.[46]

Life out of Death

Faithful witness in the context of the Latino community needs to make real for people the God who brings life out of death and hope from despair. Faith in the God of life must seek immersion in social reality. Poor Christians in Latin America and their counterparts in North American cities even now are reshaping the established church in terms of a rereading of Scripture that admits the privilege of the poor and oppressed in the reign of God (I Cor. 1:27-28; Matt. 25). Carl and Christ the King parish must realize that Jesus accompanies the poor on the village streets of Latin and North America. Thus, the church is called to advance toward the margins of society where Christ in the poor constructs a community of justice.

God's ultimate reality of justice demands delivering action from the church in a changing community. God in the form of a rejected Galilean Jew named Jesus lived at the fringe of established society. Today, from that margin Latinos teach the church faithfulness to the gospel through service to the poor and oppressed.

The church must continue the mission of Jesus Christ by recognizing in the persons rejected by the established order God's ultimate cry to construct a new humanity based on the will to community. Parish life goes well when it serves as a social force for globalization at the local level through new relationships rooted in the will to community.

Global Community in Jesus

The global community surrounding Christ the King parish is represented by Latinos whose presence is a neighborhood request to develop a new form of church. Fear of the cultural other often motivates the changing parish's resistance to change and community rebuilding. However, Peter, who learned Spanish and was able to get nearer to Latino cultural reality, knew God created human diversity as a sign of the reign of humanizing justice. Peter seemed convinced that God's Word for the church included building community with Latinos. Cultural diversity was not something to fear or reject as some of the "old timers" were prepared to do in order to block a Spanish-language Mass.

Peter's multicultural based education and immersion showed him how culture molds the meaning by which persons interpret their experience and interact with each other. Too many North American churches, however, impose their cultural values and institutions—for example, language—on Latinos. Sue Johnson represents the church that fears change. Nevertheless, change is a historical constant that defines the church as a process in time always transformed by the human diversity around it. Indeed, cultural variance represents God's universal grammar that both communicates and molds a single global field of social interaction. Ben's voice signifies the discerning church that embraces change and cultural diversity as a sign of the God of life.

Through an immersion experience in Mexico, Peter evolved positive and eye-opening values. Yet, he still thought of Latinos in North American society as mostly foreign born and Spanish-speaking. The reality is to the contrary. Many Latinos use only English to communicate their identity and the majority are born in the States.

Only 25 percent of the Mexicans in the United States were foreign born; 50 percent of all Puerto Ricans, 20 percent of Central and South Americans and 25 percent of all Cubans in the United States were born in the United States.[47] Society makes outsiders of Latinos by appealing to ethnic stereotyping that defines Latinos as drug dealers or illegal aliens.

A Spanish-language Mass would increase cross-cultural interaction and learning apt to expose negative stereotypes. For instance, I know two so-called illegal aliens from El Salvador who would welcome such a Spanish-language Mass. Luis grew up poor in a small rural village of about one hundred families. Contact with Latinos like Luis would nourish an understanding about the God of life talked about in El Salvador in Christ the King Church. Faith tells Luis that the God of life sides with the poor and feeds a deep respect for human life. In Luis's village, the sacred was defined as life in responsible community informed by faith in Jesus. He learned that the ultimate values of Christianity are justice, human rights and communal well-being.

Marina also grew up poor in a small village in El Salvador. A mother of four children, she came to the United States in the late 1980s after being brutally raped and tortured in front of her four children by members of the Salvadoran army whose training was paid for by U.S. tax dollars. She would tell members of Christ the King parish that she is not a theologian but speaks of Christ through real oppressed-suffering. As part of a multicultural parish, Marina's evangelizing voice would say, "For me to speak to North Americans of human suffering is to speak of Jesus' own suffering at the time of his crucifixion and torture." The transformed parish would become a true church of the poor by listening to the voice of Latinos and by acting in the world.

Cultural diversity as a conversation among the different histories of people in society is at the parish door. A Spanish-language Mass would change the identity of Christ the King parish. Latinos would enable church members to view history as a belief system that reveals Jesus' struggle against organized systems of oppression. Latino devotional life would generate a new community molded by a faith hermeneutics rooted in the historical experience of oppression and exclusion. Latinos who know in their flesh the meaning of human disfigurement would indicate that many biblical texts are only grasped in the context of structured wretchedness and the struggle against it. Thus, Latinos would assure that a Bible-centered spirituality would take root in the parish.

Globalization of Seminary and Church

The case urges that seminary education include cultural immersion experiences. Sustained contact with other cultural communities provides the comparative perspective out of which individuals learn to raise deeper epistemological questions about their faith hermeneutics and Christian praxis. The case also suggests that the parish is a local community institution called to engage not retreat from its changing environment. By broadening the range of human diversity in the local church, persons will learn how culture constructs theology and human behavior in response to perceived existential reality.

Local churches are not only required to be honest about social reality but to hear it explained from the perspective of different cultures, whose specific symbol and meaning systems also communicate ultimate interests. Profound honesty about social reality will lead members of the North American church to encounter the God who is identified with society's outcasts and who suffers the climate of dehumanization encompassing their lives. Christ the King parish is faced with the great challenge of recognizing in the changing community the movement of the God who liberates humanity for new relationships.

What is at stake in Christ the King parish is the gospel. Life together is ultimately depicted in the biblical tradition as a unity of all races and tongues in Christ (Rev. 5:9). Christians are not empowered to define themselves out of each others' lives. Christians are called to build a community of justice beginning with the local context. Nevertheless, this does not include absolutizing finite systems of belief or imposing cultural constructions of faith through patterns of domination. The global system of unequal development and structured death for the poor implanted five hundred years ago has already received plenty of Christian legitimation.

Globalization is an instance of evangelization when the church recognizes that

Jesus sends the church into the world to let "justice roll down like waters, and righteousness like an everflowing stream" (Amos 5:24). The church is sent to defend human life against the systems of death devised by plans of political economy that benefit a narrow substratum of global society. Christ the King parish and seminaries are called to listen to new voices on the other side of their institutional doors. Latinos challenge the theologies produced in these ecclesial settings by questioning whether or not they represent genuine Good News for the wretched humanity in the world that seeks to change the organization of society.

By overcoming the mechanisms that feed alienation between cultural communities, a clearer insight can be gained regarding the impact of organized global inequalities. As seminaries and churches like Christ the King parish engage in globalization, they will discover that cultural immersion produces "unsettling questions and tensions"; however, at a deeper level it will become clear that the mission of the church is evangelization understood as building an alternative global order nourished by Christ's promise of life in abundance, especially for the oppressed-poor. Clearly, the will to establish expanded forms of Christian community images new possibilities as it creates new directions for ministry and new questions for faith.

Evangelization implies that the church and seminary seek to do theology by marching directly to the margins of life where the God of the poor calls for a new global order of service and commitment to justice. The Good News is that God defends the oppressed by becoming one of them; thus, globalization involves awakening a new approach to social relations that calls on seminaries and churches to accompany the liberative struggle of the oppressed-poor. Christ the King Church was being invited by the shifting character of the community to renewal. The new direction taken by St. Luke's seminary and the Diocese of San Antonio indicates the refusal to harmonize the Good News of the gospel with retreat from globalizing social reality.

Notes

1. Allan Bloom. *The Closing of the American Mind* (New York: Simon and Schuster, 1987).

2. Lesslie Newbigin. *The Gospel in a Pluralist Society* (Grand Rapids: William B. Eerdmans, 1989).

3. Bloom, 1987.

4. Peter Berger. *The Homeless Mind: Modernization and Consciousness* (New York: Random House, 1974).

5. David J. Bosch. *Transforming Mission: Paradigm Shifts in Theology of Mission* (Maryknoll, N.Y.: Orbis Books, 1991), 283.

6. Reinhold Niebuhr. *The Kingdom of God in America* (New York: Harper and Brothers, 1959, first published in 1937), 192.

7. Johannes Van den Berg. *Constrained by Jesus' Love: An Enquiry into the Motives of the Missionary Awakening in Great Britain in the Period between 1698 and 1815* (Kampen: Kok, 1956), 82.

8. Wilbert Shenk. The changing role of the missionary: from "civilization to contextualization." In C. Norman Kraus, ed., *Missions, Evangelism and Church Growth* (Scottdale, Penn.: Herald Press, 1980), 35.

88   EMERGING MEANINGS OF GLOBALIZATION

9. Jonathan Chao. Indigenization of the Christian movement in China - IV: Deculturalization of the Chinese Church. *Missionary Monthly* (August/September 1987): 12.

10. Bosch, 304.

11. John Philip. *Research in South Africa* (London: James Duncan, 1982), ix.

12. W. Richie Hogg. The role of American Protestantism in world mission. In R. Pierce Beaver, ed., *American Missions in Bicentennial Perspective* (Pasadena: William Carey Library, 1987), 201.

13. Bosch, 335.

14. Wayne G. Bragg. From development to transformation. In Vinay Samuel and Chris Sugden, eds., *The Church in Response to Human Need* (Grand Rapids: Eerdmans, 1987), 20-51.

15. Linda Hutcheon. *A Poetics of Postmodernism* (New York: Routledge, 1980).

16. Jean-Francois Lyotard. *The Postmodern Condition* (Minneapolis: University of Minnesota Press, 1984), 80-81.

17. Ted Peters. Evangelization within a religious plural society. *Journal of the Academy for Evangelism* 5 (1990): 30-41.

18. Thomas Kuhn. *The Structure of Scientific Revolutions*. Second Edition (Chicago: University of Chicago Press, 1970).

19. Frederic B. Burnham. *Postmodern Theology* (San Francisco: Harper & Row, 1989), x.

20. Donald Shriver. The pain and promise of pluralism. *The Christian Century* 97 (March 1980): 346.

21. Hans Küng. The reemergence of the sacred: Transmitting religious traditions in a post-modern world. *Conservative Judaism* 44 (Summer 1988): 13-14.

22. Francis Clooney. Review of six books on Christianity and non-Christian religions. *Religious Studies Review* 15 (July 1989): 198-203. And Paul F. Knitter. Making sense of the many. *Religious Studies Review* 15 (July 1989): 204-207.

23. Bosch, 430.

24. Owen C. Thomas. The challenge of postmodernism. *Anglican Theological Review* 62 (1989): 212.

25. Peters, 33.

26. Max Stackhouse. *Apologia: Contextualization, Globalization and Mission in Theological Education* (Grand Rapids: Eerdmans, 1988), 95.

27. Peter Berger. *The Homeless Mind: Modernization and Consciousness* (New York: Random House, 1974).

28. Huston Smith. *Beyond the Post-Modern Mind* (New York: Crossroad, 1982).

29. David B. Barrett. Annual statistical table on global mission: 1990. *International Bulletin of Missionary Research* 14 (1990):27.

30. Richard Halverson. Cited in *Christ Church Lake Forest Sunday Bulletin*. October 11, 1992.

31. Bosch, 400.

32. Samuel Escobar. The elements of style in crafting new international mission leaders. *Evangelical Missions Quarterly* 28 (January 1992): 7.

33. Jürgen Moltmann. *The Church in the Power of the Spirit: A Contribution to Messianic Ecclesiology* (London: SCM Press, 1977), 64.

34. Bosch, 412.

35. Howard Snyder. *Liberating the Church* (Downers Grove, Ill.:Inter-Varsity Press, 1983), 11, 29.

36. Stanley Hauerwas and William Willimon. *Resident Aliens: Life in the Christian Colony* (Nashville: Abingdon Press, 1989), 24.

37. Lesslie Newbigin. *Foolishness to the Greeks: The Gospel and Western Culture* (Grand Rapids: Eerdmans, 1986).

38. Lesslie Newbigin. Cross-currents in ecumenical and evangelical understanding of missions. *International Bulletin of Missionary Research* 6 (1982): 151.

39. Paul G. Hiebert. Beyond anti-colonialism to globalism. *Missiology: An International Review* 19 (July 1991): 263-82.

40. It is important to note that immersion experiences by themselves do not create cross-cultural sensitivities. Many go abroad in immersion events and return as tourists, having seen the scenery, but not the people as fellow human beings. The immersion experiences of the Pilot Immersion Project were very carefully designed to expose participants to a broad range of human realities, and to introduce the participants to people in the contexts of their lives. It is this, more than going cross-cultural, that was most beneficial to those involved.

41. Talcott Parsons and Edward Shils, eds. *Toward a General Theory of Action* (Cambridge, Mass.: Harvard University Press, 1952).

42. Copyright © 1993 by The Case Study Institute. The names of persons and places have been disguised to protect the privacy of those involved in this situation.

43. See Harold J. Recinos. *Jesus Weeps: Global Encounters at Our Doorstep* (Nashville: Abingdon Press, 1992).

44. See Rafael Valdivieso and Cary Davis, U.S. Hispanics: challenging issues for the 1990s. In *Population Trends and Public Policy* 17 (December 1988), 8.

45. Joan Moore and Harry Pachon. *Hispanics in the United States* (Englewood Cliffs: Prentice-Hall, Inc., 1985), 68.

46. Mary W. Booth, Felipe G. Castro, and M. Douglas Anglin. What do we know about Hispanic substance abuse? A review of the literature. *Drugs in Hispanic Communities*. Ronald Glick and Joan Moore, eds. (New Brunswick and London: Rutgers University Press, 1990), 36.

47. See Valdivieso and Davis, 4.

[4]

GLOBALIZATION AS ECUMENICAL/ INTERFAITH DIALOGUE

ESSAY

JANE I. SMITH

Much attention has been given to an interpretation of Rodney King's often cited question in the wake of the Los Angeles uprisings, "Can we talk together?" Such a plea would seem to be a natural starting place for many of the efforts made within and among our seminaries as we press to be in communication with our colleagues in ecumenical and interfaith contexts. Why do we want to talk? What do we hope to accomplish? How do we determine the boundaries/rules/limits of such conversations and what kinds of definitions/qualifications do we posit of the persons who are partners in that dialogue? The following is intended as a modest attempt to suggest some of the dimensions of such dialogue as well as some of the things that schools of theological education may hope to achieve as we pursue efforts to understand the changing nature of our tasks as well as of our constituencies.

Since the theme of globalization is addressed in this volume under a wide range of rubrics, I will not attempt an exhaustive definition here. Let me try, however, to set a general context for this contribution to the overall discussion by suggesting several of the assumptions that I personally bring. The first is that ecumenical/ interfaith dialogue is a natural component of the globalization process in our educational institutions. It is essential, inevitable, and to be pursued both because of and in spite of its potential outcomes. A second assumption is that the category "ecumenical/interfaith" implies a concern for dialogue both with persons of non-Christian religious traditions and with those representing racial/ethnic/indigenous communities, perhaps Christian, who traditionally have not been included in our "mainline" seminary constituencies in this country. Recognizing that another chapter in this volume deals with globalization as cross-cultural dialogue, I nevertheless make reference to this dimension with some regularity because (1) interfaith and cross-cultural are often synonymous and interchangeable, and (2) even when they are not, and must be understood as separate and distinguishable categories, much of the philosophy of dialogue as I would like to develop it applies in both contexts, particularly insofar as both signify something different from what predominantly white, predominantly Christian Americans have characterized as the norm of American culture.

Third, I am assuming that the primary audience for this volume will be the traditional constituencies of seminaries and schools of theology in America. Thus insofar as the terminology "we" is unavoidably used in this presentation it is intended to refer to that audience, not to be exclusive but for the opposite purpose of suggesting that "we" need to take responsibility for generating these dialogues and learning from them.[1]

Although the Association of Theological Schools is extending the scope of its own concerns to the international arena in a number of ways, such as through its present exchange and cooperation with the World Conference of Associations of Theological Institutions (WOCATI),[2] and although many of us representing American schools of theology have been active partners in international dialogues, the present essay is intended to focus primarily on dialogue efforts in this country, both as they take place on our campuses through curricular developments and in other forums and as local and national meetings are structured for the purpose of conversation and exchange. The situation has changed from the time when interfaith dialogue almost necessarily meant "us" in this country in dialogue with "them" in other countries, either through international travel or by engaging representatives of other religious traditions who either temporarily or permanently happened to be living in America. The day is gone, for example, when the distinction between Western and non-Western in terms of geography has much meaning, although "Western" as the description of a particular kind of mindset or worldview is still a useful category. Within the United States and Canada traditions that might once legitimately have been described as non-Western are now thoroughly ensconced as part of our American society. Whether or not its members choose to see themselves as "Westernized," or even feel to any degree "at home" in this context, these unquestionably are concerns that need to be addressed as we think about the aims and goals as well as the starting points for dialogue. But ours is no longer a society that can responsibly be described simply under the umbrella of Protestant, Catholic and Jew, and we need to acknowledge that to continue to think of it as such is to offend and exclude our fellow Americans of other faiths and traditions.[3]

I. The Need for New Paradigms and Pedagogies

Considerable attention has been given recently by commentators on education in general and theological education in particular to the need for new paradigms in light of the challenges of pluralism in American society as well as within our institutions. For Christian theological schools the challenge to loosen our hold on traditional ways of thinking and doing has to be considered both pedagogically and theologically. Many educational institutions are discovering that in order to be in conversation with the persons and groups both within their walls and gathering outside of them they must take a hard look at what they teach, how they teach, and for whom they are setting educational programs. And to the extent to which these institutions share in a denominational heritage and a commitment to confessional perspectives, they are having to think seriously about their own theological commitments in light of the kinds of paradigm shifts to which some are calling.

William Shea in an article on Catholic higher education has remarked that "denominational education has displayed to the American public two things: that one can believe and yet think, and that one can serve the common good while deeply involved in the life of a particular community of meaning and value."[4] He continues, however, by lamenting the reality that denominational education at the present moment is somehow trapped between its own commitments to a particular religious tradition and its responsibility in the public realm to a pluralist vision of common life. This is exactly the predicament in which many schools of theology find themselves as they experience the tension between traditional theological affirmations and the challenges that may be brought to those affirmations through the dialogue that comes as the desired goal as well as the inevitable result of increased diversity.

I would argue, however, this may well be a false dichotomy. That is to say, some of the more creative thinkers both within the institutional structure of the church and in the field of theological education itself are responding to the challenge of diversity (interfaith and intercultural) by seeing it not as a threat to the integrity and continuity of their own theological legacies but as a highly exciting new perspective from which to consider both human relationships and theological affirmations. Dialogue with other persons and other ideas, many argue, is essential not only to understanding the faith and traditions of others but to a better understanding of ourselves and of our own individual beliefs. Many of us have come to realize that through the process of dialogue we may learn to hold our own commitments a bit more gently so that they, too, can change and grow in the process of a mutually informed search for meaning and value.

Before considering the ingredients of dialogue as such, it may be helpful to look briefly at some of the kinds of pedagogical discussions that are taking place in the academy as a whole today over questions of globalization and pluralism (also referred to in one context or another as diversity, inclusiveness, multiculturalism, etc.). Issues of multicultural education have taken center stage in the continuing debates on the national level concerning the future of American higher education. In this country we have awakened to the fact, apparently, that for too long our thinking has been fashioned by ethnocentric and androcentric assumptions that fostered an elitism and imperialism in our approach to the world that simply will no longer do. Without rehearsing all of the details of this debate, let me suggest several of the kinds of issues it seems to be addressing. I hope that this can serve as background to a look at ways in which Christian theologians and educators are beginning to think about the reality of religious (and cultural) pluralism and the necessity of engaging the conversation in dialogue with our partners.

A. Interdisciplinary Studies

Clearly related to the growing concern over issues of globalism and multiculturalism is the seriousness with which the academy is taking the need for interdisciplinary studies. As early as the 1960s some colleges, universities and divinity schools were consciously setting out to design cross-cultural courses of study, and the next several decades saw the growth of new experiments in pedagogy and curricular structures. Today one philosophical impetus for the proliferation of interdisciplinary studies seems to be the existence of various post-modernist theories, from the radical pluralism and relativism of the deconstructionists[5] to the challenges to traditional disciplinary assumptions raised by feminist theory. The methodological claims and assumptions of traditional disciplines are being seriously questioned and new attempts to work cooperatively through interdisciplinary (or sometimes multidisciplinary) means are being suggested.[6] This kind of postmodern environment in the university also fosters an interactive praxis model that can well serve, and be served by, some of the thinking of contemporary liberation theologians.

B. Anti-individualism

One of the emphases of the current concern for pluralism and inclusiveness is what is best described as a kind of anti-individualism. There are several dimensions of this anti-individualism that may be quite crucial for effective dialogue in the present context. In one sense it refers to the dawning realization that some of the accusations leveled against the West by colleagues representing other cultural and religious contexts are true. One charge is that in their insistent individualism Westerners (1) fail to understand what motivates persons of other cultures and serves as the basis of their ongoing commitments, and (2) often act to their own detriment because their emphasis and understanding are almost exclusively in terms of persons as individuals rather than persons as members of larger communal units. Women colleagues from the developing world, both Christian and non-Christian, persist in their attempts to explain to Western feminists, for example, that the term "feminism" will have meaning in their respective societies only insofar as it is interpreted less as individual rights and more as personal responsibility to the larger units of family, town or nation.

Anti-individualism can also be understood in an even broader context. There is now being developed a significant body of Western educational literature suggesting that the competitive individualism that has characterized our Western epistemology actually mitigates seriously against the possibility that we are able to have an integrated vision of the world by the fact that it sets up a kind of dichotomy (or at least a distance) between self and the context in which the self lives and operates. This theory argues that as long as the world is seen as something "out there," somehow different and apart from ourselves, we have very little chance of grasping what it is all about, and that real understanding can come only when we begin to work out a theory of relatedness. Parker Palmer has pointed to the fact that some of the new epistemologies such as feminist thought, black scholarship, ecological studies and even philosophies of the new physics are forcing us to understand that there is an inescapably relational aspect to reality.[7] Educators are starting to be persuaded by this vision. "The agenda for general education," says the Director of the Institute for Educational Management at Harvard University, "is to teach those experiences, relationships, and ethical concerns that are common to all of us by virtue of our membership in the human family at a particular moment in history. General education is nothing less than the curricular representation of society's claim on its members."[8]

C. Particularism and Prejudice

Despite the calls of our colleagues from other cultures to communal rather than individual identities and despite what may be called the philosophical vantage point of interrelatedness, it is clear that there are strong movements within American society today to acknowledge its particularities along with, and sometimes even over against, its commonalities. The pain and despair experienced by trying, without much success, to "melt" into the American pot and to achieve equal justice and equal respect have brought about what in many cases seem to be clear centrifugal movements into particularism.[9] I have argued elsewhere[10] that one of the problems for American society in general as well as for our schools of theology in particular is how to think about reconciling the competing "goods" or claims of what are increasingly separate and distinguishable groups or communities. While many might not agree with the sentiment that "particularism is a bad idea whose time has come,"[11] it is clear that too great a focus on particular or group identities can in some cases serve to undermine the concern for interrelationships and mutual understanding. To this the obvious response must be that as long as, and to the extent that, peoples, groups and cultures in this country are treated with disrespect, there is little hope of assuming that the common good can be anything more than the good of the commonality of a self-defined and self-supportive group or community. Even when forms of overt discrimination are abandoned they often give way to what are being popularly described as "micro-moments of racism," those seemingly innocent but hurtful incidents of prejudice in which things happen to people of color or of different religious traditions and persuasions that would not occur to those of us representing the "mainstream."[12]

We can learn from our partners in dialogue, if we really listen, about the importance of understanding the individual in relation to the whole both socially and ecologically, as that has been realized in many other cultures. But it is quite certain that within our American culture, both in the context of theological education and as we try to engage in dialogue in other spheres, our efforts to "hear" are foiled to the extent to which we fail to take serious account of the Western Jewish and Christian traditions' continuing history of discrimination, prejudice and both micro- and macro-moments of racism. Until we understand the experiences, and therefore the needs, out of which people think and act, it will be very difficult to comprehend how those have been translated into the beliefs and practices that characterize their respective communities.

There are various ways in which students considering the experiences of persons representing a variety of religious and ethnic groupings in America, for example, could engage in the kind of conversation that would illumine such issues. Iliff students, faculty and staff in a recent local immersion with Denver Seminary learned first hand from Hispanic women how their families had refused to allow them to learn or speak Spanish when they were growing up in order to protect them from American prejudice. A group of Iliff students visiting with members of a local Denver mosque listened in pain as they heard Muslim women tell of being called "ragheads" for wearing conservative dress and the men describe the deep antipathy and discrimination they have faced in the workplace.

There are, of course, a variety of problems that educational institutions, in this case theological schools, face when they make the attempt to be more inclusive so as to provide the context for some of the kinds of dialogue I have been pro-moting. What happens, for example, when the persons whose voices we profess to want to hear come speaking something that does not mesh easily with the very liberality that made us want to include them in the first place? My own institution is proud of a program that brings to campus one or two visiting professors each year from third-world countries. We are enjoying this resource very much, but at the same time we struggle with how to react when, for instance, an instructor from Africa treats the material of his course and the students in it in what those students perceive to be a sexist manner, or a Latin American theologian voices a theological position that reflects a kind of Christian exclusiveness that many of us are pleased to reject.

Martin Marty in a recent *Christian Century* article voiced some extremely impor-tant questions arising from the cultural climate in this country today in which basic values do indeed differ. "So what do we do," he reflected, "in a republic when my virtue does not match your virtue, when my discourse, metaphysics, ethics, theology, history, views and kind are or seem incommensurate with yours?" It is one thing to acknowledge that our culture, our society, is obviously reflective of these different values and that we do feel an obligation to allow them to be voiced and honored. It is quite a different matter, I suspect, when these differences are present and articulated in such a way as to call into question some of the most basic assumptions of our denominations, our theological schools, and our personal perspectives. How do we craft a program of theological education that comes to terms with that? How do we remain open to the possibilities of a dialogue that may illumine for us things that we do not know how to handle?

Or to put the matter a slightly different way, what if we find that by learning more about the theological perspectives of other religious/cultural traditions through dialogue we realize that we really do not appreciate them? I am reminded of Diana Eck's reference to her Hindu colleague who thought that the Christian god is quite remarkably stingy if he is only willing to send one incarnation to the world.[13] Many people may find it tempting to think that the god of Islam, who would sanction blood revenge for apostasy, must be rather mean-spirited. When in the context of dialogue we discover beliefs and practices for which we have little appreciation, when "understanding" seems to lead to distaste rather than receptivity, how are we to respond? Do we say so bluntly and risk offending our brothers and sisters of other traditions as well as prejudicing the openness of our students? Or do we keep our responses deeply buried under the phenomenological *epoche*, that bracketing of opinion that strives for a neutral stance and probably also means that we may not grow much in our exposure to other ways of thought and perception? It is part of the difficult task of dialogue to ponder these problems, and to know that working for their solution is the responsibility of all of the partners in conversation with each other.

How, then, do the current discussions in the educational world and elsewhere about multiculturalism, pluralism, anti-individualism and ethnic particularism relate to some of the ways in which Christian theologians are beginning to think about the reality of religious pluralism? It seems to me that the challenges facing the educator and the theologian are in many ways similar, which may in fact actually cloud the issue for the educator who is also theologian and for the the-ological school which is at once an academic institution and a vehicle for the transmission of the traditions, values and theological interpretations of the denomination to which it is affiliated. Academia needs to take seriously the problem of how to relinquish a claim on a set body of knowledge as somehow containing the "truth," without succumbing in the process to every current and tide of new expression. Framed differently, but perhaps coming down to somewhat the same thing, is the question facing the church of how to continue to affirm what it interprets to be the message of the Christian gospel while taking very seriously the different and often conflicting perceptions of truth and reality held so dearly by others. As Robert Schreiter put it, "In our embrace of a genuine pluralism (where difference is taken seriously), what happens to the unity and normativity of Christian faith?"[14] Put in the context of the seminary or school of theology the question may be, How does an educational institution remain true to its religious heritage and commitment at the same time that it provides a context of openness to the possibility of genuine and engaging dialogue in both the ecumenical and interfaith contexts?

There are several ways in which to think about the multiplicity of ethnic, cultural and religious groupings in this country. While "pluralism" often is used for this reality, I would argue that the fact that American society is diverse, variegated and complex is best described by the word "plurality." It is a descriptive term characterizing the state of affairs as it impinges on our social life and our institutional realities. "Pluralism," on the other hand, as Schreiter suggests above, is more appropriately an evaluative term, representing a position which holds that to the extent that different faiths and traditions embody different understandings of truth or reality, exchange among the adherents of these perspectives is a positive thing which has the potential of promoting the moral and theological growth of all participants. My own position is one that fully embraces the ideology of pluralism in that interpretation and understands it to be an important, perhaps essential, ingredient in ecumenical and interfaith dialogue.

II. Interfaith Dialogue

Let us turn now to the specific concerns of interfaith dialogue, and see how as a component of theological education it may be instructed by the insights of the current discussions on pluralism. To the extent that we are able both to help our students learn how appropriately to engage in that dialogue and even to model it in our instruction, I believe it to be an extremely important dimension of the responsibility to educate them to minister in communities of increasingly multicultural and religiously plural nature.

Dialogue, contact and conversation among the representatives of different faith communities both in this country and abroad are difficult for a variety of reasons. From the Christian perspective, many of us are concerned that there may be little to say to members of other faith traditions whose experiences, worldviews and actions often seem to be incomprehensible to us. As one whose own professional responsibilities include speaking on behalf of Muslims and attempting to explain to skeptical audiences why Muslims sometimes believe and act in ways that are quite beyond our comprehension, I know well how high the wall of misunderstanding can be. And although it may be hard for those of us dedicated to dialogue and to opening the channels of exchange to accept, the fact is that many persons of other faiths and traditions are not at present very much inclined to talk with us.

Members of these groups feel, no doubt quite rightly, that the history of encounter between them and Christians has been one in which Christians had a not very hidden agenda of trying to turn them away from their faith. They have had enough of listening to the West and often prefer to get on with their own business. In the eyes of others we have been guilty of imperialism educationally, culturally and politically; we have been intolerant and condemning of other ways of living and believing; and we have confused an understanding of the Christian gospel with the propagation of a value system that acknowledges power as residing in the hands of the culturally advantaged and the politically and economically success-ful.[15]

This is neither to disparage the good intentions of those who have witnessed to their faith and ministered to non-Christian peoples and cultures, nor to deny the genuine service that has been carried out for many centuries by Western missionaries. It is, however, to underscore the fact that the dimension of that mission that has criticized and attempted to abolish beliefs and practices of people of other religions, to say nothing of some of the more insidious aspects of colon-ialization in the name of the propagation of Western Christianity, makes dialogue, contact and conversation among the respective communities here and abroad at the present moment both crucial and difficult. Part of the educational mission in our theological institutions is to help students understand the historical context out of which mistrust and suspicion have grown as a first step toward the creation of conditions more conducive to mutual exchange.

An integral part of Iliff's newly configured three-quarter course on the history of Christianity, for example, includes major segments treating the experiences that subjugated or colonialized peoples have had at the hands of Western Christians. The history of the Crusades is studied not only through Western chronicles but from the perspective of those inhabiting the Middle East at the time, both Chris-tian and Muslim, and the influence that this legacy has left on the current rise of Islamic movements. The history of Christian mission in America is considered both through the denominational literature of the time and as it was actually experienced by the Native American peoples whose lives have been dramatically and irreversibly changed by white expansionism.

Where do we begin in the task of listening to our neighbors, especially those who have been and continue to be influenced by the legacy of Western response to their peoples and cultures? How can we both learn from them and support them as they seek to be faithful to different ways of life and sets of values that they genuinely see as alternative to those prevalent in American society? There are of course many areas in which communication among members of our respec-tive faiths is taking place. Not only in meetings sponsored by denominational and ecumenical bodies, but in smaller local and regional groups Christians are ven-turing with colleagues from other traditions into some difficult, challenging and often gratifying conversations. Those of us who have had the opportunity to par-ticipate in such conversations are, I believe, quite persuaded that they are essential on both the local and national, as well as the global levels. And certainly such attempts at mutual understanding must be a growing element in the agenda of our local churches (and thus part of the curriculum of our theological schools), as communities representing both ethnic Christian (that is to say other than the dominant white) and non-Christian traditions in America continue to grow.

Let there be no mistake about the urgency of such dialogue. If we fail to learn how to talk with each other, and I maintain that that must begin with a great deal more listening than Western Christians have found it easy to do, we will jeopardize both the possibility of working together as members of a pluralist society for some kind of common good, and perhaps even the hope for the long-range viability of the church as an effective institution in this country.

Goals of Dialogue

Living in America at the present time necessitates the self-conscious attempt of members of all denominations and faiths to try to articulate what their traditions mean to them and to interpret them so as to be able to cope with a world approaching the twenty-first century. If we accept this common concern as a starting point for conversation, it is possible to lay out some of the areas in which dialogue can take place between Christians representing what is (for the time being) the dominant culture and members of other traditions and faiths, especially insofar as we are facing many of the same challenges. Briefly, dialogue — ecumenical, interethnic and interfaith — is for purposes of (1) exchange of information, (2) working together in common cause for justice and equity, and (3) learning theologically from each other so as to enrich our own understanding of what it means to be persons of faith within our respective traditions. To the extent to which these goals for dialogue already have been acknowledged by those who have participated in institutionally sponsored dialogues, granted often with different modes of interpretation, it has been in the context of conversation between members of Christian and non-Christian faiths. I would suggest that it may be equally important to keep them in mind as possible ends to be achieved as we engage in dialogue with members of different racial-ethnic and immigrant Christian communities with and among whom conversation and mutual tolerance may, in fact, at times be the most difficult.[16]

1. Exchange of information

In the recent history of interfaith dialogue through such agencies as the World and National Councils of Churches and in other ecumenical settings, the mutual sharing of information has been a primary goal. It is a goal that increasingly is achieved as interfaith groups in many parts of this country meet today to learn about and from each other. But as indicated above, some of the members of non-Christian traditions who have been involved in these talks are frankly not much in the mood these days to engage in dialogical conversation that is genuinely dialogical. (This is also the case with some ethnic Christians in our contemporary culture.) They feel that they have had ample opportunity to hear what (Western) Christians think, and that if there is to be any conversation at all, now is the time for others to talk — to explain to Western Christians who they are, what they believe, and how they intend to live their lives in order to be faithful and responsible citizens of their own communities.

We as Western Christians, then, need to recognize that this is a time in the history of interfaith and intercultural relations when exchange may best be understood in terms of us listening and others talking.[17] To be truly open to listening, to receiving the information that others wish to give us about their faith and their way of life, means that we must suspend the natural responses of suspicion, mistrust and fear that seem often to accompany an exposure to the new and different. It also means that we must try to see, as they see of us, that what they may describe as the deepest and best qualities of their faith are ideals to be worked for and often are far from the realities of the words and deeds of those who claim to be adherents.

2. Working together for justice and equity

A second reason for engaging members of other faith traditions and cultures in conversation is to find ways in which to work together on issues of justice as well as for the resolve of concerns that may be shared in common. "Globalization should give way [as a term] to global justice," said one of the representatives of WOCATI at the 1992 biennial meetings of the ATS. "Interfaith dialogue is an expression of justice," insisted another. Better understanding of these issues helps identify a number of areas in which we can begin to talk together for purposes of living and working together. In many cases all of us who live in this culture, no matter what our communities or faith traditions, share some of the same economic, political and ethical-social concerns. On the one hand, it is increasingly evident that dialogue is not only possible but is essential as we struggle together to try to understand our common calling to live lives of ethical responsibility. On the other hand, we often can be fooled into thinking that an apparent commonality of concern presupposes a commonality of socio-economic realities. Until we become more sophisticated in our understanding that inequitable economic circumstances lead to situations of injustice which lead to different forms of religious (as well, of course, as political and other) responses, we will be ill equipped to be able to hear, let alone dialogue with, our brothers and sisters of other traditions and cultures. The case study of the Australian Aborigine community entitled "Sacred Sites" which follows this essay illustrates effectively some of the concerns that arise when the economic interests of one culture impinge on the rights, values and sacred places of another. This is but one instance of a problem that has long prevailed and now is becoming increasingly exposed in various places around the earth.

Perhaps the area in which Western Christians might find the greatest sympathy with the concerns of the members of a number of other faith traditions, including those participating in neoconservative movements, is that relating to an ever growing fear of the breakdown of moral and ethical standards in America and elsewhere. In all of the different communities of faith in this country there is deep concern for what is perceived as an impending societal chaos. People fear that their young people, if allowed to stray from the fundamental principles of their respective faiths, will become pregnant before marriage, will be involved in drugs and crime, will join gangs and fall into the other terrible traps that seem set for so many youth in contemporary Western cultures. By adopting some of the more conservative aspects of their faith, thus sometimes earning the label "fundamentalist" or "reactionary," they often are trying to cling to a way of life that they see as the only viable alternative in a deeply disruptive society.

If we want to learn about a people's faith, it is essential to know something of the life circumstances within which that faith is nurtured, challenged and changed. It is also increasingly clear to those who have tried to foster this kind of dialogue and learning that if our seminary students have any hope of understanding what it means to be Hispanic, Asian, Arab or whatever in this culture, whether that identity is developed in a Christian or a non-Christian context, they have to venture outside the classroom into the communities in which the circumstances that shape these respective life experiences prevail. In helping set up the possibility for these kinds of direct learning experiences schools of theology need to be particularly careful to avoid a perpetuation of the attitude that "we are here to help you." If different ethnic and religious groups are tired of hearing us talk, they may well be equally tired of having us prescribe for them, assuming that somehow we are able to determine the solutions for their problems. Part of the dialogue experience must be listening not only to what others would want us to know about their experiences and beliefs, but watching to learn from them the most effective means and strategies for helping bring about justice and equitable circumstances in their respective situations.

3. Theological enrichment

A recent meeting of the National Conference of Christians and Jews was devoted to a Christian-Jewish-Muslim dialogue concerning the meaning of revelation. The discussion quickly turned from the ways in which the several traditions have interpreted revelation to a sharing of the deepest purposes of dialogue. As one participant observed, such conversations are "community-forming moments which encompass all of humanity." While it is commonly affirmed that the aim of such interfaith conversations is not to come out with some form of new or eclectic religion, it was also a shared conviction at that meeting that it is in the encounter with the other that the greatest possibilities lie for personal development, change and growth, and perhaps even for the rethinking of aspects of the religious tradition of which one is a part. Here, I believe, is where the most exciting possibility may lie for understanding the importance of dialogue as part of the agenda of theological education.

Participants in interfaith dialogue recognize that the exchange of deeply held convictions among persons of different theological persuasions is a problematic business. Those who have sponsored and participated in such conversations at the national and international levels have had different views as to the best approach to take. One position, and probably that supported by the majority, is to be "objective" in trying to respond to what is heard, to assume that the most direct way to understand a different faith is to bracket one's own beliefs and to look dispassionately at what others have held to be true. I think it is fair to say that this has been the preference of the World Council of Churches as a sponsoring body of numerous interfaith dialogues. A version of this has been put forward by Frederick Streng, among others, as the most effective way to ensure understanding by students of other faiths and traditions.[18]

Another alternative involves a greater degree of personal involvement whereby one "tests" the convictions of the other against one's own deeply held beliefs, "tries them on," so to speak. Each of these positions holds its own risks. The first, some argue, actually lessens the possibility that one can really understand, precisely because of the barrier of objectivity. The second is risky in another way, insofar as it may result in some shaking of one's own theological perspectives and convictions. For many engaged in the dialogue today, however, the second option appears to be a risk well worth taking.

This is not to say that many of the partners in the dialogue are open to what might be called theological negotiation. For most of the history of Christianity the dominant theological stance vis-à-vis other religions has been that the message of the gospel is simply and basically right, or true, and to the extent that other revelations or understandings differ with that they are by definition wrong. This kind of exclusivist position not only characterizes the understanding of many within the Christian community (although certainly many would identify themselves as "inclusivist") but has been the classical stance of persons of faith in virtually all religious traditions throughout history to the extent to which they have been aware of the existence of different belief systems. And it is often the position of faithful people today, even those most deeply engaged in interfaith conversations. At a recent Jewish-Muslim-Christian discussion in which I was involved a rabbi noted that the official Roman Catholic stance in relation to Judaism has moved from absolute condemnation to saying "we wish them well in their own ways." As long as Christians profess that the only true and valid way to God is through Jesus Christ, he questioned, is such an apparent change in position really not another more subtle form of condemnation?

For some persons, however, sacrificing the possibility that the faith of others might be valid even if it seems on the surface to compromise the tenets of their own faith is not emotionally or intellectually viable. What are the alternatives for such persons? One is to try to find a ground for conversation in which common-alities are stressed and differences ignored or marginalized. Such efforts provide a way of avoiding the exclusivism of the position that says I am right and therefore you are wrong. Such efforts are, however, looked on with some suspicion by many representatives of other faith traditions. The fact is that at this particular moment in history many of them do not care much whether or not Christians find com-monality with them in experience or theology, recognizing that often what is being done by those who make such attempts is really a rearranging of the beliefs of the other to make them sound more Christian. The effort is then revealed as a kind of disguised version of the position that holds finally to the truth of one's own religious understanding and thus the relativity of another's. For many it appears as another example of the cultural/religious imperialism of which Western Christians have so often been charged.

Two processes seem to be at work here. One is the attempt to discover where commonality really lies, and the other is to see where one is willing to step outside the bounds of one's own faith tradition to see how it might feel to stand in the shoes of the other. It is with the first that interfaith dialogue generally finds itself concerned today, and the process of discovering that we really do have more in common than our histories of ignorance or sometimes of antagonism might lead us to believe is a truly exciting one. Yet sometimes nagging at the edges of our discussions is the danger of a kind of syncretism that threatens to sacrifice the vitality of our individual revelations in favor of a bland mixture of mutually pal-atable doctrines.[19] Here is where we meet the challenge of trying to find a different way in which to affirm our own understanding while still honoring the integrity of the understanding of the other.

One possibility is to shift the focus from the theological as such to the ethical, which relates back to the second goal or end of dialogue. Some very interesting work is being done on this score by feminist theologians. Marjorie Suchocki, for example, has argued that "the fundamental criterion of value and the focus of dialogue and action among religions," according to a liberationist and a feminist perspective, is justice. To assume that one particular revelation/religion qualifies as a universal norm by which to judge all others, she says, in fact leads to oppression and as such actually contradicts this norm of justice. (Suchocki goes on to argue that the superiority-inferiority syndrome that has characterized much of the Christian approach to other religions in fact has direct parallels with sexism whereby one gender is set up as the appropriate norm for all human life.)[20]

Others who are certainly not overlooking the importance of the ethical dimension still want to wrestle with the realities of seemingly different kinds of revelations. Some of them are coming to understand that it is all right to acknowledge that there are differences at the deepest levels of theological understanding which do not need to discourage our search for similarities when and if we find them. If it is not necessary to look for the common denominator, we are freed to be able to appreciate the differences and to learn from them. "The proposal is so simple and so liberating," says John Cobb, "that I am driven to ask why it is so strongly resisted."[21] Crucial to the kind of hopefulness expressed by Cobb is the insistence that to be open to the perspectives of other religious traditions does not necessarily mean that we must sacrifice our own deeply held beliefs.[22]

Those who share this perspective, and it is expressed in a variety of different ways by a number of contemporary theologians, generally acknowledge that while there are real and very significant differences among religions, each way has its own integrity and at least in a penultimate sense each has its own vision of, and thus claim on, the truth.[23] To acknowledge the integrity of different religions we have to affirm the importance of particularities and of separate revelations in a way that precludes the premature closure that often comes in the search for common ground. Oddly enough, perhaps, this "next step" in theological thinking about religious pluralism might actually provide the occasion for all of us to proclaim the unique and original truths of our own traditions with renewed vigor. But understanding those truths in the context of the reality of multiple perspectives helps keep us from falling into the trap of exclusivism. We might be greatly freed if we could begin with the assumptions that no one has a corner on the truth and that not all revelations boil down to the same thing. One could then take up the challenge of contemplating a number of sharply defined perspectives playing off against one another, greatly divergent variations that presumably would not begin to exhaust the resources of the divine imagination. As my old friend and professor Wilfred Cantwell Smith liked to say, "God is much more imaginative than we used to think." The discovery of truth by reason, an Iliff colleague recently observed, is the agenda of modernism and perhaps should be set aside for a new and more engaging agenda that opens up different possibilities for the post-modern age.

III. Concluding Comments

Thus the critical task for interfaith/ecumenical dialogue today, as it is for education in general, is a re-awakening to the crucial importance of hearing the "other" in a context of overall relatedness as a means both of attaining better and more accurate understanding, and ultimately of working toward common intellectual, ethical, and spiritual advancement. On a penultimate plane this would seem to allow both for the proclamation of the truth of the particular, in the Christian case of the revelation of the gospel, and for finding that ground upon which we can share our humanity and beginning to think together about new understandings of truth. But this alternative is not viable either intellectually or theologically unless it is accompanied by the sincere desire to hear through direct and personal encounter the perspectives of the other, and to be open through that process to possibilities not only for enhancing our own worldviews but for actually creating something new by virtue of the very exchange. As Fumitaka Matsuoka has observed, borrowing from anthropologist Paul Rabinow's terminology used in reflecting on the task of intercultural communication,[24] in such a meeting of different perspectives "both parties become conscious not only of their own cultural and linguistic worlds, but also of the liminal world that is born between them through encounter with each other's self-reflection."[25]

Insofar as ecumenical/interfaith dialogue is understood to be part of the essential task of theological education, then it needs to be an ongoing dialectical process. On the one hand, to even begin the dialogue and for it to have substance it is important to have given some thought both to one's theological stance vis-à-vis the reality that we live in a pluralistic society and a pluralistic world, and to the way that one views the particulars of another's situation and faith. On the other hand, the constant process of receiving new information, of processing that information and of reconciling it with one's own views means that there will be (or at least should be) constant changes and modifications in one's own position. This is both the most effective means of education and the most promising way to ensure that the future of theological education and ultimately of the church will be hopeful, vital and relevant.

CASE STUDY[26]

Sacred Sites

Gary Wells was troubled as he stepped on the commuter train that would take him from the prosperous suburb of Glen Lea to the city center and a meeting of his church's National Board of Social Responsibility. The meeting of the board had been called hurriedly to consider a request from the secretary for permission for him to go to Noonkanbah in Western Australia.

With other Australian church leaders and concerned citizens, the secretary wished to join the Aborigines of Noonkanbah to protest and, if possible, bring an end to the transnational Amax Exploration Company's drilling for oil on Aboriginal sacred sites in the area. Gary knew that many members of his congregation were strongly opposed to the church's involvement in such actions. What is more, he was uncertain in his own mind about what policy the church should adopt in this particular conflict. Yet in a short while he would have to vote on a specific proposal that could inevitably link the church with a demonstration that, he believed, would be considered by many as anti-government as well as antagonistic to the lawful activities of a large mining company.

Now in his mid-forties, Gary had been minister at Glen Lea for seven years. Because of their desire for continuity in schooling for their children, Gary and his wife, Carol, hoped that they might be able to stay in Glen Lea the maximum ten years permitted by denominational regulations for pastoral appointments.

When Gary entered theological college twenty years earlier, he had been very conservative theologically. During his three years of college, he fought against what he considered to be the excessive liberalism of the theological faculty. One professor in particular, Arthur Lawrence, had caused him great concern for a long time. In retrospect, Gary recognized that Professor Lawrence was probably a major influence leading to change in Gary's theological and politico-social outlook.

Following ordination and three years of parish ministry in Australia, Professor Lawrence had served for several years as a missionary in North India and then in the Pacific region. He had gone on to doctoral studies in systematic theology in the United States. After graduation he returned to Australia and was appointed to the position in systematic theology and history of religions at the seminary.

Though influenced by Barthian theology, which was in its heyday in America when he studied there, Lawrence shared with his students that he had also been deeply influenced by his encounter with Hinduism and Islam. Gary felt at the time that Lawrence was deliberately trying to shake the convictions of fundamentalists such as himself, and he resented it. He was antagonized also by many of the things Professor Lawrence taught. Lawrence used Barth's critique of religion, in which Barth included Christianity, to hold open the possibility that by the grace of God Hinduism no less than Christianity might be constituted as "true religion." Holding very firmly to the uniqueness of Christianity, Gary and his friends were deeply shocked by this teaching.

At the end of Gary's first year in seminary, some of Lawrence's students, including Gary, held a meeting to decide what they should do about the teaching they were receiving. Though Gary was uncertain about the wisdom of the decision, the students decided that their professor was such a dangerous influence in the church that they would all work to have him dismissed. They planned a campaign very carefully and took their case to the highest authorities. Though they found some support in the church, in the end they failed to achieve their objective. Since they were compelled by the curriculum to take a certain number of core components with Lawrence, they accepted the fact that they would have to endure his teaching, but vowed that they would resist his influence. Gary now knew they had not been successful in that resolve. Largely under Professor Lawrence's influence, Gary had become much more tolerant of other theological perspectives, more sensitive to people of other faiths, and more concerned about issues of justice. In his final year, he had even signed a petition to the government calling for an end to the "White Australia Policy" which restricted immigration into Australia to people of European origin. Gary had abandoned his fundamentalist theological position, but he believed that he had retained what was important in his conservatism: the centrality of the grace of God, the need for personal salvation, and a concern for evangelism. But he had added to that much more than he had lost.

Gary knew that it was his reputation as an evangelical that had gained him the invitation to the Glen Lea Methodist Circuit, as it was then called. He had been pleased with the invitation. His previous pastorates, including five years in the inner city, had all been in struggling congregations. Here at last was an opportunity to work with a growing congregation made up largely of families. He had found, however, that most of the really active members of the congregation were more conservative theologically than he was and did not share many of his social concerns.

Aurukun and Mornington Island

As he gazed out the window of the speeding train, Gary recalled the last time he had been caught up in the Aboriginal issue. It had been during the protracted struggle of the Aborigines of Aurukun and Mornington Island with the Queensland state government. Many of these black-skinned persons—the original inhabitants of the Australian continent, who had occupied the land for at least thirty thousand years before the white settlers came—had been resettled and moved onto state-controlled land over the past hundred years. However, the communities in Aurukun and on Mornington Island had remained on their ancestral lands. For most of the century, these two Aboriginal communities had been administered by the Presbyterian, and then the Uniting Church[27] as an agency of the Queensland government. But in mid-March 1978, the state government suddenly notified the church and the communities that it would assume direct control as of April 1 by which time all church personnel with the exception of a chaplain should leave. Both communities protested the decision, and the Uniting Church supported their protests.

Over the previous decade the church had followed a policy of transferring to the community elders responsibility for decision making and control in all areas of community life. A majority of members of both Aboriginal communities opposed direct government administration because they believed that under the state they would have much less independence and self-determination than they had at present. They said they were suspicious of the government's intentions for another reason. The twenty-five thousand square miles of their land included a rich bauxite deposit that the government was apparently eager to have mined. A majority of the Aurukun Aborigines declared that they did not want any mining on their land. Open-cut mining operations would destroy their ceremonial sites, scar the land with which they had deep emotional and spiritual ties, spoil their hunting, cut them off from their natural resources of fruits, roots, and seeds, and disrupt their community life.

Aurukun residents were aware of the problems that mining had brought to other similar communities. At Weipa, only a short distance away, bauxite mining had resulted in the destruction of tribal life and the decimation of the community by disease and alcoholism. They did not wish to have the result repeated in Aurukun. During the dispute they tried to explain to white Australians through newspaper and television interviews the fundamental importance of land for the well-being of Aboriginal people. "It is the source of our tribal identity and cohesion," one of them explained. "It provides not only for our physical needs, but for our spiritual needs also. Just looking at our land keeps up our spiritual life the same way reading the Bible keeps up the spiritual life of Christians."

The struggle between the Aboriginal communities and the Uniting Church on the one side and the state government on the other continued for a month with daily press and radio coverage of moves and counter moves. The federal government entered the dispute in support of the Aborigines. At the time, the land was considered "crown land" belonging to the state of Queensland, having been previously designated by the state as Aboriginal reserve land. Only minutes prior to the passage of federal legislation to acquire the land, the Queensland premier announced the abolition of the Aboriginal reserves. This in effect nullified the federal legislation, removed all state financial support from the two communities, and could lead to eviction of the Aborigines as trespassers on state land. Rather than enter into a divisive and lengthy court battle on untested issues of state and federal constitutional rights, the two governments, which were controlled by the same political coalition, effected a compromise. The Aborigines would be left temporarily in control of the land, but as lessees for a fifty-year period rather than as owners. The two communities, which had not been consulted in the decision, accepted the compromise; it was the only thing they could do. The role of the church was undercut; a powerful joint state and federal advisory board was established to counsel the two new "shires."

Throughout the dispute, ministers of the state government continually alleged that the church persons working in the communities were "do gooders," "radical stirrers," "outsiders manipulating the Aborigines," and "communists." Gary had wondered at times whether this might be true. He did not know the individuals in question, but he did know personally Uniting Church leaders whom he himself would have called "social activists." Members of the state government made similar allegations about these leaders, and Gary knew that the allegations were false. If these statements were false, it seemed to him likely that the other allegations could also be false.

Gary was pleased to note that newspaper editorials, radio commentators, and television current affairs programs were heavily in favor of the Aboriginal cause and very supportive of the church's action. Yet there had been unfavorable reaction to the Uniting Church's involvement by the congregation at Glen Lea. Gary recalled the brief conversation he had with Bob Croft during the dispute. About Gary's age, Bob was company secretary of a large Australian manufacturing firm. He was also one of the most active members of the congregation. He taught Sunday school, was one of the adult advisors to the youth program, and was convener of the Mission and Evangelism Committee of the Parish Council. Bob had opened the conversation in the vestry just before morning worship with what seemed like a humorous question:

"Can't you talk some sense into some of these ministerial colleagues of yours?"

"What do you mean, Bob?" Gary asked.

"I mean the way they are going on over this Aurukun affair. Why don't they keep their noses out of this business and let the Queensland government settle the matter?"

"Don't you think the church has a right to be involved? After all, it has administered the Aboriginal reserves for seventy years?" Gary countered.

"They should never have been involved in that sort of thing. The church's business is to preach the gospel to people, not run their affairs and turn them against the government," Bob replied.

"What makes you think the mission staff has been turning the people against the government?" Gary questioned.

"It's quite clear what they have been doing. The Queensland state premier said just this week that they are a group of social activists manipulating the people," Bob continued.

"Well, even the premier might be wrong, you know," Gary argued.

"No, I think he's absolutely right. He is a Christian man—teaches Sunday school. He knows what is best for the Aborigines and is trying to achieve it. The church is trying to keep them back in the Dark Ages—keep them separate from the rest of the nation—it's a kind of apartheid. The church leaders are always decrying apartheid in South Africa, but that is just what they are trying to create here in Australia." Bob was becoming quite agitated.

"Don't you think there is a difference between forcing Blacks to live in separate areas from Whites and allowing them, if they choose, to have their own protected reserves?" Gary asked.

"It amounts to the same thing, doesn't it? Separate development for two races within the same nation. I tell you, Gary, I am very uneasy about the leadership of the Uniting Church. They are a group of radicals who want to stir up trouble wherever they can. You never hear them talking about evangelism and the saving of souls. If things keep on like this, Celia and I will have to think seriously about transferring to another denomination."

"I hope you won't do that," Gary replied. "Let's talk some more about it sometime."

They never did take up the subject again. The dispute subsided, and Bob seemed to be carrying on his church activities as usual. Then, a conflict between the Western Australia government and the Aboriginal community at Noonkanbah began to seize the headlines. The Uniting Church was not directly involved in this dispute, but now, as the situation was nearing a climax, Gary believed some of the church leaders wanted to get involved.

Noonkanbah Station

Gary tried to recall the background of the dispute from what he had read in the papers. Noonkanbah Station was part of the tribal lands of the Yungngora people. For many years, the remaining Yungngora worked as stockmen for the white pastoralists who held a long-term lease of the land from the state. At one time the Yungngora walked off the station to protest the way they were treated, and for about five years they lived as fringe-dwellers around the town of Fitzroy Crossing though they continued to visit sacred sites at Noonkanbah. When a federal government commission, set up to settle Aborigines on their own land, purchased the Noonkanbah Pastoral Lease for the Yungngora people, the Yungngora returned to the station. They began to make good progress in establishing a profitable cattle industry on the land. Shortly after the Yungngora took over the station, a number of mining companies began prospecting for minerals, diamonds and oil on leased land. Inasmuch as the land was "crown land" — that is, it belonged to the states — and the Yungngora people only held a lease on it, prospecting could be carried on without their permission. The states also legally controlled mining contracts on grazing acreage managed by white settlers.

One company, Amax Exploration, decided to proceed and drill for oil. The Aborigines claimed that during the initial preparation Amax employees damaged several sacred sites. A bulldozer was brought in to cut long straight lines in the earth in a grid pattern. Apparently some of these lines were cut through burial and ceremonial grounds, and a tree that they believed was the home of the spirit of Friday Muller, a former elder of the tribe, was damaged. The community took action in the courts to prevent further exploration by Amax, but the action was unsuccessful. They also sent a petition to the West Australian Parliament, written on bark in their own language, asking the parliament to prevent mining or drilling on their lands. The parliament gave no public response to the petition, and in the following month the state government announced that it had given Amax permission to proceed with the drilling. The Yungngora people then voted to obstruct Amax personnel physically from coming onto the station. As a result, Amax decided to postpone operations.

Two years later the company proceeded with exploration. Claiming that the proposed drill hole would be within the sacred site complex, the Noonkanbah community sought protection through the court under the Aboriginal Heritage Act, a bill enacted by a previous West Australian government to provide protection for Aboriginal culture. This legal action failed, and it became clear from numerous press statements, as well as provision of police escorts for Amax workers entering the Noonkanbah site, that the state government saw the dispute as an important test case. Government spokesmen said that as much as a third of Australia could be closed to exploration if the Aborigines won this dispute. The state minister for cultural affairs claimed that sacred sites were not the issue and that if the Aborigines held the mineral rights to the land, they would readily negotiate with mining companies for the huge financial gain they would receive. He claimed also that the Noonkanbah people were being manipulated by "outsiders" for "political reasons."

The minister argued further that the state government could not give overriding land rights to the Aborigines. This action, he said, would be contrary to the government's policy of one Australian family with equal rights and equal opportunities for all. He said that the government was anxious to protect Aboriginal rights and all places of significance to them, but this protection must be consistent with the needs of the entire Australian community which is composed of more than a hundred different ethnic groups. Aboriginal reserves in Western Australia amounted to tens of thousands of square miles. If the Aborigines had the right to prevent mining on all these reserves, the Australian community as a whole would be deprived of needed reserves of minerals and oil, and the development of the state would be seriously impeded.

It appeared to Gary that the Noonkanbah community or a group of white activists, having lost the legal battles and having failed in all direct negotiations, might now take action outside the law. Gary was not sure in his own mind that the Aborigines really were initiators of the proposed action or that theirs was a cause he could support.

As he stepped off the train, Gary was trying to compare this dispute with the Aurukun and Mornington Island dispute. He believed he saw a difference. In that case, the church was directly involved. Here there was no necessary involvement, but, as he saw it, some church persons seemed to be trying to involve themselves — to get into the act as it were — and he was not sure what their motives were. In the previous dispute, the church's actions were through legal channels, but here it seemed that disputants were preparing to take action outside the law, not just against Amax, but against the duly elected government. In view of the strong support of Scripture in Romans 13 and 1 Peter 2:23-27 for submission to the government, how could Christians justify such action? What is more, the dispute was over protection of sites associated with a heathen religion. How could Christians be involved in protecting such sites? Would this not be like protecting idols? Surely the church's task was rather to convert these people so that they would give up their superstitions and practices. If a member of his own congregation, Bob Croft, had reacted so negatively to the church's role in the Queensland dispute, how could he and others like him react positively to this one?

Board of Social Responsibility

These questions were uppermost in his thoughts as Gary entered the meeting room. He greeted a few of his friends, but his mind was too preoccupied for small talk. The chairman called the meeting to order and opened with prayer. "You know why this meeting has been called," he said. "The motion before us is that the Board of Social Responsibility give its secretary leave to go to Noonkanbah to demonstrate the church's support of the Aboriginal struggle and that his air fare be paid by the board."

Ron Avery, the full time secretary of the board, was in his fifties. He was an ordained minister who had served in several parishes and a man whose ministry had always been strong on social issues. He rehearsed the events that led up to what he called "the present crisis in Western Australia" and put forth his case for going to Noonkanbah. Gary was familiar with many of the details, but Ron had a different interpretation of some aspects of the dispute.

Ron argued that the government had itself acted unethically in the dispute and by doing so had deprived the Aborigines of justice. The Aboriginal Heritage Act of Western Australia provided for the trustees of the Western Australia Museum to establish the location and genuineness of sacred sites. The museum had done this and had accepted the genuineness of the site in question though the museum's report had not been published. The Act also gave the minister power to direct the museum trustees to permit mining on a particular site. The minister used this power. The Noonkanbah people lost its final legal appeal on the basis of the approval that the trustees were forced to give. Ron argued that the outcome may have been legal, but was not just and fair.

"It is clear," Ron continued, "that the West Australian government is determined to have drilling proceed on the site and is prepared to stop at nothing to see that it happens. The Aborigines are clearly the poor, oppressed, and the powerless in this dispute. It was with such that the prophets and Jesus took their stand, and the church of Jesus today must do the same. There is plenty of land in Western Australia where mining can be carried out. If ever there were a modern parallel to the story of Naboth's vineyard (1 Kings 21), this is it. It may be that if the churches and other persons of goodwill support the Noonkanbah people, this desecration of their sacred site can be prevented. But even if we can't prevent it, we must demonstrate our solidarity with the Aboriginal people in their struggle. It is clear that the next few days will be decisive. I ask you to make it possible for me to demonstrate by my presence the fact that the Uniting Church cares about justice and cares about Aborigines."

Following Ron's statement, there were speeches of support for the motion, but also a number of questions were asked.

"How do we know the Aborigines are really opposed to oil drilling? The government has said they are just playing for a share of the royalties from any oil found. And how do we know this is not just a lot of trouble manufactured by social activists and stirrers?"

In reply, Ron read from the statement of Aboriginal elder, Ivan McPhee:

The old people of Noonkanbah are very upset about this mining coming onto our sacred site. This sacred site important to Aboriginal people. We got *goanna*[28] inside sacred site. That *goanna* been there from Dreamtime.[29] Long before European came to Australia. That story come from grandfather to grandfather, and now they still telling that story. Noonkanbah people don't want mining on sacred site. Already we got old man, Bob Muluby, sick by this company setting up camp on sacred site.

Ron also read from the statement issued to the press by the Noonkanbah community:

If Aboriginals give up their sites and special places, there will be no more law, no more story telling, no more initiation ceremonies. It will be like it has all gone out into space.

He referred to a statement in the press by another Aborigine, Ribnga Green. In rejecting the charge that white "stirrers" are responsible for Aboriginal opposition to mining at Noonkanbah, Green said: "It's a real insult to the intelligence of the Aboriginal people. They know what they want and are capable of making their own decision."

Another board member asked if the board was not intruding in matters where it had no right to be. "I believe," he went on, "that white people should get out of the way and let the Aboriginal people make their own protest. Support them certainly; write letters to the state premier, write to the newspapers, but it is not our job to go and organize their resistance."

This time it was the chairman who replied. "Our church has had a pastoral relationship with these people, and we have been asked to come and help them. Ron certainly would not be going to organize resistance. They are perfectly capable of organizing themselves. He would be going to stand with them and demonstrate by his presence our support for their struggle."

Gary asked if it was not very strange that Christians wanted to protect sites associated with a heathen religion. "Should we not be more concerned about evangelizing these peoples than about protecting sites associated with their pagan rituals?" he asked.

Ron replied that the churches would have no right to evangelize these people and would not be heard by them if Christians stood by and permitted them to suffer what in their eyes was a gross injustice. "If we are ever to speak to these people about the gospel, we must stand by them now," he asserted.

Discussion continued for some time. At last the chairman intervened: "I believe we have discussed this motion sufficiently to enable each person to vote responsibly and intelligently. I will put the motion to the meeting. Those in favor will raise the right hand."

TEACHING NOTE

Sacred Sites

The following teaching note could be adapted for use in either a seminary or a parish setting. Goals will obviously vary, but this case easily lends itself to discussions of how one faith and/or culture relates to another, the relationship between evangelization and justice, and different meanings of land.

I. Opening Discussion

One way to enter the case would be to construct an intercultural dialogue on the meaning of land. Divide participants into an equal number of groups of about six persons. Designate half of the groups as Aborigines from Noonkanbah Station seeking to preserve their land and half as representatives of Amax Exploration Company and the West Australian government who want to open the land for mining. Ask each of the groups to identify with the assigned designation and focus its small group discussion on what land means to it. Urge participants to include either Aboriginal Dreamtime or Christian biblical images in their conversation. (This assignment may be particularly challenging to Western-oriented North

Americans attempting to identify with an Aborigine perspective. The commentary by L. Shannon Jung which follows the case may be helpful for this group.)

After ten to fifteen minutes, ask each group to select a representative. With the case leader moderating the presentations, position group spokespersons in the front of the room and supply either a sign or some other visible way to identify each speaker as representing the Aborigine community or the corporation/government. Representatives may be asked to make brief, three-minute statements of their positions with time for one-minute rebuttals. After the case leader closes the debate, he or she should take several minutes to "de-role" spokespersons, asking them how they felt about their arguments and rebuttals.

One approach to employ the insights from the intercultural small group discussions and dialogue is to ask all participants to place themselves in the role of delegates of the Uniting Board who have received information from the Aborigine community and the corporation/government communities. The case leader may wish to assume the role of General Secretary Ron Avery requesting guidance for the decision he and the Uniting Church Board is facing.

II. Issues

The Board role play is a means to investigate the issues raised by the case. The following questions to the group from the moderator may be helpful.

A. What did you learn from the spokespersons during the dialogue on the meaning of the land?

B. What do you see as the religious roots and the theological implications of each group's view of the land?

C. What insights about economic and political power by the dominant or dominated cultures emerged from the dialogue?

D. What factors shaped Gary Wells's understanding of evangelism? How could his understanding be compatible with Uniting Church support for the protection of Aboriginal sacred sites?

E. What other significant issues do the situation in Western Australia and Ron Avery's request raise for the Uniting Church?

III. Alternatives and Actions

A. Whether or not participants have been in a group role play as the Uniting Board, ask them to vote on whether or not the church should support Ron Avery's request for support and travel funds to visit Western Australia. Record the vote. Ask participants to state *why* they voted as they did and what practical and theological rationale informed their decisions.

B. Another approach is to ask what criteria would be helpful for the Uniting Church Board to follow as the delegates decide how to respond to Ron Avery's request. Consider, for example, the implications of the Old Testament demand to "do justice"; Jesus' call to care for the "least of these"; or criteria such as expressing support but not assuming control over the Aboriginal struggle to preserve sacred sites.

C. How might the Board interpret its decision to the general membership of the Uniting Church? How can the Board address concerns expressed by church members such as Bob Croft?

D. When communities are confronted by conflicts which have interfaith or intercultural roots, what factors or approaches best generate mutual respect and understanding?

IV. Application and Resources

Consider the implications of interfaith and cross-cultural dialogue for the globalization of theological education.

A. In the North American context which groups raise issues similar to those of the Aborigines of Noonkanbah Station? In what ways, if at all, are responses of North American corporations, state governments, or churches different or similar to the responses in the case study?

B. What biblical and theological resources are available to the church in Australia or in North America to address instances of cross-cultural and interfaith conflict?

C. What ethical norms for understanding different concepts of the land might bring more sensitivity and justice to conflict management in complex cultural relationships?

D. What kind of theological education best equips women and men to minister in an increasingly interdependent multicultural global community?

V. Closing

Ask participants to share their learnings, both personal and institutional, from the case discussion.

COMMENTARY

Sacred Sites

L. SHANNON JUNG

In asking us, the readers, to take Gary's place and vote on this church action, the case invites us to do nothing less than resolve the question of how one culture and faith should address another. Recent conversation about multiculturality has made that question appear so complex that it can simply immobilize Gary—and us.

This may be a case where too much cognitive rumination prevents compassionate feeling from playing its legitimate role in decision making. To be sure, Gary (and we) must respect the perspective of the others enough to analyze the situation. Nevertheless, there remains a deep humanity that we share across cultures whether those cultures are near at hand or far away. Rural communities in the United States can be as distant as the outback.

This case does involve *analysis* of how one faith and/or culture should relate to another; that is one way of formulating the basic task of ethics on a corporate level. Recognizing the immensity of this task, let me identify many of the presenting issues in this case but focus on only two. Dr. Jane I. Smith's essay, "Globalization as Ecumenical/Interfaith Dialogue," will be helpful in this respect.

Smith claims that ecumenical, interethnic, and interfaith dialogue serves three purposes: "exchange of information; working together in common cause for justice and equity; and learning theologically from each other so as to enrich our own understanding of what it means to be persons of faith within our respective traditions." This commentary will stress the second of those purposes. It will suggest how the third purpose could be served through a common search for justice. My bet is that the third purpose will inevitably be served by pursuing the second.

There are *theological* issues here. Gary explicitly raises questions of evangelism: Should Christians be trying to convert Aborigines? What is the intention of God in relation to non-believers. How are evangelism and justice related? Does evangelism have priority over justice or the reverse? And there are questions of revelation and creation: What is the process of God's self-revelation? How intrinsic to revelation is conscious human reception and confession? Are the structures of revelation embedded in creation? Not far from those are questions of redemption: Is redemption dependent on calling upon the name of Jesus the Christ? Who is this Christ? How do the life and teachings of Jesus have impact? What might redemption mean to the members of the Uniting Church of Australia? Would it mean the same to the residents of Noonkanbah Station? The whole set of issues clustered around the relation of Christ and culture surfaces here.

Smith's essay is sensitive to the issues of religious imperialism or proselytizing (Christ above culture), but also to lowest-common-denominator thinking or syncretism (Christ of culture). We will return to her assertion that "if it is not necessary to look for the common denominator, we are freed to be able to appreciate the differences [between religious traditions] and to learn from them."

The *moral* conflicts from which this case gets its power exemplify aspects of international and interethnic relations. Theological education ignores them to its own and the church's peril. Though set in Australia, we in the United States experience the same conflicts. The land interests of Indians and rural Americans are threatened today. The case at issue exhibits the conflict between the Aborigines and the industrialized West exemplified by the Amax Exploration Company. This conflict is both economic and religious. There is conflict between legal systems. There is conflict between state and federal levels of government. There is conflict between factions in the church—both national and local. There are elements of environmental conflict as well.

Although these conflicts are framed by our perspective on the theological questions mentioned, to consider them as only theological runs a grave danger. The danger is the imperialism of theology which fails to grant social reality independent standing. That may be one reason why theology has not adequately addressed areas of human life which it defined as outside its purview—in some cases dismissed centuries earlier. To consider these conflicts primarily as moral begins to give social reality its independent due. (I am tempted to correlate theology with the church and suggest that the church fails to give God's presence in the extra-ecclesial world independent standing, but will somewhat resist that temptation.)

There are two elements in the context of the situation described that beg for attention: the meaning of land and cultural hegemony. By wrestling with these two I believe we get to the moral heart not only of the case before us but also to the core of other global conflicts—in El Salvador, South Africa, Nicaragua, Israel, Zimbabwe, and Guatemala. Furthermore, dealing with these social realities begins to open out onto theological beliefs.

The Meaning of Land

There is, in fact, a theological bias against dealing with land.[30] Part of that has to do with the wider difficulty theology has with the material world. In addition, the land is so multidimensional that it is difficult to isolate any one conception of it. This in spite of the biblical centrality of land[31] and its contemporary significance.

Integral to this case is an attenuated sense of place among citizens of affluent nations. Feminist and ecological movements are calling us to a retrieval of appreciation for land and the physical world. However, the case vividly illustrates that groups still understand the land in very different ways.[32]

From the Aborigine perspective what is being threatened is the people's identity as a culture. Noonkanbah Station is not a piece of land that is modular, interchangeable with any other. It is the source of tribal identity and cohesion. As one Aborigine says in the case, this particular piece of land "provides not only for our physical needs, but for our spiritual needs also. Just looking at our land keeps up our spiritual life the same way reading the Bible keeps up the spiritual life of Christians." Thus the land that the Aborigines are protecting is a way of spiritual and identity nourishment. It comes close to being viewed as essential to life.

In the perspective of the Amax Exploration Company, the government of the state of West Australia, and of some concerned for Australia's reserves, the land of Noonkanbah Station is primarily a commodity, a source of wealth. At best the land is viewed as a resource common to all Australians. It is striking that in the Aborigine view the land is intrinsically valuable; from the Western modern view the land is instrumentally valuable.

A little research on the meaning of their land to the Aborigine, however, uncovers that the intrinsic-instrumental dichotomy is itself a cultural product that is invalid for the Yungngora. For the Aborigine the land is both intrinsically and instrumentally valuable. The Aborigine answers the question "What is the land?" in these terms:

> The land is my mother. Like a human mother the land gives us protection, enjoyment, and provides for our needs—economic, social, and religious. We have a human relationship with the land. . . . When the land is taken from us or destroyed, we feel hurt because we belong to the land and we are part of it.
>
> To survive, [we] have to know about the land. The land contains our information about our traditional way of life. It's written there. . . . It's like a library for our people and children. It's very sad when mining wipes out our library and there's nothing left for our children to get their education from. Land is a breathing place for my people.[33]

Thus land is both economic and spiritual. This understanding is grounded in the foundational beliefs of all Aboriginal culture, the Dreaming. During the Dreaming a vast series of events occurred and continues to occur which transform the formerly featureless plains of the earth. Ancestor heroes wandered across the wide earth and in the places they rested they brought features into being—hills, valleys, rocks, pools, trees and vegetation. Sometimes the ancestors changed themselves into those features. Retracing such journeys links the contemporary pilgrim into a living relation with the Dreaming. Thus the land is a living repository of mythic accounts of creation and it embodies spiritual power in a way that is available to people today. The land is a "kind of religious icon" which represents the power of Dreamtime beings but also effects and transmits that power today.[34] The power of particular places for particular tribes is both economic and spiritual.[35] To the Aborigine the land is enchanted and the profane made religious; to the modern person the land is disenchanted and too often simply remains profane, a resource.

Theologically the Aborigine understanding of land calls for a reconsideration and revivification of the Christian doctrine of creation. It also invites us to consider how the spiritual and economic interpenetrate. Are there human dynamics which have been hidden by our insensitivity to material, spatial, and physical categories?[36]

Cultural Hegemony

The second issue grows out of the first but is distinct from it. I have tried to describe the Aborigine view of sacred sites enough to reveal its divergence from the modern Western view of land. Although it is theoretically possible for such divergences to be valued equally and mutually respected, in the case of conflicting desires and claims that seldom remains the case. Instead, hierarchial ranking appears to be the norm.

What is striking about this situation is how defenseless the traditional, oral, conventional ethnic culture appears against the modern, literate, contractual, trans-ethnic (white) culture. The Aborigine culture seems to have little voice. Indeed, the culture seems almost to have no standing. From the case description the culture and its survival depend largely on the action undertaken *for* them by the churches and the federal government.

It might be more accurate to say that the contractual, legal society does not have the capacity to hear the Aborigine culture or give it standing. That point is only academic, if we are concerned about actual consequences. Perhaps, however, if we become conscious of the consequences of how our structures and assumptions blind us to important aspects of others' faith, we could begin to give them independent standing.

The Los Angeles riots of 1992 followed the acquittal of the police officers who were videotaped beating Rodney King. Recalling the rage which resulted from the legal process with its scrubbed-up, objective, impartial procedures made me very sensitive to the operation of the legal system in the present case. The contractual nature of Western social arrangements—especially in the legal and economic realms—are formidable weapons. They have such power and have so narrowly identified the evidence that determines decisions that they can be ruthless. That ruthlessness and seeming impregnability are features of the structure that transcend human agency. By that I mean they are values carried beyond our conscious intentions. I am reminded of Reinhold Niebuhr's warning about the momentum of the immoral society and also of the way sin hides behind self-aggrandizing social structures.

On the other hand, the unconscious transmission of values and of their consequences by institutions should make us more tolerant of individual people. That does raise the question of how to check latent consequences and unintended results. We should be alert as well to the possible self-serving deception of projecting our cultural definitions or desires onto others, for example, the state minister's assumption that the Aborigines would greedily negotiate with mining companies for huge financial gains. If those rationalizations sounded familiar to North Americans, it is probably because similar devices were used to justify the displacement of Native Americans and the segregation of their cultures.[37] They continue to be used to displace many rural communities in the name of efficiency and sound economics.

James Sellers in *Public Ethics* formulated a norm relating to land which he described as distinctly, though not exclusively, U.S. American. That land-norm was freedom of self-determination in disposing of one's space.[38] That is one norm that could be used in approaching this case.

Another norm arises from the phenomenon of "environmental racism." That phrase refers to the tendency to locate landfills, toxic waste dumps, and other unsavory or unstable disposal sites in areas where Hispanics, African-Americans, or other minority groups live. The resistance such groups offer is more easily overcome, with fewer repercussions. Similarly, taking over another's land is more easily accomplished if the other is unable to prevent that. The story of Ahab and Naboth in I Kings 21 suggests that this is nothing new.

A final norm for consideration is reversibility. In these days when environmental concerns are being seen as both more pervasive and more urgent, it is important to ask whether the action we initiate today could be reversed or halted tomorrow. This is similar to the norm of sustainability and might be applicable here.

The case reminds me just how rich and complex the meaning system of any culture is. It is certainly impenetrable without a guide who is authentically an insider. The task of ecumenical or interfaith dialogue is one that should only be approached on the basis of absolute respect for both meaning systems. The goals of such dialogue is understanding the other somewhat better and understanding one's own system that much better. That comes close to being a paraphrase of Jane Smith's third purpose of interfaith dialogue. Such dialogue has incredible promise for theology but also could make a real difference in protecting one culture from the mindless hegemony of another.

I have been struck throughout this case that the need to understand issues of justice virtually demanded that I understand something of what the land meant to Aborigines. It also pushed me to understand how a traditional society operates, and what defenses it might have in the face of the legal and political instruments of modernity. It made me aware of the inability of modernity to deal with ambiguity and mystery. In both instances I felt a severe deficiency of understanding. The primary point, however, is simply that the issue of justice necessitated my drive to understand the theological meaning of land.

That is in keeping with Smith's assertion that we can be freed by interfaith dialogue "to appreciate differences." I also found that my slight acquaintance with the difference between Aborigine and Western understandings of land accomplished the second part of Smith's third purpose: "to learn from differences." It made me reinterpret what Hebrew and Christian scriptures had to say about land. In fact it enriched and expanded the human meaning of land for me.

The case also resensitized me to issues that we in The Center for Theology and Land, here in the rural Midwest, U.S.A., face on a daily basis. The gradual erosion of the economic base and independent standing of rural communities has many parallels to the Aborigine case. The subtle nature of that erosion has lulled rural peoples to an ignorance of their own powerlessness and has engendered a sense of inferiority. Rather than recognizing that external forces, such as concentrations in grains and meat industries, are undercutting their position and exercising hegemonic control over land, rural peoples have internalized those invasions. The Globalization of Theological Education experiences have demonstrated that such dynamics are not exclusively rural or urban, North American or African, Latino or Aborigine.

Questions remain: Are there any legitimate interests represented by Amax Exploration and the Western Australian government? What weight should they have? Are there positive examples of corporations, governments and indigenous peoples working together?

Is the proposed action of the Uniting Church an usurpation of Aborigine prerogative? Is it interfaith hegemony? What values should Gary's vote most reflect?

Notes

1. At the same time, and to the extent to which it is possible, we need to be wary of terminology that unnecessarily fosters a we-they dichotomy. A number of persons

active in interfaith dialogue initiatives have suggested that when the conversation finally is moved from a we-they orientation to the notion of all of us talking together, we will have grasped what the essence of such dialogue is all about.

2. The 83rd Biennial Meeting of the Association in Pittsburgh, Pennsylvania, June 15-17, 1992, was scheduled to overlap with the first international meeting of WOCATI. The theme for the Association meeting was "The Diverse Worlds of Theological Education."

3. Academics and academic presses have not failed to notice the growth of religious communities in America representing faiths other than those of the Jewish and Christian traditions; studies of such groups are among the liveliest areas of research today.

4. William Shea, "Beyond Tolerance: Pluralism and Catholic Higher Education," in John Coulson, ed., *Theology and the University* (Baltimore: Helicon Press, 1964), 259.

5. See David J. Krieger, "Conversion: On the Possibility of Global Thinking in an Age of Particularism," *Journal of the American Academy of Religion* 58/2 (1990), 223ff.

6. It is regrettable that since faculty are under increasing pressure to publish, normally within the traditional disciplinary channels, efforts at developing interdisciplinary studies are often undermined. Fortunately this is not always the case, and some excellent work is being done relating the theological disciplines to other inquiries in disciplines such as law, economics, history and international studies.

7. Parker Palmer, "Community, Conflict, and Ways of Knowing," *Change* (September/October 1990), 20-25.

8. Arthur Levine, "Curriculi-Curricula," *Change* (March/April 1990), 51.

9. Such movements Martin Marty has referred to as "the massive convulsive ingathering of peoples into their separatenesses and overagainstnesses." Martin Marty, "Among the Tribes: Realistic Hope in 1992," *The Christian Century* (January 1-8, 1992), 3. Robert Bellah *et al.* argue in *The Good Society* (New York: Alfred A. Knopf, 1991), 304, however, that the real danger inherent in our society today is not the tendency toward separatistism but the general subversion of bilingualism and multiculturalism in an effort toward homogenization.

10. Jane I. Smith, "Should Trousers Be Singular or Plural? Reflections on Pluralism and the Common Good," keynote address for *"E Pluribus Unum*: . . . . " held at the Claremont School of Theology, February 14, 1992.

11. Diane Ravitch, "Multiculturalism: E Pluribus Plures," *The American Scholar* (Summer 1990), 343. Arguing for the importance of both tolerating and appreciating the differences, Elizabeth Kristol, "False Tolerance, False Unity," in *Theology Today* 47/1 (April 1990), 61, says that "our political and social leaders are misguided in favoring the expedient route of embracing similiarity over the far more difficult task of enduring genuine differences."

12. An inner-city pastor in urban Denver, for example, recently referred to an occasion when he visited a discount department store in the city with a young Hispanic man. A case of watches, open for whites to look at, was immediately locked up when he and his friend approached. That, the pastor remarked, was one of those "micromoments of racism."

13. Diana Eck, "My Neighbor's Faith and Mine: Ordinary Christians and the Challenge of Religious Pluralism." Lecture delivered at Iliff School of Theology, January 24, 1989.

14. Robert J. Schreiter, "Teaching Theology from an Intercultural Perspective," *Theological Education* (Autumn 1989), 15.

15. "The future of mission in a pluralistic world, if there is to be a future," said

missionary Marian Bohen at the 1990 biennial meetings of the Association of Theological Schools, "will be a journey of conversion for us, and a blessing of peace for those among whom we are sent to live. . . . It will mean learning from others, sitting down with them, not standing over them." Marian Bohen, "The Future of Mission in a Pluralistic World," *Theological Education* (Autumn 1990), 42.

16. Indeed ecumenical conversations in any context present their own difficulties. See Ans J. van der Bent, "Diversity, Conflict and Unity in Ecumenical Theology," *The Ecumenical Review* 41/2 (April 1989), 201-12; and S. Mark Heim, "Montreal to Compostela: Pilgrimage in Ecumenical Winter," *The Christian Century* (April 1, 1992), 333-35.

17. "The history of the Christian churches has been at times quite shameful. Through its alliances with the ruling powers, Christianity has not only blessed exploitation and justified misery, it has sought its own perpetuation and aggrandizement. Prospective dialogue partners may well feel deep hostility toward Christianity." Marsha Hewitt *et al.*, "Education for Global Theology," *Theological Education* (Supplement I, 1990), 97.

18. See Streng's *Understanding Religious Man* (Belmont, CA: Dickenson Publishing Company, 1969), 1-12.

19. "This whole question of the creative outcome of dialogue often provokes the hallowed charge of syncretism," says John Berthrong in "A Whiteheadian Interpretation of Interfaith Dialogue." "Actually, properly understood, there is nothing particularly frightening per se about the word 'syncretism' to a process thinker contemplating the interaction of the various faith traditions. It is only thinkers especially committed to the concept of an eminently real, unmoved Godhead who find syncretism disturbing—disturbing to their concept of God." *Journal of Ecumenical Studies* 26/1 (Winter 1989), 185.

20. Marjorie Suchocki, "In Search of Justice: Religious Pluralism from a Feminist Perspective," in John Hick and Paul Knitter, *The Myth of Christian Uniqueness: Toward a Pluralistic Theology of Religions* (Maryknoll, NY: Orbis Books, 1987), 157-60.

21. "Christian Witness in a Pluralistic World," in John Hick and Hasan Askari, eds., *The Experience of Religious Diversity* (Brookfield, VT: Gower Publishing Company, 1985), 155.

22. "The basis of inter-religious dialogue," said Stanley Samartha two decades ago, "is the commitment of all partners to their respective faiths and their openness to the insights of the others. The integrity of the particular religions must be recognized." "The Progress and Promise of Inter-Religious Dialogues," in *Journal of Ecumenical Studies* 9 (Summer 1972), 473.

23. Perhaps few Christian theologians, however, would go so far as to affirm the self-consciously pluralist position of someone like John Hick, who acknowledges that his own position is one of "understanding . . . Christianity as one path of salvation amongst others, with each of the great traditions being, so far as we can tell, more or less equally effective contexts of salvation/liberation." "Straightening the Record: Some Response to the Critics," *Modern Theology* 6/2 (January 1990), 187. Anselm Min, on the other hand, argues strongly against this kind of tolerance: "A serious dialogue must do away with the . . . plea for indiscriminate tolerance of all diversity. Not all religions are harmonizable with each other in their praxis or their theology. Not all diversities are constructive and unifying; some diversities are downright oppressive." Anselm Min, "Praxis and Pluralism," *Perspectives in Religious Studies* 16/3 (Fall 1989), 201.

24. Paul Rabinow, *Reflections on Fieldwork in Morocco* (Berkeley: University of

California Press, 1977), 39, referenced in Mark Kline Taylor, *Remembering Esperanza* (Maryknoll, NY: Orbis Books, 1991), 200-202.

25. Fumitaka Matsuoka, "A Reflection on 'Teaching Theology from an Intercultural Perspective,'" *Theological Education* (Autumn 1989), 39.

26. Copyright © 1993 by the Case Study Institute. The names of Ron Avery, Bob Croft, Arthur Lawrence, Gary Wells, and Glen Lea are disguised to protect the privacy of individuals involved in the situation. The names of all other places and public figures are factual.

27. The Uniting Church in Australia, a union of Congregational, Methodist, and Presbyterian congregations, came into being in 1977.

28. A large lizardlike reptile, hunted for food by the Aborigines, but also featuring prominently in Aboriginal myths and legends.

29. "Dreamtime" is the term used by Aborigines to refer to the time long ago when according to their mythological stories or "dreaming" their spirit ancestors created the world and society.

30. For an analysis of why this is the case, see L. Shannon Jung, "Ethics, Agriculture, and the Material Universe," *Annual of the Society of Christian Ethics 1986* (Washington, D.C.: Georgetown University Press, 1987), 219-50.

31. Brueggemann's claim is that "land is a central, if not the *central theme* of biblical faith." *The Land: Place as Gift, Promise, and Challenge in Biblical Faith* (Philadelphia: Fortress Press, 1977), 3.

32. See William W. Everett III, "Land Ethics: Toward a Conventional Model," *Selected Papers of the American Society of Christian Ethics* (1979), 45-73. In this article Everett identifies and categorizes a number of the ways land is viewed.

33. Rev. Djiniyini, Badaltja, and Rrurrambu, quoted in *My Mother the Land*, ed. Ian R. Yule (Galiwin'ku Galiwin'ku Literature Production Centre, 1980), 8, 33, 10.

34. Max Charlesworth, Howard Murphy, Diane Bell, and Kenneth Maddock, eds. *Religion in Aboriginal Australia* (St. Lucia: University of Queensland Press, 1984), 9, 10.

35. See Amos Rapoport, "Australian Aborigines and the Definition of Place," *Shelter, Sign, and Symbol*, ed. by Paul Oliver (London: Barrie and Jenkins, 1975), 41-42. Quoted in Geoffery R. Lilburne, *A Sense of Place: A Christian Theology of the Land* (Nashville: Abingdon Press, 1989).

36. This understanding influenced the way in which I approached a theological interpretation of land in *We are Home: A Spirituality of the Environment* (Mahwah, N.J.: Paulist Press, 1993).

37. For another example of cultural hegemony over land, see Sam L. J. Page and Hélan E. Page, "Western Hegemony over African Agriculture in Southern Rhodesia and Its Continuing Threat of Food Security in Independent Zimbabwe," *Agriculture and Human Values VIII*: 4 (Fall 1991), 3-18.

38. James Sellers, *Public Ethics: American Morals and Manners* (New York: Harper & Row, 1970).

[5]

GLOBALIZATION AS CROSS-CULTURAL DIALOGUE

ESSAY

ROBERT J. SCHREITER

As is apparent throughout this volume, globalization has many faces. It is not a univocal concept; rather, it opens us up to the multidimensionality of human existence. This essay explores one of those dimensions in some detail, a dimension that is fundamentally simple in its conceptuality, but experientially may be the most dense of all those aspects that make up globalization. This is the dimension of culture and the crossing of boundaries between cultures.

The cross-cultural dimension of globalization, as a thematic concept, has been one of the latest to arise in the understandings of globalization. Early attempts at globalization (if one would want to take the fifteenth-century voyages of European discovery as the beginning of the globalization of the West) were more preoccupied with the expanse of a hitherto unknown world than with dealing with the diversity that their voyages revealed. This is evident in the changes in the cartography of the time. Medieval maps portrayed the world as it was supposed to be; they were not guides to trace the path from one place to another, but were ways to imagine the world properly. Not uncommonly, therefore, Jerusalem was at the center of the map. With the European adventurers discovering that the world was considerably larger than they had once imagined, a new way of conceiving the world — and the place of Europe within it — had to be constructed.[1]

The Europeans needed to account for the people and folkways they encountered in those first and subsequent travels. These were clearly different in many ways from the explorers who invaded these territories. Through the subsequent centuries, a variety of ways were developed to account for these "others." In the earliest stages, there were debates about whether those people encountered were even human at all. (Interestingly, debates about the humanity of the people of the Americas contributed to the development of a theology of the universal salvific will of God.) At another point, the non-Europeans were recognized as human, but as children in comparison to the European adult explorers. Their folkways

122

were alternately subhuman, infantile, or demonic, and so they needed to be guided toward adulthood or away from error. By the time of the development of evolutionary paradigms in the nineteenth century, non-Europeans came to be seen as primitive and in need of civilization. It was only by the late nineteenth century that they would begin to be judged as irreducibly other.[2] This was only possible when the folkways of these others could be seen as an alternative to European folkways and not simply as underdeveloped, seductively demonic, or hopelessly in error.

What was needed to bring this shift about was a conceptualization of the possibility of pluralism as the existence of legitimate alternatives and the development of the concept of culture as relatively autonomous units embodying these alternatives. The pioneering work of two thinkers, Giambattista Vico in Italy and Johann Gottfried Herder in Germany, was instrumental in laying the foundations for twentieth-century understandings of what was to become cross-cultural dialogue.[3]

Even though the foundations were being laid already in the eighteenth century, explicit reflection on what it means to cross from one culture to another did not come until the mid-twentieth century. That there was difference between cultures was immediately evident; that cultures should be understood on their own terms was apparently less so.

The language of globalization emerged around 1960 to account for the expansion of business and commerce across the boundaries of nation-states. Concern for how cultural difference was affecting this expansion seems to have come slightly later. Discussions of the latter do not appear with any regularity before the mid-1970s, when it began to become apparent to business interests that attending to culture difference within the global network fostered greater productivity. Similar conclusions were being reached among those involved in economic development work through the 1960s and 1970s. They realized that development was not only a matter of bringing technology into areas where it had previously been absent, but was also a matter of understanding how the technology would fit into a particular context.

In the religious sphere, sensitivity to culture had been an intermittent theme since the beginning of the voyages of European discovery, a theme more often than not ignored or rejected by ecclesiastical authority. The defenses of native peoples by Bartolome de las Casas and the theological proposals of Matteo Ricci in China come immediately to mind. From the mid-nineteenth to the mid-twentieth centuries, calls from missionaries for cultural sensitivity became more frequent and insistent, although still less than a full, single voice. With the coming of independence of regions colonized by Europe, calls for cultural sensitivity became lodged in the highest bodies of individual denominations as well as within the discourse of interchurch bodies such as the World Council of Churches.

The actual language of globalization came to theological education in North America about two decades after its emergence in the worlds of business and political science. Perhaps because of that later entry and because of the development of cultural awareness in missiology, issues of cultural sensitivity have been part of theological education's understanding of globalization since these discussions were first thematized around 1980.

The questions of culture and cross-cultural sensitivity occupy a privileged position in understandings of globalization for theological education. Too much of what globalization has meant and continues to mean in the spheres of business, political science, and even education (often referred to collectively as the "global culture") is really a one-way discourse from out of the powerful centers in North America and Europe directed to the rest of the world. It has to do with how the North Atlantic is going to deal with or account for the diversity found on the rest of the planet. The purpose of this discourse is to minimize friction both within this diversity, and between this diversity collectively and the North Atlantic. The purposes are seldom stated this baldly, but language of "openness" and "sensitivity" is belied by the fact that the discourse must be carried on in English, that it assumes the mobility in time and space provided by telecommunications and air travel, and that the terms of negotiation and resolution emanate from North Atlantic culture. In other words, it is the same old patter of domination under new terms. The medieval map is being redrawn, but only at the periphery and not at the center. North America may have replaced Jerusalem and North Americans may have a clearer idea about what once were *terrae incognitae*. But maps of the world as it ought to be, rather than as it has become, continue to prevail.

What place, then, does globalization as cross-cultural dialogue occupy among the four commonly designated areas of globalization in theological education (missions and evangelism, ecumenical/interfaith dialogue, and the struggle for justice being the others)? I am not suggesting that it has a privileged place in a hierarchy of values, but rather a privilege that arises out of the potential of cross-cultural dialogue for transforming the very grounds of the globalization discourse altogether. Put another way, cross-cultural dialogue can provide two important services for the entire discourse of globalization. First of all, it challenges the sometimes subtle and unconscious discourses of power and ethnocentrism that underlie honest attempts at mission, dialogue, and a justice praxis. How missions and evangelism have fallen prey to exercises of domination and ethnocentrism has already been amply documented—so much so that some theological educators even reject this area as a legitimate approach to globalization. Such a wholesale rejection is uncritical, since there have been and continue to be legitimate forms of mission and evangelism aware of this sad history.[4] Motives for ecumenical cooperation can mimic those of corporations: either to reduce conflict or create a megachurch capable of domination and conversion. And even in the struggle for justice, those who come from rich and powerful countries often miss the subtleties of reciprocity in local arrangements, or presume that mutuality can spring from their all-powerful and heavily resourced wills to bridge decades or even centuries of asymmetry between rich and poor, powerful and powerless, dominant and minority. Hence, cross-cultural dialogue calls for conversion (as do all forms of globalization), but in a special and important way.

Second, cross-cultural dialogue deconstructs the powerful, dominant culture in a special way. The other forms of globalization—evangelism, dialogue, justice—can call for a new social arrangement as the ultimate purpose of globalization: all peoples reached by the Gospel message, greater understanding and respect between peoples of different faiths, a more justly structured society. Cross-cultural dialogue has the potential for carrying this a step further and challenging a powerful culture to give over its sense of control, commit its trust, and suffer a disorienting cognitive and emotional dissonance that can lead to transformations moving beyond invitations to participate (the offer of the Gospel), containment of conflict (dialogue), and more just structures (justice). This is not intended to caricature other areas of globalization, but rather to challenge reflection about just what conversion means in the context of globalization.

It must also be said immediately that, while cross-cultural dialogue is a necessary condition for true globalization of theological education, it is in itself not a sufficient one — any more than are the other three. Cultural sensitivity can become an excuse for not examining the depth and intensity of one's own commitment to Christ and thus a way to avoid the demands of mission or the stringency of sustained dialogue. Likewise, acute cultural sensitivity may end up affirming patterns of sexism, racism, and classism in the culture we are trying to understand, because our attempt to be understanding blocks a summons to conflict. In view of this it must be said that any of the areas of globalization must stand under the same judgment: they are all deemed necessary, but none of them stands alone as sufficient. They all have a shadow side that can overwhelm them if absolutized to the point of the exclusion of others. It might make an interesting test for a theological school to look at each of the four and ask: How is this area represented and implemented in my school? What are the reasons that some areas are represented feebly or not at all? And what implications does this have for my school's discourse of globalization?

In what follows, globalization as cross-cultural dialogue is explored in some of its major themes and the issues these themes raise. Within this discussion resources to address the issues and the challenges that lie ahead in educating toward cross-cultural sensitivity and implementing this part of a globalization program are taken up. Not all that needs to be addressed can be taken up here. To give this presentation focus, two assumptions guide the discussion of themes, issues, and resources.

First, the audience envisioned is one of dominant-culture people in North America. This does not exclude people who do not count themselves as part of that dominant culture. This assumption is guided by a realization that minority cultures find themselves at a different place in discussions of globalization, especially as globalization relates to issues of culture. Minority cultures do not have the option of considering globalization or not; by dint of their position in the relationship of power, they are globalized in some measure whether they want to be or not. African Americans know that they jeopardize their promotions in the white-dominated world of business, politics, and education if they act "too black." People speaking a form of English other than Standard American run the risk of being deemed less educated or less intelligent by their dominant-culture colleagues. Minority cultures already know a lot about culture difference and cultural boundaries because they had to learn these things to survive; they cannot afford to write off the dominant-culture as idiosyncratic or ephemeral as dominant-culture persons often do to them.

This is not to say that minority culture persons are not capable of ethnocentrism, racism, and lack of cross-cultural sensitivity. They can participate in all of these. But their issues and their challenges to cross-cultural dialogue are different in significant ways from those of the dominant culture. Their situations are compounded by racism, by generational issues within their own communities if relatively recent immigrants, and by the limits on their access to power and mobility in the dominant-culture setting. The issues affecting minority-culture persons in globalization deserve special attention — not just as minorities *qua* minorities, but in the specificities of each community.[5] The discussion here will therefore focus on the group that has had the most difficulty in facing issues of cultural sensitivity and dialogue, the dominant culture in the United States and Canada.

Second, the broad expanse of culture extends beyond the reach of this presentation, as do all the concerns that may go into the affirmation of the dignity and respect due cultures. Even different modes of cultural analysis, suitable both to the settings in which they are to be exercised and the aims that are sought, represent more than can be undertaken here.[6] Rather, the focus here will be on crossing the boundaries between cultures and especially the impact it has on those who do the crossing. It is possible to study other cultures without great personal involvement, in a so-called "objective" fashion. It is also possible to participate in some measure in other cultures through travel and short-term visits. It is even possible to live for longer periods of time within another culture and yet insulate oneself from its effects (as can be the case in diplomatic, commercial, educational, and even missionary communities). What will be of particular interest here is what happens to those who try genuinely to cross over into another culture and leave themselves vulnerable to change, transformation, and conversion as a result of that transformation. This is the most difficult dimension of cross-cultural dialogue, but also the one of greatest importance.

I. Themes in Cross-cultural Dialogue

There are three themes that I want to focus upon in cross-cultural dialogue as a form of globalization: ethnocentrism, universality, and reciprocity. There are other themes that could be taken up, but these three represent central values in cross-cultural dialogue that must be treated for any of the others to attain intelligibility.

A. Ethnocentrism

Ethnocentrism — seeing one's cultural group (ethnos) as the center of the world — is a very common part of life for most cultures of the world. Indeed there are many cultures whose name for themselves is simply "the people" — describing their chosen place in the world and establishing their relation to others as outsiders (barbarians, foreigners, heathens). Ethnocentrism is so common that it probably should be seen as something nearly inevitable in the culture-forming process; it probably has to do with the identity formation of both communities and individuals. Identity formation takes the place of instinct in the more developed phyla of the animal kingdom. It is a fragile process, as every parent, minister, and therapist knows. Seeing oneself and one's community at the center of things helps create a sense of affirmation and security and helps facilitate an outreach in trust.

However, no community lives in isolation from other communities. And in a world being shaped by global structure,[7] the encounter between cultures is constant. The negotiation of those encounters elicits a range of responses, ranging from a welcoming invitation to potential friends to the creation of a fortress mentality against a malignant opponent. Basically, cultural encounter challenges an ethnocentric view in a number of ways and at a number of levels.

First of all, it presents the possibility of an alternative. The encounter with the "other" often opens up new ways of experiencing and relating to the world. Sometimes those possibilities have never been imagined; other times they represent the fringes of dream and fantasy. Yet at other times they embody the very opposite of the values cherished in the home culture.

Second, by their otherness, they challenge the arrangement of the values and relationships that make up the home culture. Those values and relationships may be superficially held or deeply rooted. They may challenge hitherto uncontested verities in the home culture or beliefs that were already conflicted in the community and under attack. At any rate, they stir up feelings never before experienced or only dimly understood to this point.

Third, by the challenges the other makes, our very sense of self and identity is challenged, particularly if we do not have the protection of a group in the cross-cultural encounter. There can be a profound sense of disorientation, loss of self-confidence, and fear of anomie. It is this third, most acute state of challenge to ethnocentrism that will be the focus of attention here, because of its pedagogical implications.

Cross-cultural dialogue is about a challenge to ethnocentrism. It can be conceived as a threat to self and community but also as an opportunity to broaden one's horizons in order to live in a changed and changing world. At one level, this is the educational aim of developing cross-cultural awareness. Unfortunately perhaps, in order to reach the opportunity that cross-cultural dialogue offers, one must go through the dark valley of the threat to get there. This will be explored more below under the issues in cross-cultural dialogue.

B. *Universality*

The plethora of cultural encounters that globalization implies can create disorientation through the quantity of options into which a person or culture comes. Are there no end to options, alternatives, variations?

The multiplicity of these encounters evokes a question that can be read and answered in different ways: Is there no universal amid this multiplicity? At a superficial level, this question can be read as an appeal to return to the old sureties of ethnocentrism: there is a center to all of this, and that center is my culture. But although this may be the panicked response of a newcomer to the conundrums of globalization, the question of universality needs to be addressed in other ways. One way of answering the multiplicity question owes a great deal to the dominant culture in North America where an ideology of plurality (as opposed to pluralism) is cultivated. In this ideology, no unity or universality is sought, since that might be construed as the triumph of one view over the others. Rather, a plurality is maintained, wherein all are allowed to coexist, provided that none threatens the existence or well-being of the other. This is in distinction to pluralism, where viewpoints and life ways engage in examination and critique of one another. The assumption that supports this ideology of plurality requires an environment that is relatively stable, where different cultures have relatively the same access to the goods and opportunities of a society. It corresponds nicely to the voluntarism and individualism that are part of North American society. In reality, of course, no such society exists in its fullness, but hidden discourses of power may foment the illusion that such is the case. The fear that those discourses may break down or that multiplicity may become an ideology to create new hegemonies surfaces from time to time. This is evident in the multiculturalism debates that are occurring in the United States at this writing.[8]

The question of universality is raised for other reasons as well. Beyond the fear of multiculturalism or of cultural relativism is a metaphysical concern about the unity of human reality. Do we live in a world that is ultimately one, created and sustained by the same God? Or, in the words of cross-cultural researchers such as Richard A. Schweder, do we live in "multiple objective worlds?"[9] The response to these questions has far-reaching metaphysical and theological consequences. It is well and good to talk of a polycentric world (and the development of communications and the style of global capitalism in which we live encourages us to do so), but what will that really mean? Is a polycentric world only possible when none is able to overtake the other or when none wishes to acknowledge the other and take the other seriously? This is a theme that has long underlain the discussion of cross-cultural dialogue and has usually been raised by conservative skeptics and opponents. For if we hold the ultimate uniqueness and autonomy of each culture, the question can then be pressed as to whether it is possible to know another culture — indeed, know the other — at all; we find ourselves lapsing into a cultural solipsism. On the other hand, a too quick granting of the grounds of universality leaves the door open for a cultural imperialism, something of which the global culture coming out of the North Atlantic is regularly accused.

We must thus ask: Why do we seek universals? What universals do we hope to find? Where do we expect to find them? These questions do not reduce this line of questioning to psychological motives or social location, as though real people don't need universals. They are intended to help us be self-critical.

In theological education, in an interest to help students and faculty see the diversity of culture and of God's world, we can sometimes fudge a bit the questions of universality, dismissing them as signs of anxiety or intransigence. But they must be there and will arise inevitably in a monotheistic tradition. Effective globalization must not only open the gates for cultural diversity, but also find ways to affirm universality.

C. Reciprocity and Mutuality

A significant concern of cross-cultural dialogue as a form of globalization is with how to relate to others across cultural boundaries. Earlier forms of globalization, as we have seen, developed relationships of dominance; some of these relationships continue to the present time. Calls are therefore rightly made to create relationships of greater mutuality.

Anyone who has ever engaged in dialogue across cultures knows how difficult it is to establish these relations. We are regularly beset with speaking different languages; our knowledge of each other's folkways is imperfect; we find ourselves vulnerable to misunderstanding by the other in the encounter. Mutuality can be further complicated by histories of racism, and current disparities raised by gender and class. But most profoundly, there are fundamental asymmetries created by the current ordering of the world that cannot be overlooked or be quickly papered over by good intentions. These are the asymmetries that persons and cultures in southern hemisphere settings experience when dealing with their richer counterparts in the northern hemisphere. As a number of Latin American commentators have pointed out, the North Atlantic was anxious to establish good relations with their poorer neighbors in the South so long as the threat of Communism prevailed. But once the state socialist economies of Eastern Europe collapsed, the North quickly began to lose interest in the South, except as a nagging debt that needed to be repaid to the North's banks, a locus for extracting certain natural resources, and an occasional source of cheap labor. Altruistic efforts were redirected to the devastated economies of Eastern Europe and away from the South.

Because of the profound asymmetries that exist, hope for mutuality seems almost quixotic at this time. Even where levels of trust are established, the contexts in which they have to be played out may be such that true mutuality—equality in participation—may simply not be possible. Dominant-culture persons may think and indeed want to offer mutuality, but may be unaware of all the things that hinder the realization of such a goal. In light of this, it might be better for a time to shift our language from mutuality and partnership (partnership in the sense of equality of participation) to the language of reciprocity. Many of our cross-cultural relations are really reciprocal rather than mutual. By that is meant they involve a going back-and-forth, but with an awareness that they are not (yet) equal. Reciprocity does not mean that the relationships cannot *become* equal, or that the participants are not equal in dignity. The language of reciprocity is necessary for the dominant-culture participants to realize how much is askew despite their wishes that it might be otherwise. It is also necessary to help dominant-culture persons realize, when they are on the receiving end (as in the case of learning about a new culture), that they cannot substitute the power of their home culture for the paucity of knowledge and appreciation they have for the culture that they are encountering. Reciprocity becomes a program directed toward achieving mutuality, and a reminder how much yet needs to be achieved.

Both mutuality and reciprocity point to the quality of the relation to be achieved. In understanding globalization as cross-cultural dialogue, the ultimate goal is not the amount of knowledge that one acquires of another culture, but what happens to our relationship to that culture and how we are transformed in that process. A good question for theological schools to ask themselves as they do an audit of their globalization programs is: How are our relationships reciprocal? From this can emerge a plan to make them more genuinely mutual.

II. Issues in Cross-cultural Dialogue

If the issues involved in cross-cultural dialogue could be reduced to a single set of themes, it would be those of *relinquishing power* and *being led through one's vulnerabilities to conversion*. Relinquishment, power, vulnerability, and conversion are themes difficult for anyone in any culture; they are doubly difficult for members of dominant cultures to address. Rather than explore these themes in a more general fashion, I would like to concentrate upon how they play themselves out in three areas: (1) crossing the cultural boundary; (2) language; and (3) travel. These three areas are discussed in terms of principles of cross-cultural dialogue and resources for entering that dialogue, and also with an eye toward pedagogies to help dominant culture persons become more sensitive persons of dialogue.

A. *Crossing the Cultural Boundary*

Crossing a cultural boundary does not assure one's becoming a person of dialogue. There are many who cross a cultural boundary, but remain relatively untouched by the experience. However, there are certain things about becoming culturally aware that probably cannot happen without the experience of crossing the cultural frontier. One does not have to travel great distances to cross cultural boundaries; they can be found in any major city in North America. But going a distance to cross such a boundary has the advantage of not being able to return to the safety of the home culture at will.

Since globalization programs in theological schools often involve going into another culture for a longer or shorter period of time, it might be helpful to chart the two movements across cultural boundaries—going out from one's home culture and coming back—since the issues in crossing boundaries become more evident in those movements. They will be presented here in terms of an individual's experience in making this back-and-forth journey. They assume normal ego strength and adult development and a desire on the part of the individual to cross the cultural boundary.

There are essentially four stages one goes through in crossing out of one's home territory and then coming back. The first stage is the *tourist phase*. The individual experiences the difference between the home culture and the new culture as exciting and exhilarating. Interest is in experiencing new and different things, supported by high levels of energy. Often there is a premature identification with the new culture—what I would call the National Geographic phase—usually emphasizing the exotic elements of the culture. Such identification is premature inasmuch as it is done on the terms of the individual, not the culture being visited. Despite the excitement, the individual remains an outsider to the culture in this phase. Often a constant change to new possibilities is important for maintaining the excitement of this phase.

The second stage is the *fragmentation phase*. After the novelty of the new culture wears off (six weeks to three months), there is a fragmentation of the ego identity and level of self-esteem. The environmental cues, rules, and routines of the new culture come to weigh heavily on the individual. The identity based upon interaction with the home culture is inadequate to the new situation. The individual's usual way of interacting with the environment becomes fragmented. Symptoms of this fragmentation are testiness, overreaction to insignificant events and things, and heightened susceptibility to illness or accident. Old, unresolved conflicts from the past reemerge as the ego shield breaks down. What is happening is that the individual now has the opportunity to cross the cultural boundary and become a relative insider to the new culture. Most will do this; others will refuse either by denying the fragmentation or by leaving and returning to the home culture.

The third stage is *reintegration*. This is the rebuilding of ego identity. The individual selects elements from the fragmented identity and elements from the new culture and begins shaping them into a new identity. The arrival of this phase (usually six months or so into the new situation) is marked by events or experiences which become paradigmatic or symbolic to the individual of the new identity. They often involve new recognitions of belonging on the part of significant persons in the new culture. There is a sense of growth and satisfaction at this stage. This is the point where one really begins to become more of an insider to the new culture.

The fourth stage is *consolidation*, where the learnings from the previous stage become part of the permanent identity of the individual. This begins about a year after entry into the culture and continues as a lifelong process.[10]

Most everyone is prepared for some culture shock when crossing a cultural boundary. What people are generally less prepared for is reentering their home culture, having developed a new ego identity. This reentry is known as *reenculturation* and mirrors to some extent the process of going out from the home culture. It ordinarily cannot be accomplished in less than six months and can take longer if there is no opportunity to deal with it directly.

The problem is that one assumes that one is returning to a familiar setting. But the home culture has changed in subtle ways in the meantime, and the individual has been changed by the cross-cultural experience, often in ways that are not entirely conscious. Moreover, the individual's family, friends, and colleagues will react to their memory of the previous ego identity of the individual rather than to how the individual now is. This creates a sense of dislocation for all involved.

The first phase of reenculturation is marked by a longing to return to the new culture and disparagement of the home culture. Again, little things about the home culture bother the individual more than would seem warranted. Illness often accompanies the early stages of the return. What is difficult for the individual at this stage is communicating the conflicting feelings that are arising, since the individual cannot pinpoint them. This is exacerbated by the fact that family, friends, and colleagues cannot pinpoint the problems either.

The best aid to reenculturation is to talk with people who have been through the same experience of coming back (though not necessarily from the same cross-cultural experience; having had the same experience between the same two cultures can be a plus, however). The reenculturation process happens in two stages: in the first stage, the individual should recount events and memories that are significant, even if it is not initially possible to say why they are significant. In the second stage, the listener helps the individual derive meaning of what has been learned from those events. This helps the individual see what changes in ego identity have taken place and allows for an affirmation of the new identity.

Reenculturation can be done on a one-to-one basis or in a group. If it is not done with other persons, keeping a journal is a possible (though less effective) substitute. If nothing is done, the process can drag on for a year or more and is often accompanied by physical illness.

From these brief remarks regarding crossing into a new culture and reentry into the home culture, one can see that there are a host of issues about power, relinquishment, and transformation that need to be discussed in a program of globalization. Many people have described the process of being a person of dialogue as similar to becoming a child: surrendering one's power as an adult and being completely resocialized by others. The experience of crossing cultural boundaries lies at the heart of globalization as cross-cultural dialogue.

B. Language

Language acquisition is an issue that does not receive the attention it deserves in the monolingual dominant culture in North America. It arises primarily in relating to specific communities where language skills are needed to carry out ministry and thus tends to get linked to "ethnic" issues. Because English is the language of the global culture created by business and communications, there is a tendency to think that one can become a truly global person without further study of language. One can pursue matters of justice, for example, because what is at stake are unjust structures and practices, not the languages in which they are encoded.

Understanding globalization as cross-cultural dialogue, however, requires a commitment to language acquisition. This is so because culture and identity are so closely allied to language. Language is more than words we use to refer to things; language represents a map of how we experience our world. Those familiar with more than one language realize how difficult it is to translate certain concepts and expression from one language to another; this exemplifies the intimate link between language and experience.

Short-term visits to another culture without learning that culture's language will yield insights and experiences for the traveller. But one cannot pretend to be an insider to that situation or that culture without learning the language (and sometimes languages) of that culture.

North Americans (and especially those from the United States) have been averse to learning languages. Unless we are willing to examine that stance, our rhetoric about becoming globalized will ring hollow indeed to the rest of the world, especially to those people in the southern hemisphere who have experienced domination at our hands. More important in many instances than achieving a good command of the language (something difficult for many people) is the honest attempt to work (and keep working) at learning a language. This becomes an important point for gauging the seriousness of our globalization programs. No one, of course, can learn all the languages of the world, but that cannot be taken as an excuse to learn none.

C. Travel

Travel broadens the mind, so the old saying goes. And travel to other cultures is seen as a central component of globalization programs. In these programs, attention is generally given to preparation, the visit itself (both its duration and intensity), and to the debriefing and integration occurring upon return to the home culture.

Visits to other cultures can be either short-term or long-term. Short-term visits (lasting from a few days up to a semester) tend to be the rule in globalization programs. A few schools are able to sponsor internships in other cultures of longer duration. What are the relative values of such visits? Short-term visits are essentially an exposure to difference. They capitalize on the differences between the home culture and the culture being visited. They often focus on the pathologies in the culture visited, since these stand out and allow for immediate critical reflection and connection back to the home situation. The duration is short and therefore understandably does not allow for deeper insight into the culture. They correspond to the tourist phase of crossing cultural boundaries that was described above. Despite their necessary superficiality, they should not be disparaged, however. Although they do not give deep insight into the culture visited, they may provoke important new insights into the person who is visiting and into that person's home culture. That is their principal strength. Preparation is of relative importance, depending upon the stated purpose of the short-term visit. If the purpose is to shock a person into new awareness, preparation may even be an obstacle. If the purpose is to investigate certain issues, then preparation is important in order to save time in the visit itself. It should be noted, however, that preparation for short-term visits is largely informational. Attitudinal preparation — beyond a general posture of respect — is very difficult to do. Likewise, the debriefing following the visit is a variable of the duration and intensity of the visit. Generally speaking, intense visits require longer periods for debriefing — usually done in a series of sessions lasting up to six months — since it takes time for visitors to realize just what has taken place.

Longer visits require greater preparation, since the visitor is likely to move through more of the stages outlined in crossing cultural boundaries. Language acquisition becomes an important part of the picture as well. One can explain to the potential visitor the stages that are likely to occur in becoming an insider to a new culture, but they are largely not comprehended until the actual experience takes place. Then it is important to have someone on site who can help the visitor understand what is being experienced. Long-term visits involve getting beyond the apparent differences between two cultures and learning to live in a situation, day in and day out, until the ego shield wears down. Only then can one begin to appreciate the genuine differences and similarities between two cultures. It involves moving beyond the immediately apparent pathologies of a culture and beginning to understand what makes a culture resilient in the face of misfortune. It is the difference, for example, between being able to identify the evil of apartheid and being able to identify what makes it possible for people to sustain hope and humanity and courage for the struggle against apartheid.

Because of both the duration and the intensity of the long-term visit, a debriefing that incorporates the elements of reenculturation (described above) is necessary.

Travel broadens the mind, but not necessarily so. It, too, does not guarantee globalization. And it can even create the opposite effect. By moving from one culture to another, the visitor can be deluded into believing that he or she somehow transcends cultural difference and is an outside, objective observer. Being well-traveled can create the illusion of being knowledgeable of many cultures. There are now studies being undertaken that critique this kind of tourism.[11]

III. Conclusion

Globalization as cross-cultural dialogue lies at the heart of a theological understanding of globalization. It requires that a powerful culture relinquish that power and be led by poorer, less powerful cultures on a journey toward conversion. Without this conversion, without this realignment of power, globalization in theological education will become merely a mirror-image of globalization in commerce and in the so-called new global culture: a new form of domination that continues what has been an oppressive fact for much of the world for too long. Cross-cultural dialogue is a summons to break that domination and establish a new set of relations with the poor and the others of our world.

CASE STUDY[12]

Text and Context

Professor George Lorimer walked out of his office and down the hall with Rachel Newton. As they stood at the top of the stairway, in front of the portrait of the first president of North Central Seminary, George looked at the pile of books Rachel was carrying, most of them borrowed from his office library.

"Rachel, don't worry about getting these books back to me. I found out this morning that Frank Svenson, the director of Field Education, is going to be in your community in January. Just send the books back with him."

Then he joked, "Since I'm giving you some of my favorite authors to add to your reading list, perhaps you'll send me some of your favorite books with Frank when you return these."

Rachel smiled. "Well, I don't have many books that I could share with you, but I do have people I'd be glad to introduce you to. Perhaps I can do that when you come to visit our tutorial in the spring."

George thanked her for her visit and walked toward his office, stopping on the way to check with the departmental secretary. There was a message from Emerson Clark confirming their lunch appointment. He looked at the time and decided to head for the Faculty Club immediately.

As he crossed the lawn and started up the sidewalk past the library, he mused about his visit with Rachel. Even though she had been enrolled in his history of theology course for three months, he had never met her before. She lived five hundred miles away, across two ranges of mountains. She was enrolled in a degree program of Theological Education by Extension (TEE) while she served as a parish minister. Every three weeks she met with five students from other communities and with a tutor. They met alternately in each other's communities and occasionally in Blaineville, the small town that was the regional administrative base for the TEE program. She came to the North Central campus twice a year; once for a two-week summer session, and once in the fall for a week of seminars and interaction with resident faculty and students.

North Central had started the TEE program five years earlier in response to requests from several distant parishes for assistance in training leaders for ministry. The program accepted only students who were recommended by their community and currently involved in ministry and was structured so that students remained in their community and ministry during their studies. Seminary faculty designed the courses and supervised the tutors who traveled into the communities to meet with the students.

George's visit with Rachel had confirmed his respect for her tutor, Janice Ingram. Janice had studied at North Central for three years and had been his research assistant for two of those years. Since then she had been engaged in parish ministry for six years and had completed two years of a doctoral program in theology. Now she was tutoring for the M.Div. program and conducting field research for her dissertation in the theology of sacred places.

Janice regularly updated him on the students in his TEE course. Her evaluation of Rachel confirmed his own first impressions. In a recent letter Janice had written,

> She is very modest about her intelligence and seems reluctant to engage in a rigorous exchange of opinions. But she has an unending curiosity and an immense capacity to see a connection between an idea from another time and place and her own situation. Just last week she commented that Anselm's essay "Why God Became Man" was about "setting things right," and she told me how her community has a traditional cleansing feast in which a wrongdoer holds a public feast to publicly set things right with the community.

George took the steps down the side of the Faculty Club to the patio over-looking the bay. Emerson was already at a table in the sunshine near the railing. After they had ordered lunch George told him about Rachel.

"She went to one of my bookshelves," he said, "and looked silently at the names of the authors. After a minute she turned to me and asked, 'Do you know all these people?' I wasn't sure how to answer. I said that I knew a few of them personally, but I knew most of them simply by what they wrote.

"Then she said, 'I don't know this many people.' I asked if she meant she hadn't read this many books, and she replied, 'No, I certainly haven't read this many books; but I also don't know what this many different people think.' "

Emerson asked, "Is this Rachel the same student you were telling me about a couple of months ago, the one who reads everything but who won't write an essay?"

"She's the one," replied George. "Perhaps it's not fair to say she won't write an essay. The program she's in doesn't really require her to write an essay. Her culture is an oral culture, and we've made a commitment to structure this program in a way that is culturally compatible. We've already made a significant concession to academic conventions by basing the course on the same readings and lectures we include in our resident M.Div. program. I tape my lectures and we send the tapes and reading materials to the students through our northern TEE center. The local tutor discusses the material with the students, but they don't write essays."

"I find it pretty hard to imagine an academic degree program without any written assignments," responded Emerson.

"Well, it's not quite that absolute," said George. "There is some writing required in the program, but it's in the form of reading reports. Let me describe the program for you.

"The whole point of the M.Div. by extension was to develop an academically recognized program of ministry preparation which is culturally appropriate for its clients and which allows the students to spend most of their time resident and involved in ministry in their communities.

"The community is part of an oral tradition, a tradition in which face to face, personal contact is the primary form of communication. Ideas and authority are personal, not necessarily individual, but certainly personal. I think that has some-thing to do with Rachel's way of seeing my library. She saw it as a gathering of people, not as a collection of ideas.

"But here's where the academic requirements come into the picture. As teachers and scholars we recognize that the perspectives we need to interact with are much broader than our personal circle of acquaintances. Reading is a way of interacting with ideas from other eras and other places. Certainly we couldn't adequately deal with Christian theology by only dealing with issues as they are raised and understood within our local community. We need to hear what the Church has thought and said throughout history and across cultures. That not only gives us a broader perspective, it also shapes our identity as part of a larger community of faith.

"But writing is different. Writing is one of the ways of interacting with the larger discussion of Christian theology, of shaping it, but it's not the only way. People also participate by speaking and acting. They can demonstrate their understanding of the larger tradition, and they can influence the larger tradition by their words and their actions. What we have to decide in any academic program is how to evaluate students' understanding of the tradition. Usually we do that primarily through written work. But that doesn't seem to fit this context well."

"Let me push you a bit on this," interjected Emerson. "Your students live within a larger cultural context in which writing is a fundamental skill. They may not write theological treatises, but won't they need to write letters, reports, and proposals? Won't they need the skill of writing, even if only to interact with the larger cultural context?"

"The simple answer is no, they won't," responded George. "You may not believe it, and even I, after considerable exposure to their way of life, find it difficult to understand because of my own cultural background; but the fact is they interact constantly with the surrounding dominant culture, and they do so orally. When something has to be written down there are always people available who have the skill to do so and either offer their services or can be hired."

"But there's more to writing than that," objected Emerson. "Writing helps a person to understand how an argument is constructed, and that makes a person a better reader. You may want to make adaptations to the usual academic writing requirements, but I find it hard to imagine a graduate degree, or any degree for that matter, without substantial writing requirements."

Emerson looked across the bay and then back to George. "By the way, isn't your Senate meeting soon to review the M.Div. program requirements? And didn't I hear that some faculty are arguing that there should be only one set of academic standards within each degree program? Doesn't that threaten your attempt to adapt the writing requirements of the extension M.Div.?"

"You've got the issues right," replied George. "I'm chairing the Academic Standards Committee next week, and we have been explicitly mandated to bring a recommendation about the writing requirements in the M.Div. to the next Senate meeting."

George squinted into the sun as it glared off a glass table behind Emerson. "You have to understand. The problem we face in writing skills in this program is not a lack of ability to write coherent sentences. Even now all students submit written reports on their reading. In fact, it was these reports that first made us aware that writing in our usual academic way could be problematic."

"What do you mean?" pressed Emerson.

"The problem is the way in which sources are used. We sense too much adherence to the structure and even wording of the sources. If you ask what an author says about a subject the answer you get back is a series of quotes from the author. The quotes often demonstrate an accurate sense of what is central to the source, but you don't usually discover if the student could express those ideas in his or her own words. It's not like plagiarism, in the sense of copying and deliberately not identifying the sources, so it's not an issue of academic honesty."

"Could it be a cultural issue?" asked Emerson. "I mean, it may be that the students are showing respect for the authority of the author. As I understand it, oral traditions place a high value on preserving the tradition as it has been passed to them from previous generations. When they add to it, they usually try to show how what they have added is inherent in or consistent with the tradition. What we usually want people to do when they write is to analyze and critique. Perhaps that's what your students are resisting."

"I'm not sure. I wish I knew precisely what the issue is. I know the students are willing to read materials from very diverse cultural contexts and to make connections to their own setting. They have made insightful connections with Plato's *Phaedo*, with the Donatist Controversy, and with Anselm's analysis of the incarnation. I want to be sure that everyone involved understands that it's not a question of competence for ministry, because all of these students, and Rachel in particular, have been strongly affirmed in their ministry.

"Here's our dilemma. We're trying to help people improve their capacity for ministry and we're doing that by offering an academic M.Div. program. A large component of an academic degree program involves writing analytical essays. Most of our evaluation of students is based on those essays. When we initiated this program we said that competence in writing would not be a major requirement. We gave our word, and the program was accepted by the community and academically accredited on that basis. The students in the program certainly are effective in their ministry and doing well in the program under the present arrangement. To insist on an increased writing requirement at this time feels a bit like introducing a new foreign language requirement into a program after a person has entered.

"We are feeling some pressure from course instructors to introduce more written requirements. They find it difficult to evaluate the quality of work being done in the program without written work from the students. The local site tutor, Janice Ingram, does most of the academic evaluation based on her regular interaction with the students. She's very good, and her assessments have always been affirmed by the regional director of the program and our field education supervisor. The faculty who design the courses and prepare nearly all of the teaching materials presently interact with the students through listening to tapes of oral exchanges between students and the tutor. They also meet them at least once a year when all of the students in the extension program visit campus.

"I think we're at a crossroads. If we opt for a traditional academic framework with written skills forming an essential basis, I'm afraid we may have to close the program down. We won't get the people in the community who are most qualified for ministry, and we'll also be perceived to have gone back on our word. If we decide that the evidence of increased skill in ministry among our students justifies this adaptation in writing requirements, then some faculty may choose not to participate in the program any longer. If several faculty don't participate in the program, we won't be able to offer the variety of courses needed for an M.Div., and that would cause us problems in our upcoming institutional accreditation review."

"So, what will the Academic Standards Committee recommend to Senate?" asked Emerson.

"I'll be able to tell you after we meet next week," answered George.

TEACHING NOTE

Text and Context

I. Goals

A. To explore the potential tension in theological education between institutional standards of certification and the need for cultural relevance.

B. To examine the role and relationship between the learning community and the teaching community with special reference to cross-cultural contexts.

II. Introduction: What Is at Stake?

A. Focus on the indigenous community:

1. What values are reflected in the educational program for which the community contracted?

2. How do you think the community will and should respond if new degree requirements are added?

3. What leadership roles might Rachel Newton or Janice Ingram play?

B. For the faculty:

1. What values are represented in the changes being considered by the faculty?

2. What options does the Academic Standards Committee have, and what are the possible consequences of these decisions?

3. What leadership role should George Lorimer play, if any?

III. Small-group Discussion

A. If one chooses to focus on the faculty decision, divide participants into several groups, each of which is divided again in two so that in each group there are three or four people to defend each of the following positions:

1. There should be *no* increase in the writing requirement for this program.

2. There should be an increase in the writing requirement.

B. Suggest that debating groups consider issues, identifying as many reasons as possible for their positions. It may be helpful for participants to consider the perspectives of various constituencies: students in the program; church communities which support these students; regular M. Div students who may object to different standards; members of the accrediting association; faculty members who want more written work; faculty who favor retaining the current arrangements; and so on.

C. Encourage the groups to draw attention to the larger historical and cultural context. For example:

    1. the legacy of promises to oral cultures being broken by written cultures;

    2. the debate about whether a group is well served by "affirmative action" which adapts standards and expectations.

IV. Alternatives

A. Reassemble full group and ask participants to state the arguments heard from their opponents which were most convincing.

B. Ask for a straw vote on adding writing assignments. Have participants offer reasons for their votes including biblical, theological, and practical considerations.

C. Discuss alternatives that could be taken by either the faculty or the indigenous community in order to address accreditation and cultural relevance.

V. Implications for Theological Education

A. Authority of written and oral sources is discussed in the case. Who should be part of the decisions about standards: candidates, community, faculty, others? What are the ecclesiological and theological implications in this case and in our own situations concerning authority and power? (Reference to commentary by Pierre Goldberger may be helpful.)

B. Are there other examples of cultural differences which might make it necessary to adapt theological education so that it could be accredited by the teaching community and be culturally appropriate to the learning community? Consider special dimensions involved in cross-cultural settings.

C. There are at least two reference points for defining educational standards. One such point is relevance to the user or customer. The other is compatibility with similar programs which facilitates transfer of credit based on mutual recognition. How can these two be reconciled in a multi-cultural world?

VI. Learnings

Ask participants to share their learnings from the case discussion. How might these learnings apply directly to one's own seminary?

COMMENTARY

Text and Context

PIERRE GOLDBERGER

Liberéz les Sujets!

C'est bon! This case study has a familiar ethos of *déjà-vu*. The setting, the atmosphere, the initial conversation under the portrait of the founding president, undoubtedly—if I judge according to my own university context—first of a sequence of other portraits of stern-looking competent patriarchs, each exuding the humble poise of self-assurance and the quiet authority that comes from presiding over proven truths in academia.

This case study sets forth the educational dilemmas of what appears to be a mainline institution of good will and acts as a provocative mirror image. To respond to a very real need, North Central Seminary no doubt did a lot of soul searching and creative hard work before going out on a limb with the TEE program. There is evidence that the extension education venture has been costly for some faculty and that every gain has been hard won. The predicament which may force the program to close reflects some of our worst traits and weaknesses imbedded in some of our best efforts to move and respond to the educational needs of the context. The case highlights not only how much further those of us in theological education need to go, but how much of a paradigm shift, of a conversion, of a "relinquishing of control and power" we need.[13] Can academia do it? Well, I hesitate. But at least it is worth a debate and a solid struggle.

Although the main issues appear to be tension between written and oral modes of learning coupled with a discussion of what constitutes a broad (school) or narrow (local context) base of knowledge and understanding, I feel that the underlying multifaceted main issue is one of *power* and *control* between the center and the periphery. What is at stake is the power to define, shape, and evaluate learning. In this situation the much needed power shift acts as a live metaphor of the power shift needed in globalized relationships and educational patterns. My remarks will thus hinge on this pivotal perception.

Qui regarde qui? ou . . . Cherchez le sujet

What is the angle of vision? The story is obviously told from the perspective of North Central Seminary. Anything wrong with this? I'll let you decide, but this fact colors everything. The school is thus *the* center of interpretation. Various actors appear and are weighted according to their relative proximity or distance to the center's institutional and power logic. The power structure of the seminary acts as the hermeneutical locus of reality which shapes the educational aims, the discourse, the pedagogical frameworks, and programs. Who is the subject of education? The seminary's institutional needs. This *punto da vista* sets the educational pecking order and somewhere down the line sets the students and their community as objects of the educational program. This order frames the encounter between "context and seminary." It is difficult to repress the feeling that Rachel, the female student, is cast as a pleasant country bumpkin who is gently patted on the head by an understanding patriarch. . . . That resembles my role. Planting the institution and its logic of control as the de facto subject of theological education entails that from the outset the community context is seen as problem and periphery which will have to fit into the seminary's predetermined categories. An attempt to meet the needs of the students in their community will be perceived as demanding "significant concessions to academic conventions."

Down the line, the question of the determination of the subject of education, or who are the referent subjects in a given context is a Christological question. Where is the Nazarene to be found walking? With the center of power or calling out from the periphery and underside? For whom does the central system work? For the gate keepers or for those who thirst and hunger? In any given context, where is the locus, the point (or points) of vantage from which the "whole" takes meaning? If one answers the Cross is that locus and, in contemporary historical terms, those who are marginalized and on the periphery (in any given context), we have then a revealing illumination (lipsis) of the whole from the *underside*, from the periphery of power. This revelation is accompanied by a sense of direction which should determine our journey in solidarity and our contextual "mission," educational or other. Reversal of the subject in accordance with the Gospel imperative sometimes appears in our mission statements but rarely in our educational structures and praxis. The dilemma at North Central Seminary illustrates the need for the reversal of the subject of education. This agenda has yet to be fulfilled by most theological institutions and calls for quite a radical epistemological rupture.

The prospect for institutional conversion does not look good. As in the parable of the rich young ruler, many schools start the conversation risking even curriculum dialogue, but more likely fail to join the company of Jesus—not the Jesuits—but the company of the poor! On the other hand, let's not throw in the towel; there is hope. The peripheral widow knows and demands her right of access, even from the iniquitous judge. She musters from her experience enough resiliency to keep knocking again and again until the law keeper, disgusted, throws justice in her lap.

On exporte qui? (Who Is Being Exported?)

The seminary as an institution, through its hierarchic mode of organization and its logic of power, not only patterns theological programs, but also exports itself into the community context. "Distance education" may then mean carrying further afield the same patterns of one-way power relationships. The patriarchal division of labor internal to the institution and the value system which is attached to it project themselves into the context. In the case study, we can see the top-down pyramid of power in action. The more one moves toward the base, the more one finds people with organic connections with the context. Inversely, the closer to the community, the less power there is to shape the design, content, and evaluation of the educational program. Thus, the Senate makes final decisions according to its own institutional logic—probably determined by marketing considerations; the faculty (mostly men) designs course and teaching material quite apart from the students; the director of field education acts as a go-between between the academic center and the community context; the gifted female graduate student works as a local tutor and has hands-on experience with the student cluster; and the students are *in situ* in the community. Even more, the community which appears to be the initial *raison d'être* of distance education is completely left out. What comes as a gift from the community context—the student and her mode of learning—when relayed up through the pyramid of decision-making reaches the top in the maimed form of a "problem." Clearly, the exportation of the seminary's hierarchic pattern to the context raises several questions. One question, for example, relates to the status and place of the field educator, who seems to be used more as a cog on behalf of the academic power center than as a person who, on the basis of praxis, experience, and connection with the field, can be a force helping to reshape the core understanding of the seminary's program. The fact that field education is often staffed by women also reveals its secondary status in a patriarchal class system.

The student and the community, which perhaps would be represented through a local "lay committee," also have no "forum" for direct input in establishing needs and evaluating programs. This case study illustrates how many of our institutions send an unfortunately too clear message. We are the experts; you are to be educated on our terms; we will try to be accommodating—within our norms.

The pyramidal sexist and classist structure has a direct impact on the context; lived out realities and learnings in the context go through filters and grids of the seminary channel of power. When questions from the community end up, for example, in the seminary, the map does not coincide with the territory. This is part of our North American theological education crisis; we are divorced from the community and context and yet are trying to relate to the community in terms of our own maps, norms, and power structure. This is a one-way street, a metaphor of global North and South relationships.

Un Sens Unique (A One-Way Direction)

A pyramidal institution such as North Central Seminary relates to its context by one-way rapport. The institution metes out educational programs in a dispensational mode: from the center to the periphery. Radical asymmetrical relationships in education (in the process of setting goals, shaping form and content, evaluating learning) are debilitating as they constitute all experience in disempowerment. The phenomenon of disempowerment is all too familiar in our educational settings where women, racial and cultural minorities, and impoverished classes can, if they have access, be exposed to liberationist course contents and material. On the other hand, they endure the painful experience of their inability, their powerlessness, to have a significant impact, to bring about change, to initiate a shift in the structure of power relationships.

A basic question before the seminary is not how much the school will extend itself into the community, but how much the community of the periphery and underside is able to effect change at the core of the institutional project. Without a two-way dialectical relationship between learning centers and community — that is, life — for both residential and distance education, the foundational learning, the sub-text, will be that of the inability to effect change. Under such conditions contextual reality will be considered a nuisance, a reality to be suffered and sometimes accommodated to.

The case study gives an all too graphic illustration of a one-way relationship. The professor meets students for the first time in seven months on his turf. The faculty raises no questions about its own need to experience the students' community context, culture, and struggles in order to be able to set standards, design programs, and evaluate results. This one-way relationship constitutes a major challenge to theological education, especially as seminaries engage in contextual theology in a global perspective.

The one-way relationship with marginalized people and communities as patterned by many of our seminaries reflects in fact a dominant mode of social organization which is patriarchal, classist, and discriminatory in terms of races and cultures. The seriousness with which seminaries address and establish two-way mutual relationships with their contextual poor and disempowered minorities and work at making the necessary power shifts for shaping together educational programs will constitute the basis of the credibility test of our venture into globalization. In what, according to Robert J. Schreiter, is fundamentally an asymmetrical world in terms of power, experiences of power shifts in learning are what graduates could have a chance to take with them from the seminary and continue to build on in a liberating praxis of ministry in their communities.

Contexte ou Prétexte

In more than one way, the context is treated here as "pretext." It is pretext inasmuch as context appears as mere environment calling for some irritating academic concessions. The student's community is totally reified and objectified. It is certainly not seriously valued as a matrix of reciprocal learning co-equal to the seminary's teaching. In a reversed perspective, paradoxically, the problem is also that the community's context and culture are not honored as being "pre-textual," that is, foundational. The life of the community always precedes reflection and "objectification" as text. Hence, we cannot ignore in theological education that under and prior to the text there is the formative pretext of the community. This understanding is not only valid for the past in dealing with textual criticism, but it is also a given of the present. The preceding living community is what gives birth to theological reflection and text. The student, Rachel, is immersed in this living foundational reality and comes to the seminary with this awareness. When she sees "books" — text — in the library, she thinks "people," life, community of exchange — pretext. Hence, the invitation to her teacher to come and meet her people, her "talking books."

The faculty, on the other hand, tends to see and dwell in text; the context as pretext is evacuated, made invisible, as if totally absorbed in the text. Classical theological education is constantly confronted with the dilemma of whether or not to take the context as the living root of text and salvation history. In this case study, the text, as held and interpreted by the seminary center, is normative and set over against the peripheral context. A deadly opposition. How does one break this enclosure of theological education? One breaks out of the enclosure through experiences deep and strong enough to create *cognitive dissonance* – the disintegration Schreiter underscores in his essay. The learning gained from such cognitive dissonance has to be given form and structure: in this case the realization of the formative locus of the community, the need for educators to be organically connected to the milieu, and the necessity to build places for participation in decision-making by the community throughout the educational process and structure. Participatory insight is necessary to transform the domination inherent in the seminary's educational process and to set modes of relationships that go beyond advocacy models.

Elevez les voix

The case study brings into the scene some enlightened advocates. One, the knowledgeable but powerless tutor, does her best to honor and interpret the learnings she encounters and enables. Another, the field educator, probably keeps justifying the need and value of practical field experience to the core faculty who possibly rate "field stuff" as mere application. But more significantly in the story, the faculty member who chairs the task force that will report to the Senate has a major advocacy role for both program and students. Obviously, we understand that this committed and enlightened teacher will *advocate* a more flexible and contextually sensitive educational program. Yet this advocacy role is part of the problem and has to be superseded.

Since the late '60s, advocacy has been the operational praxis and ideology of "liberal" mainline and middle-class churches and seminaries. Advocacy has cast the mode of relation in/with the social context. Advocates are called to be "the voice of the voiceless." Perhaps this advocacy is an unavoidable phase in consciousness raising, palliative and transitory. But it must now be superseded as a root metaphor for the use of middle- and upper-class power and influence. Through identifying their social role as one of advocacy, mainline churches and the middle class of the late '60s and '70s found *a new historical role* that both quenched our Christian conscience and justified our existence as a class. Paradoxically, while bringing about certain incremental changes, such as the distance education under discussion, advocacy as a fundamental model of relationships has comforted the status quo, left the power balance and structure unchanged, and has further disempowered the marginalized and the oppressed. Advocacy implies that the voices of the "periphery" and marginalized are never heard directly, but are carried up, so to speak, by proxy, by people, gender, classes, and cultures external to the condition for which they advocate.

What empowerment means is helping to create a space for the "voice of the voiceless," for those of the periphery to be *directly* present, heard, and making decisions. In terms of the case study, empowerment means having the contextually marginalized and impoverished erupt and participate in the use of power – here, the power of education. The educational enterprise will live a new life. The crucial question is not only how much the seminary can open up, but much more how much it can *learn* from and be transformed by the teaching periphery, marginalized, and poor. The globalization of theological education will probably remain a veneer in our seminaries if we keep locking out the eruption of the teaching periphery in the process of designing and carrying out theological education that helps set the captives free.

The case study has presented us with an all too familiar image of my seminary and university context at its best! A liberal model of education is based on the goodwill and enlightenment of those in control; this basis concerns me. As the particular case relates to "education by extension," the model will only extend so far as the limit of tolerance of those in power and as long as there are no other demands for fundamental power shifts and risk-taking other than those compatible with an advocacy model of relationship. Are we only willing to move as long as we can keep the power? Can our seminaries shed power and control? Can North America shed its power and control? The question rings: Can the leopard shed his spots? Not likely! A more potent question is: Does the persistent widow lose her resiliency and stop knocking for her rights? Not a chance! Even the unjust judge yields to her persistence.

So why can't we?

Notes

1. John Hale, "A World Elsewhere: Geographical and Mental Horizons," in Dennis Hayes (ed.), *The Age of the Renaissance* (New York: McGraw-Hill, 1967), 300-350.

2. For early developments of the understanding of the other, see Tzvetan Todorov, *The Conquest of America* (New York: Harper and Row, 1984). An excellent overview of the elaboration of the understanding of the other in terms of culture from the fifteenth century to the present may be found in Bernard McGrane, *Beyond Anthropology: Society and the Other* (New York: Columbia University Press, 1989).

3. On the development of the concept of culture, see Ton Lemaire, *Over de waarde van kulturen: Tussen europacentrisme en relativisme* (Baarn: Ambo, 1976). On Vico and Herder's contribution to the understanding of pluralism and culture, see Isaiah Berlin, *Vico and Herder: Two Studies in the History of Ideas* (New York: Viking, 1976).

4. There is a growing literature created both by missionaries and anthropologists showing the positive forces that the missionary movement has fostered to protect cultures from the corrosive forces of imperialism. Lamin Sanneh has been the most eloquent on this matter from the side of missiologists. See his *Translating the Message: The Missionary Impact on Culture* (Maryknoll, NY: Orbis Books, 1989). On the anthropological side, see John and Jean Comaroff, *Of Revelation and Revolution: Christianity, Colonialism, and Consciousness in South Africa* (Chicago: University of Chicago Press, 1991); Kenelm Burridge, *In the Way: A Study of Christian Missionary Endeavours* (Vancouver: University of British Columbia Press, 1991).

5. I try to outline some of these issues in "Multicultural Ministry: Theory, Practice, Ministry," *New Theology Review* 5 (August, 1992), 6-19.

6. One good attempt to bring together a variety of tools for cultural analysis is Gerald A. Arbuckle, *Earthing the Gospel: An Inculturation Handbook for the Pastoral Worker* (Maryknoll, NY: Orbis Books, 1990).

7. To speak of a global culture is to speak analogously. The complexities of the relation of global culture to local culture cannot be touched upon in this presentation. For some of the recent debate on this issue, see the essays in Mike Featherstone (ed.), *Global Culture: Nationalism, Globalization and Modernity* (Newbury Park, CA: Sage Press, 1990).

8. One figure worried that multiculturalism is undermining the ideals of the United

States is Arthur M. Schlesinger, Jr. See his *The Disuniting of America: Reflections on a Multicultural Society* (New York: W. W. Norton, 1992).

9. See Richard A. Schweder, "Post-Nietzschean Anthropology: The Idea of Multiple Objective Worlds," in Richard A. Schweder, *Thinking Through Cultures: Expeditions in Cultural Psychology* (Cambridge, MA: Harvard University Press, 1992), 27-72.

10. It should be noted that the times given here are relative. They depend also upon the pace of language acquisition. Rarely, however, do they begin earlier than the timeline suggested here.

11. Cf. McGrane, 114-123, on this point. He is speaking here of the training of anthropologists, but the point holds equally well, I believe, for globalization programs. Cf. also John Urry, *The Tourist Gaze: Leisure and Travel in Contemporary Societies* (London: Sage, 1990).

12. Copyright © 1993 by the Case Study Institute. The names of persons and places in this case have been disguised to protect the privacy of those involved in the situation.

13. Reference will be made throughout this commentary to Robert J. Schreiter's preceding essay, "Globalization as Cross-Cultural Dialogue."

[6]

GLOBALIZATION AS JUSTICE

ESSAY

ALICE FRAZER EVANS and ROBERT A. EVANS

The spirit of the worship service was exuberant and defiant. More than 400 South African worshippers danced as they sang hymns of praise. Twenty-three North American, mostly white, theological educators found themselves in the midst of both a service and a struggle in a black township near Cape Town. The visiting delegation had been invited to be part of an ecumenical service commemorating the June 16, 1976, uprising of young people in Soweto.

In the middle of the service, the presiding pastor announced that the church had just been surrounded by "hippos," the armored personnel carriers of the South African Defense Force. Anxiety about yet another threatening encounter in the ongoing struggle for justice filled the air. Sermons and testimonies during the service moved the congregation to tears of grief for those who had already given their lives for the struggle. There were also moments of joy when the movements of dance could barely contain the congregation's expression of faith. After the announcement, the mood of the congregation was one of resistance to the military representatives of a dominant white minority that had again invaded their community and challenged their dignity and sense of equality. During the service, the love of God and neighbor had been repeatedly proclaimed as the biblical mandate of the Gospel. Many worshippers asked themselves just what love of neighbor required in a conflict such as this.

As the service drew to a close, the presiding pastor quietly asked whether some of the overseas delegation investigating the globalization of theological education would care to express the love of neighbor in a concrete way. He invited our group to position ourselves outside the church and become a shield between the military hippos and the toitoi-ing youth who would be dancing their way back to waiting buses. The confrontation with the military was unexpected, and the request was unanticipated by host or guest. At that moment those in our group did not know how each would respond to this direct challenge about love of neighbor. The global interrelatedness of the body of Christ became more than a theological theory. On that bright and volatile June day, most members of our theological team walked out of the building first and stood in solidarity with a few of our hosts, black and white, in a thin line that separated the soldiers from the dancers.

No blood was shed, and all of the neighbors present avoided physical violence on that afternoon. As our visiting delegation left the site of the service, we were followed by the South African security police. The hands of a seminary trustee who was also a United States District Judge shook a little as he tightly gripped the steering wheel of our microbus. He said, "I just realized how boring my life on the bench normally is and how little it is immediately connected to acts of justice." A professor of theology responded that this encounter had challenged not only his faith but the relevance of his seminary teaching in a world polarized by race. "I think what we did was an act of solidarity that made a difference," declared one of the students. The evening reflection period that was part of our life together during this immersion experience in South Africa renewed our focus on the meaning of globalization as justice.

The members of the delegation did not all agree as to whether the actions of those who stood in that thin line or those who chose not to were faithful from a theological perspective. Nor was there consensus about the implications of such an act for our preparation of men and women for ministry in a world where worship can lead to confrontation. However, this day and this three-week immersion event in Zimbabwe and South Africa were to affect the lives of the individuals and the communities participating in the Pilot Immersion Project for the Globalization of Theological Education. The judge trustee returned home to take a stand on issues of civil rights. The professor has redesigned his courses to include bibliographic sources from Southern Africa and a local immersion experience focused on racial justice. The student took a pastoral appointment ministering to rural Native American communities.

The following essay will discuss the rationale for the focus on justice in the Pilot Immersion Project, raise the need for the transformation of North American theological education in order to train clergy and laity for ministry in an interdependent world, and, based on learnings from this project, propose specific approaches which can effect this transformation. These approaches include the *place* where theological teaching and learning occur, the *players* in the educational enterprise, and the *perspectives* of the institutional community. The illustration from South Africa alludes to each of these critical components.

I. The Pilot Immersion Project and Globalization as Justice

After five years, three international and one local immersion, each of the twelve seminaries in the Pilot Immersion Project experienced some institutional change. One seminary produced what faculty members described as a "paradigm shift" in the curriculum by grounding it in issues of global justice. Another institution followed a year-long faculty study of globalization with an immersion experience for the entire faculty in rural and urban areas of poverty. These experiences are leading to a new seminary focus on congregational life and mission. A third seminary developed an orientation course for all new students which directly exposes them to problems of injustice in communities near the seminary. The orientation course was designed as a result of an unprecedented coalition with a local seminary of another theological tradition. These events mirrored what one of the project consultants described as a change of seminary culture or values that made the question of globalization as justice an unavoidable issue.

The Pilot Immersion Project was one of several programs on the globalization of theological education initiated in the 1980s. Each of the twelve institutions in the project drew on its own distinctive history to devise a strategy for incorporating a global perspective. Those who designed the project did not assume that globalization as justice was the only or even the primary meaning of globalization. Essays in this volume provide eloquent testimony to the multi-faceted nature of a global perspective in the preparation for ministry.[1] However, the project did assume that one effective way of exploring institutional change for the sake of globalization was to adopt a justice-oriented understanding of globalization in the series of international and local immersion experiences in which each school participated. This orientation was not intended to block or exclude those participants who entered globalization through the doorways of evangelization, cross-cultural dialogue, or ecumenical/interfaith dialogue.

A. Why Globalization as Justice?

Several factors influenced the decision to focus the immersions on globalization as justice. First, this orientation was advocated by partners in Africa, Asia, and Latin America with whom the project was designed. The current isolation and provincialism of the theological educational process frequently stifles dialogue between North American Christians and those with a dynamic faith, especially those in the countries of the "South," "developing," or "two-thirds" world. Many colleagues in the South believe that issues of race, ethnicity, gender, class, and environment which radically affect them have been given inadequate attention by their partners in the North. Neglect leads to unjust policies. These colleagues experience governments and institutions of the North, including theological seminaries, as not recognizing the contributions of the South and not being willing to share their resources with the South. Many theological colleagues see the North as being more concerned about preserving its wealth, privilege, and power than responding to the biblical mandate to minister to the poor and oppressed. Our southern partners also express concern about global perspectives which currently permeate the geo-political and economic spheres. As the North American Church begins to re-assess its understanding of globalization, many colleagues in the South fear that globalization in theological education will take the form of domination, imperialism, and manipulation that characterize business and political patterns of the North and frequently characterized the Church's understanding of mission in the last century. It is the theological conviction of many of our southern neighbors that our lack of global awareness impedes the realization of a vision of a more just, peaceful, and sustainable world community to which the Holy Spirit calls us.

Second, the Pilot Immersion Project developed a strategic approach to globalization as justice because of the global urgency surrounding certain issues of justice. This approach is grounded in a biblical vision of applied justice which utilizes images of the Kingdom of God or the Reign of God as criteria for a just and peaceable world community. Applied justice continually challenges Christians to struggle with the implications of love of God and neighbor. The urgency of addressing specific issues of justice is graphically illustrated in studies such as the

Global 2000 Report to the President[2] or the Club of Rome study *The Limits to Growth*.[3] These reports carefully document a picture of the world which, if present trends and national policies continue, will be more crowded, polluted, ecologically unstable, and increasingly vulnerable to disruption by human conflict and natural disasters. An alarming sequel to the Club of Rome report, *Beyond the Limits*,[4] suggests that almost no progress has been made in the last twenty years in the problems identified by the original research. In fact, there have been increases in the proportions of poverty, environmental decline, and the growing disparity between the so-called rich and poor, both between nations and within nations.

The need for the Church to address the justice agenda is confirmed by global conditions cited in the World Watch Institute's report *The State of the World 1992*:

- One in three children is malnourished.
- Some 1.2 billion people lack safe water to drink.
- Nearly three million children die annually from diseases that could be averted by immunization.
- One million women die each year from preventable reproductive health problems.[5]

Probably nothing gave more dramatic emphasis to justice issues surrounding the global ecological crisis than the June 1992 "Earth Summit" held in Rio de Janeiro, Brazil. Carefully researched scientific data made it clear to most of the individual and national participants that unless widespread environmental deterioration can be stopped or reversed by the end of this century, it will be impossible to recover these natural resources in the next millennium. A World Watch summary of critical ecological issues which both North and South face includes the following findings:

- The protective ozone layer . . . is thinning twice as fast as scientists thought.
- Atmospheric levels of heat-trapping carbon dioxide are 26 percent higher . . . than when last tested.
- Forests are vanishing at a rate of 17 million hectares per year.
- World population is growing by 92 million people annually.[6]

Each of these issues seriously threatens the quality of life in the world, but those most directly and immediately threatened are the poor of the South or two-thirds world. Over-population contributes to hunger and disease, particularly in urban areas overwhelmed by massive migrations of rural poor; deforestation leads to devastating floods and the depletion of arable land in the world's poorest countries.

In order to address the justice issues heightened by the eco-crisis effectively, the Church must initiate a new partnership between the North and the South. Love of neighbor and a vision of the Reign of God call the Church and the theological education community to give leadership to a fundamental restructuring of the global society to counter critical threats to the future of our common home. Respected scholars and advocates agree that a reversal of destructive global trends demands a move to smaller families, new levels of equality between the sexes in all cultures, a move from fossil fuels to renewable energy sources, systems of transportation that reduce carbon dioxide emissions, and perhaps most difficult for those in the North, reduced consumption of non-renewable resources by the wealthy to make room for a viable standard of living for the poor.[7] Globalization as justice responds to biblical mandates and is a cornerstone of a sustainable future for the global community.

Third, a growing awareness of the need for a biblically based vision has emerged within North American theological education during the last decade. A renewed focus on questions of justice was confirmed by theological declarations and study documents from Rome, Geneva, and Lausanne in the North and from Manila, Rustenburg, and Rio in the South. The one area of common agreement in each of the major theological traditions is the focus on questions of justice. While different seminaries in the Pilot Immersion Project defined the priorities and implications of justice issues in different ways, each could point to a history and a biblically based affirmation of the mandate for justice. Other major definitions of globalization such as evangelism, ecumenical/interfaith dialogue, and cross-cultural dialogue, were seen as important, but there was less common ground than in the area described as justice, peace, or reconciliation.

This common awareness is deeply rooted in scripture. The Hebrew prophets hold up a vision of justice which characterizes the Reign of God. The vision is marked by God's special preference for and even identification with the poor, the widows, the orphans, and every person and group in the society that suffers unjustly. This biblical vision condemns injustice and inequality. Whenever a serious gap grows between those persons or communities with wealth and power and those plagued by poverty and powerlessness, God's prophets call for a biblical reversal in the unjust patterns of human relationships. Globalization as justice embodies a call for transformation, for reversal of the unjust structures of society.

Jesus draws on the prophet Isaiah as he announces his mission—a transformation of priorities with the coming Reign of God:

> The Spirit of the Lord is upon me,
> because God has anointed me to preach good news to the poor.
> God has sent me to proclaim release to the captives
> and recovery of sight to the blind,
> to let the oppressed go free, to proclaim
> the year of the Lord's favor (Luke 4:18-19, *NRSV*).

The transformation Jesus announces is described by Mennonite theologian John Howard Yoder as "a visible socio-political-economic restructuring of relations among the people of God."[8] Such societal reversals imply an accompanying spiritual transformation as well. Realignment of priorities in favor of the poor calls for nothing less than a *metanoia* that encompasses the whole person as well as the society. Globalization as justice is based in a vision of a new heaven and a new earth. Conversion does not imply that the poor and non-poor will change places; there is no historical evidence that this is possible. However, globalization as justice demands the recognition of a biblical vision of the Reign of God; the first step toward the realization of this vision is to implement new priorities. The writer of the Gospel of Luke makes the astonishing claim that in some sense the person and presence of Jesus initiated a social, economic, and political transformation.

This paradigmatic biblical account suggests that not only society, but religious communities and by implication centers of theological education must also be prepared to regularly experience conversion or transformation for the sake of justice.

"What does the Lord require of you but to do justice, love mercy, and walk humbly with your God?"(Micah 6:8, *RSV*). These themes are central to the biblical message. The challenge of doing justice calls the Church and seminary to address the conditions of the modern world. Doing justice also holds the potential for integrating, energizing, and transforming the seminary and the parish.

B. A Call for Vision and Integration

For more than a decade, extensive research and deep theological reflection have focused on the purpose and nature of theological education in North America. Recent studies such as *Christian Identity and Theological Education* sharpen the dialogue and advocate transformative education to reshape and integrate ministry and mission.[9] While many scholars argue that theological education must be transformed in order to equip men and women to be faithful servants of the Church in an increasingly interdependent world, the sobering reality is that very few fundamental changes have been made in the structure of theological education in several decades.

One of the theological reflectors for the Pilot Immersion Project, Douglas Meeks, suggests that globalization is akin to the basic question of *oikoumene*: Are the peoples of the world able to inhabit the world in mutual peace?[10] A biblically informed vision of a more just, peaceful, and sustainable world provides the basis for the Church and the seminary to focus their mission on witness and service in a new millennium in which the people of the world have no choice but to live as a global village.

Edward Farley's *Theologia: The Fragmentation and Unity of Theological Education* initiated a decade of examining the aims and purposes of theological education.[11] Farley suggested that the division of the curriculum into four classical fields left students feeling their studies were fragmented and had no point of integration. Theological education had been captured by a professional model that Farley described as the "clerical paradigm." Many students, faculty, and church leaders approached theological education in terms of the acquisition of occupational skills.

Barbara Wheeler, an evaluator in the area of theological education, found surprising agreement, at least in mainline Protestant theological education, in responses to Farley's analysis: "There is no convincing theological rationale for the basic structures and activities of theological studies."[12] While several Evangelical and Roman Catholic theologians disagreed with Farley's diagnosis of a crisis and disarray in theological education, there was general agreement that seminaries lacked direction and an integrated approach to theological education. Many seminaries and churches, while facing crises of funding and recruitment, are also asking how to minister in and to the global community. In this context a variety of globalization projects have emerged.

One must be cautious about claims for the contributions of experiments in globalization toward addressing urgent needs of the global community and integrating and energizing theological education. However, the authors propose the potential of a focus on globalization as justice for renewing, even transforming, theological education. In support of this proposal we will draw on learnings from the Pilot Immersion Project as well as from other North American experiments in globalization and programs in Latin America, the Philippines, and Southern Africa. It is clear that intentional immersion experiences in international and local circumstances which focus on justice issues motivate a critical consciousness about the content and process of theological education. Individual renewal occurs for immersion participants, and there are signs that both the structure and the culture or value system of participants' institutions can be influenced by a wave-like series of catalytic exposures that initiate a systems intervention.[13]

Paul Hiebert, an anthropologist-theologian and one of the consultants for the Pilot Immersion Project, helped many of the consultants and coordinators think about the work of individual, institutional, and cultural transformation by drawing on the research of Talcott Parsons and others.[14] An adaptation of Parsons' systems theory suggests that the behavioral changes the Pilot Project sought to achieve were on three basic levels. The first level of change is in individuals. Persons are affected by thinking, feeling, and responding. Awareness of globalization as justice can lead to an individual's recognition of responsibility for issues of justice, to the realization that the non-poor are benefactors and recipients of economic, political, and cultural systems which are primarily shaped by the North and by white males. Poor and marginalized persons most frequently experience these same systems as oppressive. Transformative education begins with an understanding and acknowledgment of an individual's place in these systems. Research indicates, however, that little change is generated by awareness at the thinking or cognitive level that so dominates present patterns of theological education. Transformation occurs more regularly at the feeling level where one's emotions are engaged. The affective level motivates the response of will which brings about behavioral modification in patterns of living. The rich ruler who sought to inherit eternal life had been cognitively persuaded to keep the commandments; the affective challenge to the ruler's will is Jesus' demand that he go and sell all that he owned and distribute it to the poor (see Luke 18: 18-25, *NRSV*). The stage of transformation that we have called a biblical reversal requires a response of will, a behavioral response.

Parsons' theory of systems change suggests a second level of change in the relationships among the members of a social system, in this case the seminary community. The nature of the relationships between president, trustees, faculty, administrators, and students is affected by (1) economic concerns, that is, the access to resources, (2) political issues in terms of power, and (3) the legal or legitimatizing processes that sustain or restructure relationships within a particular social system. Implementation of a vision of globalization as justice requires not merely individual change but an assessment and possible re-allocation of a seminary's resources. It requires modification of power relationships within and outside the classroom which are conducive to a just learning community. Implementation also calls for reappraisal of the legitimating process of theological education, for example, serious consideration of the criteria for admission, degrees, employment, and advancement.

The third basic level of change is that of culture which involves values, symbols, and ideology. A seminary globalized in terms of justice asks which symbols and rituals reflect the values of global justice at a deeper level than either the individual or the structural. What kind of language is legitimate? What themes are a regular part of the community worship experience? What patterns of equality are normative within the structure of the institution? New symbols and rituals hold the potential of institutionalizing commitments to global justice.

Our observation is that all three system levels of institutional change have been affected to varying degrees within seminaries in the Pilot Immersion Project. We are convinced that institutional change in theological education through the portal of globalization as justice is *difficult but possible.* The balance of this essay will suggest three components which seem to be essential in effecting this type of institutional transformation: the *place* where the primary energy of theological teaching and learning occurs; the *players* in the educational enterprise, including the community of learning and those who are our teachers; and the *perspectives* of those engaged in the educational process.

II. The Place of Transformative Education

Most of North American theological education occurs in secure, middle class, residential institutions. Although a shift has begun in some seminaries, a majority of courses are grounded in classical, hierarchical classroom exchanges between a teacher and students. The instructor's goal is usually cognitive or rational apprehension of a body of knowledge, not a transformation of behavior. This approach is in stark contrast to a transformative model of theological education that judges the adequacy of an educational endeavor by the degree of behavioral change in the participants and the instructors they serve.

A significant majority of teachers and students in North American theological seminaries are the non-poor, that is, those with long life expectancy, low infant mortality, and a generally guaranteed access to the necessities of life.[15] The non-poor usually exercise choice of lifestyle, vocation, and location. If the biblical vision of the Reign of God calls for social, political, and economic re-structuring of the relationships among the people of God, specifically between the poor and non-poor, North American theological education must aim for conversion or transformation of the non-poor. Sr. Marie Augusta Neal reminds us that when the poor reach out to take what is justifiably theirs—elements essential for their survival— the non-poor usually resist.[16] Transformation for the sake of justice begins with awareness by the non-poor of the needs and rights of the poor; the process Neal describes as a "socio-theology of letting go" reduces the resistance of the non-poor. Reorienting theological education, as some have urged, to focus on God's relationship to the created order would necessarily involve a series of renewals in our relationships to God and to one another. In the Pilot Immersion Project two places where reorientation and renewal consistently begin for the non-poor are in immersion experiences and in situations of openness and vulnerability.

A. Immersion Experiences

An experience of being immersed in the life and ministry of Christians struggling with poverty and oppression has been the single most important catalyst in the process of individual conversion for globalization as justice in the Pilot Immersion Project. The immersion experiences referred to in this essay and in many of the case studies in this volume had similar components. At the core of each three-week immersion were intensive experiences of exposure to communities of faithful people living in the midst of suffering as a result of poverty and oppression. Participants experienced the lives of their hosts, insofar as they were able, and sought to respond to their struggles of faith by a presence of solidarity. Demands for justice concerning food, shelter, health, education, land, and freedom were central to the hosts' social, political, and economic analysis of the conditions under which they lived.

Participant and independent evaluations reinforced time and time again that specific immersion experiences or combinations of encounters were catalytic elements in significant intentional and behavioral change for the sake of making globalization as justice central to participants' lives and to their approach to theological education. It is important to take seriously the pervasiveness of this finding. It appears unlikely, if not impossible, to "think oneself" into a conversion akin to a biblical reversal. While the cognitive is critical to both preparation and implementation, it is in fact the affective or emotive that appears essential to the process of transformation of the non-poor.

Project research points to the importance of an experiential "shock" or "radical change of environment" to challenge previous assumptions, stimulate change, and encourage the exploration of alternative patterns of living.[17] This shock often comes when one is in a different place with different people and in a different role. Immersion participants are challenged to ask how God is involved in this different reality and what is required for their hosts and for themselves to love God and neighbor in that place. The "place" of theological education for the sake of global conversion is a location in which one heightens the possibility for a fresh look at the reality of suffering, the response of faith, and the consequences of solidarity.

Place is central to the dynamic of transformation. All theological education is "experiential"; students have experiences with professors, classrooms, books, and with parishes in field education. The immersion model of education concentrates on the experience of a radical change of environment. The immersion model makes possible personal encounters with poor and oppressed people of faith in the hope that the perspective of the poor can be incorporated into a participant's world view. An immersion has an intensity and a sustainable quality that reduces the barriers of previous isolation and past assumptions. Transformation can, of course, never be assured, but initial learnings suggest that significant individual behavioral change regularly occurs.

Theological educators may ask why a greater proportion of our time and energy are not devoted to participatory and dialogical encounters with persons of faith struggling with the conditions of the modern world. Which of our courses would be more effective for transformation if we changed the place where they occur? The same question no doubt applies to educational programs of local congregations. What would change if the seminary introductory course on theology or the meeting of the board of trustees considering the church budget could take place in a shelter house for the poor or a rehabilitation center? If the non-poor do not raise profoundly and consistently the importance of the place of our education and ministry, the transformation the Gospel calls for will continue to evade us.

B. Situations of Vulnerability

Being vulnerable was the condition initially the most resisted and ultimately the most highly prized by theological educators in the Pilot Immersion Project experiences. As non-poor persons who enjoy the privilege of choice, most faculty members have a great deal of control over the educational process. Within limits, the rhythm of educational encounters, both in individual courses and in institutions, are under faculty direction. Faculty choose the content and methodology of their courses and research, and monitor accessibility of students and colleagues to their most carefully guarded possession, time. Faculty evaluate students and frequently give spiritual and vocational direction. It is no surprise, therefore, that a location for theological education that severely limits or even removes control is threatening.

Theological educators in immersion experiences often resist one of the basic premises of the program—being under the guidance of overseas or national partners whom they do not know and whom they are asked to trust with their education, health, and safety. The resulting loss of control introduces a sense of vulnerability not normally at the heart of the theological enterprise. Reflections by immersion teams regularly reveal the levels of anxiety and resistance involved in placing oneself in the midst of a ministry seeking justice that at least appears dangerous, whether that ministry is on the Cape Flats in South Africa, the shanty towns of Peru, or the mountains of Negros Oriental in the Philippines. The "place" of transforming education is in vulnerable dependency on those sisters and brothers of faith who are among the poor and oppressed within their own society.

It is precisely this dimension of risk which provides the opportunity for educational breakthroughs. The sense of danger and vulnerability for the non-poor energizes involvement in the educational enterprise and often produces a desire to investigate new alternatives. In evaluations of the Pilot Immersion Project, few things were more deeply appreciated by participants than the basic support and human companionship that resulted from living through the vulnerability of an experience of immersion and discovering the common bonds of humanity. Interdependence between the poor and the non-poor became a conscious reality.

Two Pilot Immersion Project seminars to Brazil illustrate the power of place and vulnerability as catalysts for change. Visiting delegations were directly confronted by the critical problems of protection of the environment and access and use of land. Like many areas of the developing world, the state of Para in the southern zone of the Amazon basin is in the midst of a war. Eighty percent of the land in Brazil is controlled by less than 3 percent of the population. Absentee owners of vast tracts of land, some the size of Connecticut or Rhode Island, often live in São Paulo, Brasilia, and Europe. They maintain ranch foremen and private armies to protect land for export crops such as cattle and lumber or for future investment. In the past two decades hundreds of thousands of people have migrated to urban centers after being driven from land where they once earned a living by subsistence agriculture or management of the forest as rubber tappers. In cities such as São Paulo the survival-driven peasants crowd into *favelas* (shanty towns) in a process of urbanization that threatens the sustainable development of all of Brazil.

The ecumenically staffed Pastoral Land Commission of the Roman Catholic

Church works with landless laborers to reverse the migration to the cities by assisting the laborers to form unions and occupy land for the sake of survival. The laborers are frequently attacked by gunmen hired by absentee landlords. The death rate among peasants and leaders of peasant unions has risen so dramatically that fresh graves of victims cover a good portion of the cemetery in a little village such as Rio Maria. Visitors are shocked not only by the violence but also by a slash-and-burn approach to the land that has left hundreds of thousand of acres of charred stumps in place of a once magnificent rain forest. Slash and burn was first employed on a massive scale by owners of large tracts. Invading peasants who adopted the practice on a very small scale now find themselves subject to police action and fines for "destroying the rain forest." Brazil is embroiled in two land wars. One is about access to land for peasant farmers and the livelihood of thousands of indigenous Brazilians who once lived in the forest. The other, at the heart of the eco-crisis, is about the decimation of the rain forest which could deprive the entire world of a forest that sustains the world's oxygen.

No visitor comes away unmoved from a visit to Para or by meetings with pastors such as Ricardo and José, who have become the prophetic voices for human and environmental rights. Pastor José told a Pilot Immersion Project team of educators of his accompaniment of his people in the exile from their land as the primary task of his ministry. He asked the team,"How can the land owners and their representatives be seen as neighbors to be loved by the farmers or by those of you from the North who are also injured by reckless exploitation of the land?" A member of the team asked José how he was prepared for this kind of pastoral ministry. Pastor José explained that during his formal theological education, he spent every alternate term living with and learning from people in some of the poorest and most marginalized areas of Brazil. José shared that he felt extremely vulnerable, was often terrified, and was transformed by his experiences with the people. When his class returned to the seminary from field ministry, substantial portions of the course work in the next term were shaped by questions raised by students and their people. Faculty organized their scholarly resources and their own pastoral experiences to explore with students problems posed by student field experiences.

This action/reflection paradigm for theological education involved faculty as well as students who walked with their pastoral charges. Ongoing faculty research was shaped by fundamental questions of Christ and culture. Leonardo Boff affirmed this model of education when he described to the seminary teams the process by which his own experience as a pastor and theological teacher was shaped—through his regular presence among the poor of Brazil. According to Boff, theology must emerge from the underside of history and from the center of the global eco-crisis and be built into the very rhythm and ethos of theological education.

If theological educators genuinely want transforming education, they must seek ways of heightening the degree of risk and vulnerability for participants when designing educational events. By contrast, the normative pattern of most theological education is to increase the level of security for teacher and student alike. Basic questions raised by the Pilot Immersion Project are whether security is always theologically appropriate and whether insistence on security reflects a lack of trust by theological educators in the power of conversion which can be found in communities of faith that have taken seriously Jesus' admonition: "Those who try to make their life secure will lose it, but those who lose their life will keep it" (Luke 17:33, *NRSV*). Immersion experiences with high levels of vulnerability not only result in appreciation for the educational consequences but are extremely attractive for many ministerial candidates who find current theological education inadequate and verging on the irrelevant. It will be difficult, demanding, and costly to restructure theological education so that vulnerability and immersion which are so important for transformation are built into its life. In an attempt to make a global perspective integral to the ethos of theological education in their institutions, however, several schools have already instituted and others are exploring required and regular experiences of vulnerable immersion for students accompanied by faculty.

The vision of the God of life held by courageous leaders involved in human rights and land conflicts in Brazil motivated immersion participants to seek alliances with prophetic ministries of justice in North America and to link concretely the Pilot Immersion Project's international and local immersions. The authenticity of proclamations of faith, especially those of the non-poor, will be judged on the basis of those with whom we stand. Jesus' own criterion of whether his followers have cared for "the least of these" seems especially applicable to the Church in North America. The love of God and neighbor may well be measured by the "place" in which preparation for ministry occurs and the places where the Church stands and acts on issues of global justice.

III. The Players in Transformative Education

As we seek to deepen our love of God and neighbor, those we consider our teachers or our partners in the community of learning—the players—will determine the nature and purpose of theological education as much as its place. We propose that the faithful poor, those who bring diverse perspectives to the dialogue, and those who support transformation, are critical players in the move toward a global justice approach to theological education.

A. The Poor

One of the principal learnings of the Pilot Immersion Project is that the most important teachers of a justice orientation are the poor themselves. Of all the persons whom participants met in the international and local immersion experiences, individuals and communities of those who considered themselves economically poor as well as politically and socially powerless became the most important instructors about faith, love, hope, and education for ministry. Participants repeatedly confirmed that the most memorable and motivating experiences were with oppressed people of faith struggling not just to survive but to realize visions of dignity and renewal that would reshape their communities. This consensus was held by immersion teams which also met with international political leaders, corporate executives, scholars, and religious leaders.

International or local immersions for the sake of justice are inadequate unless they encompass an exposure to the self-conscious work of communities of faith seeking to implement the Reign of God. Experiments in immersion education which merely expose students and faculty to overwhelming illustrations of injustice can in fact enervate and disable theological education and the justice ministry of the Church. The absence of an applied vision for redressing poverty and injustice often reinforces distorted images held by the non-poor whose dominant ideology of Western superiority stereotypes minorities and the poor as lazy or corrupt and unable to direct their own governance.

The Pilot Immersion Project has been blessed by overseas and local partners who are implementing concrete strategies for a more just, sustainable, and peaceful society from a perspective of faith and hope in a God of justice. Immersion participants met with Ruth Masuko, a founder of the Imbali Rehabilitation Project, who gave her life to countering the economic, social, and political consequences of apartheid. Participants were brought by Ruth and other South Africans to a more in-depth understanding, articulation, and advocacy of the needs of colleagues in Southern Africa. The poor women who organize cooperative community kitchens in Lima's shanty towns are also powerful teachers. Their vision of a more abundant life energizes them to develop concrete models to redress the injustices of discrimination which undergird the poverty of indigenous Peruvians and women. Seminar participants exposed to these persons of faith in South Africa and Peru were motivated to launch new relationships with colleagues of vision in their own urban and rural ghettoes who seek to counter the devastating effects of racism and discrimination in North America.

These teachers of faith and vision are consistently empowered by a biblical vision of a reversal, a restructuring of the social, economic, and political relations of the peoples of God and of God's creation. For them the center of the good news of the Gospel is God's vulnerable, self-emptying, incarnational act; God in Jesus Christ bears their suffering and humanity. God's identification with society's poor and marginalized is not hypothetical; it is at the very core of their daily lives. Is it therefore so strange in the logic of the Gospel that the poor should be the principal teachers of the non-poor who have inherited the mantle of the rich and powerful?

The encounter between the poor and the non-poor must be direct, personal, and sustained. Talking, eating, and living with those who suffer usually reveals the injustice of the suffering and perhaps far more important, the strength, the resources, and the gifts of the poor as they endure or challenge their own poverty and oppression. Immersion experiences from India to Appalachia have led to the discovery of a richness of human spirit and an integrity of community that are often lacking in privileged and protected circles of faith among the non-poor. The love of and trust in God expressed in the liturgy and life of vision-oriented poor communities are simple but profound. Marginalized communities of faith appear to generate a capacity to share and to express the love of neighbor even in their extension of hospitality to the visiting sojourner that puts to shame the meager attempts by the non-poor to share their abundance of resources.

The authors, along with William Kennedy, have previously raised the concept of a "controlling ideology" which functions with ideas, images, and theories to block social change as compared to a "liberating ideology" which can actually mobilize people for social reconstruction.[18] The globalization of theological education demands critical scrutiny of captivity to controlling ideologies. Our teachers among the poor, as experienced in immersion events of the Pilot Immersion Project, suggest that the privileges enjoyed by the non-poor are not only unmerited but are acquired through the benefits of economic, political, and social systems that exploit marginalized persons and block their role as participants in our communities. These privileges are enshrined in much of theological education, most of our churches, and throughout our society. An immersion experience which challenges the controlling ideology of "deserved privileges" often results in a call for the redress of inequity and injustice by the distribution of many resources held primarily by the non-poor. Redistribution of power and assurance of the necessities for survival are to be understood as acts of justice, not of mercy, acts demanded by our teachers, the poor, and required by God.

B. A Diversity of Voices

During overseas and local immersions, an essential element in the design of the Pilot Immersion Project was the commitment to be attuned to a diversity of voices. Evaluations of the international and local immersions consistently confirmed the value of encountering diverse and articulate voices from a variety of perspectives on important issues.[19] In South Africa, for example, it is as important to have dialogue with a broad diversity of political leaders as with a variety of church leaders when discussing issues such as distribution of land and amnesty for political crimes. Board members of South Africa's largest corporations and the leaders of labor unions are essential voices for comprehending the critical analysis of a leading economist from the university. A serious investment in exposure to diversity is not simply because the different players have important perspectives on an issue. They bring to the dialogue experience, memory, and hopes that are as important as the issue itself. Exposure to the non-poor who exercise control over and benefit from unjust systems also challenges immersion participants to evaluate their own role as the non-poor in North American society. Objective self-analysis is a critical step in liberation from the bonds of controlling ideology.

As Pilot Immersion Project staff, the authors sought to expose participants to a diversity of international voices; we deemed it equally important that the participants themselves represented diverse constituencies. Each international seminar was composed of teams from three to four institutions representing different theological perspectives. The vast majority of participants gave very positive evaluations of living and working intensively with those whose faith perspectives had often been treated as theological barriers. New levels of understanding and appreciation for theological traditions other than one's own resulted in some participants from quite diverse traditions establishing strong bonds of mutual appreciation and support. Project consultants observed that inter-school relationships of the seminaries with which they worked were directly affected through local immersions constructed on an ecumenical and cooperative basis with other institutions and parishes representing Evangelicals, mainline Protestants, and Roman Catholics. Strengthened alliances are shaping future cooperation between institutions. Some of the emerging partnerships would have been virtually inconceivable at the beginning of the project. Globalization as justice is based on bonds, not barriers. As many participants broke down stereotypes of other traditions within North America, they also became more open to learning from diverse international perspectives.

For North American theological education to become global, under-represented constituencies, whether the majority voices of women or the minority voices of African Americans, Latinos, Native Peoples, and Asians must also be heard from within the faculty, board, administration, and student body. Several of the articles in this volume, including those by Susan Brooks Thistlethwaite, Eleanor Scott Meyers, and Mortimer Arias, make this point emphatically. During a workshop on globalization, Canadian seminary faculty members identified without much difficulty the necessity to change the composition of faculty that contained no women or persons of color. An objection was raised that in the present economic crisis and with no imminent retirements, there was no way to address the problem. One colleague in the discussion made an obvious but shocking proposal: "If we are serious about the implications of globalized theological education, some members of our faculty must resign. With the aid of colleagues, those who resign should seek appointments in sections of the Church where our voices are needed." Although few faculty state the issue so boldly, many believe it is unconscionable to continue to assert that globalization is a priority while faculties and boards of trustees refuse to insist on diversity within their own bodies.

Here again our partners overseas become our teachers in the community of learning as they seek in limited but symbolic numbers of institutions to make essential changes in the composition of their faculties to include indigenous persons. Boards of trustees and student bodies have similar mandates for diversity. One particular institution in South Africa, for example, had been struggling with questions of academic standards which continue to deny access to black candidates who have demonstrated leadership capacity but have poor school records. A sustained debate with the university administration finally achieved a breakthrough when administrators acknowledged that the apartheid system had impoverished so-called Bantu education to the extent that it was impossible to make judgments about scholarship or a student's potential for ministry solely on the grounds of academic record. The institution began to seek other credentials more essential to leadership in questions of faith and life. New admission policies were combined with a commitment to raise additional scholarship funds, the seed money for which was provided by the personal funds of individual faculty members and finally matched by Church and academic bodies. The faculty also made a commitment to change the time, content, and style of the teaching and learning dynamic to make these more suitable to a more diverse student body. Experiments to enhance diversity are underway in some institutions in Africa, Asia, and Latin America where there is far less economic flexibility than in North America.

The new composition of faculties and student bodies will finally depend on a critical mass of decision makers committed to shifting priorities in the face of the constraints of history and economics. Where, then, does the support come from for such difficult and courageous decisions?

C. Communities of Support

The biblical vision of the Reign of God which calls for a restructuring of the relations between the people of God radically challenges the status quo. A community of support can provide the foundation for the players in transformative education to risk making significant changes. Three dimensions of support seem to be important for transformation: representative constituencies; learning covenants; and "waves" of catalytic experiences. While these dimensions may be applicable to many forms of individual and institutional change, they seem particularly important for sustaining the radical transformation required to pursue global justice.

1. Representative Constituencies

Transformation will not occur apart from the Church for which seminaries are preparing men and women for ministry. The design of the Pilot Immersion Project called for the immersion teams to include representatives from the church constituency of each seminary. These representatives, including trustees, who have special concern for the complications and the possibilities of institutional change, bring important perspectives to the discussion. The project design also called for faculty, administrators, students, and trustees to be involved at every stage of the project from approval of the project application to the establishment of goals and strategies for globalization, participation in international and local immersion experiences, and the evaluation and development of strategic plans for globalization. The power of these constituencies in the decision-making process varies from institution to institution. However, the support of all four seminary constituencies plus the presence of the Church, is necessary if globalization as justice is to become part of an institution's ethos. The daunting roles that the Church and seminary need to play in contributing to a more just, sustainable, and peaceful world community are impossible without the commitment of both to prepare men and women to be agents of change.

In North American seminaries individual faculty members committed to issues of global justice have often been marginalized. The direct involvement of a critical mass of decision makers is essential if institutional change for the sake of justice is to be widely supported. One goal of the project for an average size seminary was to involve a majority of the faculty and principal administrators in the four immersion events, with participants representing the pluralism of the institution in academic fields, gender, and race. A broad base of support is crucial for implementing new, even "counter cultural," patterns and programs. While the project involved a critical mass of faculty and administration in several institutions, the size of the project limited the number of trustee and student representatives. Even with limited representation, however, several boards of trustees and student bodies have proposed and initiated global justice events and programs that had not existed prior to the Pilot Immersion Project.

2. Learning Covenants

At the end of each immersion seminar, each participant was asked to write a learning covenant of application. The covenant identified the implications this global experience would have for: a) the individual's lifestyle, such as one's personal discipline of prayer or attention to patterns of consumption; b) institutional changes, such as the development of new course bibliographies, fresh approaches to teaching or research, or support for more global perspectives in professional guilds; and c) public policy issues at a national level. The participants selected covenant partners to support them for no less than one year and to provide appropriate accountability including forgiveness and renewal if their covenants were not met. In addition to individual covenants, most teams fashioned a school learning covenant at the conclusion of each immersion experience.

Direct exposure to the immensity of global injustices in Africa, Asia, and Latin America can be overwhelming and disempowering. When the non-poor return to comfortable middle-class communities in North America and are no longer directly confronted by injustices, it is possible to rationalize concrete responses to injustice as unimportant or ineffective. Research on the project indicates that one of the most effective means of sustaining the learning and providing support for continued response to issues of global justice is the simple process of covenants. Learning contracts ritually bind participants to the consequences of their learning as they respond in gratitude to their new teachers and partners in the learning experience.

3. Wave Theory

A third important element supporting change is based on a "wave" theory in the approach to institutional change. While this theory is applicable to any kind of institutional change, it seems particularly important to the cultural or values transformation required to pursue globalization as justice.

Each pilot institution participated in four immersion seminars conducted in a series of "waves." The first immersion team played a role in orientation and preparation of the second team. Not surprisingly, the second team of participants had clearer expectations, were generally better prepared, and had a more focused agenda. This was also true of the third international immersion team. By the time the energy and one-year covenants of application of one group were coming to an end, the next team almost invariably returned from its immersion experience with a commitment to support the work of colleagues from the previous round. As one consultant reflected, the momentum for globalization amounted to more than the sum of the four-part immersions. This exponential factor widened and deepened the base of support. Over time the values of globalization as justice are being incorporated in new mission statements that have reappropriated justice as a value of the seminary tradition. As another consultant noted, it is becoming difficult to touch any subject in the seminary without issues of global justice being raised.

The effect of the immersions in "waves" re-emphasizes the importance of an initial catalytic experience of vulnerability in an alternative environment with new partners in a learning community. Even though the immersions were in different continents and participants were exposed to different local issues, a consistency of theologically informed issues of global justice united the teams. For many participants, the result was a bonding not only with overseas partners and hosts and members of their own immersion team but also with colleagues at home who had shared comparable experiences. The "systems wave catalytic intervention theory" of institutional change which developed from the Pilot Immersion Project is analyzed in greater detail by David Roozen in Chapter 11.

The task now facing many institutions is sustaining the momentum initiated by globalization experiments spawned during the past decade. Each of the twelve institutions in the Pilot Immersion Project, as well as numerous seminaries which are independently exploring models of globalization, are facing questions of strategic long-range plans to institutionalize their learnings. How can institutions anchor the tentative bridges to globalization that span the barriers to both change and globalization? Deep, consistent, and broadly based cognitive reflection on the meaning of globalization is a valuable prelude and constant companion in the process of integrating a global perspective into the ethos of an institution. We are convinced, however, that we cannot think our way into a new paradigm; we must live it.

Transformation for global justice requires a regular relocation of the *place* of theological education to international and local communities of faith who in the midst of their suffering have a strong vision of the Reign of God. This place for theological education is staffed by women and men, primarily laity, representing voices often silenced or ignored in traditional theological education. Our seminaries and churches must come to see these new players as our teachers and partners in a learning community which focuses on the love of God and neighbor. Relocation will be both dynamic and conflictual. The vision of globalization as justice must be implemented in the midst of economic constraints and historical limitations. Communities of support and accountability within the Church, faculty, administration, student body, and boards can provide bridges out of our isolation and the encouragement to consolidate initial exploratory steps.

IV. The Perspectives of Transformative Education

Paulo Freire, first in his writings and more recently in his role as superintendent of education in São Paulo, perhaps the largest school district in the world, has worked in Brazil for the transformation of education for the sake of liberation. Freire's leadership in the creation of a public school program of education for human rights illustrates his efforts to re-think systemically the educational encounter. Freire demands that educators consider the relationship between education and power. His emphasis is on the position or perspective from which one not only views but encounters power. Freire believes that educators committed to liberation and who pursue a "question-posing" form of education (in contrast with those who engage in "banking education" which maintains an oppressive status quo[20]) must look at the "underside" of power in a process that calls for re-inventing power along with reorganizing education.[21] With a similar emphasis Dietrich Bonhoeffer inspired many Christians to think about Christology "from below." One of the learnings from the Pilot Immersion Project is the importance of the perspective one takes for empowering persons for reconciliation with justice in the churches, nations, and world in which we are called to minister.

Experiences during two pilot immersions in the Philippines helped shape our learnings about perspectives of theological education. Fr. John serves in one of the most militarized zones in the central islands of the Philippines. He is a recent graduate of a Filipino seminary aligned with the poor and oppressed of rural and urban areas. Limited transportation caused our groups, as it regularly did Fr. John, to walk the steep mountain paths in order to meet with the parishioners to whom he was assigned. His first priority was to assure that his people had sufficient basic necessities of life to survive with dignity. His ministry involved establishing and maintaining programs for sustainable food production, health clinics, and elementary schools. Fr. John's advocacy for his people's material, spiritual, and cultural needs gained the respect of local church leaders, island human rights advocates, and both government and insurgency representatives with whom he had cooperative relationships.

The parish liturgy of music, dance, and drama was one of the most moving in which many of us had ever participated. Elements of the service juxtaposed the peoples' faith and hope in God with the constant harassment and occasional torture and death which came as a result of their being trapped between warring insurgents and unrestrained government military forces. The villagers' worship and Bible study revealed a simple but profound understanding of the Gospel that sustained and empowered them. Nothing in their location or lifestyle reflected anything but powerlessness, yet they lived as a constantly re-empowered community of faith. Their priest's humble, confident ministry from the underside was an essential component in the people's empowerment and dignity.

When questioned about how he came to this form of ministry, Fr. John described himself as coming from an upper-middle-class, well-to-do Filipino family with very little exposure to either the rural or urban poverty that plagued his country. In his words his "conversion," which was not dramatic as much as it was persistent, occurred during his seminary education in Manila. Mornings were spent in the classroom for at least a portion of the year. The most formative part of his theological education, however, came from the time he spent living with people in the shanty towns and on the streets of Manila. His seminary classroom instructors were his daily partners in ministry to the city. Fr. John said he learned about reading the Bible through the eyes of the poor, not primarily from formal courses in scripture but rather from his teachers doing Bible study with Christians primarily in the slums and occasionally in the suburbs among the wealthy parishes of Manila.

The content of Fr. John's formal studies was shaped by the questions – biblical, theological, sociological, psychological, political, and economic – that arose from the problems the people faced. Living with the people provided the base from which he came to view the world and his ministry. This modest parish pastor became a powerful teacher for two groups of North American educators by sharing with us the life of the people of God whom he was called to serve. A student in one of the immersion teams asked whether a mission such as Fr. John's was the only faithful ministry in the Philippines. Fr. John was quick to declare his belief that people are called by God to different tasks. In the Philippines or North America, he reflected, the more challenging ministry may be a nurturing and prophetic role with the parishes of the suburbs or with land owners. Globalization as justice in an increasingly interdependent and unequal world will require seminary graduates and faculty to be in ministry of transforming education for the non-poor as well as in ministry with the poor.

Through strong memories of this experience in the mountains, we continue to be in dialogue with Fr. John in the struggle to follow a biblical vision of conversion which realigns the relationship of the non-poor to the poor and to God and challenges a perspective of theological education shaped by the non-poor in North America. Themes important for responding to this challenge are sufficiency, solidarity, and emancipation.

A. Sufficiency

International immersion teams encountered programs of theological seminaries and churches in Africa, Asia, and Latin America which followed the criteria of sufficiency. These programs were based on an understanding that access to the basic necessities of life for all human beings is a biblical mandate articulated by the Old Testament prophets and reiterated in the Gospels and the Epistles. Many of our international partners asked how one could live in light of the Gospel with glaring inequalities. Their own response was through ministries which sought to address issues of sufficiency through the provision of food, shelter, health care, basic education, and opportunities for emancipation. An understanding of globalization as justice is to make this mandate clear in word and action through transformative theological education.

There is, of course, the danger of being so overwhelmed with the demands of sufficiency in the mountains of the Philippines or the streets of Harlem that one is paralyzed. We are tempted to do increasingly critical analysis of the problems while taking no action because the problems are "impossible to solve." Another danger is to make human suffering private by addressing the problems of an individual or a family or even a congregation without acknowledging the unjust systems from which the poor suffer and the non-poor benefit. A goal of the Pilot Immersion Project is for participants to be able to *personalize* human suffering. Personalization involves empathizing with the pain of victims of injustice rather than blaming victims for their suffering. For the non-poor, personalization can lead to accepting some responsibility for continued participation in systems that sustain poverty and dehumanize our neighbors. Globalization as justice calls each of the principal theological disciplines to pursue the issue of personal responsibility for the human suffering which results from unjust structures.

As immersion team members returned to North America and wrestled with the vision of sufficiency, many asked whether more equitable sharing of the world's resources was a priority in their own schools and communities of faith. Many agreed, however, that there needs to be a shift in the very content of theological education itself, in experience and focus, if North Americans are to respond to the request of our partners struggling with issues of sufficiency in the South or two-thirds world. Most agreed that while a number of seminaries and churches have changed their portfolios regarding investment in South Africa, there is a significant absence of critical social, economic, or political analysis within their educational curricula. There was seldom time or motivation for faculty or students to face the problems of insufficiency and inequity that resulted in the human suffering and oppression that the teams saw on a regional and global scale.

In response to these concerns, teams of faculty and students involved in globalization programs have begun to construct courses that combine socio-political analysis and direct encounter with perspectives of the poor in North American urban and rural areas. Many of these new courses are interdisciplinary and central so that critical questions of sufficiency are not limited to elective courses on the fringes of the curriculum.

William Kennedy has described a kind of "restlessness" with structures of inequality and injustice that exists within virtually every one of the faculties and student bodies connected with the Pilot Immersion Project. Incorporation of globalization as justice does not remove the restlessness but sustains it and understands it as divine restlessness which is a gift of the grace of God. The introduction or extension of critical social and political analysis is essential for a more adequate curriculum in light of the demands of globalization as justice. However, analysis alone will be ineffective and unconvincing to our partners or ourselves without following our conclusions with concrete commitments from our institutions.

While seminaries have little immediate power to address issues of insufficiency, they can effectively contribute, for example, through restructuring endowment policies and revising educational approaches. Students in one project seminary who listened to the poor and analyzed structures in their urban community asked why seminary resources were not invested in local projects and banks. The escalating cost of the residential model of seminary education also works against the vision of sufficiency and equity. North American seminary education is increasingly limited to those who are wealthy or those willing to incur crippling debts. Theological education by extension and distance education programs being developed in Latin America and Africa provide models for seminaries and churches to address questions of cost and accessibility.

Recent educational patterns reveal increasing distance between critical reflective preparation and experiential based action. Serious attention to issues of global justice requires that reflection/action/reflection models of education need to be given new centrality in theological education. Adjusting our current curriculum to this kind of model will take creative redesign of courses. The case study "Evangelicals in a New Key" illustrates the attempts of faculty to redesign courses in light of the criterion of justice. Two of the schools in the Pilot Immersion Project have developed plans to give faculty members released time in order to develop new courses. Unless seminaries and congregations are prepared to recognize the energy and time required for the creation of new models of teaching and learning, serious attention to the biblical mandate for sufficiency will remain at the level of rhetoric not action.

B. Solidarity

Implementation of solidarity which bridges fundamental divisions between peoples requires attention to the question of power. History confirms that the simple transfer of power from the oppressor to the oppressed does not necessarily assure mutuality. Just as sufficiency and equality demand equitable distribution of resources, solidarity and mutuality require new perspectives on power. Larry Rasmussen, a seminary coordinator for the Pilot Immersion Project, reflects on this matter in "Jesus and Power."[22] Rasmussen sees power as always being relational, and, similar to a controlling ideology, power usually seeks to be "calculatedly nonmutual." As Rasmussen reminds us, human beings "seek maximum influence on the other with minimum influence upon ourselves." We exercise power "competitively and adversarially with the aim of mastery or control."[23] However, the biblical image of power is the distinctive power of God, which may be present in weakness in order to banish powerlessness. The biblical idea of power is characterized by mutuality rather than sovereignty. According to Rasmussen, the result is not "mastery, but meeting" which is marked by an understanding of shared power. There is a reciprocal relationship between two subjects which is not of "distance and domination, but rather intimacy, vulnerability, and exchange." Jesus represents the model of empowerment for, as Rasmussen reminds us, the "great charismatic leader is precisely the one who can enter into the pain of the people and articulate it, calling up for the people themselves powers of healing and change they did not know they had."[24]

Participants in the Pilot Immersion Project experienced shared power in base Christian communities in Latin America, in the "Standing for the Truth" campaign in South Africa, and in peasants' liberation movements in the Philippines. These models of ministry illustrate Rasmussen's insights:

> The reign of God requires a new understanding of power that rests unequivocally on trust in God, a total dependence on God's care and mercy as the ultimate foundation, not only of security but of life itself. Strangely enough, power is rightly exercised only when it empowers others to maximize their humanity. Power is not in holding but in relinquishing. This view of power from below measures its effectiveness in terms of service rendered not service acquired. This power is shared with love and seeks the wholeness, humanization, and emancipation of the neighbor.[25]

An understanding of globalization as justice challenges North American theological educators to adopt a radically different perspective of power within our institutions and the communities which we serve. If international and local immersion experiences have brought new insight to our understanding of power, it will be necessary to reevaluate the implications of shared power between students and faculty in the design of courses and in the evaluation of academic work. What would mutuality bring to the relationship between faculties, administrators, and boards of trustees in terms of workloads and committee assignments? What would it mean for the poor of the South to participate in decision making about the use of theological resources controlled by the non-poor in the North? The self-conscious "re-invention" of power in theological education, both reflected upon and acted out, holds important potential for achieving a global perspective with a biblical bias toward those who are poor and powerless.

C. Emancipation

The concept of liberation or emancipation was pervasive in each of the project immersions. There was general agreement among participants about the need for liberation from poverty and discrimination based on race, gender, and age that captivates both oppressed and oppressors. Emancipation became highly controversial, however, when participants discussed strategy. Which struggle has priority? To what degree, if any, is any form of violence justified in bringing about liberation? What limits are appropriate for tactics that seek to bring about emancipation from the control of a political, economic, or religious authority? In light of the domination of the seminary and the Church in North America by the non-poor, participants reflected regularly about emancipation from our own controlling ideologies of domination and superiority that have been so thoroughly a part of our socialization process.

Several immersion teams met with Brazilian educator Paulo Freire and some of his disciples who have been acting out of a new perspective on reality articulated in Freire's book *The Politics of Education.*[26] An analysis of this perspective is contained in the Introduction by Henry Giroux: "Central to Freire's politics and pedagogy is a philosophical vision of a liberated humanity . . . [achieved] by combining a dynamic of critique and collective struggle with a philosophy of hope."[27]

Freire is convinced that a process of conversion or transformation cannot occur unless it contains "emancipatory possibilities." The roots of the word "emancipate" can be traced to ancient Roman law. *Emancipare* meant to free slaves, children, or women from bondage so they could participate in the benefits of society from which they had been excluded. A contemporary, holistic understanding of emancipation, used by both Freire and ourselves, implies freedom for both the poor and non-poor from bondages that neither fully recognizes. These are bonds of bias, position, and perspective.

Theological education, in its struggle to incorporate globalization as justice, must be willing to take seriously the need for emancipation or at least a loosening of the chains of the non-poor, Western, male perspective that has dominated North American education and ministry. Many theological educators are reevaluating and rewriting their institutional mission statements. In the process they have come to a new analysis of the needs of North American culture and are questioning the seminary's role in proclaiming and witnessing to Christ in that culture. Seeing Christ as the Emancipator requires not only a new statement of mission, but a new embodiment of mission. The Pilot Immersion Project and other experiments in the globalization of theological education will ultimately be tested by the commitments and values that seminary graduates embody. One test of an integral global justice perspective will be whether or not graduates can be emancipated from the controlling ideology of Western domination to become agents of change within their churches and communities.

Effectiveness of globalization programs will also be measured by the degree to which clergy and lay leaders can empower those within local congregations to face the challenges of an interdependent global community and respond with energy to biblical demands for sufficiency, solidarity, and emancipation. The embodiment of globalization as justice cannot be undertaken, however, without recognizing the enormous power of the controlling ideology of the non-poor to resist individual and institutional changes that call for "intimacy, vulnerability and exchange."[28] Emancipation is a daunting task, but not an impossible one, which will take patience, persistence, and dependence on God's grace.

V. Conclusion

The urgency for change in theological education depends on the degree to which change is required for graduates to function effectively and faithfully in an increasingly interdependent and threatened global community. Competent preparation for that ministry may require significant re-ordering of priorities in theological seminaries. Numerous critical analyses emphasize the need for more astute social and economic understanding of culture. The failure to address the systemic needs of God's children who are poor and marginalized has become a pressing agenda in the theological debate of virtually every region of the world. The question is sometimes "why," but it is far more frequently "how" such a change in emphasis can occur which gives priority to ministries which address the needs of the poor. The rhetoric for such a paradigm shift in seminary education lacks credibility without a concrete change in the ethos of an institution including curriculum, worship, composition of faculty and student body, investment policy, and the placement of students. Adding a special course or program or focusing part of the core curriculum on justice, global evangelism, or cross-cultural concerns does not alter the basic stance of ministry of the seminary graduate. If one agrees with the premise of the need for change, then making a global perspective integral requires a substantive shift by a strong community of decision makers in a seminary.

One of the most persistent topics of discussion among project participants has been the concept of community. Few contrasts were more startling for participants in the international and local immersions than the absence of a sense of empowering community within their seminaries when contrasted to the sense of community in many of the organizations and agencies that are described in the case studies and articles in this volume. The kind of time seminary communities spend together may actually inhibit possibilities for developing bonds of community. One of the immersion participants expressed this thought in a most dramatic way, saying that he learned more about the faith and theology of his faculty colleagues in a three-week international immersion experience than he had during the past three years in his institution. Despite complaints about endless hours spent in faculty meetings and seminary committees which may also involve trustees and students — time invested in the logistics and management of the institution — we actually have very little time together to strengthen bonds with one another and with the people of God whom we are called to serve.

While virtually every seminary faculty with which we have worked has complained about a "lack of community," most attempts to address that lack have been ineffective. However, immersion experiences have had an important bonding effect for many of the participants. The quality and intensity of the time spent together may be much more important than its magnitude. The bonds of community can develop when participants are "placed" in a radically different environment and are dependent on communities which live out their faith in the emancipating Gospel of Jesus Christ. As explored in the section on "players," a seminary which understands globalization as justice must enlist the poor as teachers and partners in the learning community and endorse the importance of a diversity of voices within the seminary as well as within the communities which it serves. Immersion experiences that begin to build a community of support and accountability may be essential prerequisites for seminaries that seek to undertake significant changes which challenge the dominant patterns of theological education.

The discovery and nurture of an enabling community of support may require faculties to share one of our most precious possessions and significant powers — our time. Faculty, administrators, and students may also have to sacrifice or at least partially relinquish the personal agendas of scholarship and ministry that have increasingly shaped our lives. The quality of community that we often confess we lack may be a critical component in bringing about the institutional changes required to modify the place, players, and perspectives of theological education in North America.

We believe that seminaries, through experiments in globalization during the last decade, have taken small but important steps in the right direction. It is essential for educators to be reminded that complete trust in God and the standards of the Reign of God's justice are consistent with the re-invention of power. Our seminaries are called to rediscover this underside of history. Trust in God literally empowers one to risk her or his own life and commitment in a pattern contrary to the conforming pressures of society. Confidence in God's trustworthiness allows us to take whatever risks we do for the sake of globalization as justice.

Several of the authors in this volume have returned to the idea of community as critical to the globalization of theological education. We affirm that direction. In assuming our roles as coordinators of the Pilot Immersion Project, we envisioned linking seminaries and friends in the North about whom we cared deeply with the revitalization of community and the shared power for renewal we had experienced with partners in Asia, Africa, and Latin America. This vision has in great measure been realized.

However, it would be a mistake to suggest that individual transformation, institutional change, or community is predominantly a rational matter that can progress along paths of carefully designed implementation. Genuine community is always an experience of *communitas*.[29] Community and transformation are not material possessions that can be "created." Community and conversion are gifts from God which we can only seek and celebrate. Globalization as justice will never occur in a hierarchical or authoritarian way; it is ultimately egalitarian and reciprocal in nature. Both community and the process of conversion retain an element of mystery that will fortunately always remain beyond our control and comprehension. For us, transformation of mission and ministry and the genuine community that supports them always reflect the transpersonal embodiment of God's grace that seeks justice and reconciliation for all.

CASE STUDY[30]

Evangelicals in a New Key

Something new was going on at Mission Evangelical Seminary, and Paulo was gratified that he might be playing a role. During a conversation in his book-lined faculty office, Professor Wes Whitman had encouraged Paulo to apply their semester-long exegesis of Galatians to Paulo's own Latin American context. Not only that, but Paulo had learned that Professor Whitman had redesigned his parables course to focus on Jesus' ministry to the poor of his time and to the implications of this ministry for the traditional emphasis of the seminary on worldwide evangelism. While these changes might have been anticipated in light of Professor Whitman's first experience in Latin America, Paulo was surprised by their swiftness. Professor Whitman had only had one month to change his courses following a three-week study trip to Peru. Perhaps Paulo had to reconsider his judgments about the relevance of his education at Mission Evangelical Seminary to his own Latin American context. He wondered whether Mission Evangelical Seminary would be able to change to a more relevant education both for him and for North American students. He also wondered how his paper on Galatians might fit into his own vocational plans. After all, he had accompanied Professor Whitman on this immersion experience and with him had been deeply affected by the unspeakable poverty of the people in Lima's shanty towns and the caring responses of several base Christian communities.

Paulo was born and raised in Venezuela, an island of relative civility in a sea of civil strife. The second son of a Protestant mother and a Roman Catholic father, Paulo had eventually gravitated to his mother's Evangelical perspective, which had been nurtured by graduates of Mission Evangelical Seminary. Raised in the piety of this tradition with its stress on evangelism and encouraged by both parents to get an education, Paulo had risen to the top of his class and decided to go North to college. He brought to the Bible college in Los Angeles and later to Mission Evangelical Seminary a deep piety, a commitment to the essential truths handed down in his tradition, and a concern for social change in Latin America developed through student activism in high school. He had never considered himself poor. There had always been basic necessities in his family, and in Venezuela there were fewer of the extremes he had encountered in Peru.

What attracted Paulo to Mission Evangelical was its preaching program, its commitment to basic evangelical truths, and its openness. He was not disappointed and in his first two years immersed himself in the disciplines he would need to be an evangelist in Latin America. He especially appreciated the freedom he had to struggle with basic biblical and theological issues.

Mission Evangelical, Paulo had come to learn, was a seminary born of the controversy between fundamentalists and religious liberals in the United States during the first half of the twentieth century. He had discovered early on that the seminary was proud of its Protestant and Evangelical roots. It was Protestant in its stress on the Bible as the norm for faith and life. It was Evangelical in its traditional emphasis on conversion, evangelism, and revelation. He liked the idea that each year faculty and staff publicly committed themselves to a statement of "the great verities and abiding fundamentals of the Christian faith." With other students he dismissed some contemporary theological perspectives as "unanchored liberalism." But he also discovered that students, faculty, and staff fit no fundamentalist or Pentecostal stereotypes; that rigid ideological and interpretive positions were disavowed; and that the seminary attracted a wide range of conservative Protestants. Paulo had concluded that Mission Evangelical stood roughly at the center of the Evangelical movement in the United States, a place where he felt comfortable.

As Paulo understood the situation, the seminary had considerable experience in the international arena with its long history in world missions. In times past this experience had been largely confined to matters of individual conversion and the transplanting of the North American experience. Changes in the mission field had in recent times begun to force an expansion of traditional ways, however. Seminary-trained missionaries and faculty from the seminary who visited them had found it increasingly difficult to overlook the massive and increasing poverty in most of the Third World and the relation of United States' policy to it. In response, a social justice dimension was gradually being added to the traditional focus on individual conversion, as in his own Venezuela.

In addition, local leaders had emerged in the mission field with increasing respect for themselves and their own particular traditions. As a result, the seminary had made several alterations in its curriculum. It had also given added consideration to how local contexts interact with its Evangelical tradition. This included a re-thinking of how experiences in the field of mission might modify the seminary's traditional emphases on revelation and piety as they had developed in the North American Evangelical context. It also included listening to "other voices," women, racial minorities, and poor people both at home and abroad.

For the most part these alterations had been confined to course modifications by individual professors and to faculty discussions, or so it seemed to Paulo. Of twenty-two members of the faculty two were women, both in Christian education, and one was African American. Women made up roughly 25 percent of the student body. Third-world students like himself were a distinct minority. The racial/ethnic make-up of the seminary was still predominantly white, reflecting Mission Evangelical's constituency.

So Paulo saw Mission Evangelical to be moving toward a new synthesis, tugged one way by its traditions, the other by new experiences at home and abroad; and not quite sure how it would all work out. He was convinced that faculty and staff wanted to work between the old and the new, but a new synthesis was still in a process of development, with ample opportunity both for fruitful dialogue and divisive conflict.

The trip to Peru with its persisting images of emaciated children in miserable shanties contrasted to a well-fed elite in amply appointed houses ended Paulo's honeymoon at Mission Evangelical. The immersion in Peru altered his perspective on the relevance of his theological education and forced a reconsideration of his vocational plans. The changes began in concrete form with an objection to an assignment in one of his courses. The assignment called for an analysis of conditions in the Third World and how they affected the United States. Paulo thought the assignment was oddly reversed. Conditions in third-world countries had little to do with the United States, thought Paulo, whereas actions by the United States government and its citizens had everything to do with the Third World. Something was wrong with the assignment and perhaps even with the relevance of his education.

Paulo took his partially developed objections to his friend, Bob Wills, a local pastor who was familiar with Mission Evangelical and its particular traditions.

"It seems to me," began Paulo, "that the seminary emphasizes academics and rationality to the neglect of the practical aspects of life. Take theology, for example. In some of our classes all we learn about is doctrine, especially its rationalistic Western development, but this knowledge is divorced from real life, especially the miserable conditions people live in throughout the world. We are given answers and abiding truths and told to fit them to life. The doctrines and truths seem to have little basis in experience and even less connection to everyday questions, in particular those being asked by the poor in Latin America."

Bob shifted uneasily in his seat. Paulo thought Bob was unsure whether to listen or to engage him in dialogue. After a moment Bob said: "I understand what you are saying. I don't think this way of doing theology is characteristic of the seminary as a whole. More important, I wonder how far you want to take your criticism. Do you want to abandon the essential truths and moral absolutes of the faith which are affirmed at the beginning of each year? Don't these affirmations transcend contexts and experience and give guidance to life? Can't the primacy of experience and context go so far that you get lost in the swamp of relativism? Are the truths of the so-called white, male tradition of the West any less true for their origins?"

"Those are tough questions which I haven't quite resolved," Paulo answered. He felt a bit tentative. "You can go too far as some liberation theologians do in my Latin American context and modern interpreters do in yours. I guess I want to take a position somewhere in between. Yes, there are truths which transcend experience and context, and yes, I think those essential truths articulated by my tradition qualify. But we have to hold what fits into this category to the essentials and constantly allow experience and context to act as critics."

"And vice versa," added Bob. "The truths of your tradition should help to judge experience and context."

"Yes, by all means," responded Paulo, now more sure of his direction. "It's a dialogue I am after. What we really need to do here at the seminary and elsewhere is to add new dimensions to the propositional truths which have characterized the tradition. When I leave the seminary I should be able to take those truths in my ministry with my brothers and sisters at home and show how they relate to their experience of poverty. I should be able to discern the essential from the unessential. The seminary hasn't done those things very well. It seems to have been too occupied with confronting liberalism in the North American context to address other contexts or how missionaries should carry the Gospel to the rest of the world. Professors like Wes Whitman are themselves just beginning to learn this. They have to re-educate themselves and there is no syllabus for the course. Maybe I can use my paper in Professor Whitman's course to refine some of these ideas.

"And another thing," Paulo went on. "The seminary doesn't attend much to spiritual and character formation. No one articulates or takes responsibility for overseeing those dimensions of life. That's strange since a rich piety is so characteristic of the Evangelical tradition."

"Are you sure of that as something the seminary should oversee?" questioned Bob, a bit puzzled by what Paulo meant. "Do you really want professors and staff standing over you and checking out your every move? Do you want them forcing their own particular spirituality and values down your throat?"

"That's putting the matter in rather extreme fashion," retorted Paulo. "To be more precise, what I would like to see is the deepening and expansion of Evangelical piety to include a concern for social justice. We need more spirituality around here and we need to link it to social concerns. One of my teachers put it well the other day. He said that our tradition has so emphasized individual salvation that we have neglected corporate spirituality and social justice. Things need a better balance. Creation and redemption are both crucial."

"That makes sense," Bob responded. "And do you think we need to apply our understanding of social justice to a critique of United States involvement in Latin America?"

"Yes, that too," answered Paulo.

Paulo concluded the conversation by reflecting on the seminary's training of missionaries. "We need to hasten the change," he argued, "from a model of transplanting to a genuine model of planting. The North American model often does not transplant, but the Gospel does. It is the Gospel which should be planted and allowed to grow as it will in a different soil and climate. Missionaries from the United States should not do things for us, but with us, in particular as we address the severe social problems of the region."

Paulo spent the next weeks thinking about his conversations with Wes and Bob. He also reflected on his own vocational plans. Since he could remember, he had thought his calling was to be an evangelist in Latin America. After the trip to Peru and his doubts about the relevance of his seminary education, he had to admit to a certain refinement of that calling. He had always been committed to the poor of his region as a focus for his ministry. The question now was how to go about his ministry. Two very clear but quite different options stood out.

The first option called for him to work directly among the poor in Christian ministry, himself taking on the condition of those with whom he ministered. The second option called for him to work from above, going on for his doctorate so he would have the tools to make the systemic changes which would get at the root causes of poverty. These were two very different options, each with its pitfalls and possibilities.

He checked in with Bob Wills again, anticipating Bob's hard questions. "The first option," he explained to Bob, "seems more authentic. You are right there with those who suffer the most. The model of Jesus is so compelling that at times all other options seem to fall short of Jesus' call to pick up the cross and follow."

"Yes," admitted Bob, "but the danger is getting lost in the trivia. You will be applying band-aids and dispensing pills, not necessarily addressing the deeper causes of suffering. You may well get consumed by the enormity of it all and become deadened to the suffering."

Paulo paused to turn these comments over in his mind and then proceeded to the second option. "By equipping myself to get at the causes, I may avoid those problems and have the opportunity to make a difference in many lives, not just a few."

"And the danger?" asked Bob.

"Well, for one," responded Paulo, "there is the danger of getting bought-off, of becoming so used to the rarified atmosphere of academic or government life that I lose my roots in the people. I become one of those whom I am now committed to change. And second, the problems of injustice and poverty in Latin America may be so intractable that I end up in a futile calling, neither creating change nor helping the people directly."

"You got it, brother," concluded Bob. "Now what are you going to do about your seminary education? Will you challenge the seminary and the faculty as a Latin Christian or keep it private? And what about your vocation? It is possible that paper in Professor Whitman's course could serve as a basis for addressing both concerns? You have taken your seminary to task for its emphasis on rationality. Now that you've done the rational thing and we've discussed it, what's next?"

TEACHING NOTE

Evangelicals in a New Key

I. Objectives

A. To reflect on the relevance of North American theological education to third-world poverty.

B. To challenge North American theological educators, especially those in the evangelical tradition, to globalize their perspectives, courses, and mission.

C. To encourage an understanding of the Evangelical tradition, including its distinctive characteristics, its emphasis on global missions, and its changing patterns.

D. To explore the vocational dilemmas of third-world students in North American seminaries.

II. Opening (15 minutes)

A. Have students describe:
   1. The characters.
   2. The situation at Mission Evangelical Seminary.
   3. Paulo's own vocational choices.

B. Isolate the important issues. These might include:
   1. The challenge of globalization to Mission Evangelical Seminary and to North American theological education.
   2. The particular dilemmas of Mission Evangelical Seminary as it relates its particular traditions to the diversity of Christianity throughout the world and the injustices experienced in mission settings.
   3. Stereotypes of education in the evangelical tradition.
   4. The establishment of a coherent, integrated model of seminary education in a pluralistic world.

5. The vocational dilemmas of third-world students and faculty as they study and teach in North American seminaries and bring a challenge to orthodox theology.

III. Globalization and the Evangelical Tradition

A. Develop a role play situation between:

1. A third-world student stating the case for globalization and attention to justice issues;

2. An Orthodox Evangelical stating the case for the received tradition, biblical orthodoxy, and individual conversion;

3. A reconciler who seeks to find the connections between orthodoxy and globalization.

B. Open discussion:

1. Summarize the tensions in the Evangelical tradition between orthodoxy and globalization.

2. Ask for "bridges."

3. Ask if Evangelicals should move toward a new synthesis, and if so, what it should look like.

4. Ask what the implications are of a new synthesis for theological education.

IV. Third-world Students and Teachers

A. Open discussion

1. How do third-world students and teachers challenge North American models of theological education?

2. What dilemmas do they face moving from their countries into the North American context?

3. What criteria would be helpful for guiding Paulo's vocational choice?

V. Closing (5 minutes)

A. List significant learnings.

COMMENTARY

Evangelicals in a New Key

W. L. HERZFELD

"Evangelicals in a New Key" is misleadingly titled. The protagonist of this contemporary parable, the theological student Paulo, is experiencing a common torment. Even changing the title to "Old Key" would fail to anchor this apparent perplexity in its timeless context. Before examining the case for its ability to focus us on our contemporary quest for relevance, let's discard the notion that it is novel—it isn't. To pretend we're dealing with a new phenomenon would only distort our ability to understand it.

Upon first reading of Paulo's dilemma I thought back a generation to the ethical quandaries and apparent non-sequiturs of my own theological education. Then I thought back to the ethical paradoxes which have plagued spiritual thought (not merely Christian) for as long as the record extends. Quite a déjà vu. In "Evangelicals in a New Key," Paulo and his supporting cast re-create a dialogue reminiscent of medieval morality plays and their multiform precursors. This modern parable invites us to examine the application of faith to life—a very evangelical act, perhaps the only evangelical act.

For us to take advantage of Paulo's crisis in order to re-engage the issue of the relevance of the Good News for ourselves, let's begin by reviewing Paulo's adventures in "Evangelicals in a New Key." Professor Wes Whitman of Mission Evangelical Seminary, having recently returned from a trip to the poverty of Peru, suggests that Paulo apply his Bible study within the context of his Latin tradition. Paulo sees this as a sign of increasing the relevance of Mission Evangelical Seminary's tradition of "evangelical truth" (concentrating on conversion, evangelism, and revelation). A social justice element is being added to the mix. But Paulo is thrown a curve when he is assigned an analysis of third-world conditions in terms of their effect on the United States. Paulo takes his confusion/indignation to his friend, the local pastor, Bob Wills. Paulo sums up by noting that doctrine and truth have little basis in experience and even less connection to everyday issues, especially injustice. Bob counters with the observation that these truths transcend contexts and provide life with a framework, and that existential approaches inevitably bog down in relativism.

Paulo continues his critique by questioning the lack of focus on piety and spiritual development at Mission Evangelical Seminary. To Paulo's way of thinking this has resolved itself into a clear vocational choice, either taking on the conditions of his constituents, the poor, or working at a more remote level to address systemic changes which would seek to attack the causes of poverty. Bob confirms the conflict with the comfortless observation that either or both could well be futile.

The study concludes with the challenge to resolve the conflict, both within the structure of Mission Evangelical Seminary and in the vocational decision making for Paulo.

Within this parable the following issues surface:

- What is the relevance of traditional truth to current reality?
- What is the true path of a spiritual vocation?
- Is there an ethical imperative implied in the contrast between Western culture and third world poverty?
- What is the relationship between personal piety and good works?

All of these are familiar in the ageless debates between the abstract and the practical; between the traditional and the contemporary; between faith and action; between belief and works. But there is a danger in these dichotomies, for they trivialize the power which only comes in their combination, not separation. One hazard in a case study model, as in its ancestor the parable, is the opportunity to miss its point, to err in understanding what it is about. Parables often if not always contain a paradox. They are stories with a truth to expose, but not always only one truth, and not always only one correct truth (can there be an incorrect truth?). The point is not to find the answer but to define the question. And answers are not useful if they respond to the wrong questions.

In my judgment, the principal question for us is to re-assess the apparent dissonance between the poles of the above apparent dichotomies. I will comment briefly on two separate arenas, the contemporary life of the churchperson and the nature of theological education. The obstacle course of the Christian life differs little from that of theological education except for the fact that it might be a little easier because it is less concentrated and a little harder because it is more encumbered with other concerns. To know the Good News is to be compelled to tell it and show it. Anyone who would separate the "true Gospel" from the "social Gospel" has not heard or understood the Good News. The concept of the Evangelical in abstraction is impossible. Evangelical behavior is exclusively directed toward the real world.

In our vanity we have always sought security in the wrong places. The nineteenth-century missionary model sought to first obtain perfection and then to forcefeed it to others less insightful. It deserved its failure. We now know enough to have recovered part of the earlier understanding about our imperfections and why they must not be allowed to paralyze us. Any pretense to monopolies on truth by us are as arrogant as they are absurd.

What of the moral lessons to be gleaned from "Evangelicals in a New Key" for theological education? There are several, not the least of which is to remain tolerant of the young who are doomed (blessed?) to repeat a painful process many have endured. Is the running of the course to be abandoned because the outcome is foreordained? Isn't it the running, not the finishing, that is the objective?

The professor asked the right question (one of the right questions) and he obtained his desired objective — he forced his student to engage the issues, however misunderstood at the outset. To assess the impact of third-world poverty on the values of Western culture is every bit as relevant a task as the reverse. To phrase the question this way implies a series of ethical imperatives having to do with Evangelical behavior, or the lack of it, in the faithfulness of the Western world. While it is probably a universal economic and social truth that "the poor are always with us," what is the verdict on a culture which is poor in spirit when alternatives are available? The professor's method of raising the issue speaks directly to Paulo's problem; it is more a matter of process (action) than analysis (truth). It is the engagement that is demanded, not the verification.

And the professor proves again that there is a major distinction between the right and the wrong question, a distinction greater than that between different answers to the right question. The process of thought, debate, decision, and action is the stuff of good education, theological or otherwise. Education has little to do with content compared to learning the skills and habits which allow for the translation of experience into tools directed at its application to an ever-changing reality.

While it is false that the only substitute for experience is youth (and before our indignation goes berserk, let us reflect on our own odysseys past the perils of impatience which plagued our formative years), it is true that the only substitute for truth is wisdom. It is wisdom which understands the relativity of truth. It is wisdom which prescribes a behavior which becomes its own truth. It is men and women of wisdom rather than knowledge whom we need on our seminary faculties.

So what of the apparent polarity between vision and action? The Good News has done away with the difference. For some, it can be said that they never met a dichotomy they did not like. There are those for whom the simple is to be avoided like the plague. There are those who choose to define themselves (and others) in terms of what they are against (as opposed to what they are for). While the world is certainly not without contrasts, it is certainly filled with similarities.

Many apparent distinctions are merely apparent, and we perpetuate those distinctions mindlessly at our collective peril. Remember that the Good News is about inclusion. Our initial assumptions should be based on similarity rather than difference. It makes it so much more difficult to judge negatively because of difference. With this skill and habit, it is easier to recognize and practice social justice. Therefore let us go beyond the dichotomies to become agents of social justice. Let us understand the necessary connection between faith and works, between truth and justice, between vision and action. They only make sense, they only have life, they only fulfill our purpose in living if they are understood to be inextricably linked. That we lack the clarity we seek is given, but no excuse for our inaction. Let us raise these questions, let us reject their false compartmentalization, let us practice what we preach.

In our critical, fragmented, litigious world, we are quick to judge. Fault-finding and blame are too facile. A case could be made to show the weaknesses in each of the characters in "Evangelicals in a New Key" and in the seminary itself. But what would be the point? Is Paulo too innocent or impatient, the professor too enigmatic or insensitive, Pastor Bob too rational or traditional? Who cares? "Evangelicals in a New (or Ancient) Key" provides us with another welcome opportunity to revisit an old dialogue, to reject anew a tempting but ultimately destructive dichotomy between vision and action; to reaffirm our determination to go boldly into our world living the intrinsically socially just Good News.

Ours is an inquisitive ethic. We will be always questioning, forever revising, constantly listening — and above all — always in action. Rejecting false dichotomies, let us practice what we preach. Confident of forgiveness, we can risk error. Confident of love, we are incapable of inaction.

Notes

1. For an overview of current globalization issues see S. Mark Heim, "Mapping Globalization for Theological Education," *Theological Education* 26, Supplement I, Spring, 1990, pp. 7-34.

2. *Global 2000 Report to the President*, vol. I, Washington, D.C.: U.S. Government Printing Office, 1980.

3. Donella H. Meadows, et al., *The Limits to Growth*, New York: Universe Books, 1972.

4. Donella H. Meadows, Dennis L. Meadows, Jorgen Randers, *Beyond the Limits*, Post Mills, VT: Chelsea Green Publishing Co., 1992.

5. Lester R. Brown, et al., *The State of the World 1992*, New York: W. W. Norton, 1992, p. 4.

6. *Ibid.*, p. 1.

7. World Commission on Environment and Development, *Our Common Future*, Oxford: Oxford University Press, 1987.

8. John Howard Yoder, *The Politics of Jesus*, Grand Rapids: Eerdmans, 1972, p. 39.

9. See Joseph C. Hough and John B. Cobb, *Christian Identity and Theological Education*, Chico, CA: Scholars Press, 1985.

10. See M. Douglas Meeks, "Globalization and the *Oikoumene* in Theological Education," *Quarterly Review*, Winter, 1991, pp. 63-80.

11. Edward Farley, *Theologia: The Fragmentation and Unity of Theological Education*, Philadelphia: Fortress Press, 1983.

12. In Kenneth A. Briggs, "Probing the 'Whys' of Theological Study," *Progressions*, Indianapolis: The Lilly Endowment, vol. 4, issue 2, April, 1992, p. 5.

13. See David Roozen's essay in this volume which puts forward a theory of institutional change and William Bean Kennedy's essay which addresses the pedagogical implications of immersion experiences.

14. Talcott Parsons and Edward Shils, eds., *Toward a General Theory of Action*, Cambridge, MA: Harvard University Press, 1952.

15. Alice Frazer Evans, Robert A. Evans, William Bean Kennedy, *Pedagogies for the Non-Poor*, Maryknoll, NY: Orbis Books, 1987, p. xi.

16. Marie Augusta Neal, *A Socio-Theology of Letting Go*, New York: Paulist, 1977.

17. William Kennedy, "Ideological Captivity of the Non-Poor," in *Pedagogies for the Non-Poor*, p. 250.

18. Robert A. Evans, "Education for Emancipation: Movement toward Transformation," in *Pedagogies for the Non-Poor*, p. 268.

19. While they indicated appreciation for the variety of contacts, some participants in the initial seminars expressed the desire to meet more frequently with representatives of theological traditions with which they identified. Some were concerned that we met with a dominance of mainline Protestants in Southern Africa and a dominance of Roman Catholics in Latin America. The coordinators sought to broaden the representation in subsequent seminars.

20. Paulo Freire, *Pedagogy of the Oppressed*, New York: Herder and Herder, 1972, pp. 57-74.

21. See Paulo Freire, *The Politics of Education*, South Hadley, MA: Bergin & Garvey, 1985; and Paulo Freire, " Conversations with Paulo Freire, " in *Pedagogies for the Non-Poor*, pp. 219-31.

22. Larry Rasmussen, "Jesus and Power," an address at Union Theological Seminary, New York, September 12, 1985.

23. *Ibid.*

24. *Ibid.*

25. *Ibid.*

26. Paulo Freire, *The Politics of Education*, South Hadley, MA: Bergin & Garvey, 1985.

27. *Ibid.*, p. xxiv.

28. Rasmussen, "Jesus and Power."

29. R. Evans, "Education for Emancipation: Movement toward Transformation," in *Pedagogies for the Non-Poor*, p. 284.

30. Copyright © 1993 by the Case Study Institute. The names of persons and places in this case have been disguised to protect the privacy of those involved in the situation.

PART TWO

IMPLICATIONS OF GLOBALIZATION

[7]

LIBERATION: GENDER, RACE, AND CLASS

ESSAY

TOINETTE M. EUGENE

We weren't doing anything. We hadn't hurt anybody, and we didn't want to. We were imbibing freely of the fun of vacation as well as the fun of investigation for globalization; we thought we were thinking theologically and acting "un-touristy." We had studied maps of the city and taken hundreds of photographs. We had walked ourselves dizzy in the "people's" part of town and stammered out our barely Berlitz or newly reclaimed versions of a beautiful language. We had marveled at the convenient frequency of the Metro and devoured vegetarian crepes from a sidewalk concession.

Among ourselves, we extolled the seductive intelligence and sensual style of this Paris, this magical place to celebrate the two hundredth anniversary of the French Revolution, this obvious place to sit back with a good glass of wine and think about a world lit with longings for *Liberté, Egalité, Fraternité*. We toasted the famed African American ex-patriots who had been here before us — Baker, Baldwin, and those whose heritage (my own among them as a French Creole, Louisiana Catholic woman) linked us to this place in some mystical or mysterious way. It was raining. It was dark. It was late. We hurried along, punch-drunk with happiness and fatigue. Behind us the Cathedral of the Sacred Heart glowed ivory and gorgeous in a flattering wash of artificial, mellow light.

These last hours of our last full day in Paris seemed to roll and slide into pleasure and surprise. I was happy. I was thinking that the more things change, the more things change. I was thinking that if we, most of us black, all of us women, all of us deriving from peasant/immigrant/persecuted histories of struggle and significant triumph, if we could find and trust each other enough to travel together into a land where none of us technically belonged, nothing on earth was impossible anymore.

But then we tried to get a cab to stop for us, and we failed. We tried again and then again. One driver actually stopped and then, suddenly, he sped away almost taking with him the arm of one of my companions who had been about to open the door to his cab. This was a miserable conclusion to a day of so much privilege

185

and delight, a day of feeling powerful because to be an intentionally global person is to feel completely welcome and at home among strangers. And that's the trick of it. No one will say no to freely given admiration and respect. But now we had asked for something in return—a cab in which to go "home." And with that single, ordinary request, the problems of our identity, our problems of power, reappeared and trashed our globalization glow of confidence and joy.[1]

Catching a Cab Home

I am looking for a way to catch a cab home to renewed and revitalized contents and forms of theological education in North America. I am looking for an umbrella big enough to overcome the theological, tactical, and ethical limitations of "identity politics"—a process based on preferential gender, class, or race. I am searching for a language and a potential rooted on a different consciousness of identity as my basis for achieving a womanist ethics of care and as a theological praxis for "doing the human good."[2]

M. Shawn Copeland offers some significant lessons on just how to flag down this cab, and on how to acquire the umbrella which I suspect that more folk might need than those few of us stranded on a Parisian boulevard a while back. In proffering a theoretical and theological framework for getting at the structure and praxis of human good, Copeland claims,

> If theology mediates between a cultural matrix and the significance and role of religion in that matrix, then the theologian needs some framework by which to attend concretely to the cultural matrix as it is in process. This tool ought to anticipate and apprehend the operations, cooperations, complexities, and differentiations within the cultural matrix.

Relying on Bernard Lonergan's notion of the human good,[3] Copeland comments on how the structure of human good charts progress and change as well as decline and breakdown. "Progress is rooted in self-transcending human . . . persons struggling to live attentively, intelligently, rationally, and responsibly. Their decisions and choices, their evaluation of proximate and future costs and benefits to themselves, their groups, and other societal groups promote progress."[4]

Decline contests progress. Egoism and ethnocentrism are embedded in human evaluation and decision. Surrender to short-term costs and disregard for long-term benefits manifest the refusal of self-transcendence and undermine intellectual, moral, social, and religious praxis. The implications of globalization for theological education depend and impend on our ability to promote long-term progress in the ethics of care and the human good.

The tripartite structure of the human good as developed in general by Lonergan, and in particular by Copeland and other womanist social scientists, theologians, and ethicists supplies a field theory,[5] a set of fixed terms and their relations through which to grasp concretely and to interpret critically the function of the basic variables of race, gender, and social class status within a cultural and theological matrix. Racism, sexism, and classism are principal manifestations of breakdowns in just what the human good is.

Womanist ethics and theology, as disciplined commentaries about the nature of God and the human good, intimate a critical posture toward sexism, misogyny, and the objectification and abuse of black women, both within African American communities and within the dominant patriarchal culture. Womanist ethics and theology agree with black liberation theology in its critique of white racism and the need for black unity, and they agree with feminist theology in its criticism of sexism and the need for the unity of women.

Womanist ethics and theology also emphasize the dimension of class analysis, since historically most African American women have been poor or are negatively affected by the unequal distribution of capital and gainful employment as a direct consequence of the economic system operative in the United States. Consequently, womanist ethics and theology must be based on a tri-dimensional analysis of racism, sexism, and classism.[6] As such, womanist ethics is able to serve as an umbrella with which to forge ahead toward greater globalization in theological education. Womanist ethics is one effective way to catch our cab home.

Womanist ethics and theology, as they are appended to and appropriated as implications of globalization and theological education, provide concrete form and content to the praxis and the structures of thinking, teaching, and learning globally while acting and reflecting locally in reference to gender, race, and class. Many of us function on the basis of habits of thought that automatically concede paramount importance to gender, race, or class. These ways of thinking may, for example, correlate race with class in monolithic, absolute ways; that is, white people have, people of color have not, or poor people equals people of color. Although understandable, these dominating habits of thought tend to deny the full and positive functions of gender, race, and class.

If we defer mainly to race in our habits of thought about doing the human good, then what about realities of class that point to huge numbers of poor white people or severe differences of many kinds among various, sometimes conflicting classes of black people? Or, if we attend primarily to factors of class in formulating an ethic of liberating care, then we may mislead ourselves significantly by ignoring privileges inherent to white identity, per se, or the socially contemptible status of minority-group members regardless of class. Both forms of analysis encourage exaggerated — or plainly mistaken — suppositions about racial or class grounds for political and theological solidarity. Equally important, any exclusive mode of analysis will overlook or obviate the genuine potential for unity across class and race boundaries.

Habits of racial and class analyses also deny universal functions of gender which determine at least as much, if not more, about any person's psychological, economic, and physical life force, well-being, and progress toward the experience of human good. Focusing solely on racial or class or gender attributes will yield only distorted and deeply inadequate images of ourselves. Traditional calls to unity on the basis of only one of these factors — race, gender or class — will fail, finally, and again and again, I believe, because no single one of these components provides for a valid fathoming of the complete community and individual.[7]

And yet, many of us persist in our isolated race/class/gender habits of thought. And why is that? We know the negative, the evil origins, the evil circumstances that have demanded our development of gender, race, and class analysis. For those of us born into a historically scorned and jeopardized status our bodily survival testifies to the defensively positive meanings of gender, race, and class identity because we have created these positive implications as a source of self-defense.

We have wrestled, we have invented positive consequences from facts of unequal conflict, facts of oppression. Facts such as I am African American, or I do not have much money, or I am Somalian, or Serbian, or I am a girl and my father mends shoes, become necessary and crucial facts of race and class and gender inside the negative contexts of unequal conflict and the oppression of one group by another, the oppression of somebody weak by somebody more powerful.

Race and *class* are not the same kinds of words as *grass* and *stars*. *Gender* is not the same kind of noun as *sunlight*. *Grass*, *stars*, and *sunlight* all enjoy self-evident, positive connotations, everywhere on the planet. They are the physical phenomena unencumbered by our knowledge or our experience of slavery, discrimination, rape, and murder. They do not presuppose an evil any one of us must seek to extirpate.

It is helpful to reflect on some common descriptions of racism, sexism, and classism in order to consider how they are principles which seriously affect the development of a praxis that benefits the teaching and learning of globalization in theological education.[8] Racism, sexism, and classism are primordial breakdowns in just what the human good is. Racism, sexism, and classism are aberrations which index just how pervasively dramatic, individual, group, and general bias are acquired; they catalogue social decline and anesthetize religion.[9]

Racism is "the generalized and final assigning of values to real or imaginary differences, to the accuser's benefit and at [the] victim's expense, in order to justify the former's own privileges or aggression."[10] Sexism is the subjugation of women to men on the basis of biological difference; it projects male superiority over against intrinsic female inferiority. By way of female biology and social roles, sexism coaches culture to define women as closer to nature than men, and hence, means and objects to be subordinated, controlled, and manipulated for the ends of the culture (men).

Taken as the economic productive and distributive exploitation of a powerless class by a powerful one, classism is a marked feature of modern capitalism. Classism is characterized by commoditisation of an individual's capacities and skills; by distortion of roles, duties, obligations, institutions, and social cooperations; by deformation of individual orientation and liberty; by the inflation and protection of one group's interests and opportunities at the expense of another. Indeed, racism, sexism, classism, and capitalism are inseparable according to Copeland, William Julius Wilson,[11] bell hooks, and Cornel West,[12] and other African American critics of the dominant and oppressive culture, who employ economic analysis as well as social science tools in their assessment of how to catch that cab home, how to open the umbrella for the empowerment of more individuals and social and religious institutions who want to engage in "doing the human good."

Womanist ethics and theology remind us that racism, sexism, and classism are not "out there"; they sink into consciousness, suffuse the concrete human set-up, penetrate all relations, and mediate meanings. Copeland, Cannon, and others contend that the racist, the sexist, or the elitist fabricates and inhabits a worldview so structured by racism, sexism, and classism that to behave otherwise is deemed abnormal. And hence the very humanity of all of us is disfigured.[13] Racism, sexism, homophobia, and classism, embedded in our institutions of theological education, are the principal reasons why we cannot catch a cab in order to "get home from here."

I am wondering if those of us who began our lives in difficult conditions defined by our race, our class, or our gender identities can become more carefully aware of the limitations of race and class and gender analyses, all the while utilizing the strengths of these different kinds of insights. I believe that there is another realm of possibility, political and socio-theological unity, and human community based upon concepts that underlie or supersede relatively immutable factors of race, class, and gender: the concept of justice, the concept of equality, the concept of an ethic of care and tenderness. Theologian Carter Heyward puts it quite succinctly in her characterization of this concept as one of "justice/love."[14] I believe that creative alternative ethics for doing the human good emerge when such difference in habits of thought are acknowledged and encouraged. bell hooks concurs in her work, *Talking Back: Thinking Feminist, Thinking Black*:

> Working collectively to confront difference, to expand our awareness of sex, race, and class as interlocking systems of dominations, of the ways we reinforce and perpetuate these structures, is the context in which we learn the true meaning of solidarity. It is this work that must be the foundation of the feminist [and womanist] movement.[15]

I believe that one way home, a major method for catching the cab, or of opening the umbrella in order to fend off the effects of the reigning orthodoxies of racism, sexism, and classism, lies in the way we choose to renew our moral imagination. I choose to do this by claiming and explaining an ethic of solidarity and of honoring our differences as essential aspects of the theological education we must re-create in order to survive as well as to be sources of transformation and redemption with all God's people on this fragile globe.

The Renewal of Moral Imagination

To say that the entire world needs to be the context of theological education says something both very important and yet quite broad and indeterminate. To say that the entire world needs to be the context of theological education does not answer how we should balance global contexts with local contexts. As Don Browning observes,[16] we also live and have our education and ministries in local contexts, and it is the height of both forgetfulness and arrogance to become so preoccupied with the problems of Africa or Latin America or Asia that we overlook the particularity of our own social location or the continuity between the two. Hence, to be attentive to the term *globalization* demands that we ask, how do we implement globalization in such a way as to meaningfully participate in the "renewal of the face of the earth"?

My answer to this question suggests itself as an ethical description of the "renewal of the moral imagination." This is my twist on the term created by David Tracy in his work *The Analogical Imagination*. To link the particular and the universal whether in theology, in ecclesiology, or in any other contextual framework for learning is to argue for a perspective which does not ignore structural evil either in the world or in the beam in our own eye.

To argue for the renewal of moral imagination in theological education is to concur with the creative analysis of *The Analogical Imagination*, which suggests a complementarity between three theological disciplines, each mainly (but not exclusively) addressed to three distinct publics and motivated by three distinct orientations.

Foundational Theology	Academic Public	Truth [Metaphysics and dialectics]
Systematic Theology	Ecclesial Public	Beauty [Poetics, Rhetoric]
Practical Theology	Social Public	Good [Ethics, Politics][17]

My own particular concern is with the convergence of the foundational and the practical, since the forms of expression for classical systematic theology often fall outside the boundaries of liberation theology, and thus avoid any renewal of any imagination, moral or otherwise.

To argue for globalization as a matter of the educating power of particular human relationships across cultural lines is to commit ourselves to the renewal of an ethic or a moral revisioning which is primarily characterized by a redefinition of responsible action or praxis which must accompany our theologies of social salvation and social change in the face of social sin and social evil. The renewal of moral imagination through a redefinition of responsible action toward the achievement of globalization does not mean the certain achievement of desired ends, but the creation of the conditions of possibility for desired changes.

This important task of renewing our moral imagination also may be described as the delineation of an alternative ethical system which provides a foundation for critiquing predominant notions of responsible action. My thinking on this matter is in agreement with the approach of the philosopher Michel Foucault, who claims that the intellectual work most suited to our current political and intellectual ferment has two features: an attempt to describe the fractures that are developing in dominant systems of thought and action; and an articulation of alternate systems actually present and operative in political struggle. Such work, he states, is more suited to our time than the work of the "universal intellectual," the person who develops an ideal construction of what thought and actions should be. By describing an alternate system of thought and action that exists already, that we can see operating in people's lives, we participate in constructing what Foucault calls an alternative politics of truth.[18]

The reality and exigencies of responding effectively to the oppressions of racism, classism, sexism, homophobia, and all the other ideologies resident in dealing with our response to globalization demand that we acknowledge our dissimilarities in order to create new shared images and heritages of persistence, imagination, and solidarity for a positively oriented global future.

In this essay, it is my expressed purpose to provide a broad framework for praxis, and to make a few basic recommendations on "getting home from here." But I can only get there by remembering the past in order not to encourage a continued repeating of past mistakes.

I want to get to the edge of the future which beckons us, to the dawning of a brand new day for women and men in a global ecclesial context. I want to realize and to claim collectively the true universal nature of the church. But I cannot get from here to there by sliding softly around the hard issues of racism, sexism, classism, and all the other issues and ideologies of domination which oppress persons all over the world.

It is necessary for me "to tell the truth, and to shame the devil," as my old grandmother would say, if I want to be able to announce with you and in the words engraved on Dr. Martin Luther King's tombstone, "Free at last! Free at last! Thank God Almighty, I'm free at last!" This is the privileged and liberated home to which Jesus calls and invites us to come together as friends and disciples; this is the renewed context to which theological education and moral imagination compel us both from the perspective of the past and from the hope for a renewed and far more inclusive future of leadership for the church and the world.

To this end, I want to share with you a truth told in an African American proverb:

> We ain't what we oughta be;
> we ain't what we wanna be;
> we ain't what we gonna be;
> but thank God, we ain't what we was![19]

This African American proverb expresses the reality, yearning, and hope of a people still in formation. African American Christians along with other people of color, women, and related oppressed communities are painfully aware of negative forces or obstacles that work against our becoming what we "ought to be."[20] These obstacles to a renewed moral imagination include all ideologies of dominance and subordination, the glorification of a Rambo or *machismo* mentality, but also the demoralizing personal self-hate and low self-esteem that depress the human spirit.

But despite the complexity of contemporary social and moral issues that surround the freedom and empowerment of which I speak, the overwhelming message of this proverb remains: God is still at work today in the minds and souls of all the oppressed and disenfranchised of the globe, renewing and mending broken lives and forever calling us to faithfulness and accountability. In the storytelling and oral tradition of the elders in the black churches, we can proverbially affirm — with shouts of divine praise — that "we ain't what we was!" For brothers and sisters to say this together, to act it out institutionally and systemically in an effort to reshape our own theological education is to begin the hopeful journey home.

Implications of Globalization for Gender, Race, and Class

Although geography, culture and time are not the same, we do know that pain and persecution are universal. Pain knows no barriers of time, ethnicity, or gender. Surely, women know pain. Some pain we share universally with all humanity. Like Job, we know how it is to have our children taken, to suffer ill health, to be taunted that it's our fault. Like Sarah, we know what it is to have our men hide behind our skirts. Like Paul, we know what it is to be misunderstood and to suffer abuse. Yes, we share pain universally with all people.

But consider for a moment the metaphor of pain as "the world in my eye."[21] As an example, African and African American women know a degree of pain that is quadrupled in its intensity. By the time the general pain of human struggle reaches us, it has been passed down from the white man to the white woman to the black man to the black woman—solidified now, fourfold. Frequently, ours is pain of the scar tissue—wounded and "rewounded" in mass brutalization of social, political, economic, and religious strata. I start here only to reaffirm that one's way to the universal can only be informed and renewed through an examination of the particulars of one's history and experience, without flinching from what that means, but also with a readiness to utilize that context for personal and social change.

Not only does the black woman—and by extension, women of color in general—bear the white world's burdens, she is a virtuoso burden bearer. Alice Walker observes that generally this woman was the "mule of the world." Her person, her unique spirituality and creativity have been systematically suppressed—she has never really had a "place" of her own to come home to, despite the gains of womanist theology and ethics. Instead, she is most often handed everybody else's burdens to the exclusion of her selfhood.

When she has asked for simple caring, she's been given empty appellations and stuck in the farthest corner. When she asked for love, she was given children and left alone with the responsibility of child rearing, her home characterized as broken, weak, and unsuitable for raising children. She is even criticized for her insightfulness and held suspect if she's smart. She has been taught not to trust herself or anyone else. If she issues a complaint about how she's treated by the masses, her sanity is questioned. Her labors of love and fidelity are knocked down her throat.

Yes, hers is a congenital pain, deeply rooted in its disfiguring scar of mass neglect, abuse, and brutalization. She's always seen life through her scars, bruises, and wounds. What I am describing here are the primary and deeply painful places where the renewal of moral imagination and solidarity from seminary trained and theologically educated leaders must make itself more adequately and appropriately felt, like a balm in Gilead, for globalization to have a more nuanced meaning in order to make the wounded whole.

"The World in My Eye"

The point is vividly made in Alice Walker's true story of a childhood accident in which one eye was wounded. Her brother shot her with a BB gun (the facsimile of a white man's weapon, passed on to an unsuspecting black boy who injures a black girl). Throughout childhood, Alice was made to feel ashamed of that eye. It just sort of stared out at you from a gray, bead-sized dead spot in its center.

One night, as she prepared her three-year old daughter, Rebecca, for bed, Rebecca noticed her mother's eye for the first time. She cupped Alice's face in her tiny hands. Embarrassed, Alice tried to pull away—afraid that even her own daughter would find the eye offensive. After all, children can be innocently cruel sometimes. But Rebecca insisted upon looking at that eye.

Rebecca's favorite television show, "The Big Blue Marble," featured at its beginning a whirling globe set out in space, surrounded by billowing, bluish-gray clouds. With this point of reference, and after what seemed like an eternity, Rebecca spoke, "Mommy, you've got a world in your eye. Mommy, where did you get that world in your eye?"[22] And what was once shameful, painful, and dead, in the eyes and hands of love became a new life—a new world.

So many women, black and white alike, have tried like Alice to protect ourselves from our child's discovery of our woundedness, to hide our scars behind our intelligence, our apparent strength, our acquired influence, the shallow sisterhood of sororities, clubs . . . and yes, our men; we are afraid of being found out that we are like everybody else, fragile and vulnerable because there has been no protection for those vulnerabilities. And there was no place and no contentment. Even in Alice's displacement and discontentment, she was found.

Out of the broken homes of prophetic as well as marginalized communities of resistance to evil, and for those who long for alternative redefinitions of responsible ethical praxis to attend our theologies of solidarity and resistance, God creates what I call the potential *ekklesia* of our future. Here, in a realized eschatology, scars are transformed into new life and hope. In the midst of this affliction, in fact, we are also given an entirely new address for the "cab drivers" of theological education. We are given a new way home to share with fellow travellers, much like the magi in the account of the Christmas epiphany.

Rosa Parks reached that home on the day she refused to stand up so a white man could have a seat and so that she might accommodate the demands of an unjust law. Both theological education as well as the church militant must find concrete ways of adopting and imitating the stance of this African American woman who is a mystic—one who can truly hear and respond to the word of God. My great-grandmother reached that home when, in defiance of expediency, she refused to allow someone else to write her name. Langston Hughes's mother reached that home when from old and aching knees she told him, "Don't you set down on the steps 'cause you finds it's kinda hard."[23]

The renewal of moral imagination in solidarity with these women and other oppressed communities demands that globalization in theological education be present there with them in some specific, person-oriented ways, in some intentionally liberational ways in which we are able to follow their direction and their leadership. This means that we as the church and theological seminaries representing power, wealth, or prestige can no longer just feel bad, or just offer electives which are marginal to the required curriculum or which are ancillary and not at all at the core of our training for *all* persons participating in our theoretically inclusive program of theological education and professional preparation for globally responsible ministry.

But what if we find that we cannot readily identify with the way those "others" get home from here, those who creatively construct a liberational ethic of care by which everyone is entitled not only to ride the freedom bus, but also to share in the taxi cab of theological education? What if we need not stories and proverbs from the oppressed but from the lives of the "oppressors" in order to say that this is our situation, and from this perspective we must learn solidarity?

In my Pilot Immersion Project trip to Zimbabwe to diverse centers fostering ecumenical and social justice ministries, and in my visitation to South African theological and denominational centers of power and influence which claim solidarity with the oppressed and the outcast, the blindness of the "world in my own eye" began to bother me considerably. As we lived with, spoke, and shared from the largesse of our often economically indigent hosts, several points became increasingly clear and focused.

Critical questions began to flow like healing and cleansing tears from the world in my eye. What would happen if the theological centers of the mainline and old-line religious institutions finally decided that we really "ain't what we wanna be," and told the truth and made a real commitment to "what we gonna be"? What if our desire to really be globalized and for solidarity with those who experience oppression principally because of their gender, race, and class began to be matched by *consistent* and *significant* responsible theological and educational praxis that made a difference?

Moral Imagination: Moving toward the Home of Solidarity

Depending upon our social location, some of us might better be able to identify with the women and the churches, and the theological faculties of privileged South Africa before the days of the end of apartheid and before the days of our own conversion in the here and now of North America. For those of us who need the antithesis and an alternative perspective than that of Alice Walker's vision and experience of scars, there are other ways of utilizing the categories of gender, race, and class as a basis for revisioning an ethic of solidarity and difference, of care and tenderness.

A powerful parable offering just such an example appears in the pages of South African novelist J. M. Coetzee's *Age of Iron* when we meet Mrs. Curran. In Cape Town, this white, wise, old woman — a retired classics professor — is dying as breast cancer carves into her bones. She writes an extended letter to her daughter, who has shaken the dust of her home in South Africa and its apartheid system from her feet and has gone to live in the United States. Mrs. Curran has always abhorred apartheid, but until these latter days of her life she has been shielded from the flesh and blood of its horror and its rage, of the malignancy killing her country as surely as cancer is eating away at her body.

First, a homeless black man shows up in the alley down the side of her garage. This unsavory man — he smells of urine, sweet wine, moldy clothing — becomes her companion and confidante, the only person to whom she can confess her swelling sense of anger and grief at what she witnesses. He cradles her into death at the book's end.[24]

Mrs. Curran has two words for us as we withdraw from our own latest World War and as we seek to establish a more real solidarity and globalized theology in company with those who already know the negative implications of gender, race, and class at this time in our salvation history. The first word Curran speaks when she is cold and wet. She has been out all night searching with her domestic servant for this woman's son, and has witnessed the burning of a black township. Together, they finally find Bheki: a dead body stretched out in a rain-soaked school hall. Stunned and shunned by the Blacks she has been with, she stumbles up to several young Afrikaner soldiers. Later, she writes to her daughter:

What did I want? What did the old lady want? What she wanted was to bare something to them, whatever there was that might be bared at this time, in this place. What she wanted, before they got rid of her, was to bring out a scar, a hurt, to force it upon them, to make them see it with their own eyes: a scar, any scar, the scar of all this suffering, but in the end my scar, since our own scars are the only scars we can carry with us. I even brought a hand up to the buttons of my dress. But my fingers were blue, frozen.[25]

In these times of ecumenicity and world diplomacy when neutrality and numbness are taken to be true signs of humanity, when a public relations man garbed in desert camouflage can stand in an air-conditioned hotel lobby half-way around the world to tell us we are innocent of the blood of Iraqi women and children because our intentions are good, it is time to find a new way home, to claim a new address and context and content for theological education in place of what we currently hold. It is time to risk our vulnerability in a continent that values competence and control and confuses both with virtue. It is time for the churches and bastions of theological education, and for our separate and self-sufficient denominations, to tell the truth of our own battlefields memorialized by each scar and every suture of women and others whom we have oppressed, in order that we might become better participants, partners, and real recipients of justice and peace.

From South Africa, Mrs. Curran's second word for us is written when a friend of her domestic servant's dead son—a defiant young man—shows up one night. She writes to her daughter as some of us might well write to our local congregations and churches:

So this house that was once my home and yours becomes a house of refuge, a house of transit. My dearest child, I am in a fog of error. The hour is late and I do not know how to save myself. As far as I can confess, to you I confess. What is my error, you ask? If I could put it in a bottle, like a spider, and send it to you to examine, I would do so. But it is like a fog, everywhere. I cannot touch it, trap it, put a name to it. Slowly, reluctantly, however, let me say the first word. I do not love this child. I love you but I do not love him. ... That is my first word, my first confession. I do not want to die in the state I am in, in a state of ugliness. I want to be saved.

How shall I be saved? By doing what I do not want to do. That is the first step: that I know. I must love, first of all the unlovable. I must love, for instance, this child. Not bright little Bheki, but this one. He is here for a reason. He is part of my salvation. I must love him. But I do not love him.

Nor do I want to love him enough to love him despite myself. It is because I do not with a full enough heart want to be otherwise that I am still wandering in a fog. I cannot find it in my heart to love, to want to love, to want to want to love. I am dying because in my heart I do not want to love. I am dying because I want to die.[26]

What would happen if we told the truth? What would happen if we admitted along with a real commitment to renew our moral imagination in theological education that "we ain't what we wanna be, we ain't what we gonna be"? Yet!

What would happen if we told the truth as our old ancestors and relatives sought to do? Poet Muriel Rukeyser says that if just *one* woman told the truth about her life the world would split apart. Let it be so! Let this world become a wilderness split apart. Let us live with this much renewal of our moral imaginations.

What shall we do with the theological heritage of the Civil Rights movement and the memory of a Martin Luther King who said and understood that we will be unable to solve our problems until there is a radical redistribution of economic and political power in the United States? King said that the black freedom struggle was "exposing the evils that are deeply rooted in the whole structure of our society. It reveals systemic rather than superficial flaws and suggests that radical reconstruction of society itself is the real issue to be faced."[27] This is a central aspect which we must deal with in our contextualized version of the globalization of theological education.

"Getting Home from Here"

Now we face the question: What shall we do about the renewal of moral imagination in conjunction with the globalization of theological education? Are we fully prepared to face and to deal with what contemporary prophets have called "the real issue . . . the radical reconstruction of society itself"? Or is this too much for the churches and centers of theological education to bear in order to renew our moral imagination and to be in solidarity with all those others who are unfairly and unjustly marginalized, disenfranchised, and victimized in our country and throughout the world because of our lack of leadership in addressing the implications of globalization for gender, race, and class?

Is it possible that our best theological education can begin as we examine with utmost seriousness our most radical hopes, and ponder what they mean for our lives? Is it possible that the state of our nation and our world now demands that we who consider ourselves part of the church universal must commit ourselves to press forward toward that fundamental transformation of ourselves and of theological education in America that is even more necessary in these days than ever before if we are to believe the likes of Edward Farley, Joseph Hough and John Cobb, Max Stackhouse, and the Mudflower Collective,[28] to name a few well-known proponents of globalization?

In the words of the prophet Micah, "What then, does the Sovereign One require of us?" (Micah 6:8). I do not presume to answer for the Almighty. Nonetheless, what I do wish to offer in conclusion are a few broad applications on how we may carry out the ethic and lifework of a renewed moral imagination as it is envisioned and lived out by an embodiment of the term "solidarity" with all those for whom God has shown special predilection and a preferential option.

The implications of globalization for gender, race, and class call for a "radical revolution in values" and a kind of moral imagination which is deeply personal as well as profoundly social and political. This radical revolution in values, which a renewal of our moral imagination will require, is a lifetime of metanoia, of death and resurrection, of total conversion in our lifestyle and in our communities of security and of support.

In this context, I conclude by offering these modest reflections and broadly worded recommendations as to how we might begin again to live according to a global ethic of care and kinship, of profound respect for pluralism and difference while fostering dialogues, communities, and friendships.

1) If we believe that the renewal of moral imagination and the praxis of responsible action for the sake of the Gospel has its place in the Christian ethic, then it is necessary for institutions of theological education to embody it more concretely in faculty, administrative staffing, and student recruitment. Concrete expressions of our renewal of moral imagination require renewal of adult methods of teaching and learning, of creative competency-based curricular planning, and contextual and congregational models of experience-oriented education. The intentional inclusion and recruitment which helps to balance gaps in representation based on gender, race, and class difference count considerably toward making theological education into an entirely different home away from home.

2) We will earn the right to speak of Jesus, of reconciliation, of community, when we too embody a similar ministry. We must practice what we preach, that is, become genuine friends and fellow disciples with those who experience injustice, by making their lot and their cause our own. That is the only way that the message of a renewed moral imagination which can bridge the gaps between the academic public, the ecclesial public, and the social public will have any credibility in our time.

3) To strengthen our praxis of responsible action in theological education we must join forces with the victims who are struggling for justice here and abroad. To struggle for justice is the only way to eliminate violence and vengeance and to establish peace. There can be no peace without justice. And there can be no justice apart from the creative input of the history and culture of the victims of domestic and international violence.

As we struggle for peace and justice, it is necessary to remember that the Gospel demands that we take sides with the weak, the disenfranchised, the disinherited. For as Reinhold Neibuhr has said, "Neutrality in a social struggle between the entrenched and advancing social classes means alliance with the entrenched position. In the social struggle we are either on the side of privilege or need."[29]

Thus we may need to listen more closely to alienated voices and viewpoints within the seminary as well as within the churches. We will need to be present in the local churches in order to contextualize our learning and to glean the Gospel as it is lived in the places where we may be in the process of outpricing ourselves or removing ourselves or indicating in subtle ways "no access" to those who may seek or benefit from our purpose and "product."

4) Through its long history, the western churches and theological education have taken, more often than not, the side of those in power rather than the side of the poor. That is why those who struggle for justice are often anti-Christian or at least suspicious of the churches and of seminary-trained pastoral leaders who know all about things such as process theology and post-modern critical theory but who do not know Jesus and who cannot be close to those whom Jesus loves most — the little, the weak, the lost, the oppressed. This was reinforced for me in South Africa; it is also reinforced for me in the times I spend in dealing with urban non-white, and fundamentalist, evangelically oriented congregations.

If we expect to create a renewed moral imagination and responsible praxis to match our theology and mission, then the burden is on us to prepare, support, and sustain ministerial leaders who are willing to struggle in solidarity with others for the sake of a transformed church and society. Our own field education sites and CPE units must be more risky, inclusive, and creative than the traditional, safe, sterile, and predictable places which many students expect, compete for, and in which the renewal of moral imagination is virtually impossible.

5) In a time when the major world powers are engaged in a nuclear arms race that can only mean death for us all, we must responsibly act so that this madness be ended. It is not the violence of those oppressed by racism, sexism, and classism that has created the risk of nuclear holocaust; it is the insanity of so-called civilized persons in authority. If Christians expect to end the cycle of violence, it is necessary for us to express our unqualified solidarity with those who are victims.

Peace studies and conflict resolution courses ought to enjoy a privileged status in our curricular reform and as core requirements for competency in ministry. Community organization skills are necessary tools of theological education for globalization. These are most often omitted or neglected along with courses which provide emerging ministers with a depth of spirituality and a devotional, contemplative life to match their desire for social transformation, and which is also able to balance their theologically intellectual formation.

6) We must become careful that we do not let the powers of violence and the power brokers of the status quo create despair in our struggle for justice and peace. They will try to make us think that there is nothing we can do to make a difference in the realms and realities where we are — students about to graduate, faculty on the line for tenure or promotion, administration in transition or reorganization.

7) Finally, as we struggle against the principalities and powers, let us remember that we do not struggle alone. The God of Abraham and Sarah, of Moses and Miriam, of Deborah, Esther, and Ruth, the God of Jesus and Mary is struggling with us. It is God's global presence in and with all the oppressed that empowers them and us who choose solidarity with them.

God's presence in the struggle, however, is not a replacement for human initiative. Rather, God dwells with the oppressed so that they will know that their struggle is not in vain. In the black community of faith, my people do not deny that trouble is present in their lives. We merely contend that trouble does not have the last word. And we believe that "God don't always come when you want Her, but She always comes on time!"

Perhaps the time is now ripe to begin to retrace our path home by a new way and to a renewed community based on a profoundly humane, inclusively theological foundation for education. This is a vital way to reclaim the world in our eye, to heal and restore our own wounded and fragmented selves, and to be with others in genuine gestures of renewal and reconciliation.

I believe that the movement that we shall take toward a new society and a renewed moral imagination for theological education must be such that it will bring us into solidarity with all who seek for the gift of their land, who seek for food for their children, who attempt to break the combination of despoiling, exploiting classes and institutions everywhere.

Then, returning to the source, always, necessarily, our struggle must be such that it opens us to a new sense of ourselves with others who share also the created universe and its Creator Spirit. I believe that there is a route out of the paralysis of identity politics, even here, in the ugly heartbreaking crisis of the Middle East, in the Middle European States' breakup, in middle America where racism, sexism, and classism continue to reign supreme in many ways. There is available to us a moral imagination, a moral attachment to a concept beyond gender, class, and race. I am referring to the concept of justice/love, which I am prepared to embrace and monitor so that justice shall equally serve us all. It is to that concept and that praxis that I am willing to commit my energies and my trust.

Returning to the rainy evening in Paris, I am still hopeful of acquiring an umbrella big enough to overcome the tactical and moral limitations of identity politics. Yes, I am exhilarated by the holiday I enjoyed with my friends and am proud of the intimate camaraderie we shared. And I also believe somebody, that is to say somebody in addition to those of us who know how it is to be left in the lurch, needs to be talking, sisterly and brotherly, with the obdurate and resistant cab drivers in the world, as well.

CASE STUDY[30]

To Go Home Again

The question for Dalton DuBose—it was enough to trouble her sleep—was what was she going to do when she graduated from seminary? Her question was not simply about a job, although she acknowledged that was part of it, but it was more. It was which road to take, which world to walk toward, and which world to try to leave behind. At least that was how she tried to describe her question to Ben Palmer, her faculty advisor.

Dalton's question about life after seminary was complicated by her life before seminary. The child of affluent, respected, and progressive parents, she had grown up in a home where kindness and the acceptance of civic responsibilities were cardinal virtues. After following her grandmother and mother to their alma mater, where her mother still served on the board, Dalton had married a man from a prominent men's college and raised two children. By the time she entered seminary, her oldest child was in college, the youngest was a freshman in high school, and her husband was well-established in his law firm. Dalton served as president of her Junior League, spent one day a week working in a downtown soup kitchen, and was an elder in her church—a large, affluent, downtown congregation in a Southern city. She had come to seminary because, as she put it on her application, she "wanted to help people with their problems," and she believed that counseling from a Christian perspective was the way she could be of most help.

While her first year at seminary had been challenging in ways that strengthened her faith and long-cherished commitments, her second year had produced a crisis. The seminary required all M.Div. students to take a course that placed them in a significantly different social context. Dalton selected a three-week January immersion experience in Central America. It was this course and the reflections which followed that raised the question about what she was going to do when she graduated. She had not been prepared for such an outcome from what she called "the most powerful and important learning experience of my seminary career."

It was not that she wasn't prepared for the course. During the fall term her Central American group had met regularly, read articles, seen videos, and heard lectures on the geography and history, politics and economics, religious and cultural life of Central America. Dalton's group had even met with students who had gone to Central America the previous year, had seen their slides, and heard their stories. She had listened to them talk about what a "life-changing experience" the immersion had been for them, and she had wondered what that meant.

"I was really prepared for an intellectually challenging and emotionally demanding experience," she told her Central American group one afternoon during the spring term while they reflected on their January together. "But what I was not prepared for was its outcome. I went to Central America convinced that the United States was a Christian nation. I knew that we had our problems; I had seen them vividly at the soup kitchen. But I knew that on the whole, and compared to other countries, we had done a lot of good in the world. Before January, I felt called to work in a suburban congregation, especially to help people with their family problems and to try to get the congregation involved in community affairs. But now I am not sure about any of that. Now I don't know what to think about the United States, or what it means to be a Christian here, or where God is calling me."

With tears in her eyes, Dalton told how she could not forget images from their Central America trip: the hospital for amputees in Nicaragua with the young men sitting in a long row waiting for an artificial arm or leg; the mother telling about her daughter being killed by the military; the children in the streets unable to get simple medical treatment because of a U.S. embargo. Dalton recalled with mixed feelings the different interpretations of what had been happening in Central America—the official interpretations given by the political officer at the U.S. embassy and by the spokespersons for governments supported by the U.S., and then the quite different interpretations given by local ministers, parish priests, and lay leaders. But what had disturbed her the most had been her conversation with Judith, a young woman in Guatemala who had been to the United States with a church group. "What did you think of the United States?" Dalton had asked her. Judith's once clear English, Dalton reminded the group, had given way to her native Spanish. Dalton continued, "Judith spoke of rooms where the Guatemalans were hesitant to sit on the elaborate furniture or where the houses were so very large for only two people. Her pain and distress were obvious." Clearly troubled, Dalton asked her friends, "How can we ever understand?"

The group listened to what she said, and they began to share their own struggles. The January experience had been deeply moving for them all, but most felt they were to continue on the paths they were on, only with the new insights gained from their encounter with Central America. Robert Howe, a professor of church history, who had been the faculty member with the group, said he intended to try to bring new perspectives to his classes and see if he could help students come to grips with the realities that had confronted him in Central America. Dalton said again she was not sure what it all meant for her.

Later in the spring term, Dalton had entitled her final reflection paper for the course "All That is Unresolved." She had begun one section of the paper with the line from the old hymn: "Spirit of the living God, fall afresh on me." "Maybe," she asked, "the question is how do I understand the words of this song." She noted that "images of a white-robed Jesus standing at a garden door have long given way to the image of Jesus in the soup kitchen line. The sketchings of the *campesino* Christ in the Stations of the Cross are now vivid." But what troubled her now was how alienated she felt from all that had been so familiar, the discomfort she had with "big churches with American flags in the chancel, $4 million capital campaigns, and my own easy jaunts around the country." Moreover, the "rhetorical confessions of 'Give us this day our daily bread' " now seemed merely rhetorical "when the bread I eat is more than daily and more than bread." Dalton mentioned a book entitled *How Then Shall We Live?* "I've never read the book," she wrote, "but the title is haunting. Maybe it has become my foremost theological contemplation since Central America. It does not speak only to what I may or may not choose to spend money on, but how do I understand God's story? How do I tell it to others, not just with words but with my life?" "I want," she confessed, "to push away from the Central American experience and say there cannot be a correlation between what I saw there and how I live here. This is a different time and place and context. But push myself away to where?"

It was "But push myself away to where?" that was the haunting question for her, she later told Ben as she struggled to decide what to do after seminary. Was she to push away from Central America to home, to forget what she had heard and seen in Central America, to repress the questions that had been raised, and continue to live a life marked by kindness and the acceptance of civic responsibilities? Or was she to abandon the road that led smoothly from her past, from her home and place, give up the assumptions about the nature of the United States and her place in it, and adopt some radical — God knows what — ministry in solidarity with the poor? Or was there some middle way, some way to avoid extremes?

The closer she came to graduation, the more Dalton wondered why the seminary had put her in such a situation. Was it, she finally asked Ben, fair or right to require such a course of her? Was the course intended to do anything more than produce "liberal guilt" in her? Or did the seminary, with its growing endowment, really expect her to make radical changes and become alienated from her family and the congregation that had nurtured her? She didn't see any of her professors doing that. So, at night, she had trouble sleeping.

TEACHING NOTE

To Go Home Again

I. Goals

A. To help administrators, trustees, faculty, or students "live" the questions and problems of globalization.

B. To explore the complex issues associated with a required course that sends affluent North American theological students into a developing world immersion experience.

C. To provide an opportunity for participants to clarify their own thinking and feeling about the purposes of such immersion experiences.

D. To provide an opportunity for serious dialogue about the nature and purpose of theological education in North America at the end of the twentieth century.

II. Getting into the Case

Construct the following scenes:

A. Ask each person in the group to close his or her eyes and imagine the home where Dalton grew up. Imagine the dining room. What is served for dinner? What kind of dinner table conversations take place here? What might it feel like to be part of such a home?

B. Imagine Dalton walking into the hospital for amputees in Central America. What does she see? smell? hear? What does she do as she walks past the long row of young men waiting for new arms and legs? What is she feeling when she walks out of the hospital?

C. Imagine Dalton in her own home, talking at night in bed with her husband, trying to tell him about what she experienced in Central America. What does she say? How does she feel? What does her husband think, and what emotions does he feel when he hears his wife's story?

III. Issues

A. Have the entire group brainstorm the following questions:

What are the issues in this case for Dalton? What are the issues for theological education?

B. Divide into small groups.

Each group: Referring to the issues raised and adding others, put these issues in order of priority. Analyze the connections between issues for Dalton and issues for theological education. Each group put on newsprint the three most fundamental issues; be prepared to state why these are the most important. Post newsprint and have the small groups study other papers.

IV. Implications

Regroup. Identify the common themes from the small groups. Then reflect on the following:

A. Should all North American M.Div. seminarians be required to have an immersion experience in some significantly different socio-cultural context?

B. If such an experience is required, what assumptions need to be clear? What should be included in the experience? the preparations for it? the follow-up to it?

C. If such an experience is not required but offered, what assumptions need to be clear? What should be included in the experience? the preparations for it? the follow-up to it? Are these different from your response to question B? Why or why not?

COMMENTARY

To Go Home Again

DANIEL SPENCER

Spring 1992. Los Angeles is in flames again. Two days following the acquittal of four white policemen in the brutal beating of a black man, a beating captured on videotape and broadcast throughout the world, the long-smoldering rage of another discarded urban population has exploded — again. Los Angeles is burning, turning in on itself, and other cities threaten to follow suit. It seems we have learned little and changed even less since the long, hot summers of urban riots and police backlash of the 1960s.

I find I cannot respond to the case study, "To Go Home Again," without asking, "Whose home?" We can no longer avoid acknowledging that there are many "homes" in "America." The case study makes clear that home means one thing in Central America and quite another in the United States of America. But the events of Los Angeles also make it abundantly clear that within the United States there are at least two very different Americas: the America of Whites, the America of persons of color; the home of the powerful and increasingly affluent, the home of the powerless and increasingly poor.

In responding to the case, "To Go Home Again," I want to keep this question in the background of the analysis: To whose home do we return?

The question of "whose home" is particularly critical for those of us involved in seminary education where justice and liberation are understood to be central to the Christian Gospel. In a society characterized increasingly by chronic mobility, dislocation, social isolation and skewed economic opportunities, can seminary education enable us to examine critically our own contexts and work to transform social realities that contradict our witness to the liberating reality of the Gospel?

Globalization projects based on immersion-style pedagogies have emerged as one attempt to respond to this question. What are the key issues at stake in this effort, and what challenges and resources can we identify to contribute to a constructive response? In this commentary I will use these questions and the challenges posed by the events of Los Angeles to analyze and identify six key issues that emerge from "To Go Home Again" before concluding with some suggestions to further and deepen the work begun in globalization programs.

I. Analyzing the Case Study:
Issues Present in "To Go Home Again"

The situation of Dalton DuBose following her immersion experience in Central America is common to many travel seminar participants: returning home and viewing the United States from the perspective of someone else's home brings about a crisis of meaning, faith, and vocation. Many find it impossible to proceed as before, pretending nothing has changed. The dissonance these experiences produce is one of the key components to immersion-style pedagogies; it offers the opportunity to distance ourselves momentarily from the socialization patterns that have shaped us to see more accurately where we are located in society and how this shapes our understanding of the world. As in the case of Ms. DuBose, this can cause a crisis of values and meaning, as well as vocation. Let us look more closely at some of the dynamics involved in this crisis of returning home, when one's understanding of home can never again be the same.

A. Whose Home? Importance of Social Location

All of us view the world through lenses shaped by our experience — a product, in part, of where we call home. Our worldviews are shaped by where we are located in society with respect to social differences based on factors such as race, class, gender, sexuality, and physical ability. These experiences influence us to see the world a particular way, building up around us what William Kennedy has termed an "ideological cocoon" that serves to filter reality, reinforcing interpretations that conform to the dominant societal views and eliminating or obscuring those that differ.[31] Dalton DuBose's upbringing indicates a particularly thick cocoon reflecting a social location of economic affluence and societal prestige combined with liberal social values. That her life after seminary has become "complicated by her life before seminary" is an indication both of the strain of maintaining a worldview shaped by this social location when the realities of others — in this case, the poor of Central America — begin to break in, and how difficult it can be to break out of a cocoon shaped by social and economic privilege.

B. The View from Home: How We See the World Determines How We Respond

Ms. DuBose's socialization into a reality that emphasizes civic responsibilities and kindness (at the cost of acknowledging and confronting conflict) reflects a characteristically liberal worldview that presupposes both the basic goodness and soundness of society and access to power to bring about reform when it is needed. These values are reflected in her motivation to attend seminary: one-on-one counseling "to help people with their problems" presupposes that the problems are the individual's (rather than society's); an appropriate avenue for ministry, therefore, is to help people adjust themselves to a basically good society. Absent from this goal is any analysis or awareness of how society is *structured* differently for different people and how this affects one's ministry and one's view of the world.

C. Entering Other Homes: Confronting Incompatible Worldviews and Breaking through Ideological Cocoons

Seeing the world from the perspective of a different home produces a crisis of belief for Ms. DuBose. She finds herself confronted by two incompatible worldviews shaped by very different social locations — affluence in the United States *vs.* poverty in Central America. Prior to this, the liberal social values of her upbringing helped her to be open to learning about Central America during pre-trip preparation, and what she learned influenced and challenged her views.

It did not, however, fundamentally alter her worldview of the basic goodness of the United States as a Christian nation and positive actor on the global stage. Rather, her ideological cocoon allowed her to assimilate and accommodate this new information without calling into question her overall perspective and beliefs. It is not until she encounters another reality fundamentally different from her own that her cocoon is shattered momentarily, forcing her to consider a different way of viewing the world. Her pre-trip study may have been important to prepare her for this encounter with a radically different view of reality, but it is the encounter itself that breaks through the many layers of ideology and socialization to enable her to see the world from the perspective of a home very different from the one she left behind.

D. Feeling Homeless: Trying to Reconcile the Irreconcilable

As Ms. DuBose begins to grasp both the incompatibility of the view of the world she held before, especially of the United States, with the claims made by people in Central America, she is troubled by the dissonance this awareness produces. Conscious now of the gulf in experiences and social location that shapes such widely divergent views, she experiences confusion, mixed feelings, and ambiguity in deciding how she can reconcile what she has learned with what she has believed. While most of the other group members seem content to continue in a reformist model, "only with the new insights gained from their encounter," this no longer seems a viable option to her to resolve the tension between the two, fundamentally different understandings of reality. In addition, the contradictions she experiences are connected to her faith. Her earlier shift in images of Jesus from "white-robed, standing at a garden door" to "Jesus in the soup kitchen line" showed her movement from a spiritualized faith that supports the status quo to a liberal faith that shares its resources with the needy, but the rupture of both of these with the new image of "the *campesino* Christ" has left her feeling alienated from her old sheltered world and understanding of her faith.

E. Home Ties That Bind: Continued Ideological Captivity and the Need for Engagement in the "New" Home

Ms. DuBose's experience illustrates a common occurrence in how we are socialized in society: our ideological cocoons often shield us most effectively from those contradictory views of reality that are closest to home. Despite her initial breaking out of her protective cocoon that leads to feelings of alienation and dissonance, Ms. DuBose's inability to connect the experiences and challenges she had in Central America to the social reality *within* the United States illustrates how difficult it is to escape the ideological captivity of our social locations. This inability is glaring at several points in her story. The most basic question for her (and for all of us), is *Why did she need to leave the United States to experience the dissonance of different worldviews shaped by radically different social locations and access to societal power?*

Why, for example, did it take the testimony of Judith, the young Guatemalan woman, to cause her discomfort at the wealth of resources in our large homes, when immersing oneself even briefly in the worlds of domestic laborers in the United States would reveal a similar disparity? She is reluctant to admit a correlation between what she saw in Central America and how she lives in the United States, but totally absent in this question is any correlation between how she lives here and *how others live here.* Her contrast between Central America and "home" reveals how restricted and limited her understanding of home remains; it is still a segment of society with people of her own social station, relatively shielded from the underside of societal divisions along lines of race, class, gender, and sexuality.

The choices Ms. DuBose poses—either to remain within her familiar world, capitulating to its values and assumptions, or to opt for "some radical, God knows what, ministry in solidarity with the poor"—further reflect her remaining ideological captivity to a liberal worldview. Implicit in these two alternatives is the assumption that to address the problem one must go "out there," away from "home" and among the poor, rather than re-think what home means now from this new worldview. To reconceptualize home this way would force Ms. DuBose to face the difficult challenge presented at the beginning of this article: recognizing the extent to which the problems of the poor and other marginalized persons, in Central America *and* within the United States, come from her section of this home, and that truly going home means not abandoning her own social group, but confronting it in order to transform the values, assumptions, and practices of this powerful group.

F. The Seminary Home: Institutional Complicity and Compromise

The dissonance experienced in recognizing conflicting understandings of home and the understandings of reality they produce is a key learning moment in immersion-style pedagogies. Working to resolve this dissonance can provide the opportunity, energy, and motivation to re-think long-held assumptions about the way the world is structured and our place in it. As Ms. DuBose herself has recognized, however, this task is made more difficult and confusing by the institutional investment her seminary has in the dominant reality. This contributes to her paralysis in the face of now-exposed social contradictions. Neither the practices of her professors nor of the institution as a whole demonstrate a radical commitment to the kinds of change confronting her, and she rightly questions the motive of the seminary in requiring involvement in an immersion experience designed to radically confront one's worldview when the seminary is unwilling or unable to do the same.

This is a critical component of immersion-style pedagogies too often overlooked or ignored by the institutions that try to implement them. When taken seriously, these kinds of educational programs should force the seminary to reexamine its own motives, social location, and relation to power, and how these affect the educational mission of the institution. When this does not happen, globalization programs can serve to disempower rather than empower the participants. Without institutional self-critique and commitment to change, including follow-up programs that facilitate individual and institutional engagement at home, a dynamic is set up that reinforces individualism. In effect, it blames the individual participant for her or his paralysis without recognizing that the way society is structured, and the institution's place in society, make it very difficult for persons as individuals to take the next step in commitment to transforming society.

It is true that once aware of being confronted by irreconcilable worldviews, only Ms. DuBose can decide for herself how she will respond. Yet whether she receives institutional and community support may be decisive in determining how profound and long-term her response will be. The analysis above suggests that while she has made an important breakthrough from the confines of her ideological cocoon, a certain degree of captivity continues as does the temptation to return to her restricted view of home in order to avoid having to deal with the dissonance. She will need the support of others with similar experiences and questions to avoid succumbing to this temptation.

G. How Do We Live in a New Understanding of Home?

Ms. DuBose has raised the important question of how then shall we live once we become aware. That is a topic for another essay. I suggest, however, that any consideration of this question should follow the logic of the oft-repeated (but seldom analyzed) phrase, "Think globally, act locally," and include the following:
1. Identify Your Own Places of Social Marginalization.
2. Identify Your Own Places of Social Privilege.
3. Clarify Your Relation to Societal Contradictions of Class, Race, Gender, Sexual Preference, Age, and Physical Ability.
4. Count the Cost of Working for Change.
5. Build in Support: Work Together with Others.
6. Explore Possibilities of Power-Sensitive Coalition Building.

Finally, a word to those engaged in seminary education. While the above commentary addresses specifically the case study involving one individual, Dalton DuBose, the analysis and suggestions are equally applicable to those involved in seminary education and to the seminary itself as a social institution. As educators we must become much more critically self-aware of how social location and institutional and ideological captivity shape our work and contradict in practice much of what we teach. This is not an easy task, but it must be absolutely central to those of us committed to teaching and practicing the liberating message of the Gospel. Immersion-style pedagogies offer a powerful tool for beginning and deepening this process. But they are only a first step. Whether or not they are ultimately successful in meeting their goals depends on the follow-up engagement here at home that seminaries must model and individuals must risk.

II. How Then Shall We Live?

Dalton DuBose has begun to do the first part, to challenge her sheltered worldview by thinking globally. This is insufficient, however, without connecting it to acting at home, making the connections between global and local problems.

A. Identify Your Own Places of Social Marginalization

An important first step in building effective solidarity and sustaining efforts at social transformation is to become aware of marginalization and suffering in your own life caused by societal contradictions. How are your personal experiences of suffering connected to societal structures and attitudes? How has this changed historically, and what are the dynamics currently at play? For Ms. DuBose, as a woman seeking ordination in the church, an institution structured historically by patriarchal attitudes and practices, the contradictions experienced by gender may be one place for her to begin this reflection.

B. Identify Your Own Places of Social Privilege

Hand in hand with identifying and understanding your experiences of margin-alization, and often more difficult, is examining the ways we experience social and economic privilege in society, and how this is predicated on the suffering and oppression of others. Ms. DuBose has begun to raise these questions for herself in correlating what she saw in Central America with her lifestyle in the United States. What is needed now is to connect personal experience and lifestyles to societal structures and attitudes. One way of beginning to identify privilege is to ask what are the parts of the way society functions that I can afford to be blind to or remain ignorant of that others cannot? Why is this?

C. Clarify Your Relation to Societal Contradictions

After identifying personal experiences of marginalization and privilege, it is critical that each of us go on to examine and clarify our relation to the multitude of societal contradictions such as class, race, gender, sexual preference, age, and physical ability that divide U.S. society. How are you harmed personally by each of these? What is your self-interest in challenging each? What are the risks? Which are most frightening and why? One way to get at this is to begin to examine how you and your family have been shaped historically by each of these factors. What has your family's relation to poverty and class been, and how have you been affected by society's strong pressure toward "class amnesia" to hide this through shame or memory loss.[32] How has your family's social position been affected by slavery? By patterns of land ownership? Rather than using these and other ques-tions to instill further "liberal guilt," such social analysis highlights the structural dimension of society without erasing personal accountability for our own actions in this social matrix.

D. Count the Cost of Working for Change

Jesus counselled his disciples to count the cost of picking up the cross before joining him. Working for social transformation, for an alternative vision of the world, necessarily comes at a cost. It is important that all of us are clear about what is at stake for each of us, that we acknowledge the risks and envision the gains. For people in the church we must be able to connect this to our vision of the Gospel and ask what resources our faith provides. Here I find St. Augustine's understanding of hope to be instructive. Sixteen centuries ago Augustine wrote that Hope has two daughters: Anger and Courage. Anger at the way things are; Courage to work to change them.

E. Work Together with Others

Absolutely critical to finding the support one needs and being able to sustain one's efforts over the long haul is working in community with others. In a society that bombards us with messages of rampant individualism, it is also one of the most difficult things to find, build, and sustain. It is better to start with a small group and begin modestly, and to incorporate moments of work, play, study, and prayer together. As this group forms, it needs to be aware, too, of its social location and how this shapes its view of the world. While working to transform the values and practices of one's own social class is critical (the problem begins at home), it is important also to work in coalition with people from other social groups who can help us identify our blind spots.

F. Explore Possibilities of Power-Sensitive Coalition Building

As you gain clarity of the needs you seek to address and your own commitments, join others who are working on similar issues. Here it is critical to be conscious of how one's own social location, relations to societal power, and access to resources and information affect the dynamics of working in a coalition. In coalition work, not all actors are equal — either in how they are affected by the issues being addressed (such as access to adequate health care) or in the power and perspectives brought to the work. Feminist historian and activist Donna Haraway stresses that each coalition has an "animating center" made up of those most directly affected by the issues and with whom others in the coalition must work to build a shared vision and effort.[33] Coalition work is not easy. As Gregory Baum has noted, the dynamics of our society actively resist efforts toward solidarity. Here continuing the process of identifying marginalization and privilege in our own lives begun in the earlier steps is critical to facilitating work in coalitions with those different from ourselves so that we do not simply reproduce the power dynamics already present in society.

Notes

1. This reflection is drawn from a speech delivered by June Jordan at the eighth annual Gender Studies Symposium at Lewis and Clark College, Portland, Oregon, April, 1989.

2. M. Shawn Copeland, in a trenchant and seminal article, "The Interaction of Racism, Sexism, and Classism in Women's Exploitation," in *Concilium: Women, Work, and Poverty*, ed. Elisabeth Schüssler Fiorenza and Anne Carr (Nijmegen/Edinburgh, 1987), pp. 19-27, discusses in detail the cognitive discord resident in the polarities of racism, sexism, and the human good. This article is enormously useful for filling in the more technical theological and ethical gaps not addressed in this present essay.

3. This theoretical framework comes from the work of Bernard Lonergan, *Method in Theology* (New York, 1972), especially chapter 2, and *Insight: A Study of Human Understanding* (New York, 1970).

4. Copeland, p. 20.

5. See Katie G. Cannon, *Black Womanist Ethics* (Atlanta, 1988) for extensive commentary on the means by which womanist analysis and methodology critiques and

challenges the infrastructures of racism, sexism, and classism. See also Jacquelyn Grant, *White Women's Christ and Black Women's Jesus: Feminist Christology and Womanist Response* (Atlanta, 1989); Delores Williams, "Womanist Theology," in Judith Plaskow and Carol P. Christ, eds., *Weaving the Visions: New Patterns in Feminist Spirituality* (San Francisco, 1989), and by the incomparably detailed text of Patricia Hill Collins's *Black Feminist Thought: Knowledge, Consciousness, and the Politics of Empowerment* (London, 1991).

6. See Toinette M. Eugene, "Womanist Theology," in *A New Handbook of Christian Theology*, ed. Donald W. Musser and Joseph L. Price (Nashville, 1992), pp. 510-12.

7. See Toinette M. Eugene, "On 'Difference' and the Dream of Pluralist Feminism," *Journal of Feminist Studies in Religion* (Winter 1992-93), pp. 95-102.

8. I draw heavily on the descriptions provided by M. Shawn Copeland (cf. "Interaction of Racism, Sexism, and Classism") as the most succinct and clarifying research on how the definitions and descriptions of the infrastructuring of racism, sexism, and classism can affect our ethical response to the implications of globalization for and in theological education.

9. Copeland, p. 21f.

10. Albert Memmi, *Dominated Man* (Boston, 1968), p. 185, as cited in Copeland.

11. See William Julius Wilson's *Power, Racism, and Privilege: Race Relations in Theoretical and Sociohistorical Perspectives* (New York, 1973), and his more recent analysis of the declining significance of race, *The Truly Disadvantaged: The Inner City, the Underclass, and Public Policy* (Chicago, 1987).

12. See bell hooks and Cornel West, *Breaking Bread: Insurgent Black Intellectual Life* (Boston, 1991). hooks and West speak to the critically thinking masses inside and outside of academe, calling for greater politicization and critical engagement in the process of transforming contemporary culture and politics.

13. See Patricia Morton, *Disfigured Images: The Historical Assault on Afro-American Women* (New York, 1991) for a more explicit and scholarly commentary on the multitude of dehumanizing constructions of reality embedded in racist, sexist, classist studies of the history of black women in particular.

14. See Carter Heyward, *Touching Our Strength: The Erotic as Power and the Love of God* (San Francisco: 1989).

15. bell hooks, *Talking Back: Thinking Feminist, Thinking Black* (Macon, 1986), p. 101.

16. Don S. Browning, "Globalization and the Task of Theological Education in North America," *Theological Education* 23:1 (Autumn 1986), p. 43f.

17. David Tracy, *The Analogical Imagination* (New York, 1981), pp. 339-404.

18. Michel Foucault, *Power/Knowledge: Selected Interviews and Other Writings, 1972-77* (New York, 1980).

19. Roger D. Williams, *Positively Black* (Englewood Cliffs, N.J., 1970), p. xi.

20. I am indebted to and encouraged by the work of Enoch Oglesby in *Born in the Fire: Case Studies in Christian Ethics and Globalization* (New York, 1990), from whom many of these examples of proverbial wisdom and alternative methods of responsible praxis are taken.

21. This metaphor is inspired by Alice Walker's essay, "Beauty: When the Other Dancer Is the Self," *In Search of Our Mothers' Gardens: Womanist Prose* (New York, 1983), pp. 384-93.

22. Ibid., p. 393.

23. Langston Hughes, "Mother to Son," in Arna Bontemps, ed., *American Negro Poetry* (New York, 1963), p. 67.

24. I credit Melanie May, dean of gender and women's studies at Colgate Rochester/ Bexley Hall/Crozer Theological Seminary, as the source for these broad-ranging observations and sentiments, which I have adapted for this essay.

25. J. M. Coetzee, *Age of Iron* (New York, 1990), p. 106f.

26. Ibid., p. 136.

27. Martin Luther King, Jr., "Beyond Vietnam: Dr. Martin Luther King's Prophesy for the 80's" (New York, 1982), p. 8.

28. Edward Farley, *Theologia: The Fragmentation and Unity of Theological Education* (Philadelphia, 1986); Joseph Hough and John Cobb, *Christian Identity and Theological Education* (Chico, 1985); Max Stackhouse, *Apologia: Contextualization, Globalization, and Mission in Theological Education* (Grand Rapids, 1987); Mudflower Collective, *God's Fierce Whimsy: Christian Feminism and Theological Education* (New York, 1985).

29. Reinhold Neibuhr, *Love and Justice: Selections of the Shorter Writings of Reinhold Neibuhr*, ed. D.B. Robertson (Philadelphia, 1957), p. 40.

30. Copyright © 1993 by the Case Study Institute. The names of persons and places in this case have been disguised to protect the privacy of those involved in the situation.

31. See William B. Kennedy, "The Ideological Captivity of the Non-Poor," in *Pedagogies for the Non-Poor*, ed. Alice F. Evans, Robert A. Evans, and William B. Kennedy (Maryknoll, NY, 1987), pp. 232-56.

32. Beverly Harrison uses the term "class amnesia" to highlight the effect of societal pressures and shame to filter out family memories of poverty and "lower" class experience in favor of "success stories" that reconfirm the mythology of equal access for all to the American Dream.

33. See Donna Haraway, "The Promise of Monsters: Regenerative Politics for Inappropriate/d Others," 1990 paper prepared for *Cultural Studies Now and in the Future*, ed. Paula Treichler, Cary Nelson, and Larry Grosberg.

[8]

IMPLICATIONS OF GLOBALIZATION FOR BIBLICAL UNDERSTANDING

ESSAY

CRAIG L. BLOMBERG

I. Introduction

Most students of biblical hermeneutics now agree that presuppositionless exegesis is impossible.[1] Some, therefore, deny the possibility of finding any objective truth and eschew attempts to assess the relative legitimacy of competing interpretations of given texts. Few, however, can consistently live by this philosophy. More convincing is the model that outlines a hermeneutical circle or, probably better, a spiral, in which one tests one's pre-understandings by applying identifiable hermeneutical criteria to texts and comparing those results with the exegeses of diverse traditions and communities. Then one alters one's pre-understanding on the basis of the encounters with the text and traditions and continues to repeat the process.[2] The implications of globalization for biblical understanding are thus best summarized as a product of the process of one's coming to the text with a fresh set of questions, based on the agendas of religious and secular communities worldwide, which are less commonly raised in one's own tradition of reading the Bible, and then being open to allowing answers to those questions that emerge from the text to alter one's interpretations.

Staunch Calvinism should thus regularly interface with Arminian objectors. Process theologians should regularly test their views against Barth. Atheists need to moderate their interpretations in view of theistic exegesis. North Americans must listen to Asians. But in terms of the agenda items most consistently raised under the banner of "globalization," five stand out: liberation theology, feminism, pluralism, economics, and contextualization. Though space permits only suggestive and programmatic remarks, each of these five topics deserves brief treatment. Each brings questions to the text, which Western Bible readers have not traditionally raised as often as other questions. Each elicits fresh answers which should have

213

an impact on theological education. At the same time, it is worth stressing that a vocal minority of proponents in each of these arenas of theological reflection has so emphasized particular concerns that increased globalization *for the minority* must mean balancing its agendas with the concerns of still other parts of the world (including those of more traditional First World conservative Anglo-Saxon Protestants). To borrow an analogy from the study of world history and literature, the solution to a historic imbalance in favor of "DWEM's," as they are being called (Dead White European Males), is not the automatic demeaning or neglect of all such individuals. Reverse discrimination may seem to create a balance longitudinally, but latitudinally it merely replaces one injustice with another.

Even as pre-understanding informs exegesis, several presuppositions will limit the parameters of this discussion. First, it will be assumed that "biblical understanding" refers to interpretations which arise out of the Protestant canon of Scripture. The results of this discussion would not seem to be materially affected by the inclusion of the deutero-canonical material accepted by Roman Catholic or Orthodox communions, so it is best to focus on that on which all three major branches of Christianity agree. Of more concern is to avoid appeal to various kinds of "canons within the canon," in which objectionable material is *de facto* jettisoned. Precisely by the definition of the hermeneutical process outlined above, it is those passages which most challenge an individual's cherished conceptions on a topic that requires closest scrutiny. Biblical exegesis which purports to be Christian must, by any recognizable historic definition of that adjective, accept the authority of at least the basic sixty-six books. It may determine that the theological principles behind certain texts require quite different applications in new contexts, but it may not reject views it believes the Bible puts forward as transcultural simply because they are out of step with contemporary fashion or personally distasteful. A canonical interpretation further means that questions about the pre-history or authorship of texts will not be raised here. Though interrelated, authority and authenticity are separable issues.[3]

II. Liberation Theology

The challenge of liberation theology comes primarily from Latin America, Southern Africa, and East Asia. It calls for a restoration of focus on this-worldly aspects of biblical salvation in contexts in which they have not been given adequate attention.[4] Globalization for liberation theologians who stress these social-physical-material benefits to the virtual exclusion of spiritual liberation and life after death requires a restoration of balance in the opposite direction. A sympathetic encounter with all the biblical data suggests that the proper synthesis may be similar to what Ron Sider has called "an evangelical theology of liberation."[5]

The Exodus provides a proper starting point for this paradigm.[6] The Israelites experienced spiritual liberation and freedom from physical oppression by the Egyptians. But the Exodus was quickly followed by Sinai. Israel's liberation invested in them the greater responsibility of the Law—to model before a watching world the standards of God's righteousness and to point people to the one true God of the universe, Yahweh. Herein lies the heart of the promise to Abraham with which the patriarchal narratives begin (Gen. 12:1-3), the ultimate fulfillment of which Paul will argue comes with Jesus of Nazareth (Gal. 3:8). The majority of the historical narratives of the Hebrew Scriptures centers on the cycles of temporary and partial fulfillment of the promises of land, progeny, and blessing, contingent on Israelite obedience to the Law.

But the New Testament consistently applies the more exclusive texts of the Hebrew Scriptures in more unrestricted ways.[7] Whereas the Psalmist promised faithful Israelites peaceful existence in the land once called Canaan (Ps. 37:11), Jesus quotes the identical Psalm to declare that his true followers ("the meek") will inherit the entire earth (Matt. 5:5). When the Samaritan woman raises questions of sacred geography, Jesus looks ahead to the time after his exaltation when such issues will become irrelevant. Rather, "God is spirit, and his worshipers must worship in spirit and truth" (John 4:24). Revelation 20-22 warns against spiritualizing the promises concerning peace and justice in the land to the point that they exclude a literally re-created earth from God's eschatological purposes. The inaugurated eschatology of the New Testament more generally should prevent one from limiting this re-creation to a coming age, and inspire Christians to work, with the help of God's Spirit, for the greater fulfillment of God's righteous purposes in society in the present. But it should also temper utopian enthusiasm that expects, short of the end of this age, the appearance of any long-lasting "new world order" which is strikingly better than what human history to date has experienced.[8]

Jesus' teaching should be thought of as a kind of revolutionary protest, but it eschewed both violence and nationalism in favor of love.[9] His social involvement challenged his own religious authorities more directly than it did Roman politics. The universal focus of the New Testament of the church as uniting Jew and Gentile in Christ and creating a heavenly citizenship (Phil. 3:20) should similarly prevent one from exalting any one nation, political entity, or people group as more or less a part of God's plans for history in the present era.[10] These observations call equally into question: (1) common American evangelical equations of Christianity and republicanism (or of the restoration of the state of Israel with God's will), (2) common Western liberal identifications of "progressive" or "developed" cultures as the products of moral evolution and hence superior to so-called "primitive" or "developing" cultures, and (3) common liberationist dogmas of the inherent goodness of political freedom, of the moral superiority of socialism to capitalism, or of ethnic autonomy as necessarily desirable, apart from any of these factors drawing people closer to service of the true and living God now made known through Jesus Christ.

Careful analysis of the biblical wisdom literature again suggests a balance between opposing emphases.[11] The Psalms and Proverbs continue the theme of prosperity as a reward for righteousness. But they also begin to introduce the equation of poverty and piety, a theme continued in the prophets, with their call for justice and righteousness which reaches its zenith in Isaiah 40-66 (but cf. also 1:17, 9:7, 11:4, 14:30, 33:5, etc.).[12] So when Jesus quotes Isaiah 61:1-2, claiming that in him is fulfilled the prophecy concerning the Servant of the Lord whose mandate was "to preach good news to the poor . . . to proclaim freedom for the prisoners and recovery of sight for the blind, to release the oppressed," and "to proclaim the year of the Lord's favor" (Luke 4:18-19), these terms may be restricted to neither spiritual nor physical liberation.[13] Luke's "blessed are you who are poor" (Luke 6:20) does not contradict Matthew's "blessed are the poor in spirit" (Matt. 5:3); both draw on this dual background of the Hebrew word *ana-wim*.[14] Against many evangelicals, Matthew does not have in mind the economically rich who are spiritually humble; against many liberationists, Luke is not referring to the economically poor who take no thought for God.[15]

So too the Law and the Prophets combine a strong emphasis on social justice, denouncing the sins of Israel's corrupt, oppressive leaders and enacting legislation to put limits on consumption and provide care for the dispossessed, with equally strong calls to serve God alone (climaxed in the credo of Deuteronomy 6:4-9). Social justice in the service of false gods is no more commendable than orthodoxy without orthopraxy.[16] In the same vein, the epistle of James contains some of the strongest New Testament denunciations of rich landlords of poor Christians in a context strikingly parallel to the oppression of many modern-day Latin American peasants at the hands of traditional Catholicism, corrupt governments, and huge multi-national corporations (see esp. Jas. 5:1-6).[17] But James also makes plain, in ways not usually highlighted by liberation theologians, that God's "preferential option for the poor" is not for all the economically impoverished irrespective of their spiritual condition, but "for those who love him" (2:5).[18]

Indeed, throughout the rest of the New Testament, this "both/and" witness persists. Jesus' teaching focuses on a coming Judgment Day and an age to come, with eternal perfection for his followers, in ways which cannot be dismissed as merely metaphorical language for a better quality of existence in the here and now (see esp. Matt. 25:31-46).[19] People who deny him in this age will be denied before his heavenly Father (Matt. 10:32-33; cf. Mark 8:38). He is concerned to heal people's physical ailments, but the forgiveness of sins takes on even greater priority (Mark 2:1-12).[20] As these references demonstrate, it is not just the Johannine Jesus who speaks this way, though the Fourth Gospel is the one which contains the greatest number of references to eternal life (see esp. John 5:24-30 for the classic balance of realized and future eschatology). Luke, on the other hand, is the Gospel writer with the greatest social concern, highlighting Jesus' compassion for the outcasts and disenfranchised of society, most notably women, prostitutes, the poor, lepers, Samaritans, tax-collectors, and other notorious "sinners." But his salvation, too, remains holistic.[21] Luke's Jesus comes "to seek and to save the lost" (Luke 19:10) in the context of the salvation of Zacchaeus, who welcomed Jesus gladly, but also gave half of his possessions to the poor and restored fourfold the finances of those he had defrauded in his toll collecting. If it is often overlooked that the "parable" of the sheep and the goats is most likely depicting Christ's judgment of people's response to his emissaries ("brothers"),[22] it is also often forgotten that the Good Samaritan generalizes the command to help materially needy Christians to include their enemies, particularly those of other religions and races (Luke 10:25-37).[23]

Despite Paul's staunch insistence on justification by faith, he does not betray Jesus' holistic view of liberation. Romans 8 provides a ringing climax to the progression of salvation described throughout Romans 1-8 and includes a restoration of all creation, which has been groaning in its oppression (Rom. 8:19-22). The unity of the church, so central to Ephesians, will prove a witness to the principalities and powers of its day (Eph. 3:10), which must include evil governments as well as the more overtly demonic realm. Here is surely a mandate for opposing systemic as well as personal evil.[24] The two major, competing readings of Peter's first epistle demonstrate how balanced his perspectives are. On the one hand, the epistle may plausibly be read as a call for Christians to provide "a home for the homeless" as a kind of refuge from a hostile world.[25] On the other hand, it may just as plausibly be seen as a call to Christian involvement in society to "seek the welfare of the city."[26] Romans 13, finally, must always be balanced with Revelation 13. Governments may be ordained by God, or they may be demonic. And the consistent biblical subordination of Satan to God makes possible the additional conclusion that in some instances both of these may be simultaneously true!

Perhaps a translation of Jesus' oft-repeated declaration, ἡ πίστις σοῦ σέσωκέν σε (Mark 5:34, 10:52; Luke 7:50, 17:19), which renders his words, "Your faith has made you whole," best encapsulates the biblical theme of liberation.[27] God in Christ is concerned to heal our physical as well as our spiritual sicknesses, but neither is ever more than partially accomplished in this life. Christians, and theological institutions in particular ought to be working for and preparing others to bring about social justice in this world and fellowship with God in the next. Definitions of evangelism are truncated and biblically incomplete if they focus merely on bringing a person to pray a prayer of repentance and faith or merely on sensitizing an individual to cross-cultural oppression. "Pro-life" movements are myopic if they battle abortion without simultaneously becoming advocates for the poor and marginalized who have already been born, just as "peace and justice" movements are incomplete if they do not also seek justice (and therefore life!) for unborn children.[28]

The biblical balances which emerge when the questions of liberation theology are addressed to the canonical texts take one beyond most contemporary liberation theology and beyond most contemporary evangelical theology to a holistic mandate which is bigger than both. Immersion in Two-Thirds World contexts of extreme poverty drives this point home powerfully. A traditional Gospel of merely spiritual salvation lacks credibility in situations of intense physical suffering, while an offer of merely physical help, when many will die anyway, leaves people without hope for the eternal fellowship with God which far more than compensates for even the greatest suffering of this life (Rom. 8:18). Of many contemporary models which approximate this balance, a good example in the English-speaking world is the "Heart for the City" focus of the "Church Unleashed" movement, originally inspired by Frank Tillapaugh.[29] Among Latin Americans, the writings of Orlando Costas and René Padilla prove particularly balanced and programmatic.[30]

III. Feminism

From one point of view, feminism is simply one branch of liberation theology, just as in certain senses also are black theology, gay theology, Asian theology, and a variety of other subdisciplines, which limitations of space prevent treating here. But feminism's size and significance as a movement, the size of the "minority" it represents, and the uniqueness of some of the hermeneutical questions it raises all justify at least brief comment. If one wants to interact with marginalized voices from cultural traditions around the world other than those which have dominated modern biblical scholarship, one must dialogue with feminism. The major questions feminists ask others to pose of the biblical texts deal with issues of equality and roles in the church, society, and home.[31] They understandably see the stories of Scripture that narrate the violation and exploitation of women as "texts of terror"[32] (for example, the obvious cases of the rape of Dinah and Tamar or the seduction of Bathsheba, but also "milder" prejudice such as Paul's command regarding submission of wives to husbands in Ephesians 5:22-23). Feminists point to biblical examples of women in leadership (such as Deborah and Huldah, Phoebe and Junia) and statements about equality in Christ (most notably Galatians 3:28) as support for their claim that patriarchy is evil and that women have historically been unjustly oppressed in being denied equal access to leadership positions in the church and family.[33]

Globalization for non-feminists thus requires a careful re-reading of these portions of Scripture to see if the vast majority of church history has been guilty of a monstrous repression of women and to the extent that it has, to seek redress by vigorously advocating women's rights. Conversely, globalization for committed feminists must involve a rigorous re-examination of their readings of Scripture and their personal motives to see if they adequately account for biblical texts which seem to mandate male/female role differentiation (e.g., Eph. 5:22-33, 1 Tim. 2:8-15, 1 Pet. 3:1-7) as well as those which call Christian women *and men* to relinquish their rights as a counter-cultural testimony to a world bent on seeking only selfish advancement (e.g., 1 Pet. 2:11-25, Tit. 2:9-3:2).

The arguments for the two sides are, in fact, more finely balanced than most on either side usually admit. On the one hand, there are striking parallels between many arguments for patriarchy or hierarchy and the classic "Christian" arguments on behalf of slavery.[34] If, as virtually everyone in North America and Europe today admits, slavery is wrong and unbiblical, surely it would follow that any kind of mandatory role differentiation between men and women must be equally undesirable. On the other hand, there are no biblical texts which say that persons of color could not or cannot do anything which other individuals may. To be sure, advocates of slavery and apartheid have drawn unjustified theological inferences from certain passages of Scripture, but that is quite different than if specific texts had read, "I do not permit a black person to teach or have authority over a white person" or "Native Americans, submit yourselves to Europeans as unto the Lord."

There are, therefore, at least four clearly definable options. (1) Some find Scripture so thoroughly permeated with a patriarchy promoted as normative that they cannot accept any form of Christianity which is biblically based.[35] (2) Some try to salvage the supposedly egalitarian portions of Scripture by setting up a canon within the canon and simply refusing to countenance any normative value for patriarchal texts, even though they admit that the biblical authors themselves viewed patriarchy as transcultural.[36] (3) Another group, usually calling itself biblical feminism, accepts the authority of the entire canon, but denies that it ever explicitly promotes patriarchy. What "discrimination" is present is descriptive and not prescriptive; commands to subordination are culture-bound and not transcultural. Only the egalitarian strains were ever intended to be timeless.[37] (4) The most conservative group agrees with the first two that part or all of Scripture is "irredeemably androcentric"[38] but does not view this as a problem to overcome. This group finds a wholesome, divinely ordained aspect in role distinctions, often citing the growing number of secular, social-scientific studies which stress not merely physiological, but psychological, emotional, and cognitive differences between men and women, while at the same time admitting that historically many Christians have gone far beyond biblically defensible distinctions in their discrimination against women.[39]

The most attractive option for one committed to the blend of evangelical and liberation theology already articulated is clearly the third view, as currently represented in North America by the rapidly growing organization, Christians for Biblical Equality. The fact that the other three views agree that part or all of Scripture promotes some kind of transcultural distinction between the genders, however, gives one pause.[40] Perhaps there is a fifth option, still remaining to be explored in detail, which would rigorously assert the full, essential, or ontological equality of men and women without denying possibly God-ordained role differentiations in certain settings.[41] Some would deny that it is possible to maintain functional differentiation without implying essential subordination, but it is not clear that collegial experiences in other arenas of life demonstrate this possibility. If leadership can be recognized, biblically, to involve servanthood more than authority, responsibility more than privilege, then one who assumes leadership of a church or home should promote the welfare of those being led above self.[42] And if it is recognized that roles of leading and being led are voluntarily assumed, then nothing need be inferred about essential inequality of the various individuals participating in the specific group. For example, it is at least arguable that the interpretation which best accounts for the combination of cultural and transcultural elements in 1 Timothy 2:8-15 is that which prevents a woman from performing the role of an ecclesiastical office (what Paul seemingly interchangeably designates as elder/presbyter/bishop) if and only if (a) she is married, (b) her husband is a member of that congregation, and (c) the nature of her office is to exercise authority over him. The rationale then would probably be to guard against inappropriate domestic relationships, inasmuch as the church is to model the fellowship of the family. But this interpretation would not prevent the ordination and pastoral ministry of unmarried women, of married women ministering in other contexts, or of team ministry of husband and wife together. Put another way, no woman would have to be excluded from ministry except in certain situations which she could choose to avoid.[43]

Such a "compromise" currently fits into no well-established ecclesiastical patterns. Feminists have very little time for anyone who would put any restrictions on them, notwithstanding the fact that the Bible's description of Christian discipleship more generally is characterized by the voluntary relinquishing of one's personal rights. Non-feminists in general fear that society has already become too feminized, and they blame most of the destructive forces affecting today's families and churches on that process of feminization. Few evangelical churches have moved anywhere close to a liberal position as this compromise would articulate, and many are now seriously trying to reclaim a greater emphasis on men in positions of leadership in the family and home than they currently maintain! Meanwhile, statistics of men's physical abuse of their wives and children, indeed even of the frequency of incestuous relationships, frighteningly mounts in conservative Christian circles, while more liberal Christian circles find it increasingly difficult to attract men to active discipleship and balanced models of servant-leadership. In many such churches these models are almost totally absent. So perhaps it is not completely naive to suggest that none of the main, current models is working or faithfully reflecting the "whole counsel" of God's Word. Internationally known

Anglican evangelical John Stott, however, has articulated and implemented a very close approximation to this proposed paradigm, with a plurality of leadership of men and women in team ministry even through his team leaders have remained male.[44]

Immersion in non-Western cultures would seem to confirm the need for such a "compromise." On the one hand, the vast majority is more traditional in recognizing a variety of valuable role distinctions between men and women. Western liberal feminists sometimes are surprised that their agenda for women's liberation is not met with the expected enthusiasm by women from other cultures.[45] On the other hand, the diversity of these role distinctions suggests they are functional and not ontological in origin. Many, for example, in evangelical circles prove more open to women in ministry than their North American counterparts, leaving missionaries in the paradoxical situation of promoting a double standard. What women are denied access to "at home," they are permitted and even encouraged to do abroad![46]

A quite different effect of cross-cultural immersion is the realization of the remarkable role of women helping to meet the needs of the poor in Two-Thirds World contexts, particularly where men are unable or unwilling to help. Visitors to these situations often speak of seeing in such women "the maternal face of God." This raises the whole question of the appropriateness of inclusive (or even exclusively feminine) language and imagery for the Godhead.[47] This question lies largely beyond the scope of this study, but it is worth at least noting that one's views on women's roles should logically correlate with one's approach to the Godhead. If there are never any functional distinctions among husbands and wives, then there should be no objection to calling God "Mother." In fact, such forms of address should be promoted since almost certainly one of the reasons the Bible consistently applied the language of "Father" to God was to underline his authority and sovereignty.[48] The fact that evangelical feminists, for the most part, have refused to take this step reflects an inherent inconsistency in their position. On the other hand, if it seems inappropriate to render all of the biblical language for God in inclusive terms,[49] then, because husband-wife relationships are modeled after the relationships within the Trinity (1 Cor. 11:3), perhaps there is a transcultural, desirable role for husbands as servant-leaders after all. In either event, we may heartily applaud and support women's work among the poor and stress the imagery of Scripture, which applies attributes to God more commonly associated with women than with men [50] even if we may have to agree to disagree on other questions which feminists raise.[51]

IV. Religious Pluralism

Returning to the broader themes of liberation theology: if there is a biblical balance between what has traditionally been called evangelism and social action, then pressing questions are raised about what some deem the most crucial issue of globalization for the 1990s and into the twenty-first century—the issue of religious pluralism. In other words, if the Christian mandate involves not only calling women and men to a saving relationship with Jesus Christ but also striving to create a world more filled with peace and justice for all people, then to what extent may Christians continue to speak of the uniqueness of Christianity or of any truth which it exclusively contains? Globalization forces these questions on North Americans as they personally encounter for the first time people of various religions, often, given current patterns of immigration, without leaving their suburban enclaves. But the same is true for individuals of other religions. Much of the current struggle in the Middle East stems from the cognitive dissonance of Shi'ite Muslims trying to reconcile the claims of the Qu'ran that Islam has superseded Judaism and Christianity with their ongoing experience of a vibrant Jewish presence in Israel and of Christianity among the Palestinians, Egyptians, and Lebanese.[52] And if evangelical Christians find it increasingly difficult to believe that all those who have never heard the Gospel are automatically consigned to hell,[53] liberal Christians are having to explain the remarkable, global resurgence of evangelical Christianity, which according to their paradigms should represent a regression in the evolution of religion.

The major trend in worldwide ecumenical circles in the last half-century has been consistently to move further and further away from acknowledging any exclusive truth-claims for Christianity. Dialogue is good; proselytizing is taboo. Relativistic presuppositions render conversion unnecessary.[54] It is hard to square this trend with any viable understanding of the biblical data as normative.[55] Israelite religion clearly puts forward the Jews as God's uniquely chosen people. Their God, Yahweh, is unrelentingly monotheistic. The Credo which summarizes the heart of Judaism focuses on Yahweh alone as God (Deut. 6:4-9). The most serious and besetting sin of the Israelites over the course of their history is idolatry — serving other gods besides Yahweh. Animism, polytheism, pantheism, and henotheism are never countenanced as viable alternatives but as damnable sin. Paul in the New Testament articulates this exclusivism even more bluntly (Rom. 1:18-32).

The New Testament consistently applies the language of Israel as God's elect nation to the church as God's "new chosen people."[56] Gentiles as well as Jews now have equal access to God, to his special revelation, and to salvation, and on identical terms. But in another sense, the New Testament portraits of Christ are more exclusivist than Israelite religion, because they now declare that one cannot have God without also having Jesus. Such claims are attributed to Jesus himself (John 14:6, Mark 8:38, Matt. 10:32-33) and persist throughout the entire New Testament period (cf., e.g., 1 John 2:22-23). The major missionary thrust of the early church, epitomized in the ministry of Paul, is inconceivable without the conviction that people who had not heard the kerygma about Jesus were in desperate need of the liberating message of the Gospel. The proliferation of texts about hell or eternal punishment makes the jettisoning of the doctrine that those who reject the true Gospel of Jesus Christ will be eternally separated from God, in a state of existence which it is desirable to avoid, incompatible with an approach that acknowledges the authority of the entire canon.[57]

At the same time, none of this requires assent to the common evangelical notion that one must consciously hear the story of Jesus and respond in faith in order to be saved. Obviously all faithful Israelites had not heard of Jesus; they were judged on the basis of trust in God's promises and appropriately obedient responses to the revelation they had received. Romans 2:6-7, 14-16, and 27-29 probably have such people primarily in view and suggest that all who have not yet heard the Gospel may be viewed similarly: God will judge them on the basis of their response to whatever vestiges of true special revelation they have received as well as on the basis of the natural or general revelation he gives to all people (1:19-20, 32).[58] If the watershed between true and false religion has to do with the age-old dichotomy between faith and works,[59] that is, if what sets Christianity more clearly off from all other religions and ideologies is its clear affirmation that humans cannot earn God's favor through any effort or merit of their own,[60] then it would seem that persons who have not heard the Gospel but trust in God as they understand him rather than relying on any alleged goodness of their own might well be accepted by him.

Texts such as John 14:6 and Acts 4:12 do not preclude this possibility. Jesus declares that no one comes to the Father except by him, that is, on the basis of his atoning work on the cross and triumphant resurrection over death. He does not state that one has to have heard of him to be a beneficiary of his gracious gifts. So too, when Peter declares "there is no other name under heaven given to people by which we must be saved," he is using "name" in its Semitic sense of "power" or "authority." If anyone is saved, it is by Jesus' power; but the question of whether such people must have heard of Jesus remains unaddressed. And if it is possible that some who have never heard the Gospel may yet not be damned for all eternity, it is also worth asking if some who have rejected what was presented as the Gospel may in fact be identical to those who have never heard, because of the badly truncated nature of that "Gospel" as it was either presented or incarnated in the lives of the evangelists. One thinks, for example, of "Christian" German attitudes toward Jews before and during World War II or of traditional Roman Catholic alliances with oppressive Latin American regimes against the indigenous peoples they were claiming to evangelize.[61]

The objection that such concessions relieve believers of any missionary mandate lacks force on two grounds. First, careful study and interaction with devotees of the world's other religions (including secular "isms") demonstrates how profoundly ingrained performance-based ideology remains in every sector, including within professing Christian circles. The numbers of people who have not heard the Gospel who might yet find eternal fellowship with God based on faith rather than works do not seem to be overwhelmingly large. Second, the assumption by those who hold the door open to salvation for at least some who have not encountered the true Gospel is that no one will reject authentic Christianity who would have been saved without it. Rather, "redemptive analogies" prepare the way in certain (though not a majority) of non-Christian cultures for a rapid, positive reception of the Gospel when it is presented.[62] But those who embrace Christianity in such settings often raise the question of their recently deceased relatives who believed just as they and who, they are confident, would have equally warmly embraced Christian faith. The common evangelical appeal to Genesis 18:25 ("Will not the Judge of all the earth do right?") scarcely proves satisfactory; on the basis of God's justice none would be saved! An appeal to his mercy is more appropriate, in which one trusts in his grace in treating those who have died without hearing of Jesus at least as mercifully as he does those who do hear.

At the same time, dialogue in ecumenical circles needs to include a discussion of the most fundamental issues which separate representatives of competing religions. Too often, in the name of politeness and tolerance, the most crucial differences have simply not been raised. Of course, evangelizing dare not employ coercive or heavy-handed techniques; God's people ought to respect human free will at least as much as he does! But in a world in which powerful parties scarcely hesitate to try to promote their economic, political, and social agenda, and outspoken conservative representatives of the various religions prove equally strident in advocating theological and moral claims, less dogmatic adherents of various ideologies simply consign themselves to growing irrelevance if they do not make very clear what they believe, why they believe, and why they believe others should change and in what ways. They must grant others the freedom to reject those claims, but ecumenism is never advanced when discussions center only on a lowest common denominator of mutually agreeable positions or when disagreements are treated in ways which never permit Muslims to tell Hindus that they really believe they should convert to Islam (or Christians to Judaism, or Jehovah's Witnesses to Mormonism, and so on).

What is ironic in the "liberal" West, particularly in educational settings and in the media, is how consistently most every religious voice but evangelical Christianity is given a fair hearing in the name of religious pluralism. The irony increases when one is globalized and recognizes that in many parts of the once Communist world Christianity is given greater public consideration in universities and schools than it is in the supposedly democratic United States. Many Americans have so distorted the constitutional freedom preventing the *establishment* of any one religion in the public arena that they prohibit even a neutral *presentation* of the claims of historic Christianity in many sectors. Anglican bishop Lesslie Newbigin's works, *The Gospel in a Pluralist Society* and *Truth to Tell: The Gospel as Public Truth*, jointly released by an American evangelical publisher and the Swiss headquarters of the World Council of Churches, offer hope that a growing sector of people in the ecclesiastical world may be prepared to move beyond the current impasse to become advocates of a "committed pluralism," which denies neither the truths which inhere in parts of all world religions nor the uniquenesses of Christianity nor the legitimate rights of all religions and ideologies to compete with civility in the public marketplace for adherents.[63]

V. Economics

For those who already profess discipleship to Jesus, another arena integrally linked with liberation theology and the experiences of globalization involves how best to respond to the massive poverty, starvation, and, in general, economic inequities in so many parts of the world. James bluntly declares that those who see their Christian sisters or brothers in material need and refuse to help cannot themselves claim in any legitimate sense to have salvation (Jas. 2:14-17). John proves equally forthright: "If anyone has material possessions and sees his brother in need but has no pity on him, how can the love of God be in that person?" (1 John 3:17). As on each of the three previous issues, Christians tend to be polarized in ways which do not adequately account for the abundance and diversity of the biblical data on wealth, poverty, and stewardship. Conservatives tend to think capitalism is more Christian than other economic structures; liberals and liberationists frequently believe socialism or Marxism better incarnates biblical mandates. It is not at all clear that either of these assumptions is true or that Scripture promotes any one system which can easily be equated with current economic institutions.[64]

Wealth, as part of God's created world, is by nature good, but humans have corrupted it and used it to exploit one another. The Mosaic Law recognized the validity of private property, but enacted much legislation to prevent gratuitous consumption or the accumulation of wealth at the expense of the poor—hence the institutions of Sabbath, Jubilee, tithing, and gleaning. The Law and the Prophets regularly epitomized social justice as caring for the most dispossessed in the land including the alien. The wisdom literature recognized that prosperity could be the reward for righteousness or the result of greed and the oppression of others. Proverbs 30:8-9 expresses a mediating ideal: "Give me neither poverty nor riches, but give me only my daily bread. Otherwise, I may have too much and disown you and say, 'Who is the Lord?' Or I may become poor and steal, and so dishonor the name of my God." Tellingly, Jesus commands the same petition in his model prayer for his followers: "Give us today our daily bread" (Matt. 6:11). Lest these texts be confused with a justification for the "middle class," it needs to be recalled that virtually all who so label themselves today have accumulated enough goods to last them far longer than twenty-four hours![65]

The New Testament eschews even the rudimentary economic structures which the Hebrew Scriptures established. Here appear no tithes but many commands to voluntary, sacrificial giving to the needy (classically 2 Cor. 8-9), which should thus doubtless significantly exceed ten percent of the average Westerner's income. Here all Sabbaths and Jubilees, like Israelite holy days, festivals, and rituals more generally, are fulfilled in Christ, rendering their literal observation unnecessary (Col. 2:16-17).[66] But instead of laws enforced by a theocratic government, Jesus' disciples create a voluntary association (the church) which is committed to having no needy persons among them (Acts 4:34).[67] The implications of a similar commitment on the part of the contemporary Western church, whether liberal or conservative, are staggering. Personal and ecclesiastical budgets would require substantial modification to create truly sacrificial giving to the poor, while global institutions and structures which prevent fair distribution of goods to the needy would have to be challenged. And, lest anyone protest that these texts speak merely of a responsibility to the Christian poor, one need reply only that (1) estimates suggest that upward of 200,000,000 *Christians* live marginalized existences beneath any reasonable poverty line, and (2) texts like Galatians 6:10 make clear that our responsibility to do good is to all people, even if a certain priority attaches to those of "the household of faith."

At the same time, as stressed in the section on liberation theology, Christians with an acute social conscience must always guard against focusing only on meeting people's material needs at the expense of their spiritual needs. Further, it has become commonplace in certain circles to hear claims such as "it is impossible to be both rich and Christian," with appeal made to parables such as the rich fool (Luke 13:13-21) or the rich man and Lazarus (16:19-31), to Jesus' encounter with the rich young ruler (Mark 10:17-31), or to the entire epistle of James.[68] Yet it is clear that the rich man has not only neglected Lazarus, but has also never repented (Luke 16:29). The rich fool has not only selfishly accumulated crops which could feed others, but he has taken no thought for God (13:21). As the evangelist most concerned for the poor, Luke nevertheless makes relative the extent to which one may apply Jesus' command to the rich young ruler to sell all and give to the poor (Luke 18:22) by juxtaposing the otherwise unparalleled accounts of Zacchaeus

(19:1-10) and of the parable of the pounds (19:11-27). In these passages, other disciples give up only half or none of their possessions (in the latter case investing the money instead for their master's work). And though they are in the minority, there are well-off Christians within James' churches (Jas. 4:13-17, and probably 1:9-11[69]) as also in Paul's (1 Cor. 1:26, and probably 11:20-21[70]). What is valid to say is that the New Testament knows no rich people who may legitimately call themselves Christians who are not also generous with their goods in giving to support the holistic ministry (spiritual and physical) of God's people to the neediest of his world.[71]

Immersion in poverty-stricken parts of the world makes one aware of the terrible injustices of capitalism, especially in its purer, unchecked forms, which are not always visible to Americans accustomed to minimum-wage laws, relatively inexpensive public education, the benefits of the welfare system, however inadequate it may still be, unions, collective bargaining, and so on, all of which are the products of socialism. Compassion for the victims of unchecked capitalism, however, makes one that much more concerned to offer realistic, viable alternatives. A look back over nearly a century of Marxist experiments around the world does not inspire confidence that Communism in its purer forms offers any greater hope. Again, progress probably depends on mediating alternatives, perhaps more akin to the democratic socialism or socialist democracies of certain European and British Commonwealth countries, and perhaps even more likely to become incarnate in some entirely fresh combination of structures.[72] Yet Christians must never lose sight of their mandate: they must first of all focus on creating *within the church* the counter-cultural examples of sharing and compassion, peace and justice, which can then model before a fallen world the unique possibilities of God's redemptive Spirit at work in and through his people.[73] To this end, Ronald Sider's suggestions concerning "graduated tithes" prove suggestive; so too Tom Sine's practical examples of the possibilities of Christian stewardship in his newest volume of Christian futurism.[74]

VI. Contextualization

Perhaps the most pervasive effect of globalization on biblical understanding, irrespective of one's commitment to evangelical or liberal, liberationist or pacifist, American, African, European, or Asian theologies, is the regular discovery that one's interpretations of biblical passages have been so colored by one's culture that it is difficult to discern what genuinely inheres in the meaning of a text and what reflects unnecessary "cultural baggage" which has become attached to it. The process of removing such baggage, which may well have been very helpful in a previous culture, and where appropriate replacing it with analogous material in a new culture is what is often called contextualization. Put more simply, contextualization may be defined as "that dynamic process which interprets the significance of a religion or cultural norm for a group with a different (or developed) cultural heritage."[75] This process requires an assessment of the culturally limited and transcultural elements of Scripture as well as an astute "exegesis" of contemporary cultures to determine phenomena in them sufficiently analogous to the culturally limited portions of Scripture to enable contemporary applications of texts containing those elements.[76]

An awareness of the process of contextualization offers a sober reminder that every attempt to systematize the biblical data or to extrapolate the most essential, unchanging elements of the Gospel is itself a product of changing cultural forces. The ancient creeds, the Reformation confessions, nineteenth-century systematics, and contemporary liberation theologies all disclose as much about the nature of the worlds in which they were formulated as they do about the abiding truths of Scripture. Still, there are limits on this diversity, and cross-cultural similarities of emphasis remind one that contextualization need not (and should not) lead to pure relativism. But as with the hermeneutical spiral more generally, contextualization does call every interpreter to subject his or her views to the scrutiny of persons from very different backgrounds to see what additional truths may have been missed or distorted and to assess what may have been put forward as biblical which is in fact merely cultural. Immersion (through research) in the cultural worlds of the Bible is equally crucial to these ends and a part of globalization (across the centuries) not often adequately perceived by advocates of cross-cultural immersion in the present.

Surprisingly, most of the rigorous theoretical reflection on contextualization has come not from biblical scholars or students of hermeneutics but from missiologists, anthropologists, and linguists.[77] Biblical scholarship has tended to focus primarily on what the text meant rather than what it means in various contexts today. Contemporary hermeneutics has tended to focus so exclusively on reader-centered approaches that it eschews any cross-cultural objectivity in determining application or significance. But practitioners of these other three sciences have moved to a third phase beyond the more objective study of what a text meant in the past and beyond the more subjective study of all the possible things a text could mean in the present to a search for meta-critical models of application which combine objective and subjective components. Only then may result what Bruce Nicholls calls "the translation of the unchanging content of the Gospel of the Kingdom into verbal form meaningful to the peoples in their separate cultures and within their particular existential situation."[78]

The Bible itself reflects contextualization as the Laws of Exodus are restated but also altered in the Deuteronomic code to reflect the changing influences of a more sedentary life in the Promised Land over against wandering in the wilderness. The tabernacle later gives way to the temple, which in Jesus is so "spiritualized" as to be literally unnecessary (Matt. 12:6). Later prophets repeat and re-contextualize earlier prophetic material. Chronicles redacts Kings; the Synoptic Gospels modify their sources (which in part include each other) to make the Gospel more relevant for their distinctive audiences. The first creation account in Genesis is stylized at least in part to demonstrate Yahweh's supremacy over Baal; so too are many of the Hebrew Scriptures' miracles.[79] The New Testament quotes the Hebrew Scriptures selectively and creatively to demonstrate Jesus' own claim that all of the Hebrew Scriptures are fulfilled in him (Matt. 5:17). Paul's evangelistic sermons to Jews at Pisidian Antioch and to Greeks at the Areopagus are strikingly different (Acts 13:16-41, 17:22-31), yet both share a common strategy and core kerygma.[80] The Pauline epistles are characterized by their "occasional" nature; remarks are clearly tailored to the specific circumstances of each church, and yet a Christo-centric focus pervades them all.[81]

As with each of the preceding issues, one must forge a precarious path between two opposing quagmires—the danger of imposing one's cultural norms on a text and promoting those norms as transcultural and the danger of jettisoning transcultural principles as temporally limited and no longer necessary. Because methodological reflection in this field is still relatively young, it is not clear that any major works have yet clearly identified this mediating perspective; most tend to fall off the path on one side or the other.[82] Many of the contributors to recent international evangelical congresses on contextualizing the Gospel, however, seem to be striking a viable middle ground, so perhaps there is hope for a growing consensus at some time in the future.[83] Surprisingly, of all the regional and ethnic theologies being developed and promoted, those most neglected are the ones which are emanating from the Bible lands themselves, particularly the Middle East. Interestingly, New Testament study has seen a virtual renaissance of interest in Jewish backgrounds and has swung the pendulum almost completely away from the first half of this century's preoccupation with Hellenistic origins. Perhaps more attention to the small but growing body of literature emanating from Israel and her neighbors—from Jewish, Muslim, and Christian (both Jewish and Palestinian) circles—might suggest fresh contextualizations of biblical material which are being neglected by West and East, North and South alike. And to the extent that indigenous cultures in the Middle East preserve traces of customs and mindsets common to biblical times, the sifting between cultural and transcultural elements may also be enhanced.[84]

VII. Conclusion

In each of the five areas explored, tensions between traditional conservative and liberal theologies may be discerned. It is increasingly clear that neither of these traditions, as classically advocated, offers a way forward in a healthy globalization which will enhance biblical understanding while remaining faithful to biblical authority. A pessimist would call attention to the major trends in liberalism to grow increasingly more radical and less bound to Scripture, particularly in North American society, and of a widespread retrenchment, more bound to tradition, in more conservative circles. If either of these trends predominates, authentic Christianity will lose out. An optimist, on the other hand, would point to the smaller but significant movements within conservative Christianity to move more toward what may be called "progressive evangelicalism"[85] and within liberal Christianity to move more toward a centrist position and engage in serious dialogue with those more conservative than themselves.[86]

Plowshares Institute and its Pilot Immersion Project, of which this chapter is in part a product, has the potential to be an important example of this latter tendency and to become one of the most encouraging developments in the area of globalization of theology today. If there are conclusions in this article critical of that program, it is hoped that they can be read as constructive criticism in the midst of a critical evaluation of theologies of both the right and the left. If all Christians could agree to subject their doctrinal and ethical formulations to the bar of Scripture, taken in its canonical entirety, and to subject their Scriptural interpretations to the reality of the contemporary world, taken in its cultural diversity, then a certain unified agenda for theological education, and for Christian belief and praxis more generally, would doubtless emerge, even if agreement to disagree on numerous important details would inevitably remain. A balanced view of the nature of God's work among his people in the present age offers hope that such a consensus may in part be forged, but makes it unlikely that it will ever transform the world in entirely revolutionary ways. But to the extent that God's Spirit enables even partial fulfillment of these goals, we remain grateful and continue to strive for his ideals.[87]

The nature of this essay by definition has been primarily hermeneutical and exegetical in nature. Inasmuch as this entire volume impinges on theological education, however, certain personal illustrations of the impact of globalization on my teaching in a Christian seminary, in the five areas discussed here, may prove apposite. In teaching a variety of required New Testament survey courses, elective English Bible book or theme studies, and required and elective Greek exegesis courses, I try to dwell more heavily on key teaching passages on the topics discussed here. Choices for topics to research for term papers include a liberal dose of issues related to liberation, women, and minorities, and wealth and poverty. Required inductive Bible studies regularly assign texts like Ephesians 5:18-27 or 1 Timothy 2:8-15. One of our three required Greek exegesis courses deals solely with the book of James; required texts include both evangelical (Davids and Moo) as well as liberationist (Tamez) commentators. One quarter of the final exam in that course involves an integrated essay responding to the latter.

An elective on the parables of Jesus concludes with a field trip to meet personally and talk with leaders and participants in Mile High Ministries — a Denver inner city partnership of suburban and urban church and para-church organizations running a street school, home for unwed mothers, outreach to gays and lesbians, and the like. That field trip is led by one of our graduates, who gave up suburban ministry and residence for the inner city, in part, he claims, due to research on Luke's view of the poor for a seminar I taught on the theology of Luke-Acts. An English Bible elective on Matthew uses as one of three primary texts the cross-cultural commentary by the Roman Catholic priest and former missionary George Montague.[88] Input from international students, women, and minorities in all classes is sought and valued. Guest speakers from divergent perspectives are periodically invited. Examples could be multiplied; the possibilities are enormous, and I do not claim to have done more than scratch the surface.

CASE STUDY[89]

Affirmation of Life

Hector Gonzales closed the door to his office, retreating from several lively conversations in the seminary hallway. Hector realized he was also trying to gain some distance to put into perspective the recently completed faculty presentation on long-term investment in a North American foundation. An $80,000 grant to the seminary, sitting in a New York bank, gave urgency to the decision.

As dean of the faculty of the Central American Biblical Seminary (CABS) in Panama, Hector had an important voice in decisions regarding seminary funding. The seminary was unique in that there was no external board of trustees. The fifteen faculty members, three administrators, and two student representatives served as a governing board and made decisions together on seminary policies. There was a strong history of consensus on significant decisions. But the seminary was in a period of great ambivalence about the ethical principles involved in long-term funding.

Hector saw the current impasse as a result of several factors, the new curriculum being the most significant. Although adoption had taken several years of intense study and debate, the new course of study was now enthusiastically embraced by the faculty. In the words of one faculty member, the primary thrust of the program was "the affirmation of life."

Hector picked up the position paper the faculty had developed. He believed the paper described the program's goals quite well: "As persons committed to the task of theological education in Latin America, we feel an enormous responsibility as we consider the conditions of life and death among our peoples and the limitations of ministry and mission of our churches." The paper described the seminary's mission as the formation of pastoral agents "able and committed to accompany, build up, and guide their churches and ecclesial communities and agencies in evangelization and social action toward holistic service among their peoples in faithfulness to God's reign and God's justice."

Seminary administrators and faculty had profound questions about accomplishing their goals through traditional models, some stating that previous models had been "totally inadequate." Their position paper described the faculty's attempt to articulate biblical premises and develop the framework for a liberating model of theological education which could best achieve the seminary mission:

The faculty affirms that the biblical message, which Jesus proclaimed and incarnated, speaks very directly and powerfully and holistically to our Latin American reality. During recent years biblical scholars at CABS, in other parts of Latin America, and in other regions have been able to recover important dimensions of the message and background of the Bible. They have taught us that the central events of the Exodus, the conquest, the exile, the return, the ministry and death and resurrection of Jesus, and the birth of the church have major economic, social, and political implications. We see that the ministry of Jesus created conflict precisely because he was confronting very deliberately the religious, political, and economic structures that oppressed his people. His message about God's reign denounced those oppressions and announced liberation for fullness of life.

Now we understand that from Genesis to the Apocalypse God reveals God's grace as the creator and defender of life. This option for life is manifested in God's preferential option for the poor, for widows and orphans, for the oppressed, for women and children, for sinners and lepers, for foreigners and Gentiles. God calls all to newness of life in justice and peace. In Christ the unjust are justified in order to follow him in building up his body where this new life is manifested, and in building just communities and societies, where the basic conditions to sustain life and the human rights of all are established.

We should recognize first that God's reign proclaimed by Jesus appears not among the rich and powerful, but among the small and weak, among children, sinners, women, and other marginalized people. Likewise, the peoples who have experienced God's reign and God's justice are not the more developed and the more educated but the oppressed and exploited. Churches and ecclesial communities and their agencies are not called to enlarge themselves with bigger evangelistic campaigns, structures, and programs, but to be in solidarity with the most despised sector of our communities and societies. Thus the pastoral agents that the seminary tries to reach and incorporate in its formation program are those who have already demonstrated a calling to follow Jesus in his way of service, humiliation, sacrifice, and death.

The faculty members developing the various courses sought to use the most advanced approaches to pastoral studies, theology, and biblical studies in order to strengthen churches and agencies working primarily with the popular base. Central to the new curriculum were the analysis of the context of ministry, including current social, economic, and political factors; re-reading the Bible in light of this context; and implementing pastoral models based on the analysis and biblical study. The focus on the intellectual development of pastoral agents was balanced by a focus on spiritual formation, training in a variety of pastoral skills, and sharpening of commitments toward issues of justice. The faculty was convinced that this type of education could not be accomplished in the classroom, but must be incorporated into daily life and into direct pastoral work with carefully selected local tutors.

Hector and his colleagues had found that traditional theological education led to the formation of intellectual elites with high professional expectations and resistance to working with poor grassroots communities. In most of Latin America, because of the distance between seminaries and the cost of tuition and board, residential theological education was often limited to the most privileged in a society. Those young people from rural villages able to attend residential seminaries were dependent on church or seminary scholarship aid. However, after three or four years of living in comfortable dormitories and studying within a stimulating and diverse urban environment, some students were unwilling to return to their villages. While in seminary, they experienced several years of freedom from hard labor and were expected to return to communities where most pastors were "tent-makers" earning a meager living alongside their parishioners. Those students who did return home were often so "deculturalized" they could no longer relate to their own people or accept their former lifestyles.

In order to counter these dangers, the seminary designed its diversified course with a major component of a pastor's training taking place in extension education programs in or near their own communities. This design made the program both contextual and much more accessible to those whom the seminary sought to reach. The new model required candidates and their ecclesial communities to do self-studies of their faith journeys and their goals for the future. Upon being admitted to the program, students would negotiate with the seminary an individualized course of study based on the self-studies and on the counsel of their communities and seminary personnel.

While offering significant freedom to construct the most appropriate course of study for each student, the total course included traditional areas such as Bible, church history, systematic theology, ethics, Christian education, and pastoral studies. These courses were to be taken in a logical progression and with a nucleus of essential subjects taught primarily through correspondence, assisted by a local tutor, and through theological centers in students' own countries. CABS had formal relationships with thirty-five theological centers in eighteen Latin American countries. They were currently in conversation with another fifty centers. In theory each CABS faculty member was committed to travel and teach at extension centers twice a year. However, these courses were at the initiative of the centers. Some faculty members would have a year with no travel, while others would teach in the extension centers four or more time in a year. To deal with increasing international air fares, the faculty would try to make course arrangements in conjunction with other church or academic meetings scheduled abroad.

Students in the new program would come to the CABS campus in Panama for a maximum of four two-month periods of intensive study. This component facilitated the integration of experience and study and assured that students were meeting academically rigorous standards. The seminary could educate four or five students in the new program for the cost of one student in the traditional residential program.

The new program was introduced into the traditional format of the seminary in stages. Initially the residential students resisted the intensive courses, required for both residential and diversified students, as students were required to study much harder than in longer, full term courses. Gradually, however, both students and faculty came to express their enthusiasm for working with the broad diversity of Indians, Blacks, Pentecostals, and poor women who came from throughout Latin America to participate in the diversified program. Hector was convinced that the seminary community was benefitting from the insight, energy, commitment, and depth of experience of the new students. They were not only "adequately" prepared, but often outshone the residential students.

The faculty was challenged to learn creative new teaching approaches, to draw on and integrate the experience of their new students, and to be able to understand questions about the Gospel raised by radically different voices. Hector recalled a conversation he had with professor of New Testament Jorge Nuñez, as he discussed the challenge of explaining the "Kingdom of God" to Indians whose only context for "king" was Spanish kings who had supported brutal colonization, or the image of God as Father to women who had been raped by their fathers. Nicaraguan students who had lost family, land, and community raised very different questions about faith from the white, middle-class, male, residential students from Costa Rica. The faculty began to share insights and teaching models with one another as they attempted to adapt to their new constituency. One course was using material developed by two of the diversified program's women students. Hector smiled as he recalled Jorge's words: "Things are not as clear as in the past. In the past the answers were important. Now it is the questions." In spite of these challenges, or because of them, Hector felt the seminary was filled with renewed energy and anticipation

In the 1970s and '80s Hector saw political and ideological polarization as a primary challenge for many Latin American churches. He saw the challenge of the '90s to be the development of a pastoral ministry able to respond to the growing poverty and disempowerment of the present hour. Earlier, conservative denominations and congregations in many parts of Central and Latin America had been offended by the ideological stance of the seminary, which they considered radical. Now, however, many church bodies were adopting the same agenda as CABS, recognizing the need for pastoral agents who could work directly with poor and marginalized communities. Churches did not see the future in professional theologians but in lay pastors who could minister in a broad variety of areas. The seminary now had fifty-five students in the residential component of the diversified program and over 1,000 students enrolled in the regional network of institutions and centers.

The biblical and philosophical stance of the diversified program was with the poor and oppressed of Latin America. The seminary was training pastors to accompany those who were not part of the establishment and to work with them for a new society. Yet Hector wondered about putting new wine into old wineskins. Could the seminary move toward a new vision of fullness of life for all of God's children while reaping the benefits of investment in the old society?

Having been a faculty member for many years at CABS and now an administrator, Hector had been privy to diverse conversations regarding funding. He knew that the seminary president, Enrique Alvarez, was not only hesitant about international investments but, based on his biblical understanding of the church, was unsure of the ethical need for any institutional endowment. Hector recalled Enrique's words shared privately just last week:

> For years the seminary depended on funds "sufficient to the day." The poor whom we serve live this way, with nothing for tomorrow. They find many alternatives to survive. The church must be this way, too. The church should not be rich. There are other seminaries in Latin America whose teachers live and work among the poor; this model is consistent with the theology we espouse. I don't think that we should have large savings. Just watch out for our future if we have a million dollars in U.S. banks. This would be a serious challenge. How can we hold a preferential option for the poor while we secure our own position? When people are too secure, they start to change their minds about mission.

Hector was aware, however, that Enrique did not feel free to tell the faculty how strongly he felt. "I do not believe that presidents should overstay their ministry. I will be here only a short time longer, and I don't want to impose my views. We have almost always worked as a community, in consensus, and I respect the other positions."

Hector recalled the former president, José Cruz, who was as esteemed by the community as Enrique, but who had a significantly different philosophy of funding. One of José's goals had been for the seminary to become not only financially secure, but also independent from foreign mission support. The seminary was located near the center of Panama City on valuable commercial property. With the possibility of either selling or leasing the city land for long-term income, the seminary invested in less expensive land on the edge of town where a new, modest campus could be built.

José had also initiated a major funding drive through churches in Europe and North America to endow chairs for Latin American faculty. At the time the drive began, almost one-half of the faculty were foreign nationals, primarily from the United States and Europe. Most of the expatriate faculty members were appointed and financially supported by their own mission boards, often with significantly higher salaries than the Latin American faculty. Ten years later the endowment program was reaping impressive results. The seminary's chair of theology, held by a professor from Ecuador, was completely supported by funds from this program; a second chair was nearly three-fourths funded.

Anita Estaban, professor of Church History, was convinced that the seminary should maintain a secure financial base, not simply for its long-term security but to provide the scholarship aid which was so critical to the new program. "I am most concerned that we continue to be able to support women like Maria. She is a woman with a deep faith and a strong call to ministry." Hector knew that Maria was a widow with three children who sold vegetables in an open market to support her family. Like other women in the diversified program, Maria faced great opposition from her church when she enrolled. She was told by the male church elders in Bolivia that she was abandoning her children, that it was not worthwhile to spend the church's money on women who should marry and raise families, and that a woman who would travel alone to Panama had loose morals. Maria had initially used her church address to receive correspondence materials from the seminary. She lost a year of study because her pastor confiscated all of the study packets without telling her they had arrived.

Maria's commitment held firm. Hector remembered her telling him that her journey began when she had urged the church to help the needy people who surrounded the church. "One day I said that we should gather an offering of love for them, but the church said, 'No. This offering is for our church.'" Maria then told the elders about a poor woman with a fever who had five children and no money for medicine. She could not nurse her baby. "I reminded them about the Christians in the Book of Acts who shared with one another. The church again said, 'No, we do not help people directly with money.'

"This is when I took hold of myself. I needed to understand more about God. I began to study the Bible. At the church the pastor only spoke about theology that didn't mean anything. When I began your correspondence course, I used a dictionary to look up many words, but I learned that theology is about a relationship with God. Working with my seminary tutor, I began to understand more and more. My goal is to take the church to women in the mountains where my parents come from. I speak their language. I want the women to understand what theology means."

Half of the seminary's scholarship aid was reserved for women and indigenous people. Anita Estaban reminded Hector that "financing is a powerful tool. It gives us a chance to work a few cracks into the system and equip women like Maria to minister to her people."

Alfredo Morias, who taught ethics and theology, said that one of the issues the seminary must face was not whether to invest their funds, but where to invest. "People in Latin America continue to experience the disastrous effects of North American capitalism and the brutal restructuring policies of the International Monetary Fund. A handful of elites in Central America are becoming increasingly wealthy while poverty for the masses is growing. I am also deeply concerned about investing funds in the United States, no matter how profitable. U. S. taxes support a massive military machine that has invaded Central America for two centuries. For us to profit from a system that continues to subjugate us lacks integrity."

Anita Estaban challenged Alfredo's position. "We have to live in a real world — a world of contradictions. We can't force our institution to face the guilt for the whole system. We are in the midst of global economic transitions. The dramatic changes in Eastern Europe make European funding uncertain, and the recession in the United States has slowed mission contributions in mainline denominations. We need to move away from dependence on Europe and North America and build independent institutional stability for the future. Some have suggested that we should redirect our investments to our own country. But if we invest in Panama's banks or businesses, which could fail at any time, we could lose everything. Our government's policies are too erratic. Where and how we invest is a central issue, so I suggest we invest responsibly in stable international funds which don't support the U.S. military."

"We talk about autonomy, but no organization within society can achieve more than relative autonomy." Carmela Molina, one of the student representatives on the governing board, had spoken with Hector during a tea break in the recent presentation. "We may always be economically dependent, but our goal should be to be ideologically independent. If the seminary tries to be politically and economically 'pure,' it will be unable to take money from anyone. This stance would make it impossible for the seminary to survive, much less offer scholarships, provide a library, or hire tutors in other countries. Taking money from churches which attach 'strings' to their support and challenge the teaching of our professors is more dangerous than receiving money from investments of our choice. The best option would be to take a much lower rate of return and invest in churches and agencies that provide housing and services for the poor."

Hector glanced again at the bank statement which had arrived from New York in the morning mail. The $80,000 had been in a savings account for the past ten months, earning less than 4 percent interest. If the funds had been wisely invested in the international stock market during this time, they could have earned nearly $6,000 for the seminary — enough to provide tuition, room, and board for fifty students in the diversified program. The North American foundation representative implied that through his program the return could be even greater.

Hector opened his Bible. Apparently conflicting images came immediately to mind. In his ministry Jesus accompanied those who were outcast and downtrodden; he chastised those who laid up treasures on earth, warning, "For where your treasure is, there will your heart be also." Jesus had called his followers to "take up your cross and follow me." Wasn't this the basis of being in solidarity with the poor which the seminary was declaring as the heart of the Gospel? Yet Jesus also admonished the servant who had not wisely invested his master's money. Hector wondered which models were most faithful for the seminary as it sought to witness to God's reign with integrity. He also wondered how he could help the seminary move to a responsible consensus.

TEACHING NOTE

Affirmation of Life

I. Goals

A. Investigate the elements of a model of theological education by extension that seeks to be "life affirming."

B. Explore the biblical and theological assumptions that inform a particular model of theological education.

C. Discuss the structures of support for and opposition to a change in theological education that calls into question traditional Western European patterns of seminary and church life.

D. Examine the implications of connecting an institution's witness and mission policies to its investment strategies.

II. Teaching Design

A. Opening Exercise

1. Begin with a period of reflection. Ask each participant to share with another one phrase, such as "affirmation of life," which best summarizes the mission of the seminary with which he or she is connected (as student, faculty, supporter, etc.) Which elements in the life of the seminary inform this image? What is the biblical basis for the mission? Are there specific societal needs the seminary seeks to meet with its mission? What are the implications, if any, if one is unable to state the mission of a seminary, identify guiding biblical principles, or relate the mission to the needs of the society?

2. An alternative approach: Ask participants to write out their thoughts privately, then share with a neighbor their most immediate response to the question: If seminaries did not exist, how would you design theological education?

B. Issues

The following questions may help identify some of the major issues in this case.

1. Identify the central components of the extension program at Central American Biblical Seminary (CABS). Discuss the biblical understanding which informs the new program. Which elements in the program seem most directly related to this biblical understanding?

2. What are the strengths and weaknesses of the CABS extension education approach to theological education? Why were some students threatened by the new program? How does a seminary maintain integrity in academic competence and spiritual formation in an extension program when students are in residence for only limited periods?

3. A central component of the CABS model of theological education is the "analysis of the context of ministry ... re-reading the Bible in light of this context, and implementing pastoral models based on the analysis and biblical study." What are the practical implications of this approach? How would you expect students and faculty to respond to a curriculum such as this?

4. How do residential or extension programs help theological students relate to their denominations and former congregations in light of educational programs which concentrate on transformation of the church? This question may relate to issues such as "deculturalization" as well as to educating women in male-dominated church bodies.

5. What is the relationship between the new program and long-term investment policy at CABS?

C. Persons

List the major players in the case. Ask participants to identify persons by their role in the seminary and the various arguments concerning the seminary's investment policy. What biblical and theological arguments support autonomy from the power of provincial or dominating mission churches? Which support policies of liberation from a capitalist system that some declare brings death not life to Latin America? How would each person identified advise Hector about the seminary's investments?

D. Alternatives

If you choose to focus the discussion on the investment problem, analyze in greater depth positions of specific persons in the case: Enrique Alvarez, José Cruz, Anita Estaban, Alfredo Morias, and Carmela Molinas. Establish a short group role play asking participants to give Hector suggestions for developing a faithful and responsible seminary investment policy that is consistent with the new curriculum. Ask each person to note what biblical image or theological assumption informs his or her advice.

E. Closing

Ask participants to reflect privately for a few moments about seminary education. What mission themes stay with them? To what degree should/are investment policies a part of the mission of the seminary?

COMMENTARY

Affirmation of Life[90]

ELSA TAMEZ

To undertake theological education as an apostolic mission is to enter into a process of constant restructuring. The intrinsic components of theological education become dynamic and globalization occurs.

The case study illustrates this reality. One perceives from the brief description that this seminary is obliged to make radical revisions in its program because it takes into serious consideration diverse economic, cultural, social, ecclesiastical, theological, and ideological challenges. Motivation for these revisions certainly does not emerge from a desire to modernize or to make innovative changes but from the longing to respond to many who want to prepare themselves theologically to share the message of the gospel of liberation in the context of their struggle for a just life.

In the case study theological education is projected as an affirmation of life. By integrating life with its teaching ministry, the seminary cannot conceive of theological education apart from daily life and the macro-structures of society. It is also not possible to think of theological education in a uni-dimensional manner, according to traditional academic concepts or residential seminaries whose curriculums are frequently imitations of First World universities. Theological education as apostolic mission becomes complex and dynamic, offering challenges with many risks, yet gratifying because of the fruits that emerge. Through this case one observes that much ability and commitment are needed to face the different challenges that appear as theological education opens and integrates itself into the concrete dimensions of existence, spirituality, ecclesiastical community, society, and culture.

That is why the members of the community of CABS are forced simultaneously to consider several diverse issues. This consideration will inevitably influence the development of the curriculum and programming of activities (use of times and spaces) in relation to the candidates, didactic techniques, fund raising, and so on. The seminary faces the following challenges:

1) The greatest challenge is the reality of poverty and the struggle for life. There is a conscious discomfort in the seminary community due to the abyss between the cost of theological preparation and the context of bare economic, social, and cultural survival. To narrow the gap radical changes are necessary in the seminaries.

2) On the other hand, Hector's ethical concern is valid. He seeks to be consistent with the stance that denounces the financial mechanisms of the market and at the same time to acknowledge the economic necessity of increasing income in order to help more students with scholarships.

3) Theologically, the grace and mercy of God for those who are excluded are assumed. At this very point the question arises concerning the incongruity between university theological academia and the growing illiteracy in the interior of the country which CABS serves. Students and professors face a constant challenge to create pedagogical techniques in harmony with the content of liberating theology and the context in which it is shared.

4) An additional challenge that is not raised by the case is that today many indigenous people question the occidental rationality in theological education and Christian theology itself. To meet this challenge requires a reformulation of Christian thought from its roots, utilizing non-Western categories.

5) Women have been able to make inroads in theological education, and this has presented CABS with challenges that are revealed at different levels: *machismo* among students, churches that reject the ordination of women, the need for scholarships for women with children, and more. Anita Estaban is concerned with the situation of women caused by the "patriarchalism" which exists in many churches.

6) The ecclesiastical aspect is another concern that is always present. Students are sent by churches whose members are humble and often conservative. In the course of their studies, the students grow intellectually and in their sense of solidarity; CABS then must frequently build bridges between the students and their churches so that instead of being out of synch, the students can return home and be a part of their churches' transformation into authentic signs of the Kingdom.

7) Not the least of the challenges which the seminary must face are the ideological currents against solidarity, the option for the poor, the struggle for the defense of human rights. Attacks by people with closed minds become wearing obstacles to the efforts of change. In other words, the changes promoted by the seminary must be worked out in the midst of criticism, slander, self-defense, pessimism, clarifications, or explanations that never cease. This is all in a context in which the future for many is hopeless due to the economic and ecological situation.

My observation is that when theological education assumes the hermeneutical principle of God's option for the poor, or takes the poor and excluded as a theological reference point, the classical structures of seminaries totter. When spiritual life and academic theological preparation seek to be integrated, traditional models enter into crisis. That is why I would affirm that when challenges arise from daily realities of suffering and struggle, theological education acquires characteristics of apostolic mission.

In 2 Corinthians 4:1-15 Paul helps us understand an aspect of the significance of assuming an apostolic mission in the service of Jesus Christ. Paul sets his ministry within the new alliance inaugurated by Jesus, the Messiah. We are dealing with an age in which grace takes supremacy over the law and human beings over the Sabbath. Obviously this radical revision brings with it many difficulties for various opponents. Some cling to the holy statues of the old covenant; others distance themselves from history's conflicts and difficulties, thinking that they already abide in the Kingdom of God. These opponents do not submit to following Christ the Crucified; other leaders of the community of Corinth question Paul's apostleship and request from him letters of recommendation.

Second Corinthians 4:1-15 is written in the midst of a polemic situation. Paul is defending his apostolic ministry and tries to give an account of the significance of that ministry. In the first part, verses 1-5, Paul unfolds the objectives of his mission: to make evident the truth (v.2). This task can easily be manipulated and converted into arrogance and law that kills. Paul does not permit manipulation. He speaks of God's truth and not his own; he remembers that his apostolic mission is derived from the mercy of God (v.1); it is not his person that he is defending before the attacks, but his ministry. Neither is he preaching of himself, but Jesus Christ as Lord. Paul presents the truth as he believes it according to his conscience before God. His ministry does not seek to reflect his own image but the glory of Christ which is the glory of God (v.5). His understanding of the truth comes from the Gospel of the glory of God. So Paul boldly presents himself without weakening and at the same time is conscious that it is Christ who has illuminated him for Christ's glory.

In order to carry out his mission effectively Paul does not remain silent; he rejects the intrigues and does not falsify the Word of God for personal ends (v.2). Following Paul's example, it is very important in every ministry that involves an institution to maintain the balance between presenting the truth with all certainty and confidence, and at the same time recognizing that one's strength comes from God. This implies no weakening, having total confidence in what one believes. Paul's recommendation to the Corinthians is not based on letters but on his own testimony.

Paul realizes that some people will be unable to perceive the Gospel (v.4). According to him, the "god of this world" has blinded their understanding, and they do not have the capacity to decide or discern.

Pauline ministry is like a treasure, but it is in very fragile vessels (the ones who carry it). That is why the extraordinary strength that emerges from ministry proceeds from God and not from people or institutions. In the second part of this passage of Scripture, Paul writes of the actual risks of his apostolic mission. These risks can become agonizingly deadly, but there is always the hope of conquering death. "We are afflicted in every way, but not crushed, perplexed, but not forsaken; struck down, but not destroyed" (v.8-9, NRSV). The apostolic ministry implies participation in the death of Jesus and in his life. One who ministers is willing to take these risks to give life to others, even at the cost of dying like Jesus.

Paul concludes in verse 13 with the force that is given to him by the faith that undergirds his ministry. "We also believed, and so we speak" (v.13, NRSV). The belief that God who resurrected Jesus "will raise us also" gives Paul the boldness to continue in his apostolic ministry. Paul continues so that many people may reach God's grace and so that grace becomes superabundant (v.14).

The socioeconomic, cultural, ecclesiastical, and theological context in which the CABS carries out its task of theological education requires that it be assumed as an apostolic mission. The primary motivation of theological education should be to make evident the truth of the God of life and, consequently, the lie of an economic system that poses as an idol or as "god of this world" and is killing many by excluding them from fundamental necessities. Seeing theological education as an apostolic mission also signifies that the CABS should be capable of discerning the mechanisms utilized by the society and the culture to exclude women, Blacks, and indigenous people, and proposing new mechanisms for including all. The community of CABS must believe in the truth that it communicates and must realize that it will be judged by God. The truth of the Gospel of freedom, justice, and peace is at the core of the CABS educational mission; this truth propels the community to remodel its mission permanently.

Theological education as an apostolic mission bears its task with passion, with compassion, and with patience. It does not let itself be crushed by the slanders, the criticism, the repressions; it does not flag; it is not silent in the face of shameful reality. The CABS community should always keep in mind that it is responsible not only to itself; nor should it waste time defending the institution. The community must defend its ministry of theological education by affirming the life of all. That is why it organizes its institution with the intention of affirming the life of all, especially the lives of those who are threatened, since Jesus is the giver of abundant life. Desiring to include the most despised, the community finds it necessary to reformulate the models of education, the propitious times and spaces, and the necessary pedagogies.

All institutions are fragile and can easily become corrupt or lose their mission. That is why an institution's community life should be of constant self-evaluation. Also, many obstacles emerge in the process of radical change. At times one will have to say like Paul: "We are afflicted in every way, but not crushed, perplexed, but not forsaken; struck down, but not destroyed" (v.8-9, *NRSV*). Theological education rendered in those terms participates in the life and death of Jesus, in order to make the life of others reign, although the promoter of that life dies, while believing by faith that resurrection overcomes death.

Hector must consider the logic of law and the logic of faith as he considers the issue of financing. He must stay on the level of the logic of faith. The apostolic mission is ruled by the logic of faith, the logic of the Spirit, and not by the logic of the law or the laws of the market that enslave. These two logics are present in the world, and they may not be mutually exclusive if the logic of faith comes before that of the law. The Sabbath and the human are not mutually exclusive unless the Sabbath enslaves humans. If the logic of faith comes before the logic of the laws of the market, and if there is freedom to decide, then one can discern with maturity where to invest the funds in order to benefit many.

Notes

1. The classic study was Rudolf Bultmann, "Is Exegesis without Presuppositions Possible?," in *Existence and Faith*, ed. Schubert M. Ogden. London: Collins, 1964, pp. 342-51.

2. The fullest methodological analysis of the process is now Grant R. Osborne, *The Hermeneutical Spiral*. Downers Grove: IVP, 1991.

3. Contrast, e.g., Itumeleng J. Mosala (*Biblical Hermeneutics and Black Theology in South Africa*. Grand Rapids: Eerdmans, 1989), who recovers liberationist strains in the biblical texts despite purported later canonical attempts to cover these up, with Norman K. Gottwald ("The Exodus as Event and Process: A Test Case in the Biblical Grounding of Liberation Theology," in *The Future of Liberation Theology*, ed. Marc H. Ellis and Otto Maduro. Maryknoll: Orbis, 1989, pp. 250-60), who questions a liberationist understanding of the Exodus on precisely these grounds of competing layers of tradition-history.

4. The classic exposition is Gustavo Gutiérrez, *A Theology of Liberation*. Maryknoll: Orbis, 1988, rev. For the best survey of implications for biblical understanding, see

Christopher Rowland and Mark Corner, *Liberating Exegesis: The Challenge of Liberation Theology to Biblical Studies.* Louisville: Westminster/Knox, 1989.

5. Ronald J. Sider, "An Evangelical Theology of Liberation," *Christian Century* 97, 1980, pp. 314-18; for a detailed exposition of the biblical basis of this perspective, cf. Thomas D. Hanks, *God So Loved the Third World.* Maryknoll: Orbis, 1983.

6. Cf., from what otherwise contain very different perspectives, J. Severino Croatto, *Exodus: A Hermeneutics of Freedom.* Maryknoll: Orbis, 1981; and Elmer A. Martens, *God's Design: Focus on Old Testament Theology.* Grand Rapids: Baker, 1981.

7. See esp. W. D. Davies, *The Gospel and the Land.* Berkeley: University of California, 1974.

8. For this balance, cf. the numerous works of George E. Ladd; see esp. *A Theology of the New Testament.* Grand Rapids: Eerdmans, 1974; and *The Presence of the Future.* Grand Rapids: Eerdmans, 1974.

9. On which see respectively Richard J. Cassidy, *Jesus, Politics and Society: A Study of Luke's Gospel.* Maryknoll: Orbis, 1978; and Bakole wa Ilunga, *Paths of Liberation: A Third World Spirituality.* Maryknoll: Orbis, 1978.

10. This perspective accounts in part for what today would be perceived as the general lack of patriotism on the part of Christians in the pre-Constantinian era.

11. See esp. R. N. Whybray, *Wealth and Poverty in the Book of Proverbs.* Sheffield: JSOT, 1990; Sue Gillingham, "The Poor in the Psalms," *Expository Times* 100, 1988, pp. 15-19.

12. Cf., e.g., R. N. Whybray, *Isaiah 40-66.* London: Marshall, Morgan & Scott, 1975, pp. 239-46.

13. See esp. Robert B. Sloan, Jr., *The Favorable Year of the Lord: A Study of Jubilary Theology in the Gospel of Luke.* Austin: Schola, 1977.

14. Cf. Robert A. Guelich, *The Sermon on the Mount.* Waco: Word, 1982, p. 75: these are "those who stand without pretense before God as their only hope."

15. Cf. Frederick D. Bruner, *The Christbook: A Historical /Theological Commentary — Matthew 1-12.* Waco: Word, 1987, p. 135: "If we say that 'blessed are the poor in spirit' means 'blessed are the rich, too, if they act humbly,' we have spiritualized the text. On the other hand, if we say that 'blessed are the poor' means 'poor people are happy,' we have secularized the text. . . . Jesus said something incorporating both Matthew's spirituality and Luke's sociality."

16. Cf., e.g., John F. A. Sawyer, *Prophecy and the Prophets of the Old Testament.* Oxford: Oxford University Press, 1987, pp. 40-44.

17. See esp. Elsa Tamez, *The Scandalous Message of James.* New York: Crossroad, 1990; and Pedrito U. Maynard-Reid, *Poverty and Wealth in James.* Maryknoll: Orbis, 1987.

18. Cf., e.g., Peter H. Davids, *The Epistle of James.* Exeter: Paternoster; Grand Rapids: Eerdmans, 1982, pp. 111-12.

19. Contra, e.g., M. Douglas Meeks, *God the Economist: The Doctrine of God and Political Economy.* Philadelphia: Fortress, 1989.

20. For an overview of the functions of physical healing in the Gospels, see Craig L. Blomberg, "Healing," in *Dictionary of Jesus and the Gospels,* ed. Joel B. Green, Scot McKnight, and I. Howard Marshall. Downers Grove and Leicester: IVP, 1992, pp. 299-307.

21. The best and fullest study of salvation in Luke remains I. Howard Marshall, *Luke: Historian and Theologian.* Exeter: Paternoster; Grand Rapids: Zondervan, 1989, rev.

22. For a history of interpretation, demonstrating the predominance of this view in

past generations, and for exegetical arguments for and against, see Sherman W. Gray, *The Least of My Brothers, Matthew 25:31-46: A History of Interpretation*. Atlanta: Scholars, 1989.

23. Of three major foci, love for one's *enemy* predominates. Cf. Craig L. Blomberg, *Interpreting the Parables*. Downers Grove: IVP, 1990, pp. 232-33.

24. Cf. Markus Barth, *Ephesians 1-3*. Garden City: Doubleday, 1974, p. 365: "Following this verse the church would unduly limit her task if she cared only for the souls of men or for an increase in membership. Rather she has to be a sign and proof of a change that affects the institutions and structures, patterns and spans of the bodily and spiritual, social and individual existence of all men."

25. J. H. Elliott, *A Home for the Homeless: A Sociological Exegesis of 1 Peter, Its Situation and Strategy*. Philadelphia: Fortress, 1981.

26. Bruce Winter, " 'Seek the Welfare of the City': Social Ethics according to 1 Peter," *Themelios* 13, 1988, pp. 91-94.

27. See Craig L. Blomberg, " 'Your Faith Has Made You Whole': The Evangelical Liberation Theology of Jesus," in *Jesus of Nazareth: Lord and Christ*, ed. Joel B. Green and Max M. B. Turner. Grand Rapids: Eerdmans, forthcoming.

28. See esp. Ronald J. Sider, *Completely Pro-Life*. Downers Grove: IVP, 1987.

29. Frank Tillapaugh, *The Church Unleashed*. Ventura: Regal, 1982.

30. See Orlando E. Costas, *Liberating News: A Theology of Contextual Evangelization*. Grand Rapids: Eerdmans, 1989; C. René Padilla, *Mission Between the Times: Essays on the Kingdom*. Grand Rapids: Eerdmans, 1985.

31. On the implications of feminism for biblical studies, see esp. Letty M. Russell, ed., *Feminist Interpretations of the Bible*. Philadelphia: Westminster, 1985; and Adela Yarbro Collins, ed., *Feminist Perspectives on Biblical Scholarship*. Chico: Scholars, 1985.

32. The term comes originally from Phyllis Trible, *Texts of Terror: Literary-Feminist Readings of Biblical Narratives*. Philadelphia: Fortress, 1984.

33. The classic work of this genre is Elisabeth Schüssler-Fiorenza, *In Memory of Her: A Feminist Theological Reconstruction of Christian Origins*. New York: Crossroad, 1983.

34. See esp. Willard M. Swartley, *Slavery, Sabbath, War and Women*. Scottdale and Kitchener: Herald, 1983.

35. See esp. Naomi R. Goldenberg, *Changing of the Gods: Feminism and the End of Traditional Religions*. Boston: Beacon, 1979.

36. See esp. Elisabeth Schüssler-Fiorenza, *Bread Not Stone: The Challenge of Feminist Biblical Interpretation*. Boston: Beacon, 1984.

37. See esp. Gilbert Bilezikian, *Beyond Sex Roles*. Grand Rapids: Baker, 1985.

38. A label borrowed from David J. A. Clines. "What Does Eve Do to Help? and Other Irredeemably Androcentric Orientations in Genesis 1-3," in *What Does Eve Do to Help and Other Readerly Questions of the Old Testament*. Sheffield: *Journal for the Study of the Old Testament*, 1990, pp. 25-48. Clines himself is not an exponent of this position.

39. See esp. John Piper and Wayne Grudem, eds., *Recovering Biblical Manhood and Womanhood*. Wheaton: Crossway, 1991.

40. Cf. Clark H. Pinnock, "Biblical Authority and the Issues in Question," in *Women, Authority and the Bible*, ed. Alvera Mickelsen. Downers Grove: IVP, 1986, p. 55: "The radical feminists and the traditionalists both argue that such texts (e.g., Col. 3:18) are not feminist in content, and I suspect that their view, agreeing as it does with the 'plain sense' reading so widely held, will prevail and not be successfully refuted by biblical feminists. Of course, the biblical feminist interpretation is possible; the

problem is that it does not strike many people, either scholarly or untutored, as plausible."

41. For more detail on the relevant biblical data for such a position, see Craig L. Blomberg, "Woman," in *Evangelical Dictionary of Biblical Theology*, ed. Walter Elwell. Grand Rapids: Baker, forthcoming.

42. See esp. James E. Means, *Leadership in Christian Ministry*. Grand Rapids: Baker, 1989.

43. For a defense of a quite similar interpretation, see E. Earle Ellis, *Pauline Theology: Ministry and Society*. Grand Rapids: Eerdmans, 1989, pp. 53-86.

44. John Stott, *Issues Facing Christians Today*. Basingstoke: Marshall, Morgan & Scott, 1984, pp. 234-57.

45. Cf., e.g. Christine Gudorf, "Peru: Women's Agendas," *Christianity and Crisis* 48, 1988, pp. 393-94.

46. For a thorough survey, see Ruth Tucker, *Guardians of the Great Commission: The Story of Women in Modern Missions*. Grand Rapids: Zondervan, 1988.

47. The programmatic study in defense of this inclusivism is Rosemary R. Ruether, *Sexism and God-Talk: Toward a Feminist Theology*. Boston: Beacon, 1983.

48. See the detailed documentation in G. Schrenk, "pathvr," in *Theological Dictionary of the New Testament*, vol. 5, pp. 945-1014.

49. As defended well in Roland M. Frye, "Language for God and Feminist Language: A Literary and Rhetorical Analysis," *Interpretation* 43, 1989, pp. 45-57.

50. For a good survey, see Virginia R. Mollenkott, *The Divine Feminine: The Biblical Imagery of God as Female*. New York: Crossroad, 1981.

51. Herein lies the greatest obstacle. More conservative evangelicals and more radical liberals alike refuse to recognize this as an issue on which disagreement may be tolerated. Even people who adamantly reject creedal or dogmatic theology become curiously inconsistent and dogmatic on this issue. On this trend in the ecumenical movement more generally, see Michael Kinnamon, *Truth and Community: Diversity and Its Limits in the Ecumenical Movement*. Geneva: WCC; Grand Rapids: Eerdmans, 1988. For equally inappropriate conservative dogmatism, cf. Wayne Grudem, reviewing E. Margaret Howe, *Women and Church Leadership*. Grand Rapids: Zondervan, 1982 in *Journal of the Evangelical Theological Society* 27, 1984, p. 227.

52. Cf. David Dolan, *Holy War for the Promised Land*. Nashville: Thomas Nelson, 1991.

53. Witness the diversity reflected among the all-evangelical contributors to recent volumes such as William V. Crockett and James G. Sigountos, eds., *Through No Fault of Their Own? The Fate of Those Who Have Never Heard*. Grand Rapids: Baker, 1991; and William V. Crockett, ed., *Four Views on Hell*. Grand Rapids: Zondervan, 1992.

54. A recent culmination of this movement is the anthology of John Hick and Paul F. Knitter, eds., *The Myth of Christian Uniqueness: Toward a Pluralistic Theology of Religions*. Maryknoll: Orbis, 1987.

55. For a detailed discussion of the relevant biblical data, see the first six essays in Andrew D. Clarke and Bruce W. Winter, eds., *One God, One Lord in a World of Religious Pluralism*. Cambridge: Tyndale House, 1991.

56. The title of a programmatic study of the biblical doctrine of election from a corporate perspective (William W. Klein, *The New Chosen People: A Corporate View of Election*. Grand Rapids: Zondervan, 1990).

57. See esp. the catalog of texts and discussion in Neal Punt, *Unconditional Good News: Toward An Understanding of Biblical Universalism*. Grand Rapids: Eerdmans, 1980, pp. 23-30.

58. Cf. Klyne R. Snodgrass, "Justification by Grace—to the Doers: An Analysis of the Place of Romans 2 in the Theology of Paul," *New Testament Studies* 32, 1986, pp. 72-93.

59. As stressed particularly in the Pauline writings. A recent paradigm shift in certain circles denies that this is a fundamental contrast between Christian and Jewish thought in the work of Paul, stimulated by E. P. Sanders' ground-breaking work (*Paul and Palestinian Judaism*. Philadelphia: Fortress, 1977). There is no doubt that Luther overstated this distinction, but "the new look on Paul" has swung the pendulum too far in the opposite direction, as demonstrated particularly by Stephen Westerholm (*Israel's Law and the Church's Faith: Paul and His Recent Interpreters*. Grand Rapids: Eerdmans, 1988).

60. See esp. Norman Anderson, *Christianity and World Religions: The Challenge of Pluralism*. Leicester and Downers Grove: IVP, 1984.

61. For a book-length defense of this position from an evangelical perspective, with detailed interaction with alternative views, see John Sanders, *No Other Name: An Investigation into the Destiny of the Unevangelized*. Grand Rapids: Eerdmans, 1992.

62. See esp. Don Richardson, *Eternity in Their Hearts*. Ventura: Regal, 1981.

63. Lesslie Newbigin, *The Gospel in a Pluralist Society*. Geneva: WCC; Grand Rapids: Eerdmans, 1989. See also Newbigin, *Truth to Tell: The Gospel as Public Truth*. Geneva: WCC; Grand Rapids: Eerdmans, 1991.

64. See the survey of the biblical teaching in Craig L. Blomberg, "Wealth," in *Evangelical Dictionary of Biblical Theology*, forthcoming.

65. A brief but balanced survey of Hebrew Scriptures' perspectives on possessions is Hugh G. M. Williamson, "The Old Testament and the Material World," *EQ* 57, 1985, pp. 5-22.

66. See esp. D. A. Carson, ed. *From Sabbath to Lord's Day: A Biblical, Historical and Theological Investigation*. Grand Rapids: Zondervan, 1982.

67. See esp. Richard J. Cassidy, *Society and Politics in the Acts of the Apostles*. Maryknoll: Orbis, 1987.

68. The classic expression of this perspective is perhaps José P. Miranda, *Communism in the Bible*. Maryknoll: Orbis, 1982.

69. Douglas J. Moo, *The Letter of James*. Leicester: IVP; Grand Rapids: Eerdmans, 1985, pp. 66-70.

70. Gerd Theissen, *The Social Setting of Pauline Christianity: Essays on Corinth*. Philadelphia: Fortress, 1982.

71. Cf. Robert H. Gundry, *Matthew: A Commentary on His Literary and Theological Art*. Grand Rapids: Eerdmans, 1982, p. 388: "That Jesus did not command all his followers to sell all their possessions gives comfort only to the kind of people to whom he would issue that command."

72. Some programmatic suggestions appear in Andrew Kirk, *The Good News of the Kingdom Coming*. Downers Grove: IVP, 1983. Humberto Belli and Ronald Nash (*Beyond Liberation Theology*. Grand Rapids: Baker, 1992) adequately document the anti-capitalist excesses of earlier liberation theology and the more moderate approach of much recent liberationist thought. It is not clear, however, that their attribution of all the weaknesses of what passes for capitalism in the West as due to interventionism, protection, or statism, is valid, nor that the solution is to become even more purely capitalist than we already are.

73. See esp. Stanley Hauerwas and William H. Willimon, *Resident Aliens: Life in the Christian Colony*. Nashville: Abingdon, 1989; Ben Wiebe, *Messianic Ethics*. Waterloo, Ont.; Scottdale, PA: Herald, 1992.

74. Ronald J. Sider, *Rich Christians in an Age of Hunger*. Dallas: Word, 1990, rev.; Tom Sine, *Wild Hope*. Dallas: Word, 1991.

75. Osborne, *Hermeneutical Spiral*, p. 318.

76. A good recent example of Third World readings of Scripture, reflecting a variety of forms of contextualization, some more persuasive than others, is R. S. Sugirtharajah, ed., *Voices from the Margin: Interpreting the Bible in the Third World*. Maryknoll: Orbis, 1991.

77. See respectively, Harvie M. Conn, *Eternal Word and Changing Worlds: Theology, Anthropology, and Mission in Trialogue*. Grand Rapids: Zondervan, 1984; Paul G. Hiebert, "Critical Contextualization," *International Bulletin of Missionary Research* 11, 1987, pp. 104-12; and Eugene A. Nida and William D. Reyburn, *Meaning Across Cultures*. Maryknoll: Orbis, 1981.

78. Bruce J. Nicholls, "Theological Education and Evangelization," in *Let the Earth Hear His Voice*, ed. J. D. Douglas. Minneapolis: World Wide, 1975, p. 647.

79. See respectively Conrad Hyers, *The Meaning of Creation*. Atlanta: Knox, 1984; and Leah Bronner, *The Stories of Elijah and Elisha*. Leiden: Brill, 1968.

80. Gerhard Krodel, *Acts*. Philadelphia: Fortress, 1981.

81. On this unity of NT theology more generally, see Eugene E. Lemcio, "The Unifying Kerygma of the New Testament," *Journal for the Study of the New Testament* 33, 1988, pp. 3-17; 38, 1990, pp. 3-11.

82. Cf., e.g., Charles H. Kraft , *Christianity in Culture: A Study in Dynamic Biblical Theologizing in Cross-Cultural Perspective*. Maryknoll: Orbis, 1979; with David J. Hesselgrave and Edward Rommen, *Contextualization: Meanings, Methods, and Models*. Grand Rapids: Baker, 1989.

83. See esp. John R. W. Stott and Robert Coote, eds., *Down to Earth: Studies in Christianity and Culture*. London: Hodder & Stoughton, 1981; Mark L. Branson and C. René Padilla, eds., *Conflict and Context: Hermeneutics in the Americas*. Grand Rapids: Eerdmans, 1986.

84. See esp. Kenneth E. Bailey, *Poet and Peasant: A Literary-Cultural Approach to the Parables in Luke*. Grand Rapids: Eerdmans, 1976; and idem, *Through Peasant Eyes: More Lucan Parables*. Grand Rapids: Eerdmans, 1980; Tim Matheny, *Reaching the Arabs: A Felt Need Approach*. Pasadena: William Carey, 1981; and Phil Parshall, *New Paths in Muslim Evangelism: Evangelical Approaches to Contextualization*. Grand Rapids: Baker, 1980; Brad H. Young, *Jesus and His Jewish Parables: Rediscovering the Roots of Jesus' Teaching*. New York: Paulist, 1989; and most all of the issues of *Jerusalem Perspective*, representing Arab-Christian, Muslim, and Jewish perspectives, respectively.

85. Timothy P. Weber, "Premillennialism and the Branches of Evangelicalism," in *The Varieties of American Evangelicalism*, ed. Donald W. Dayton and Robert K. Johnson. Knoxville: University of Tennessee, 1991, p. 13.

86. For example, in the jointly authored volumes pairing evangelical and liberal writers such as Delwin Brown and Clark H. Pinnock, *Theological Crossfire: An Evangelical-Liberal Dialogue*. Grand Rapids: Zondervan, 1990; or David L. Edwards and John Stott, *Evangelical Essentials: A Liberal-Evangelical Dialogue*. Downers Grove: IVP, 1988.

87. I am grateful for numerous helpful suggestions from my colleagues for revising an earlier draft of this essay, particularly from Drs. R. Alden, P. Borden, B. Demarest, W. Klein and G. Lewis.

88. George T. Montague, *Companion God*. New York: Paulist, 1989.

89. Copyright © 1993 by the Case Study Institute. The names of persons and places

in this case have been disguised to protect the privacy of those involved in the situation.

90. Translated by Karen Sue Hernandez, Master of Divinity student, McCormick Theological Seminary, Chicago/Seminary Intern, The Fourth Presbyterian Church, Chicago and F. Ross Kinsler, Seminario Biblico Latinoamericano, Costa Rica.

[9]

GLOBAL ECONOMY AND THE GLOBALIZATION OF THEOLOGICAL EDUCATION

ESSAY

M. DOUGLAS MEEKS

"Globalization," as construed in this essay, has the same sense as the ancient question of *oikoumene*: Will the peoples of the earth be able to inhabit the earth mutually in peace with justice?[1] If we raise this question theologically, we ask how the triune God is working for the redemption of a world which has become at once enormously diverse and yet threateningly uniform.

Seldom, however, is "globalization" approached theologically. Its more natural home is economies where it arose within the universe of discourse ruled by multinational corporations centered in the United States, the European Common Market, and Japan. It recognizes that local and national economies are increasingly tenuous, that is, that governments are less and less capable of holding economic actors accountable to the humanity and dignity of the people in their sphere of influence.

Globalization from this economic perspective means that there is one global economy and that those who can comprehend or control the household rules of the global economy — its language and logic, its resource allocation, its markets — will survive and be secure. Those who do not globalize increasingly become victims of an irreversible historical process. And thus we have the recent self-congratulatory claim of a major multinational corporation, "We globalized forty years ago."

What, however, does a global economy mean for the two-thirds of people in the global household — the majority of people in Asia, Africa, and Latin America, and an increasing proportion of marginalized persons in the First World — who are systemically excluded from the global household, and hence threatened with death? Is it merely an irony that within North American theological education "globalization" is a current rallying cry?

Global economy, to say the least, may be the most difficult aspect of the globalization of theological education. Important strides have been made in addressing the global questions of plural cultures and religions; of racial, gender, and political subjugation; and of the degradation of nature. The human misery that results from injustices in the global economy, however, is so profound, and our modern theological and economic traditions so inadequate in recognizing and actively dealing with conditions of economic injustice, that this aspect of globalization tends to take a back seat in seminary deliberations and decisions. It is not just that the economic problems seem so intractable; it is also that in their modern cast theology and church are not supposed to be responsible for the questions of the public household. Theology and church have more and more confined themselves to the realms of meaning and purpose for the internal life, to the sphere of the private and of the cultural free choices of leisure. How to put economy and theology together in any significant sense is a major conundrum of globalization.

Global economy is beginning to emerge in North American consciousness just as apprehension about the post–Cold War age is growing. The central struggle of the five-decade-long Cold War has served so many powerful interests so well for so long in so many different ways that it is difficult to imagine new economic realities. It can be argued that the political economy of the North Atlantic won against stubbornly slipshod economies engineered by repressive states. But there is little sense that the "victory" is realizing great dreams. There are casualties of the long conflict for all. The nearly half-century mobilization, with a two-trillion-dollar U.S. arms buildup during the 1980s, has profoundly distorted our economy.[2] We have seen the hemorrhaging of investment funds and the draining of creative energy from the nation's cities, infrastructure, and education of its people.[3] The government has been willing to deceive in the name of national security, while political parties were becoming weak and the political process denigrated. We do not yet know the long-lasting effects of producing and testing nuclear armaments on the bodies of two generations of people (not to speak of the ecosphere), nor the Cold War fear of nuclear holocaust on their psyches and spirits. The "victory" does not take into account the anxiety of millions of middle-class people whose families fought for four generations to get into the middle class, but who now are fearful of losing all semblance of economic security.

What is clear in this time of *perestroika* in the West is that we do not have to go to Third World countries to find Third World economy. Third World economy exists right here in the United States, in depressed areas such as Appalachia and many sections of our metropolitan regions.[4] The economy of McDowell County, West Virginia, and of southeast Washington D.C. are adumbrations of economy everywhere in North America if current trends are not turned around. The point is that we live now in a global economy. The U.S. economy is still the strongest economy in the world; it can and does effect much that happens throughout the global household. Nevertheless, the U.S. economy is now part of a global economy; people who live in the American household are subject to many of the same economic dynamics that people in Zaire, Ecuador, and India suffer.

I. The Market Society and the Absence of God

An expansive dream has flourished ever since Adam Smith wrote *The Wealth of Nations*. It is the dream that economy can function without politics and without community. It is a powerful dream. But it is a false dream that, unfortunately, has everything to do with the separation of theology and economy in the modern world. Up to the seventeenth century, theology and economy were pursued together. But for at least two centuries now, it has been considered logically impossible, unwise, or even dangerous to think of God and economy together. Economics and theology, it has been assumed, belong to two entirely separate universes of discourse.

What separates modern economics from traditional economics, so that it is assumed that modern economics is in fact an entirely new science, is that God is presumed absent from the market.[5] Because God had traditionally been the epitome term of power and community, the Deism which arose at the same time as the modern market assured by abstracting God from the world that economics would not have to be encumbered by the necessity of dealing with politics and community. No traditional understanding of God's presence or God's law can be allowed to deter the science of economics from following its own internal laws.[6]

What separates most of modern theology from traditional theology is the tendency to construe God in ways that leave the laws of the market intact. In fact, one might say generally that modern liberal theology is that kind of theology that speaks of God under the conditions laid down by the theory of natural liberty and the laws of the modern market. God can only be and do what the modern market logically allows God to be and do. Were the church able to make a genuine historical contribution to the massive questions of economy, which are ever more urgently challenging the world's order and peace, it would have radically to rethink God and economy. But God (at least biblically rendered) and economy cannot be thought of together without the significant transformation of our conceptions of both.[7]

"Economy" is not a word invented by modernity; it belongs to antiquity, including the language and culture of the Bible. The Septuagint speaks of the *oikonomia tou theou* (economy of God).[8] The word "economy" means literally "the law of the household" (*oikos + nomos*). In its ancient sense economy is about the relationships of those in the household for life.[9] It is about access to what it takes to live and live abundantly.[10] As the arrangement that makes it possible for the household or community to live, economy was bound to community.[11] In fact, it was clear that economy existed to serve community.

The difficulty with modern economics, especially with the rise of neo-classical economics at the end of the nineteenth century, is that the ancient question of *livelihood* has dropped out of the center of economics.[12] This eclipse of the question of access to livelihood, of access to life, is the impoverishment of modern economics, in spite of its accomplishments in other respects.

Economics claims to be an autonomous area of life. As a science seeking to approximate the clarity of physics, it claims to study the workings of the unalterable laws of the market. Its abstract mechanistic way of thinking disregards everything not measurable and manipulable. No one can doubt the great gains in economy due to the creation of the modern science of economics that focuses on the laws of the market and the measuring of various flows of the market according to the criteria of these laws. The astounding rise in productivity and in the living standards of millions of people seems to justify the official absence of God and human livelihood in the thought and practice of the market. The promises of the market are so great that its language, concepts, and mechanisms represent the most universal reality. Is there anything to which more people in the world look for the future of the world more than the market and its science? And, yet, despite the great gains of the science of economics, millions of people around the world feel powerless economically and resigned to poverty as though it were destiny.

Even though economics claims to be the "hardest" science, much about the great project of market science remains utopian. When awareness of the horrible suffering of people throughout the world, people excluded from household and therefore subject to death, comes into consciousness, it is usually claimed that once the assumptions of the market actually prevail and the rules of the market are observed, all economic problems will be solvable. But can the assumptions and rules of the market ever be universally and historically realized in the global household? Questions about how to form and sustain community, and questions about how the members of the household are related to each other are in modernity divorced from questions of economy. In this context, it is assumed that community exists to serve economy. This is a truncation of the older meaning of economy. It is a truncation that threatens the lives of peoples and the earth itself.

II. The Market Logic

The difficulty of juxtaposing theology and economy is this: the absolute prevailing logic of our society is the market logic. Robert Heilbroner says that the nature of our society is accumulation of wealth as power, and that the logic of our society is exchange of commodities.[13] Everything dances around these realities. We believe them so implicitly that we are willing to serve them and shape our lives according to their logic. Perhaps the only thing that approximates a universal presence today is the market logic. The market is spreading into and in one way or another affecting, even if only negatively, every village of the world. It is the language with which all people are fascinated. It is increasingly the logic through which people expect life, security, and future.

The market logic is in and of itself good. It is perhaps the most successful human social device ever conceived. No one can deny its awesome effect in modernity. But we do need radically to criticize many of the so-called capitalist assumptions of the modern market. These assumptions destroy the possibility of Christian discipleship within economy and are increasingly narrowing the public space in which the church can exist. They destroy the possibility of democracy shaping property, work, and consumption in ways that preserve equality, participation, and access to livelihood and community. The market can flourish without these assumptions and many of the institutions to which they have given rise. It is not the market per se but rather what Karl Polanyi calls "the market society" that I am opposing.[14] That is, I am criticizing a society in which all the spheres in which social goods have to be distributed are controlled by the market logic itself.[15] All social goods are produced and distributed as if they were commodities. This means the decisive question about economy today is a cultural question.

If the Household of Jesus Christ has a memory, we know that there are certain social goods that should be distributed according to a different logic because these social goods are themselves not commodities. Food, healing, learning, the generation of the generations, belonging, justice, respect should not be commodities or exhaustively commodities. The market is the greatest mechanism we have ever devised for producing and distributing commodities. But if something is not a commodity, should it be distributed according to the market logic, or is there another logic for the distribution of those things necessary for life and life abundant?[16] What is necessary for life cannot be a commodity or exclusively a commodity. In the market society, however, there is nothing that cannot, in principle, be distributed as a commodity. Market economists even suggest that air pollution can be solved as soon as we learn how to make air a commodity.

III. Global Economy

Modern economy has been thought under the banner of the "wealth of nations." We are entering an age in which we have to think economy in terms of the global household and have to try to understand what is happening to people in all parts of the household precisely because the economy is global.[17] There may be ways to counteract some global trends but certainly not without understanding them and what they are doing to persons and communities within the global household.

It is increasingly difficult to speak of "national" economies. Few American firms or industries compete against foreign firms or industries. Much more typical now is the

global web, perhaps headquartered in and receiving much of its financial capital from the United States, but with research, design, and production facilities spread over Japan, Europe, and North America; additional production facilities in Southeast Asia and Latin America; marketing and distribution centers on every continent; and lenders and investors in Taiwan, Japan, and West Germany as well as the United States. This ecumenical company competes with similarly ecumenical companies headquartered in other nations. Battle lines no longer correspond with national borders.[18]

In this global economy the economic well-being of persons in a nation depends on the value they add to the global economy through their work, skills, and insights.

Robert Reich divides income earners on the global level into three categories: 1) routine producers, 2) in-person servers, and 3) symbolic analysts.[19] Routine producers, once the backbone of high-volume, heavy industrial production, usually work among large numbers of people doing the same thing according to standardized procedures and rules. In-person servers, though they also are paid by the hour for the amount of work done, are directly related to the beneficiaries of their work. Thus their services are not sold world-wide. If they have to be as punctual, reliable, and flexible as routine producers, they also have to be pleasant in personal relationships. Symbolic analysts engage in problem-identifying-solving and strategic brokering. The products of their work are traded world-wide, but these products are not standardized things. Rather, they are "manipulations of symbols — data, words, oral and visual representations."[20]

Though natural and historical conditions in the United States are vastly different from most places in the world, these three classes of workers represent the emerging worldwide division of labor. The trends in the relationships among these three functional categories, which include three-fourths of American jobs, can provide a microcosm through which we can see the global household relationships between those who are growing richer and those who are growing poorer.

In the global economy the interlocking character of the symbolic analysts world-wide is accompanied by their decreasing dependence on other economic actors in their own country and region. The income of symbolic analysts has increased dramatically in the last fifteen years, while the income of routine producers and in-person servers has dramatically declined. Decline in their income has meant less access to good education, health care, and job training for the latter two classes and thus increasing exclusion from what it takes to become a symbolic analyst. In the United States the wealthiest one-fifth of all households, the symbolic analysts, owns three-fourths of all assets and earns almost half of all income. Economic growth and affluence have not eliminated significant levels of poverty.[21] Over 32 million people are poor in this country. The cessation of progressive tax reform and public investment by government has diminished the infrastructure on which all but symbolic analysts depend for communication, transportation, education, health-care delivery, and safe and commodious living.

The burden of poverty has always fallen disproportionately on a few groups, such as people of color, children, and women heads of households. African-American and Hispanic families are nearly three times more likely to be poor than white families. The rate of poverty is even higher among Native Americans. One fifth of all children in this country live in poor households. But in the global economy we have also an increasing segregation by income. The number of working poor is growing everywhere. National household and the global household are dividing up in ways that make it impossible to give all people access to what it takes to live and live abundantly.

Perhaps most frightening in the global household is the way in which those with economic power are dropping out of the community, the commonweal. But participation in community is the pre-condition for the political transformation of economy toward justice. Symbolic analysts "are quietly seceding from larger and diverse publics of America into homogeneous enclaves, within which their earnings need not be redistributed to people less fortunate than themselves."[22] This leads to two separate cities, two residential patterns, two school systems, two systems of health care delivery, and two systems of welfare and security.

On the global scene the three major economic blocs in the First World—the European Community, North America (with Mexico in tow), and Japan (closely associated with South Korea, Taiwan, Singapore and until 1997 Hong Kong) are withdrawing from a household whose rules would assure the inclusion of the world's poor. "This foreshadows the development of a two track world economy, with these three regions in a fast track and most others in a slow one which will fall further and further behind, to the point of being effectively excluded from the dominant economic systems."[23]

For the twenty-nine year period following 1960 the richest 20 percent of the world population increased its share of the global gross product from 70.2 percent to 82.7 percent, while the poorest 20 percent of the world population suffered a reduction of its share from 2.3 percent to 1.4 percent.[24] At a global level, the disparities in income are enormous and increasing. Low-income countries in Asia, Africa, and Central America, with nearly half the world's population, account for only 5 percent of global income. Over a billion people live in abject poverty.

The clearest index of poverty is hunger. Although the world food supply can provide enough for all, some 700 million people do not get sufficient food for an active and healthy life. In their first five years of life one out of every three children is undernourished. Forty-two thousand children die each day of starvation. Persistent hunger throughout the world dooms new generations of children to the lifelong problems caused by severe malnutrition at an early age. Nearly two billion lack potable water. Nine hundred million cannot read or write.[25]

The secession of symbolic analysts is continuing apace in the global household, but here, especially, the exclusion of masses of human beings from the household shows up our tragic inability to imagine evil. On a recent trip to Lima, Peru, I found myself seeking to comprehend dreadful poverty. Fifteen years ago Lima's population was about one million. Now it is almost eight million. For twenty years people have been coming to Lima because they could not find livelihood in the countryside. They squat on land and begin by building the barest shelter. The first shanty town I saw in Lima is literally built on the top of an immense garbage mound. People are living all over it. Scratch the surface and you can see and smell the garbage. At the heart of this garbage heap is a fire caused by fermentation.

The only thing that seems to be keeping these people alive in degrading conditions is something like a community, a household. Where it comes from is hard to say. These people live outside and against the formal economy. They can expect nothing from it. They expect nothing from the state. But somehow there are household rules that are keeping them alive. This picture is repeated all over the world. We have to ask ourselves whether simply extending the market logic as we know it will save these people, or whether extending the market logic into these settings would destroy the community that is keeping the people alive. It is a very serious decision that we are faced with. It can give one an awesome sense of despair in face of a possible unimaginable destruction of human life.

The market as increasingly controlled by symbolic analysts in all parts of the world is spreading into every region of the world. But the spreading of the market logic without household rules that protect the living of the poor exacerbates human suffering. Fluctuating commodity prices create cycles of economic crisis for nations whose economies depend heavily on a few export prices. Many of the products of the South have fallen in price due to the North's stranglehold on the producers of raw materials and the North's production of artificial goods that no longer require the natural resources of the South. Artificial sweeteners have replaced cane sugar, oil derivatives have replaced rubber, satellites in space have replaced copper communication cables. Zambia's rich deposits of copper at one time gave it a promising future but now lie idle in one of the neediest countries. In the decade of the 1980s the non-fuel commodity exports of developing countries declined by about 40 percent. The stabilization of raw material prices and ways of creating diversification require extensive international political cooperation that is not yet a reality.[26]

Another problem hindering the inclusion of the poor in the global household is the high level of debt and austerity programs mandated by the International Monetary Fund and World Bank that make it difficult or impossible for many poor countries to finance effective internal development programs.[27] Needy countries must devote more of their land and resources to export crops or minerals, which earn more hard currency.

These conditions create a cauldron of resentment in barrios and ghettoes and are leading in the last decade of the twentieth century to new levels of dislocation, immigration, and homelessness in many parts of the world. In the United States ownership of land by working farm families and rural community life are deeply threatened. The flight of capital and factory closings have left whole communities without a means of livelihood. Northern countries try to make a distinction between political and economic immigration, but generally accept the more talented persons as well as workers willing to accept wages much lower than the standard in the host country.

As is the case ever since Cain spilled the blood of Abel upon the earth, nature groans from the injustice of the human economy. An example of this can be seen in the purchase of small seed-supply firms by multinational chemical firms, especially in the United States and the Netherlands.

> The avowed purpose of the chemical firms is to develop highly productive strains of seed. As a result, strains requiring a lavish use of artificial fertilizers and pesticides have been promoted most, which is profitable, of course, for the chemical industry. In the process, however, not only is a wide range of different seeds eliminated but the use of such quantities of artificial fertilizers and pesticides also has incalculable ecological consequences.[28]

Small farmers become increasingly dependent on industrial products which they cannot afford because of unfavorable exchange conditions between industrial products and agricultural products. The trend is exacerbated by the development of hybrid seed strains whose harvest is unserviceable for future sowing, so that seeds always have to be bought from the large seed firm whom lending institutions support when farmers apply for loans. These relationships encourage monocultures and export-oriented farming. The result is that Kansas farmers are on food stamps and Brazilian peasants raise soy beans rather than the black beans on which they have subsisted for decades.

IV. Democracy, Community, and Free Trade

If we mean by democracy the systematic criticism of privilege so that all may have an equal opportunity of participation in decisions about their living and the fulfillment of their lives, then we are speaking of an instrument that has a rough analogy to God's Torah and Gospel concern to create economy that serves communities of life against death. One of the strongest institutions assuring the continuation of the present practice of the market is free trade. But this institution is increasingly threatening the very being of democracy.[29] Free trade generally means that goods, services, and capital can flow across national boundaries as easily as they flow within a single country.[30]

> Today, concretely, it means that transnational corporations can invest freely where and for what purposes they will and that governments give up the right to regulate them. "Free trade" is the means whereby the most important decisions about human welfare are shifted from the political sector to the market, and that means to the major players within the market.[31]

The result is that the very livelihood of people the world over is made dependent on a trade whose terms are set by others.

The argument for free trade begins with the assumption that only the market can make decisions that lead to the efficient use of resources and thus to the sufficient supply of desired goods. As a second step the argument claims that the larger the market the better. Only ever greater specialization in ever larger markets makes increased efficiency possible. It therefore seems logical to conclude that only the global, that is, all-inclusive market, can assure the most rapid possible growth in gross world product. The ethical justification for this argument is that humanity suffers from a massive shortage of goods. If the well-being of the whole depends on expanding free trade, then governments would seem immoral to support certain populations of special interests rather than free trade proposals.

We arrive, then, at the familiar inevitability of the single global market. Since there is no alternative, the best one can hope for is the amelioration of the harmful effects of free trade. But we then quickly encounter the equally familiar inadequacy of any political body to exercise authority over the market in such a way that even a small amelioration of harm to human beings and nature can be effected. In any case, the globalization of political authority to meet the globalization of the market has an ambiguous history. Up to this point history gives no assurance that a world government would not be controlled by those very economic interests it was meant to control.

What would be an alternative to the control of the world economy by multinational corporations and a global political authority unresponsive to the poor and ordinary citizens? An alternative vision may require questioning the largely unexamined assumptions of free trade. Is it true that the greater the increase of gross national product, the better? The increase of GNP in expanded markets can be connected with the increase of the wealth of the rich but not with improvement of the welfare of the poor. The market does not measure the price of Third World people taking on the market culture and modes of behavior overnight, as it were, when in point of fact it took First World people decades, if not centuries to become adept. Nor does it measure the close connection between growth of this kind and the exhaustion and pollution of resources.[32]

The growth of the gross national product does not necessarily measure improvement of human welfare. Per capita gross product is not even an adequate measure of economic welfare.[33] Alternative indices of economic welfare have shown that welfare has not grown proportionately to per capita GNP in recent decades. If economic welfare in the broadest sense rather than increase in gross product is the ethical goal, then there is no ethical compulsion to increase the size of markets. In fact, ethical considerations count strongly against it.

An alternative to free trade would be a system of relatively self-sufficient markets in relatively small regions. In each of these regions the community can organize through political and social institutions to make certain that its members are included in the household. A market economy without bureaucratic planning can accompany the community's establishing of rules, applied equally to all members of the public household, designed to support the public good in health, environmental well-being, and the conditions of labor and to assure that its members have access to what it takes to live and live with fulfillment. Contemporary forms of communal autarchy will have to ensure that those who played by these rules are not forced to compete with other producers who play by less demanding rules in other markets. The market, for example, will have to be complex enough to ensure competition in as many sectors as possible. If such conditions do not exist, businesses will be closely regulated or even owned by the community.

In this kind of public household ordinary people have a much more realistic chance to belong and to participate in significant decisions than is true in global governance. In the alternative vision each community could survive without trade, and therefore it would trade only when the terms of trade were advantageous to it.

Because many issues cannot be solved locally, relatively self-sufficient communities would have to organize themselves in what Martin Buber called "communities of communities" up to the global level. The minimum rules for regional economies that must be enforced are that no community should be free to export its pollution to others, including products that ruin the health of other communities, or to exclude minority groups from participation in the community's own life. Communities of communities would, of course, require considerable power to enforce such rules. But the power should emerge from the community itself.

V. Church, Power, and Community

In a market society there is decreasing space in which the church and its expectation of the reign of God's righteousness can exist. The fascination of the modern market is that it can shape mass human behavior without force or authority, and thus the violence of the state and the authority of the church can be replaced by simple exchange relationships. The result is a set of economistic laws that make decisions for us. The market is an organizing (and conveniently invisible) mechanism that is automatic. It allows us to avoid public encounter and decision-making, and trades citizenship in a polis for consumership in a market. But, in point of fact, economy can be transformed only through politics and community. One works either from the direction of politics or community, but in the end both are needed.

If our best chance for a global household of justice is the democratization of economy, this would require radical changes in the way we form, accumulate, and distribute capital; in our understanding of property, work, and consumption; in our tax, insurance, welfare, and security systems. These changes can only be made politically. But where are the communities which could envision and bear such a politics? The church is not meant to be such a political community itself, but it is meant to be a community to make such communities possible.

The ominous fact of which we North American Christians are only barely conscious is that the church itself is also more and more governed by the market logic. Even our church institutions, including the seminary, have joined the move from traditional accountability to accountancy. If the church is actually meant to be the living economy of God, then we should go no further without saying that to make a genuine contribution to alternative economy in the world, the church itself would have to be radically restructured and "recultured" by its own Gospel, sacraments, diakonia, and koinonia for mission. The great task facing the church toward the next century is how and where to find the actual free space in our market society to become the *oikonomia tou theou*. No other question is so urgent for the globalization of church and seminary.

VI. The Conditions of Globalization in the Seminary

It is next to impossible for the North American church and seminary to engage in globalization. We do not have the conditions for globalization, namely, criticism[34] and innovation.[35] What would have to happen in Christian theological schools for the conditions of criticism and innovation to be established? There would, to be sure, have to be a curriculum governed by praxis, agency, and strategies for change. The life and work of the seminary in its entirety would have to intend projects of transformation.[36] But since, for the seminary, all significant references of praxis, agency, and strategies for change are ecclesial, the primary question is how the church can be transformed for engaging in God's mission of transforming the world.

Whatever we would expect to be, the character of the praxis of globalization in the church would be normative for globalization in the seminary. For the North American church this means above all the question of how the church can be free from its culture for the sake of God's passion for the world and its new creation.[37] This would require a complex ecclesiology that understands the church and globalization as functions of the history of the triune community of righteousness.[38]

It is true that both criticism and innovation stem from what we may call the power of suffering. But seminaries will not be changed by the mere experience of the poor and poverty. Modernity's pervasive liberalism can absorb and coopt any experience of the negative. In fact, the routinization of poverty and of the experience of the poor is a function of the same social sciences by which we have shaped persons to be professional ministers and teachers of professional ministers. What we have thought we do best may in fact preclude what is most needed for globalization within a market society.

In the sphere of individual selves evil thrives in alienation, resentment, guilt, and violation stemming from idolatry. In the social sphere evil occurs when a group's self-absolutizing of its particularity violently utilizes other groups.[39] The peculiar power of evil is that it separates the spheres of the self and of the social from the interhuman, thus rendering redemption in any sphere impossible. Market relations, once they determine all relations, separate communities of face from selves and social entities, agencies, and strategies, and become seemingly benign masks of subjugation. Because idolatry and self-absolutizing can be overcome only in the interhuman, redemption takes place in the sphere of the mutual co-inherence of human beings with each other and with nature. If culturally mediated norms for regulating human action as sedimented in the market culture can be criticized and changed only in the sphere of the interhuman, then we should search for globalization in the depth of the community of face.

Communities of face express themselves in relatively constant modalities or relationships and they call forth strategies and practices, agential and political disciplines. What are the distinctive disciplines of the church's practice under its own criteria of face? I would argue that the peculiar community of face of the ecclesia is the alternative economy of the household of Jesus Christ formed at the Lord's Table.

VII. Globalization in Eucharistic Practice

The eucharistic economy of God expresses itself in patent, objective table manners, which create the ethos and ethics of globalization within the community of face.

Table manners are as old as human society itself, the reason being that no human society exists without them. Every society obeys eating rules.[40] The rules of eating are simple: if you don't eat you die, and no matter how large your meal you soon will be hungry again. If you want to get invited to dinner, you have to know and keep the table manners of the someone who is in the position of inviting. Table manners are thus life and death concerns, and every meal is ritualized according to those ends.

Manners assure sharing and prevent violence. With the occasional exception of a few species like chimpanzees, human beings are the only creatures who bring food home to share with adults as well as children. It is this sharing that is at the heart of table manners. There can be no community without table manners.

But table manners also exist because of the fundamental threat of violence. As soon as human society existed there were manners which assured that at meal times we eat rather than are eaten. Eating is aggressive by nature and the implements required for it could easily become killing instruments around the table. Table manners are social agreements devised precisely because violence could so easily erupt at dinner.

Every community, of course, also distorts itself through table manners, for they can be used not only to make sure one is included at the table, but also to exclude others from the table. Table manners can be used to serve snobbery and class systems.

The strange table manners at the Lord's Table are practices of the *oikonomia tou theou* and thus intend more than prevention of violence and sharing of what is necessary for life. They embody the perichoretic and oikic relationships which actually constitute life against death, evil, and sin. They are expressions of the interdivine, interhuman relationships created by the logos/logic of the Gospel in the power of the Holy Spirit.

At the Lord's Supper we have the same questions of manners and rituals that any meal has: Who is the host? Who is invited? How are hosts and guests greeted? What should be served? How should we serve it? What is the seating arrangement, and how should the weakest be assured of their portion? When should we start eating? What should we talk about? How should we thank the host? How should we depart? What provision for the next meal should be made? These of course are the primary questions of economy, notwithstanding their eclipse in modern economics; that is, these are the primary questions of relations of the household toward life against death. The way in which these questions are answered in practice in the community of face determine the possibility and shape of globalization for North American church and seminary. What follows can only be suggestive of this claim.

A. Memory, Hope, and the Host

The perichoretic, oikic relationships of globalization depend on the real presence of the host, Jesus Christ, to create the community of face in which idolatry and subjugation can be overcome. The real presence of Jesus Christ means the mediation of the past of Jesus (including Israel and creation) and the future of Jesus (including the reign of the Triune Community's righteousness over death, evil, and sin). The market society/culture eclipses memory and hope. Without those household functions which stimulate memory and hope there is no possibility of oikic community of face which grounds the possibility of criticism and innovation. Much of what is currently passing for globalization in terms of deconstruction of tradition is itself undermining the possibility of globalization in church and seminary.

B. The Stranger's Face

Globalization depends on who is invited to dinner. If we do not eat with the stranger, we will never be able to establish oikic relationships with the poor in any conceivable way that approximates the intention of the Triune Community's righteousness/justice. Conventional moral norms sedimented in North American culture are thoroughly egoistic. The theology and life forms of church and seminary reflect these criteria functioning in market society: self-possession, individual as one's own hermeneutic and arbiter of truth, and humanity judged as most human insofar as one distinguishes oneself from the other. In such a privatistic culture all public responsibility has to be defended in terms of self-interest in some kind of social contract.[41] The church is merely a voluntary association of likeminded people who help each other with individual choices.[42] Globalization in this context can also be conceived in terms of egoism: the other completes me, helps me to come to my own self-understanding, makes me more human. The market culture retrieves with ardor every ethical argument for egoism; we are profoundly predisposed to understand rights in terms of prudence. Such "globalization" is still a form of egoistic prudence. There is no wonder, then, that the discourse of justice is so strife-torn. All speak of justice, but do they mean the same thing by it?[43]

Only the encounter with the stranger can break self-absolutism. The encounter of the stranger at the Lord's Table is the beginning of life, the possibility of justification before God, the stuff of redemption.[44] There are two ways to encounter a stranger, someone who is radically different. The great philosopher of individual freedom, Jean Paul Sartre, claims that when we encounter a stranger we come upon a *look*, a look that threatens us, because the other might define us and take away our identity and freedom. Thus Sartre says, "Hell is other people." On the other hand, the Jewish philosopher Levinas asserts that when we encounter a stranger we come upon a *face*. A face is the expression of the way another person is in the world, of his or her way of experiencing the world. Levinas says that the face of a stranger shocks us, to be sure, but it is our one chance of becoming truly human. Our salvation is wrapped up in the face of the stranger. We don't discover ourselves and our salvation by self-discovery, by looking deeper into ourselves, but in encountering the face of the stranger. The other's call or appeal is the beginning of life; it is the other's appeal that gives me the opportunity to be free and just. The call or appeal of the other is the only way to break absorption in agency or institutional forms and policy.

C. Scarcity, Satiation, and Gift

Globalization is deterred in the North American church by the numbing effect of the experience of artificial scarcity and satiation. The deepest and most necessary assumption for the practice of market logic is scarcity. The effect of the practice of the market logic is satiation. Both deaden the spirit and impede life with the other. Artificial scarcity spawns the lottery culture: the others may not make it, but I may. Satiation slakes the thirst for righteousness. Scarcity and satiation leave only one possibility for the distribution of what is necessary for life and life abundant: the logic of exchange. The genuinely other cannot appear in this logic. If globalization means anything, it must mean the encounter with the other.

Eucharistic oikic relationships begin with forgiveness and thereby create a new economy and a new logic of distribution called grace. What is served at this meal is the gift of God's own life, the body and blood of Jesus Christ, which above all is the gift of God's forgiveness as the sole power which can break the bonds of sin, evil, and death.[45] Those who are forgiven are capable of extraordinary love (Luke 7:36-50). Those who are forgiven little, love little. They hoard, for they have constantly to justify themselves and construct their own immortality. If we are forgiven and loved so much that God gives God's own life for us, then much is expected of us. And so we leave this meal, not just having shared with each other and having prevented violence, but we leave as new creatures empowered to live with the other.

The eucharistic modality is joy so great that it judges and transforms, a judgment that is so absolute that we cannot help but be thankful that it is gift. Joy and judgment are the beginning of globalization; they make us outraged by poverty because of the endless generosity of God and shock us with the recognition that not being in the mode of gifting and being gifted is blasphemous. Globalization depends upon the retaught and relearned generosity of God, upon gifts that give in being given and create dignity in being received. Only the gratuitous language of praise can break the suspicion and hatred of gifting and being gifted in our public household. No one in our public household wants to be "much obliged," for it would mean by definition the loss of freedom for exchange. But unless we will mean by globalization only what the market intends (we should remember that "globalization" was originally a word of the multinational corporations), the miracle by which we understand ourselves and our community as gift to be gifted will have to take place.

The table manners at the Lord's Table become our manners for the whole of our lives. Our manners at this table are meant to be our manners at all tables. The Lord's Table is connected with our dining room table, our seminar tables, and with tables of all people who eat and live this day. If the question of the Lord's Table is the question whether everyone in Atlanta, Beijing, and Lima will this day eat, then churches and seminaries committed to globalization would become trustees of political responsibility. They would practice responsible life together, the life of common decision that includes the face of the radical other, the life of conference, the life of conciliar and synodical existence with the stranger.

The globalization of ourselves as the body of Christ in the market society is a project so awesome, complicated, and next to impossible that we should not even think about it far removed from the Stranger who invites us all to a meal in which the earth and all its creatures are promised home.

Ho, everyone who thirsts, come to the waters; and he or she who has no money, come, buy bread and eat! Come, buy wine and milk without money and without price. Why do you spend your money on that which is not bread, and your labor for that which does not satisfy? Harken diligently to me, and eat what is good, and delight yourselves in fatness. Incline your ear, and come to me; hear that your soul may live; and I will make with you an everlasting covenant, my steadfast, sure love for David (Isa. 55:1-3).

CASE STUDY[46]

A Place for Reconciliation

"These kids are time bombs," Thulani declared to Professor David Myeza as they stared out the window at the half-dozen boys, age fifteen to nineteen, who stood on the street corner and shared a single cigarette. "As co-chairperson of the Township[47] Reconciliation Committee, I feel a special responsibility for this so-called 'lost generation' of youth. These kids sacrificed more than their education for the struggle against apartheid. They have probably donated their future to the cause as well. Ironically, they were the leaders of the violence as well as the leaders of the peace initiative.

"My friend Ruth Masuku, who has training in mediation skills, has agreed to co-chair the Committee. We figure we have about six months to give some sign that reconstruction and reconciliation are possible. If we can't do that, the community will return to violence even worse than the first round. Our community has endured two thousand deaths. Thirty percent of our housing has been either destroyed or severely damaged. David, you're a key leader in a seminary that claims to be committed to a Gospel of reconciliation and to the needs of the poor and oppressed. If our peace initiative is going to be successful, the Committee needs the seminary's help in two areas. Will the faculty sign a letter of endorsement to support the Committee's application for a foundation grant, and will the seminary provide a meeting place for us?"

David took a deep breath and paused for several moments before responding to his friend Thulani Khumalo. "You know that I completely support you and the community, but asking the seminary to become involved again is a different matter."

"I don't see how you can refuse," replied Thulani. "Because of the legacy of apartheid, all of South Africa desperately needs reconciliation and reconstruction. I am convinced that reconciliation is the only route to stopping the sub-culture of violence we are experiencing. Violence creates the conditions for its own self-perpetuation and has the potential to derail the construction of a new society. Perhaps equally important, without creative intervention the abandoned work force, made up primarily of youth, will soon reach the point where it will be uncontrollable.

"The time has come to empower the communities. If political parties, such as the ANC[48] of which I am a prominent member, are unwilling or unable to halt the violence and meet our specific local needs, we will have to rely on the resources of the community. The seminary is clearly one of those resources."

Thulani continued, telling David that his own perspective changed by seeing political leadership actually created by the violence. The same young people who started out defending the community, ended up using their weapons and strategies to attack members of their own community who questioned their leadership. The former students and workers of the community became heroes of either the ANC or IFP[49] on the basis of their violent activity.

"The final straw for me," Thulani declared, "came when both sides finally forced the schools to close." He recalled that whenever people died in the violence, schools closed for a two-week mourning period, and more young people were on the streets to participate in the violence. Those youth who had first freely offered protection began to barter their protection services. People were killed, crippled, and injured, and the shops in the township were closed because of looting. The post office, the schools, and transport were all shut down. The community was on the verge of chaos.

It was during this time, Thulani reminded David, that four seminary faculty members gave sanctuary to several unarmed young people who were fleeing from an armed group. During the same period, a number of seminary faculty who were ordained clergy conducted funerals for members of the community.[50] "David, I realize that a few people in the community were upset with the seminary's role, but through you, the church made an important statement about solidarity with the people. The people will listen to you now if you openly support the reconciliation process."

"Thulani," David replied, "You must remember that some members of the community believed the faculty had taken sides. The 'few people' you say were 'upset' gathered in the street and threw stones at the seminary. For the security of our students and faculty, we had to suspend classes and lock the seminary gates. The tension surrounding this incident was then compounded several weeks later when a number of our Methodist students gathered and marched to their church in celebration of Hero's Day. Their singing and toyi-toying[51] attracted a large crowd of young people. Before long the march turned into a political demonstration. The demonstration led to another violent attack on the seminary, including strong complaints from local churches who were upset with what appeared to be a political stance."

"David, the seminary was challenged when it appeared that students or faculty had taken sides with one political faction or another. I am asking you to take the side of *all* the people for peace. The most important issue facing us is not which faction is right or wrong, but how to make peace in the midst of ongoing violence. Think back on how we moved to this current truce. The problem that confronted us last year was how to bring together people who had become justifiably suspicious of one another. With all the destruction, people had become so suspicious they believed that anyone who advocated peace must be biased toward one side or another. Advocacy of reconciliation was interpreted as betrayal.

"As you well know, our township was one of the birthplaces of the violence that has spread to virtually every part of the country. It was this spiral of violence, and especially the crisis in the schools, that led to the necessity for intervention. Several members of the community, including a member of the seminary faculty, asked me to intervene in the situation. I gathered a small group of friends to discuss ways to stop the violence. We decided to focus on one primary school and appeal to both ANC- and IFP-affiliated parents. Based on my experience in the liberation struggle, I thought it might be possible to 'talk beyond' the current struggle."

Thulani reminded David that the selected primary school was located in an ANC-dominated area. Most of the IFP children had been forced to stop attending school by February 1990. The violence was at its height in March and April. By

July virtually all the ANC children were also out of school. A crisis was precipitated by the fact that school exams were set for mid-November. There was a general conviction that without the reopening of the primary school and an enormous tutoring effort, there would be no chance that the children could pass the examinations. Thulani tried several times to gather support for reopening the schools. Finally, with exams a little more than a week away, he persuaded a representative group of students and young people to gather at the school. Initially the IFP parents assumed that the ANC parents would vote to take the exams in November since their children, having attended school longer than the IFP children, would have an advantage. However, after much negotiation, parents, teachers, and representatives of the education department agreed to postpone the exams for four weeks, until mid-December. The two groups of students were to study together with special tutorial help from teachers and the support of parents. There was at least the possibility that all the children might pass their examinations.

"It was a rough several weeks," Thulani confided to David. "There was great concern for the safety of the IFP children coming to school in a predominantly ANC area. The children, of course, harbored the same suspicions as parents of either political group. I found myself making speeches to students and parents that reflected my understanding of reconciliation. I insisted that it was now more important to identify oneself as a member of the community and only after that as a member of any political party. I suggested that the kids needed to separate politics from education and concentrate on being a community of scholars preparing for their examinations. Otherwise they were in danger of destroying their future."

As Thulani arrived at the school to accompany some of the children home each day, he observed that groups of young people of different political persuasions were gathering in the school yard to talk not only about their studies, but also about peace. They expressed growing concern about the violence that affected their school and community. About three weeks after the community initiated the reopening of the primary school, a group of about fifty children were meeting in the school yard discussing issues of peace when the gathering erupted into a spontaneous peace demonstration. The youths marched to the headquarters of the township IFP leader who was also a member of the Kwa-Zulu Legislative Assembly. They insisted that he summon other IFP youth so they could discuss peace. The crowd of young people began to grow. Finally, they began a march through the township, toyi-toying and singing, not about violence, but for peace. Ultimately about five thousand young people from throughout the community participated in the demonstration.

In the days and weeks that followed, there was still a great deal of suspicion among older people about overcoming the polarization between ANC and IFP. There was virtually no official support for the peace movement from the regional leaders of major political groups.

"There are, of course, many variables," Thulani said. "Most local political leaders secured their posts based on their resistance to apartheid rather than on skills of reconstruction. At the time they came into power, it was impossible to deliver a program or develop local infrastructure. There is also the inevitable temptation of corruption. A leadership role lends itself to power brokering, and some local leaders really became war lords. Leaders also resist losing a position of power when their time is past."

Thulani then reminded David that after the demonstration a group of young people asked him to work with them to start a rehabilitation program. At the heart of this group were Christians committed to peace. Declaring the importance of addressing the basic issues of the community—violence, housing, and education— they formed the Township Reconciliation Committee. There was a great deal of enthusiasm for addressing the problem of rebuilding the community's infrastructure—getting the schools, the shops, the post office, and the transport system functioning again. Committee members were particularly anxious to rebuild some of the destroyed houses so that rehabilitation would have a concrete, constructive side. Before calling for a community-wide meeting, the Committee decided that small groups of young people would go into both the IFP and the ANC areas to talk with people at the grass roots level about what it would mean to cooperate and make peace. The young people distributed pamphlets and canvassed support. As a result of the truce brought about by the young people, the community celebrated Christmas for the first time in nearly five years. People could attend their churches and function in an almost normal way. The culmination of the young people's efforts was a mass meeting in the township stadium attended by over six thousand people. This meeting was in February, about three months after the spontaneous peace demonstration by the young people.

Thulani reported there had been no significant act of violence in the community since the mass meeting, but reminded David that the community truce was very tenuous. "For lasting peace the churches must become directly involved. As you know, many church leaders have been supportive of the process, both the peace demonstration and the Reconciliation Committee. But they did not initiate the process and are not giving significant leadership. There are seminary students in numerous congregations throughout the township, yet they tell me the seminary will not allow them to become involved. I acknowledge that the churches are vulnerable. During the past five years when some churches provided shelter for refugees, they were attacked by one or another of the opposing political factions. However, the churches must now begin to play a critical role if we are to have peace. We need Bible studies about what it means to become human beings in community rather than warring political factions. The church needs to help us develop a new form of consciousness about the community. Apartheid has created an ethos of violence and repression. Peace depends on an ethos of respect and freedom."

Thulani again looked out at the group of young men standing on the street corner. "Looking at these idle young people, I believe the most urgent question is whether we can maintain this fragile peace. How can we turn it into a period of genuine reconciliation and reconstruction? It will take at least two million rand to begin the process of housing reconstruction. That money is obviously not available in the community. This is why we have to turn to outside agencies. Once we have enough money for basic materials, we will depend on sweat equity, the human power in our community, to rebuild.

"Underlying the question of rebuilding houses is the issue of the so-called 'lost generation' of young people. Now that the violence that temporarily gave meaning to their lives has stopped, how can they begin again? They are unemployed and have little education. Family members of most of the children have been killed during the violence. Many children are living a hand-to-mouth existence, surviving on gifts of food and shelter from relatives. They don't have the money for uniforms, books, school fees, or transport to return to school. Many of them need basic technical skills in order to earn a living. The formal entrance requirements of our technical schools don't reflect the societal disruption we have been through. There is the continued danger that these young people will be co-opted by elements within one of the political groups or the security forces or even a 'third force'[52] that wants to disrupt progress toward negotiations and a new nation. These young people are vulnerable to bribes for antisocial behavior at the very moment when they are in a struggle for survival and freedom."

Thulani confided to David his conviction that there was a limited time for the Reconciliation Committee to prove that rehabilitation is actually possible. "The Committee needs to build models offering some hope for the future. We must begin to move people into employment, education, and preparation for a trade. We need a base of support to carry on this overwhelming task of rehabilitation. David, the seminary is a strong symbol of the church in our community. With your support the local congregations would be encouraged to join in the reconciliation movement. Offering us a place to meet would be a concrete sign of your support. The seminary's endorsement of our funding proposal would give credibility to our organization."

David agreed to consult with his colleagues and get back to Thulani. He watched his friend leave the seminary and saw the open smiles of the boys on the street as they greeted him. David knew Thulani as a courageous and outspoken Christian, deeply moved by the pain and suffering of his people and committed to the dangerous path to peace. He was also convinced that Thulani and Ruth had the energy and integrity to lead the massive reconstruction the community so desperately needed.

As he considered the best approach to raising Thulani's requests with his faculty colleagues, David reflected on the concerns he had not felt free to share with Thulani. Faculty members had been united when the seminary had come under direct attack, but they continued to be divided about the role the seminary should take in the community. The seminary was a predominantly black institution; funding was precarious and depended on the support of numerous church bodies and congregations, both black and white. A number of the traditional and conservative clergy were strongly opposed to liberation and contextual theologies and had expressed their disapproval of those faculty members who taught what were considered "progressive" courses. Some of the progressive faculty members, referred to by some as "radicals," were those who had been most directly involved in offering seminary refuge to young people and conducting funerals in the heat of township violence.

Some of the strongest resistance to community involvement, however, came from within the seminary. When the faculty members most active in the community were challenged, they acknowledged that the youth who were given refuge were all members of either the United Democratic Front or the ANC, after it was "unbanned." The same was true of the family members who requested funerals. The faculty involved countered that had IFP members asked for asylum or funerals, they would have been supported. However, those faculty who were affiliated with IFP were clear that the ANC support in the seminary, particularly among the students, was so vocal that they had become hesitant to have their political sympathies known.

David felt that the strongest voice opposed to involvement in the community was a senior professor of biblical studies. Jacob Sibeko was a conscientious scholar and dedicated teacher who attended every faculty meeting and was always well prepared for his courses. Jacob spoke persuasively in faculty deliberations: "We are called to teach students in the seminary; others have been called to serve in the community. There is a lot to be done here. For most of our students, who come from very poor backgrounds, this is the only concentrated period of theological study they will ever have. Their education must be our primary concern." Jacob was particularly distressed by some of the more liberal faculty. "Liberation theology, with its focus on *praxis*, does not go deep enough. If students learn only from situations, when does the Bible come in? As Christian scholars, we must teach our students to *start* with the Bible."

It was after very negative comments from some congregations about the student march and demonstration that the faculty, with Jacob's urging, had decided that student pastors would not be allowed to become involved in political activity so long as they were enrolled in the seminary. The seminary announced at the same time that it would no longer harbor any political refugees. This decision was made in the midst of the township violence.

David believed that Thulani had brought a valid proposal to the seminary. The community was in a fragile period, and the seminary might be able to play an important role in helping transform the truce into long-term peace. David had agreed to bring Thulani's requests to the faculty, but he was unsure of the most faithful way to present the issues. He opened his Bible to 2 Corinthians 5 and reread the passage which entrusted all Christians with a "ministry of reconciliation." David wanted to remind his colleagues that to act for "the least of these" was to act for Christ himself. He was convinced that faith and economics, reconciliation and rehabilitation were linked. How could the faculty turn its back on the costly discipleship of peacemaking?

David was a professor of theology and a scholar who had invested many years in intensive study. He suspected, however, that he probably taught his students more through his actions and personal responses to them than by his carefully prepared lectures.

As David turned to his computer to jot down a few notes for his proposal to the faculty, the phone rang. The voice on the line was strained. "David, Ruth Masuku, the co-chair of the Reconciliation Committee, has just been assassinated in a restaurant parking lot. This peacemaking is a dangerous business. I understand your friend Thulani may be next on the list."

TEACHING NOTE

A Place for Reconciliation

I. Goals

This case can be used in several ways.

A. To analyze the issues and raising alternatives for a community caught in a spiral of violence, or to focus on the role of a seminary within such a community. Although the case takes place in South Africa, a case leader may wish to make comparisons with situations of urban violence in North America.

B. To deepen sensitivity to a variety of perspectives of persons involved in community violence, explore barriers and bridges to reconciliation in areas caught in violence, develop viable options for township youth and investigate creative alternatives for bringing long-term peace to disrupted communities.

C. To explore the role of the seminary in each of the categories noted above and discuss the educational and theological implications of the direct involvement of a theological institution in community concerns.

II. Setting / Situation

A. Review or post in advance on board or newsprint the critical steps leading up to the case situation: township near chaos; plan to focus on exams in one primary school; spontaneous peace demonstration by youth (November); formation of Township Rehabilitation Committee with focus on rebuilding homes; small group of young people canvass support; mass demonstration (February); current state of "truce." (Ask if there are any critical steps omitted from above list.)

B. Review the evolving role of the seminary in the community disruption from the time that a few students and faculty offered sanctuary to political refugees to the faculty decision to prohibit students from all political involvement.

III. Persons

A. Begin the discussion by exploring the attitudes and feelings of some of the persons in the case:

Thulani: David commented that Thulani had been "personally reconstructed" by recent experiences in the township. Explore what this phrase means. What is Thulani's primary concern? What role does Thulani see for local churches in establishing long-term peace? What roles do "economy" and "community" play in the restoration of the youth and relationships in the township?

Political leaders: Although Thulani is himself a community political leader, he speaks very negatively about some leaders. Why? Put yourself into the shoes of a regional political leader. Why might you be hesitant to support the peace process?

Community youth: Think about the young people on the street corner. Imagine what they must be feeling. What are they most concerned about? How could they be emphasized?

Ruth Masuku: How might her death affect the persons discussed above?

B. Focusing on the seminary, consider the approaches and feelings of the following persons:

David Myeza: Discuss David's role in the community. How might he have felt when the seminary faculty voted to bar students from political activity and to refuse political refugees? Elaborate on his theological and educational understanding of why the seminary should be involved in the life of the community.

Jacob Sibeko: Elaborate on Jacob's understandings of theological education and seminary involvement in the community. Do you agree with his concerns about liberation theology? Why or why not?

Faculty: What would it mean for the faculty to think about the economy and the community in terms of the "Eucharistic community of God"?

Students: How might those students who were deeply involved in the community conflict feel about the prohibition on participation in political activities?

Members of local congregations: Why did members of some congregations attack the seminary? What might be the basis for Thulani's vision that the churches are a key to long-term peace in the community?

Ruth Masuku: How might her death affect the persons discussed above?

IV. Issues

A. As Thulani seeks lasting peace in the community, what do you see as the primary issues in the case? (Possible responses: spiral of violence; political polarization; resistance to reconciliation; the role of the community; identity with community before identity with political party; "lost generation" of youth; education; rebuilding the township.)

Identify and discuss at greater length the critical problems of the young people: unemployment, lack of education, etc. What possibilities exist for their future?

Discuss at greater length the issue of reconciliation: Do you agree with Thulani that reconciliation is the only way to stop the violence? Why or why not? What are some of the barriers to reconciliation in the community? (e.g., historically negative connotation of "reconciliation" in disempowered communities, power of the political leaders, etc.). What are the most effective bridges to long-term reconstruction and reconciliation? What are the most effective roles for political leaders?

B. Identify the primary issues that David and the seminary community are facing. Consider the role of theological education in a divided society, the role of the church in peacemaking, the meaning of sanctuary in the midst of violence, etc.

V. Alternatives

A. Divide the participants into several small groups of four to six persons. Ask each group to develop a response to Thulani's question: "How can we turn this fragile peace into a period of genuine reconciliation and reconstruction?" Ask each group to identify and list the most effective ways to bring lasting peace to the township. Build a specific plan of action. Be creative and concrete.

Groups should write their plans on large newsprint and post them around the room. Give groups fifteen minutes to discuss and write; another ten minutes to study other plans. If there are numerous small groups, ask each person to study at least three other plans.

B. David is deeply concerned about the role the seminary might be able to play in helping transform the community truce into long-term peace. Follow the procedure cited above, asking small groups to develop a possible approach for David to bring his concerns to the faculty. Are there creative approaches David might take which would not involve the faculty? Urge participants to support their suggestions with theological and educational rationale.

VI. Closing

Regather the groups in plenary. Ask participants to identify any patterns or central themes in the plans developed.

What resources can Thulani and the young people draw on to help the community move forward?

What resources can David draw on either to engage the seminary directly in peacemaking or personally follow his biblical understanding of the "ministry of reconciliation" through other channels?

What would be required to move toward economic and political rearrangement of the society and the church as urged by Meeks and Mosala?

COMMENTARY

A Place for Reconciliation

ITUMELENG J. MOSALA

Introduction

Ironically, Christian activists in South Africa had to deliberately abandon their belief in reconciliation in order to be able to speak and act relevantly about their faith in the context of apartheid. For many years, talk of love, peace, and reconciliation formed the basis of white Christians' political defense of the status quo. Blacks had, therefore, to search for other conceptual weapons of the Christian faith in order to make sense of their opposition to white colonial rule.

Since the late 1980s and early 1990s, however, the call for reconciliation is on the lips of many, not least some noteworthy black Christian activists.

Reconciliation, of the sort that the Bible gives testimony to, a far cry from the white Western Christian version, has always been relevant to the situation in South Africa. It was inevitable, though, that in the context of the political and ideological conditions existing in the late 1960s and 1970s reconciliation would be treacherously misinterpreted and abused.

The pivotal role of the notion of reconciliation will be kept in mind throughout this commentary. In the context of thinking about reconciliation, this commentary will address the key issues raised by the case study: the "lost generation" of young people; violence; and the church's role in the political struggle in South Africa.

The Lost Generation of Young People

The loss of schooling for many black young people in the 1980s was lamented by many in the black community. The African National Congress through its internal wing, the United Democratic Front, had popularized the slogan "liberation first, education later." This development turned out to be unfortunate, and even some in the ANC camp admit to having been foolish. It is important that the developments that led to what subsequently came to be called the "lost generation" of young people should be seen in proper perspective.

Firstly, the destabilization of black education in South Africa predated the ANC/UDF ideological errors of the 1980s. The white apartheid regime itself had been bent on ensuring the lack of education for black people as a matter of policy. In particular, in the 1980s this policy stance of white South Africa was buttressed by military and police occupation and disruption of black educational institutions and systems. The army literally camped in schools, colleges, and universities — all black institutions. It is, therefore, not just a generation which is lost; it is a whole nation which has been intentionally lost by the way white people dominated and ruled black people.

Secondly, black parents and professionals have always seen the crisis of black education in proper perspective. They never characterized the crisis of black education in terms of a "lost generation." Those could never be their words. The reason is simple. Every black dropout that apartheid produces must be seen for what he or she is: a constructive dropout, to use the words of Martin Luther King, Jr.[53] The question, therefore, is whose characterization is "lost generation" and what are the real political and ideological implications of this characterization.

Assessment of the crisis of black education in terms of a "lost generation" has a close affinity to the response of the white South African regime's ritual response to black people's revolt against unjust institutions: "It is your own future you are destroying." Black people successfully resisted this ideological blackmail for a long time. "Whites cannot be both the destroyers and the messiah of black people's future," we retorted. The fact, however, that by the 1990s a growing number of black activists and professionals began to imitate white people in describing the crisis in black education in terms of the "lost generation" is evidence of a new ideological crisis in black politics.

The implications are paralyzing. If nothing else, they reflect a deep-seated political reformist streak, especially on the part of those who carry a reputation of erstwhile political involvement. This ideological shift calls for a re-articulation of Amilcar Cabral's warning concerning the opportunism of petit bourgeois groups within the oppressed community:

> We must, however, take into consideration the fact that, faced with the prospect of political independence, the ambition and opportunism from which the liberation movement generally suffers may draw into the struggle individuals who have not been re-converted. The latter, on the basis of their level of education, their scientific or technical knowledge, and without losing any of their class cultural prejudices, may attain the highest position in the liberation movement. On the cultural as well as the political level, vigilance is, therefore, vital. For in the specific and highly complex circumstances of the process of the phenomenon of the liberation movements, all that glitters is not necessarily gold: political leaders — even the most famous — may be culturally alienated.[54]

Violence and the Role of the Church in the Struggle for Liberation

Again, until the 1980s, violence in the black community, excepting criminal violence, was always the result of the apartheid regime's overall strategies against the black community. This situation was never vociferously identified by the Christian churches whose dominant structures were, of course, part of the apartheid setup. It was not until the rise of the black consciousness movement that clergy and Christian activists spoke out fearlessly against this situation and against the idolatry of its theological underpinnings. The white church, the white state, and the white community were made by black and African theologians to share in the blame for the violence perpetrated by them on the black community.

The rise of courageous leaders such as Desmond Tutu, Frank Chikane, Allan Boesak, and their simultaneous co-option into the populist politics of the international media and solidarity groups heralded a new era of the church's role in the struggle for liberation. In these leaders and other "prophetic" characters of the time, the black community and the black struggle had, in the apt words of Todd Gitlin:

> elevated leaders; the media selected for celebrity those among them who most closely matched prefabricated images of what an opposition leader should look and sound like: articulate, theatrical, bombastic, and knowing and inventive in the ways of packaging messages for their mediability.[55]

Ironically, the church and therefore some of its institutions such as seminaries were to be negatively implicated in the new political violence that gripped the black community. As millions of dollars poured into South Africa to help "progressive" movements, the party political partisanship that came as a result of the populist politics of the 1980s required a divisive dealing with the black community. Frankly put, to be politically progressive became synonymous with being a member or supporter of the African National Congress (ANC). Money that came through churches and church structures like the South African Council of Churches (SACC) and the Catholic Bishops' Conference favored programs and organizations linked to the ANC over against any others in the black community. The result was deep division in the black community and in particular among many black professionals and leaders. The problem between Thulani and David in the case study must be seen in this light. So must the crisis between Inkatha and the ANC. The integrity of the church and of church institutions such as the seminaries suffered irreparably.

Reconciliation

What does it mean to talk of reconciliation in the situation presented by the case study? The fruitless attempts to stop violence since the time when it was confined to Natal indicate that the role of the church must be viewed skeptically in this regard. SACC leaders, bishops, and other leaders have made their bid at peace. It has not worked, and it cannot work.

There are two reasons why current attempts at reconciling the South African society cannot work. Firstly, the church and Christians in general have always been and are seen as part of the status quo. In the words of Steve Biko, they cannot therefore be both part of the problem and part of the solution. In other words, the church cannot simply view itself as an agent of change in South Africa. It is itself an object of change. Unless the church undergoes some serious transformation, such as that starting under the impact of the black and African theology movements, it is discredited and can only make errors of judgment and practice. For the church to become an agent of change is not simply a matter of the self-immersion of the church, as implied by the case study; the church must possess a theological arsenal that powers it into constructive action.

Secondly, reconciliation is possible only if it is seen and understood in the biblical sense, that is, as restitution and repossession in the spirit of Jubilee in Leviticus 25 and as fundamental transformation in the manner of Micah 3:4 – hammering swords into plowshares.

This kind of reconciliation is the result of political rearrangement; it is not a matter of mere constitutional tinkering of the sort currently being pursued. Unless black people take over political power in South Africa, they cannot construct a democratic system and a just economic order. Only power will enable them to do so. The current route will lead them only to the kind of economic blind alley represented by the idolatry of the markets which M. Douglas Meeks so well exposes. He writes poignantly:

> The assumption of the liberal theory of liberty that domination is eliminated by market arrangements is false. Domination enters into exchange and production relationships by means of the determination of property and work. So dominant is the market regime that logic of distribution within the market controls many, if not all, of the other spheres of distribution within the market society.[56]

Notes

1. See M. Douglas Meeks, "Globalization and the *Oikoumene* in Theological Education," *Quarterly Review* 11/3 (1991), 63-80.

2. At least 138 Congressional districts are dependent on military contracts.

3. Barry Bluestone and Bennett Harrison, *The Deindustrialization of America* (New York: Basic Books, 1982); idem, *The Great U-Turn* (New York: Basic Books, 1988).

4. For a superb novel that graphically tells the story of Appalachian economy see Denise Giardina, *The Unquiet Earth* (New York: W.W. Norton, 1992).

5. For a more extensive argument see M. Douglas Meeks, *God the Economist: The Doctrine of God and Political Economy* (Minneapolis: Fortress Press, 1989).

6. The most influential North American "theologian," Andrew Carnegie, declared in 1889 that it would not behoove Christianity to say anything about the actual processes of economy—production, distribution, and consumption—for, he said, they are lodged in the incorrigible laws of nature, such as tooth-and-fang competition. Christianity, he said, could only enter the picture after money had been made and reinvested and there is a little left over. Christianity could then advise how to disperse one's leftover money. He even provided us the rules: give money only to the deserving poor and only to those who support the system from which the money was made. He thereby defined what we call American philanthropy or charity. Andrew Carnegie, "Wealth," *North American Review*, 1889. See also Andrew Carnegie, *The Gospel of Wealth and Other Timely Essays* (New York: Cambridge University Press, 1962). This is often what the church has taken over as its theology of economy.

7. Meeks, *God the Economist*, pp. 29-45.

8. For biblical and Hellenistic usages of *oikonomia* see John Reumann, *The Use of Oikonomia and Related Terms in Greek Sources to about A.D. 100 as a Background for Patristic Applications* (Ann Arbor: University Microfilms, 1957); John H. Elliott, *A Home for the Homeless: A Sociological Exegesis of 1 Peter, Its Situation and Strategy* (Philadelphia: Fortress Press, 1981).

9. Other words that derive from the root *oik-* are *ecology* and *oikoumene*. Ecology asks whether nature will have a home. Nature's way of protesting homelessness is to die. Thus Rachel Carson spoke of the "silent spring." We are slowly learning that if nature dies, so will human beings. The ancient question of *oikoumene* is not just whether the Lutherans and the Baptists are going to get together. That is an important

question. But the fundamental question of *oikoumene* is whether all the peoples of the earth will be able to inhabit the earth mutually in peace.

10. Meeks, *God the Economist*, pp. 29-45.

11. See Aristotle, *Politics*, Book II.

12. Karl Polanyi, *The Great Transformation* (Boston: Beacon Press, 1957).

13. Robert Heilbroner, *The Nature and Logic of Capitalism* (New York: W.W. Norton, 1985), pp. 31-32, 141-48 and passim.

14. Karl Polanyi, *The Livelihood of Man* (New York: Academic Press, 1977), p. 9 and passim.

15. Cf. Charles E. Lindblom, *Politics and Markets: The World's Political-Economic Systems* (New York: Basic Books, 1977).

16. For a discussion of this question see Michael Walzer, *Spheres of Justice: A Defense of Pluralism and Equality* (New York: Basic Books, 1983).

17. Robert B. Reich, *The Work of Nations: Preparing Ourselves for 21st Century Capitalism* (New York: Alfred A. Knopf, 1991).

18. Reich, *The Work of Nations*, p. 171.

19. Reich, *The Work of Nations*, pp. 171-84.

20. Reich, *The Work of Nations*, pp. 177-78.

21. Kevin Phillips, *The Politics of Rich and Poor: Wealth and the American Electorate in the Reagan Aftermath* (New York: Harper Collins, 1990).

22. Reich, *The Work of Nations*, p. 268.

23. "Abundant Life for All: Christian Faith and the World Economy Today" (Geneva: World Council of Churches, 1992), p. 22.

24. United Nations, *Human Development Report*, 1992.

25. United Nations, *Human Development Report*, 1990.

26. For a helpful discussion of "development" and "dependency" theories see Rebecca M. Blank, *Do Justice: Linking Christian Faith and Modern Economic Life* (Cleveland: United Church Press, 1992).

27. Susan George, *The Debt Boomerang: How Third World Debt Harms Us All* (London: Pluto Press, 1992).

28. Ulrich Duchrow, *Global Economy: A Confessional Issue for the Churches?*, tr. David Lewis (Geneva: WCC Publications, 1987), p. 143.

29. Richard J. Barnet, *The Lean Years: Politics in the Age of Scarcity* (New York: Simon and Schuster, 1980).

30. The Uruguay Round proposals for revision of the General Agreement on Tariffs and Trade and U.S.–Mexico Free Trade Agreements will assure that those who live from the investment of capital will gain by increasing the size of markets, and labor now living above the global subsistence level will lose. All may suffer through the decline in health and environmental protection, the exhaustion of resources, and the pollution of the environment.

31. John B. Cobb, Jr., "Ethics, Economics, and Free Trade," *Perspectives* 6/2 (February 1991), p. 13. I follow Cobb's argument here.

32. See Hazel Henderson, *The Politics of the Solar Age: Alternatives to Economics* (Garden City, N.Y.: Doubleday, 1981).

33. Herman E. Daly and John B. Cobb, Jr., *For the Common Good: Redirecting the Economy toward Community, the Environment, and a Sustainable Future* (Boston: Beacon Press, 1989). Daly and Cobb have criticized the GNP as an inadequate economic measurement and have worked extensively at alternative ways of measuring human economic welfare.

34. By "criticism" I mean the fulsome treatment given by Michael Walzer in *The*

Company of Critics: Social Criticism and Political Commitment in the Twentieth Century (New York: Basic Books, 1988).

35. By "innovation" I mean the project that intends the radical transformation of conditions that determine the quality of life of peoples globally.

36. Cornel West, *The American Evasion of Philosophy: A Genealogy of Pragmatism* (Madison: The University of Wisconsin Press, 1989).

37. Were we to follow recent Latin American liberation theology, we would speak here of globalization and spirituality. See Gustavo Gutiérrez, *We Drink from Our Own Wells: The Spiritual Journey of a People*, tran. Matthew J. O'Connell (Maryknoll, N.Y.: Orbis Books, 1984).

38. I have made an initial attempt at this in *God the Economist*. Other endeavors in this direction are Jürgen Moltmann, *Trinity and the Kingdom: The Doctrine of God*, tran. Margaret Kohl (San Francisco: Harper and Row, 1981) and *History of the Triune God: Contributions to Trinitarian Theology*, tran. John Bowden (New York: Crossword, 1992); Leonardo Boff, *Trinity and Society* (Maryknoll, N.Y.: Orbis Books, 1988); Catherine Mowry LaCugna, *God for Us: The Trinity and Christian Life* (San Francisco: Harper, 1991). These theological projects are presently developing new perspectives in pneumatology: Jürgen Moltmann, *Der Geist des Lebens: eine ganzheitliche Pneumatologie* (Munich: Chr. Kaider, 1991) and Michael Welker, *Gottes Geist: Theologie ded Heiligen Geist* (Neukirchen-Vluyn: Neukirchenet Verlag, 1992).

39. Edward Farley, *Good and Evil: Interpreting a Human Condition* (Minneapolis: Fortress Press, 1990), pp. 260ff.

40. Margaret Visser, *The Rituals of Dinner: The Origins, Evolution, Eccentricities, and Meaning of Table Manners* (New York: Grove Weidenfeld, 1991).

41. See, for example, John Rawls, *A Theory of Justice* (Cambridge: Harvard University Press, 1971).

42. M. Douglas Meeks, "Hope and the Ministry of Planning and Management," *Anglican Theological Review* 64 (April 1982), 147-62.

43. Alasdair MacIntyre, *Whose Justice? Which Rationality?* (Notre Dame: University of Notre Dame Press, 1988).

44. See Meeks, *God the Economist*, pp. 82-89; Michael Ignatieff, *The Needs of Strangers* (New York: Viking Press, 1985); Thomas W. Ogletree, *Hospitality to the Stranger: Dimensions of Moral Understanding* (Philadelphia: Fortress Press, 1985), pp. 35-59; Walter Brueggemann, *Interpretation and Obedience: From Faithful Reading to Faithful Living* (Minneapolis: Fortress Press, 1992), pp. 290-310.

45. See Farley's helpful reflections on forgiveness in *Good and Evil*, pp. 247ff.

46. Copyright © 1991 by the Case Study Institute. All names and places have been disguised to protect the privacy of the persons involved in this situation.

47. South African "townships" were established by South African laws of apartheid as geographically defined areas adjacent to white urban centers in which Blacks are allowed to live, but not to own property. Many townships have several hundred thousand residents crowded into two and three square mile areas.

48. African National Congress (ANC). A South African political party "unbanned" in 1991. Nelson Mandela is president of ANC.

49. Inkatha Freedom Party (IFP). A political party under the leadership of Kwa-Zulu Chief Minister Mangosutho Buthelezi.

50. Between 1986 and 1990, while South Africa was under a "State of Emergency," open political gatherings were outlawed. Funerals were the only legal avenue of political protest in most black communities. Township funerals, drawing hundreds of mourners, frequently became highly politicized events.

51. "Toyi-toying" is South African group dance movement used in black political marches and rallies to express solidarity.

52. There is substantial evidence that conservative and radical elements, outside the ANC and IFP and in collaboration with the South African government's security forces, have fueled the violence in many townships. Between 1985 and 1990 more than six thousand South Africans were killed in factional violence.

53. Martin Luther King, Jr., *Strength to Love* (New York: Harper and Row, 1963).

54. Amilcar Cabral, *Unity Struggle* (London: Heinnemann, 1980), p. 145.

55. Todd Gitlin, *The Whole World is Watching* (Berkeley: University of California Press, 1980), p. 154.

56. M. Douglas Meeks, *God the Economist*, pp. 58-59.

[10]

LIBERATING PEDAGOGIES IN THE GLOBALIZATION OF THEOLOGICAL EDUCATION

ESSAY

WILLIAM BEAN KENNEDY

The Pilot Immersion Project sent nine groups of representatives from twelve seminaries abroad to learn from local people and their situations. Each seminary also took representatives into local immersions for intercultural involvement at home. For those who participated and for their institutions these experiences outside normal academic activity raised questions about modes of learning and teaching in theological education.

What can be learned from those experiences that can contribute to more vital pedagogies? These questions may help us improve how we learn and teach in North American seminaries.

I. Identity

A. Who Am I? What Do I Bring from My Background to This Experience?

Every mode of learning connects new experiences to old ones, according to how each of us has been shaped in the past. Our self-formation conditions each of us to learn in certain ways. It sets up filters that affect how we perceive reality and influences greatly what and how we learn or do not learn. Our knowledge and our ways of knowing are social constructions of reality. We learn where we walk, with the persons with whom we share ongoing life experiences. As we grow up, our modes of learning and knowing become patterned much like those of the persons and groups with which we associate, all of which reflect the society and culture within which we live.

In our early years those modes of learning are fashioned in us as we live in a matrix of multiple relationships with other people and things. In our individualist-oriented culture it is easy to perceive ourselves as separate beings, who have to *do* something to relate to others and to nature. More helpful perhaps is to think of ourselves as the center of a large number of relationships which converge on the nexus which is myself. Distinctiveness and individuality are there because no two persons share the same set of relationships. Lewis J. Sherrill wrote that "the self is formed in its relationships with others. If it becomes de-formed, it becomes so in its relationships. If it is re-formed or transformed, that too will be in its relationships."[1]

The self is historical, that is, I keep changing as the relationships change during my life. Although outside forces strongly influence those relationships, I do have some continuing choices of relationships as my self-nexus moves through time. Whatever image of a matrix I have needs to be moved along the time line of my life. Studies of stages of growth or learning readiness can also seem simply fixed and sequential, whereas if the matrix is moving through time, different relationships reflect changing needs and circumstances. Particular stages call for special attention, but the potentialities for human development remain present in different ways through all the changes.

Educationally, an immersion experience intentionally places persons in new and strange situations where their particular matrix of relationships is radically expanded and re-formed. The result is a shaking of the comfortable patterns formed by the ongoing regularities of life and work. The experience opens up new relationships and ways of seeing and knowing. It raises questions about how we learn as we continue to become re-formed or trans-formed or de-formed. The Pilot Immersion Project set out to provide different cultural contexts for those changes and to help participants learn in the process.

A first step in transformative learning is to affirm and use our own past experience as a valid source of knowledge as well as a fundamental influence in all our learning. Our pedagogies must develop ways to help persons bring that patterning into consciousness where it can be recognized, analyzed, and utilized. Ways to help that happen include:

(1) Have persons make lists of roles by which they would identify themselves; then, have them suggest a stereotype for each role listed; then list a phrase or word to counteract each stereotype. In small groups discuss each person's list.

(2) Analyze the formative social forces in one's own ideology by combining personal and social ideologies.[2]

(3) In pairs or threes discuss: How would I describe myself as a learner before I go on the immersion (or as I begin an academic course)? Then discuss the same question after returning (or when the course ends).

(4) Ask participants to locate themselves in regard to their socio-economic class by sharing their family's relation to land over the last three to five generations. In small groups discuss how these memories affect our learning.

B. *Who Are* **We?**

What is the group identity in which the various individual backgrounds now come together? In what ways do commonalities and differences among members of a group experience enrich or inhibit learning?

It is important to focus on the diversities in each group as persons enter the immersion (or course) experience and later reflect on it. What background diversities are there? In what ways are members open to modes of learning other than the familiar ones? Too great a diversity without common commitments or trusting ongoing relationships can block shared learning and openness to those who are different. Nevertheless, there can be enriched understanding and empathy if the group can sense its commonalities and build relationships that provide trust and security for members. When that happens, they can more easily take the risks of openness which may threaten personal identity and self-worth.

Smaller sections of large courses, led by professors or tutors, offer excellent opportunities for this kind of enrichment to occur. Professor Susan Davies of Bangor Theological Seminary is experimenting with how to utilize the background diversity of incoming students to enrich their theological education.[3]

An immersion experience can develop a close sense of community among participants as together they encounter new and strange situations that challenge and threaten their customary ways of doing and learning. Bonding relationships often develop, which skillful management of the group experiences can facilitate. Such facilitation needs to occur early in the orientation process and be carried out through the entire immersion. Then attention must be paid to analyzing how diversity can enrich the event and how learnings from the process can then be brought home into the pedagogical styles of participants.

One very important commonality in the Pilot Immersion Project was that all participants belonged in one way or another to academe, as professors, students, board members, and administrators. In what ways has an academic cognitive rational approach dominated their ways of learning? What resistances have women and minority members experienced to the power of an academic mode of learning? Do lay persons among the trustees share that academic approach? Focused reflection on such questions during and after the immersion can lead to new understandings about how persons learn.

What happens when academicians are put in situations where they cannot control their schedules, when they face unfamiliar threats, and when they encounter a wider range of stimuli than they know at home? From it all, what can they learn about the dialogue for which they strive in their teaching, the dialogue between the content of their disciplines and the knowledge students (and they themselves) know and bring to it from their own lives?

II. Participation

A. Why Did I Participate?

It is important to share at the outset the fears, anxieties, and excitement participants bring into any new learning experience. Such discussion encourages awareness of what is at stake for different persons and what anticipations they have for change in future activity.

What common and diverse expectations do they bring to the experience? What special interests seem important to recognize? For example, what if it was the first trip to a Third World country, a first or rare adult experience of living in community settings, of sleeping in a dormitory or in a rural village shanty? What of

African-Americans going to Africa for the first time? Is there expectation of trans-formation? If some persons hope for conversion or liberation from a vaguely sensed provincialism, how is the threat of that deep change manifested? dealt with? Leaders need to provide support and perhaps counseling as persons are undergoing such changes. And how do we nurture carryover of these learnings into the pedagogies we use in theological education?

Such questions are important also in seminary classrooms. Conscious recogni-tion of the aims for education brought into the concreteness of a particular aca-demic course helps deepen the learning possibilities for all. When academicians become aware of how immersion experiences stimulate or shock a person's learn-ing, they can reshape the dialogue they hope for with the materials presented or assigned in a course. Even more, in planning the curriculum, the kind of field education offered to students gains from the establishment of clear aims which are understood by those involved. When the drama of an event fits within the expectations, its values increase; when it does not, reappraisal of aims can take place. When professors and students reflect upon this combination of aim and process, their "back-home" teaching and learning intensifies.

B. Why Did We Participate?

The community question requires exploration of group motivation. What insti-tutional pressures, rewards, and punishments may be factors? Was the seminary's articulated goal clear for its members? Did having to pay for the experience change anything? Was institutional change part of the "assignment" as participants were chosen to go? Was there a "commissioning" by the community that reinforced their motivation and directed the goals that were set? Learning is enhanced greatly when personal and institutional aims cohere.

Institutional consciousness of goals provides context for pedagogies. Analyzing the institutional and community expectations of educational programs can help clarify the mission of a seminary, construct a curriculum that resonates with the expectations of students and constituencies, and encourage support for improved teaching and learning.

A helpful way to analyze expectations and commitment is to put the aim or mission of a particular course on the chalkboard or on posted newsprint, and ask the students to write their personal aims for the course on a sheet of newsprint. Then have those aims posted on the walls, and have everyone walk around and read them. Ask for suggestions about how aims that are alike can be grouped, with reflective comments. Then have everyone look for similarities and differences between groupings of student aims and the seminary's goals.

III. Experience

A. What Did I Experience?

Participants need some way of recording their experiences for later recall and reflection. They need to note sequences of events; talk about them; and be able to share what they have seen, heard, and smelled, their feelings and thoughts. If journaling is proposed as a way to do this, time must be set aside for it each day or two.

Comparing the exercise of taking notes from class lectures or reading assignments with the recording of a hurried exposure to unfamiliar sounds, smells, and situations can bring fresh insight into the dialogue between different sources of knowledge. In traditional academic classroom learning "new" and different human experiences and understandings are brought to students mainly through printed books and articles written by specialists who have analyzed situations and codified some portion of human experience into print. Professors' lectures bring to the student the specialized knowledge of many such written sources, related to and enlivened by the lecturer's own lived experiences.

A major purpose of education is to bring into dialogue those experiences from outside and from the past with the present ongoing experiences of learners. The fresh challenge to make some sense of relating the feelings and insights of the immersion experience to one's own previous knowledge is like the activity of relating the codified knowledge of others' experiences with one's own personal knowledge. An immersion participant's experiential knowledge emerges in a demanding schedule in a strange situation. That knowledge therefore lacks the comfortable patterning that helps us carry on and interpret our ordinary lives back home.

We need to reconstruct our ways of knowing to encompass the fast-paced "new" into our fabric of ideology, our framework of interpretation. That challenge stimulates professor and student alike to re-engage traditional courses with a livelier respect for what each brings into the dialogue with past or "outside" knowledge and for the richness latent in the common sharing of contemporary experiences and insights of others in the class.

Scheduling of the immersion to provide pedagogical variety and time for reflection requires jealous protection of relaxed and reflection time. It is important to avoid an overload of lectures and information and to find a balance of direct experience with people, in small groups, and time for personal and group reflection. Overseas it is understandable why local hosts want to pack a schedule with all possible information and exposure. Stateside leaders must work with them to set priorities and be realistic about the energy required for successive new experiences and the consequent need for careful scheduling.

Back home, the American system of course credits forces learning into quarter- or semester-long packages that often overwhelm students' overcrowded schedules with impossible amounts of assigned reading and papers.[4] Reflective thinking about how the parts connect to the whole and to one's ongoing life is squeezed out or detrimentally delayed. Immersion experiences can encourage seminaries to reorganize the curriculum to realistic expectations and to explore better ways of reflecting during a course or a semester. Perhaps a class can expand the review and evaluation process of mid-term tests or papers with some small group discussion that allows student response and reflection to improve the rest of the course.

B. What Did We Experience? What Was the Corporate Experience?

Since there is no guaranteed automatic community result from an immersion experience, it is necessary to arrange helpful ways of sharing, such as providing for pairs to talk about events as they travel around. Arranging small groups in which members can reflect on experiences enhances learning on immersions as well as in classroom assignments and processes. Along with small group discussions, plenary reflection needs to include conversation about what was seen, how participants felt about it, and how they can interpret it.

When tutorial sessions in large classes foster such sharing, the learning is enriched by the diversity focused on common questions as students get to know one another better. Group assignments and research projects encourage such sharing. For effective pedagogy on overseas and local immersions, and in seminary classrooms, different combinations of participant relationships should be arranged in order to enhance the learning that comes through one another's backgrounds and bodies of knowledge.

Attending to what is experienced raises questions Elliot Eisner asks in "The three curricula that all schools teach."[5] First, there is the *explicit curriculum*, the one described in the catalogue that lists courses. The second, the *implicit curriculum*, the ethos of the institution that in its total life, administrative patterns, student activities, and inherited assumptions has a tremendous influence on what is learned. The implicit curriculum reinforces but also challenges the modes of learning of all the institution's participants and constituencies in ways that often are more fundamental to the shaping of graduates than the "content" knowledge of classrooms and academic assignments. Insofar as immersions provide different experiences and challenges than those ordinarily included in a seminary program, they raise questions that need to be addressed in the explicit curriculum. Some of the institutions involved in the Pilot Immersion Project have entered into curriculum revisions as a result of their involvement.

The immersion experiences have an effect also on the implicit curriculum, inasmuch as the participants bring back into community life different kinds of expectations and energy for multicultural and global aspects of chapel, "extracurricular" activities, and service commitments outside the seminary.

The immersion also raises major questions about Eisner's third point, the *null curriculum*. What is not included in the explicit and implicit curricula that the experience has exposed? What is left out, either consciously or unconsciously, that can remind us of the necessary but ideologically selected narrowing of particular knowledge? If political economic criticism of North America from fellow Christians abroad comes as a surprise, what does that say about what and how contemporary theology, ethics, and church and society, are taught? If the inability to listen attentively to what seems radically "other" in the experiences is lacking, what does it say about the lack of concern in the seminary community for developing that essential gift for any serious multicultural and multiethnic understanding? If biblical interpretation among Christian scholars and lay people in other countries is not like what is taught at home, have important hermeneutical principles and processes been ignored or avoided? We cannot assume that other approaches are simply wrong. Every pattern has cultural specificities that cannot be overlooked. Differences and contradictions that emerge in the immersion experiences offer powerful openings to our provincial North American cocoon, and challenge U.S. and Canadian theological education to pursue those openings with commitment.

The corporate experiences from immersions can have revolutionary impact on the three curricula of North American seminaries.

IV. Learnings

A. *What Did* I *Learn?*

Going into a quite different political, economic, cultural, and social situation requires dealing with new "content" knowledge. Where people experience poverty, hunger, brutality, and other forms of oppression, a visitor from the relatively protected world of North American theological education has to confront knowledge that may be known lightly but not deeply. New knowledge of that sort forces new kinds of appropriation. Well-planned immersions focus on helping that learning occur.

One of the major contributions of Paulo Freire to educational and theological thinking in our generation is his affirmation of the wisdom of ordinary people. In *Pedagogy of the Oppressed*, possibly the most widely read book on education in our lifetime, he addresses the issue of the knowledge that emerges when ordinary people, the "oppressed" by the political economic and social systems of the modern world, discuss together their situation and what actions they might take to transform it. "The starting point for organizing the program content of education or political action must be the present, existential, concrete situation, reflecting the aspirations of the people."[6] The point extends to students and their experience as well as to ordinary people, the peasants:

> Through dialogue, the teacher-of-the-students and the students-of-the-teacher cease to exist and a new term emerges: teacher-student with students-teachers. The teacher is no longer merely the one-who-teaches, but one who is himself taught in dialogue with the students, who in turn while being taught also teaches. They become jointly responsible for a process in which all grow.[7]

Immersion experiences in many ways address such changes by focusing on the learning that comes from listening to people in other cultures and listening together with a diverse group of learners. Immersions call for and encourage conscious effort to discover implications of these deep changes in the pedagogical practices of theological education.

B. *What Did* We *Learn?*

It is useful to concentrate on the group experience, on how and why different people learned differently. In what ways did personal backgrounds influence *what* was learned? How was that prepared for? utilized? From such reflection clues can be noted for experimentation back home in seminary courses and in curriculum approaches that take advantage of the potentially enriching diversity of background "wisdom" in any group of persons. Similar awareness can enliven and deepen any group study in local congregations where seminary graduates will serve as leaders.

Here is a place for the hermeneutical and theological dimension to be consciously addressed and enhanced, as participants set up the conversation in themselves and with one another between their own backgrounds and sets of responses, and the new data experienced and observed in light of the theological tradition to which they belong. The particular potential and problems of academically oriented participants need to be analyzed, in order for the contribution of their specialized knowledge to be bridged creatively with the new knowledge and the knowledge of others. Creative learning comes from affirmation of both types of knowledge, awareness and utilization of both the cognitive and affective aspects of learning, and skillful structuring of the processes by which persons can learn together and from historical or absent others. In such conversations about learning and teaching, the immediately experiential and the codified experiential of the tradition can come together in exciting moments of fresh insights and commitments.

How do different ways of learning new knowledge on a trip relate to the usual seminary patterns? Personal evaluation and analysis can illumine for the participants what factors best contributed to or blocked their learning. It is useful during the experience, as well as later, to explore and analyze different modes of learning. For example, compare academic, rational, and book-oriented with more direct experiential, holistic, and active-reflective learning; discuss the pros and cons and varieties of each type in relation to different kinds of insights or perspectival transformations gained.

In my courses on multicultural teaching I have found it helpful to use Kolb's Learning Style Inventory as a way of opening up discussion and awareness of different ways persons learn.[8] It is a simple, brief test that reflects a person's stronger and weaker modes of learning. The inventory also can be used for discussion in class as a means of helping self-understanding and fostering ability to listen to others.

In retrospect, the *encuentro* I led in Buenos Aires in 1971 for the Assembly of the World Council of Christian Education failed to take full advantage of the opportunity to learn from one another in the immersion experiences. My report on those seventeen *encuentros* reflected the experience of our group, which included participants from all six continents:

From [his or her] background each person reflected upon the Latin American situation. The mixture of those reflections added another dimension to the analysis. Critique from North America was tempered by that from Africa or Asia; European assumptions vis-à-vis the Latin American scene were modified and enriched by other cultural approaches. The resulting effort, though not always neat in its results, invariably proved highly stimulating and challenging to participants. Whatever views of education they held upon arrival they left a week later with much less confidence that their patterns could be simply transferred to another culture or easily adapted into another situation. As a result they went on to the Assembly [in Lima the second week] and returned to their countries with a vastly greater appreciation of the varieties and complexities of education around the world and with some radically new options to consider and perhaps implement in their own situations.[9]

V. Change

A. *What Can* **I** *Change?*

Myself? in what ways? My teaching? My studies? My relationships with those from other cultural backgrounds? These questions recognize the value and the potential for personal refreshing and refashioning of one's ongoing academic activity that can come from an immersion experience and pedagogical reflection on it.

In North American society and in theological education there is growing concern about multicultural and multiethnic education. An immersion project can make a great contribution to addressing that concern in two ways: by giving selected groups of seminary persons direct experience in another culture, overseas or locally; and by structuring that experience in a diverse group with processes that pay pedagogical attention to the differences in background and learning modes of participants.

B. *What Can* **We** *Change?*

What institutional or societal changes were aimed for? accomplished? What new and ongoing commitments were made? Were they sustained?

The communal dimension broadens questions about change by focusing on the institutional structures and processes of theological education. Social and ideological analysis of the patterns of traditional theological education can lead to new ways of conceiving and organizing the curriculum and course syllabi. As recent writings have emphasized, inherited patterns seem to be increasingly inadequate for the kind of theological education that would fit contemporary needs. One aspect to which attention has been called in recent studies is the inherited gap and assumed sequence of theory and action.[10] The questions of epistemology and hermeneutics related to the analysis of the direct experience of participants in immersion events are part of a larger inquiry into how persons know and how different sources of knowledge contribute to knowing.

Theological education has much to learn from analyzing its pedagogical patterns and possibilities in light of the immersion experiences and other activities of the Pilot Immersion Project. To summarize, here are several principles that may continue to stimulate thinking about learning and teaching in seminaries and about implications for the institutions involved. Theological education should:

(1) Affirm and make conscious pedagogical use of both the past and immediate experiences of participants as being sources of knowledge as well as shapers of their ways of perceiving the total experience.

(2) Affirm the importance of sharing life stories in the preliminary orientation to an event or course, balanced with information about the context and expectations, in order for participants to know one another and thereby to enhance the shared learning.

(3) Pay attention to what the immersion situation (or seminary context) teaches, and how the new knowledge can be put in dialogue with what

persons already know about the "big picture" and how it affects the lives of people.

(4) Recognize the value of recording events and impressions as they are being experienced, in order to deepen the possibilities of reflection and to develop ways of understanding and using the related processes to codify and articulate that knowledge.

(5) Affirm the value of quiet relaxed time for journaling and reflection on immersion events or for pacing the assignments during a course.

(6) Analyze the rhythm of learning to enhance the process of dialogue in learning through note-taking from lectures and books as well as through personal recording of events, feelings, and insights.

(7) Develop a sequence of theological reflections that builds toward implications and commitments for the ongoing life of group members and their institutions.

Many books on pedagogies and planning for learning and teaching in academic institutions elaborate on such principles.[11] What immersion projects add is immediate experiential and unfamiliar modes of learning, where involvement forces changes that reflection can expand into fresh and different ways of learning and teaching in theological education.

CASE STUDY[12]

More Questions Than Answers

How would Joe Seramane teach this course? What would he say? Where would he begin? Mike Reardon sat with his class notes before him as he prepared to teach the fundamental moral theology course, a course that he had taught many times in his nine years on the faculty. Once again he found himself reflecting on the story of Joe Seramane. It was a story that haunted him since his return from South Africa. The man, the story and the questions were as present to him on this cold snowy evening in Minneapolis as they had been on that August evening in Johannesburg. Six months had passed since his return from South Africa, but the impact of the experience was still very much with him.

Mike thought back to the day he received an unexpected call from the dean asking if he was still interested in joining the team of five persons from his school who were preparing to travel to southern Africa as part of a pilot project concerning globalization and its impact on theological education. Mike's school, along with two other theological schools in the area, were participating in the program. A major component of the project was to provide carefully prepared Third World immersion experiences for faculty, administrators, and others who could influence the ethos, curricula, and orientation of the school in relation to global awareness. The team for the trip had been selected weeks before, and Mike had dealt with his disappointment in not being selected for this particular immersion. He knew eventually he would have an opportunity to participate in the program because he was one of the few persons on the faculty who had had very little cross-cultural experience. In spite of his disappointment, he had let go of his wish to travel to Africa. Now, just as the group was about to begin the immediate preparation for travel, one person dropped out. Mike did not hesitate to step in. In the few weeks of hectic preparation that followed Mike sometimes wondered if he had made the right decision. He was both excited and challenged by the adventure that lay before him. South Africa was a long way from the heartland of America, the place he had always called home.

Mike Reardon was born and raised in Ohio. As a high school student he was drawn to the vocation of priesthood and entered a Roman Catholic religious community of men. He attended a college in Indiana sponsored by his religious order and in 1974 moved to Chicago to begin studies in preparation for ordination to priesthood. In addition to completing the Master of Divinity degree, Mike also earned an M.A. in ethics as part of his program of preparation for priesthood. This was to set the course for his future work. Two years after his graduation from seminary Mike was asked by his superiors to leave his position as a high school teacher to begin doctoral studies at Notre Dame in the area of moral theology.

Nine years had passed since he completed his doctorate and began his teaching career at Holy Cross Theological School. The school had an enrollment of approximately 250 students, some preparing for Roman Catholic priesthood, others preparing for lay ministries. The student body had changed in the nine years Mike had been there. When he began teaching, most of his student were white middle-class males belonging to various religious orders. In time, more and more international students preparing for ordination as members of missionary communities came to the school. More recently lay students from various urban minority groups were attracted to a new emphasis on black and Hispanic studies. Given all of this and as a result of his trip to South Africa, Mike found himself looking back and asking if he needed to view his teaching and research with new eyes.

The trip to South Africa had awakened something within him. While he had always made efforts to do a good job, he now recognized that he had approached his classes with a certain complacent attitude. He had taught with blinders on, dealing with a perspective of truth narrowly focused as if it were the whole truth. The experience of South Africa had thrown him off balance. It changed him. Somehow he knew that he could not be honest to the moment at hand or to teaching well if he did not reconnect with what he had seen and heard in South Africa. But just how to do that eluded him.

Thinking back, Mike was amused at how nervous he had been at the start of the trip. He remembered the many "what if" questions that stayed with him even as the plane made its way across the Atlantic. What if he got separated from the group? What if he lost his passport or money? What if the group members did not get along with one another? Mike had heard from those who had gone on an immersion experience the previous summer that various personal agenda and individual differences had been an issue. In the preparation sessions the group seemed to work well together. Expectations had been shared. A covenant of learning had been developed. Mike knew that he and his travel companions were invested in the process, but what if . . . ?

For Mike, the time in South Africa fell into two segments, the time before and the time after hearing Joe Seramane's story. It was a story unique to one man, but in reality a story repeated in the eyes and voices of all the other black South Africans he met during the remainder of his time in South Africa. He knew that for him and for his travel companions the power of Joe's story was linked to what they had encountered in the first part of their journey. And its meaning unfolded as they reflected upon the experiences that followed.

During the first segment of the immersion the group spent time in Zimbabwe. They visited villages, shared in worship with the people of an independent African Church, the Zion Apostolic Church, and learned about cooperatives and land issues. Time was spent meeting with political and religious leaders who helped the group to learn about the political and economic reality of Zimbabwe in relation to the countries of the northern hemisphere, especially the United States. Mike found the discussion with the faculty of theology and religious studies at the University of Zimbabwe particularly helped him to appreciate the struggle and difficulty that was a part of developing a more contextual and indigenous theology. Being on the faculty of a school that educated many African students and also prepared students for international missionary work, Mike realized the importance of the issues involved.

The first afternoon in South Africa was spent at the headquarters of the South African Council of Churches (SACC) in Johannesburg. In meetings with General Secretary Frank Chikane and Vice President Sheena Duncan, the group received an orientation concerning the situation in South Africa at that time. The church leaders spoke of the crucial priorities and potential problems that lay ahead for South Africa.

It was on that first evening, Friday, August 10, that the group met Mr. Joseph Seramane, director of the South African Council of Churches, Department of Justice and Reconciliation. For Mike and for others in the group this particular meeting was clearly a highlight of the entire travel experience. Just thinking about it put Mike back in the basement of the retreat house in Johannesburg listening again to the most remarkable, memorable, mesmerizing man he had ever met. It seemed ironic to Mike that this man had ended up heading a department on justice and reconciliation. Joe had been a victim of injustice for so many years that his own heart had for a while grown hardened with hatred. Now he lived and worked for reconciliation.

Joe Seramane had been raised a Christian but fell away from the church when he couldn't understand how white people could pray on Sunday and mistreat Blacks during the rest of the week. That disillusionment gradually grew into antipathy for all things religious and even for God. He wasn't sure if he believed in God, but if God did exist, Joe despised God. For six years Joe was a prisoner in South Africa's notorious Robbin Island Prison. He had been a teacher and was arrested for helping to organize other teachers to stand against substandard educational conditions for black children. Twenty-eight months of his imprisonment was in solitary confinement. Mike vividly remembered Joe's intensity as he told the group that the only way to survive in such circumstances was to forget the world, forget loved ones, forget all those held dear. Survival meant not letting the world become any bigger than the four surrounding walls. During his time in prison, Joe was tortured regularly. He described to the group the beatings, the electric shocks, and how it felt when, to keep him from screaming out in his pain, a cloth was stuffed in his mouth. Joe told of feeling that he was passing from the plain of life to the plain of death, consoled only by the fact that he was dying for his convictions and by the justice he hoped would come to South Africa.

As Mike remembered the story, he again felt a type of stillness deep within. The turning point of Joe's story was in some way a turning point for him also. Mike wondered aloud, "Why did it touch me so deeply?" Thinking back he remembered Joe saying that it was exactly at the point of greatest suffering, when he was certain he would die, that life began its most extraordinary change. Certain that he was dying, Joe, who had turned away from God, heard himself whisper, "God, I offer you my soul." And at that moment when he could literally taste death, he heard another voice whisper to him about life. It was a voice that said, "I have created life, and this life that is you they are not going to take away." It was from that point on that Joe began to understand the meaning of reconciliation even in the midst of sin and injustice. Things changed. The guard who had been most vicious and brutal in torturing him befriended him. He told Joe that he could no longer torture him because he no longer saw hatred in Joe's face. The guard changed from beating Joe to helping him and praying for him. And Joe's change continued too. He knew that whatever life he had left would be spent trying to understand the upside-down ways of God, trying to learn them, fathom them, and practice them. The experience forever changed Joe's life. It gave him new life and, in a real way, made Joe a new person.

Mike knew that having heard Joe's story in the context of the travel experience in South Africa, he, too, was changed. Coming home felt strange. He remembered being somewhat disoriented. Things looked the same but nothing felt quite the same. He was amazed that he had been away only three weeks and yet found "re-entry" to be an issue. He missed the folks he had traveled with. They had shared an intense, memorable experience. Coming back to business as usual was not easy.

While other faculty members and those he lived with expressed interest in hearing about the trip, it felt superficial to Mike. He appreciated their interest but knew that he could not easily convey all that had taken place for him. He was glad that some others in his school had had similar experiences in cross-cultural situations. It helped. He felt more connected to efforts being made toward glob-alization and also had a better appreciation of the multicultural student body. There had been faculty discussion and some heated arguments about the use of terms like globalization, cross-cultural, contextual theology, and so on, but Mike had felt outside of these discussions. Now he realized that the questions others had raised were also his questions.

Mike knew that his attitude had changed in regard to the diversity he encoun-tered in the classroom and in the practicum groups with which he worked. Prior to the trip, he had accepted as a given the fact that there would probably be students from various cultural backgrounds in his classes. He viewed it as a chal-lenge since a missionary emphasis was a central focus at the school. If students had difficulty understanding what he presented, Mike would go out of his way to explain it to them. He wanted them to grasp what he was teaching. But now something was different. He found that he wanted to listen to them. He was more interested in hearing their point of view. One instance in particular came to mind. In the fall semester immediately after his return Mike taught a course entitled "The Ethics of Thomas Aquinas." When he was lecturing on Aquinas's notion of charity as friendship, an African woman challenged his understanding of friend-ship, pointing out that her experience of growing up in Africa gave her a different perspective. She questioned the notion of friendship as a virtue to be reached for, nurtured, or developed by an individual. For her it was a given. Friendship was part of the experience of being human. One did not choose to be a friend, but rather was born into a circle of friends, one's family, and the larger community. Rather than simply explain what he meant and expect her to understand, Mike listened and entered into conversation with her. He found that as the course developed they had several discussions that enriched and challenged them both. He learned from her as well as taught her. As he thought about these conversa-tions, he realized that their most fruitful exchanges had taken place outside the classroom. Now the challenge was to find ways to foster that kind of dialogue as part of his teaching. His approach of carefully prepared class lectures carried the content of the subject at hand and that was important, but something more was needed. How to accomplish that "something more" still eluded him.

Beyond a growing awareness of cross-cultural issues in his own school, Mike felt more invested in the efforts that were being made among the schools in the area. The group with which he had traveled continued to meet both on a formal and informal basis. Their times together always generated more questions than answers. The discussion was lively, the practical outcomes few. All this reinforced his own conviction that the implications of globalization were far reaching and that it was important that he and others continue to struggle with the issues involved.

Mike knew that he could not teach any of his courses in the same way as he had taught them before South Africa. As he began to rethink the fundamentals course, he struggled to name just how it would be different. In the past he had taught that good moral action is grounded in community and not in an individualistic misuse of human freedom. That was still fundamental. However, his experience had pushed him to see new implications behind the notion. He suspected that in the past he had taught the course in a disembodied way, laying out a basic approach and understanding of ethics before even raising the question of justice. He now knew that the central focus of his teaching had to be justice. It was not one issue among many that needed to be addressed, something to be attached to Christian ethics. It was the heart and soul of ethics. He began to recognize that he, himself, had moved from being aware of justice to having passion for justice. But, how do you teach this?

Something else pushed into his awareness. He wanted to convey to his students that any viable Christian morality must have a strong global dimension. The interdependence of all peoples had to be a consideration. He wanted them to realize what it means to live justly in the real world, not the small provincial world that was familiar to the majority of his students. To do this he had to make an effort to avoid an overemphasis on intellectual arguments and elaborate systems. He needed to root his approach in the power of stories. Looking again at the class notes before him, Mike knew what he wanted to say, how he must begin. He picked up his pen and began. . . .

I want to draw us into the world of Christian ethics through the door of justice, and to do that I want to begin with a story about a man named Joe Seramane. What I would like to suggest is for all of us to let his story stay with us throughout the course, to allow it to become a background chorus to all our considerations, something to which we need continually to return and by which we must measure everything we do. We must let this memory work itself out in our study of Christian ethics. We must reckon with it, honor it, respond to it. How does the story of Joe Seramane and all the people he represents, not only in South Africa, but all people denied life throughout the world, all the people who are told they do not matter, that they are expendable, that they can be diminished so that others may prosper, shape and direct our understanding of what Christian morality involves? Put differently, how would Joe Seramane or the people of Soweto teach this course? What would they say to us? Where would they begin?

Mike put his pen down and reread what he had written. The question echoed within him and reached farther. What did all this mean for him personally, for him as a scholar, and just as important, for his institution? It had to be more than just nice sounding words.

TEACHING NOTE

More Questions Than Answers

The challenge to unexamined assumptions that Mike experienced as a result of his exposure to an unfamiliar context is not unlike the disequilibrium experienced by many as they are confronted with the rapid changes that are occurring in local and global realities. In particular, this case raises issues for persons grappling with the impact of a changing world context on the teaching of theology. The teaching of the case might include the following objectives:

- to examine the implication of disorientation as an aspect of the learning process;
- to challenge educators to examine the epistemological assumptions that are operative in one's approach to teaching;
- to prepare students/faculty to engage in a cross-cultural travel experience;
- to stimulate discussion concerning the issue of globalization of theological education and its impact on curriculum design.

I. Opening

Have participants complete the sentence: The farthest place from home I have traveled to is _____.

In pairs, have persons discuss briefly the understanding of the word "home" used to complete the sentence. Ask if different assumptions were operative and why.

Examine the idea of home and its influence on Mike prior to his travel experience in Southern Africa. On newsprint or board list assumptions that, given Mike's background, might have influenced his view of the world, the church, and his teaching prior to the trip.

II. Development

A. Invite the group to identify points in the case when Mike experienced disorientation.

B. Using the grid on page 294, compare the experiential learning process for both Joe Seramane and Mike.[13]

C. Using the stages in the grid on page 294, have participants recall a similar, even if less dramatic, learning experience. Share in pairs.

III. Conclusion

Have persons reflect on their own risk-taking or willingness to enter into disorientation as part of the teaching and learning process.

	Joe	Mike
1. Disorientation		
2. Self-examination		
3. Critical assessment of assumptions: epistemic socio-cultural psychological		
4. Recognition that others have had similar experiences and have managed change		
5. Consideration of new roles, different approaches		
6. Plan for new course of action		
7. Reintegration based on new perspective		

COMMENTARY

More Questions than Answers

HEIDI HADSELL do NASCIMENTO

According to the case study, Mike's transformative experience in South Africa has led him to an unanticipated re-evaluation of his task as an ethics professor. There are a number of elements relevant to this re-examination, several of which are closely related and can be grouped under two kinds of topics: those that are epistemological, and those having to do directly with the proper content of courses in ethics.

I. Christian Ethics and the Nature of Knowledge

The epistemological assumptions that professors like Mike as well as their students bring to the classroom are often unexamined and remain so throughout the duration of any course. Before his immersion experience Mike had a dual set of epistemological assumptions that as a result of his meeting Joe Seramane in South Africa he is now beginning to question. His first assumption concerned the extent to which, in a pedagogy of Christian ethics, it is possible to be "objective" and to teach what might be called The Truth. The second assumption concerned Mike's unexamined notion that the classroom is where and how theological education takes place. I will briefly discuss each of these.

A. *The Question of Perspective*

Mike now realizes that until his meeting with Seramane he, as The Professor, unilaterally developed and presented his course material to the students as The Truth, repressing or ignoring the insight that rather than one truth with a capital T, in ethics as in most of life there is no one truth but rather multiple perspectives on truth. Mike was suddenly grasped by this insight during his South African immersion, in which radically different human perspectives were overt, powerfully displayed, strongly polarized, and plain to all, including outsiders. Mike brought this new realization home with him from South Africa; it now enables him, even forces him, to see new perspectives on moral truths directly in front of him in his students.

In order for Mike to shape a pedagogy reflecting this new epistemological insight, he realizes that he must go beyond the limitations of his own education. He must begin to question the epistemological assumptions with which he was socialized in his church and, particularly, in his graduate education. Most centrally Mike knows now that he must question the fundamental assumption that what he was taught was not considered a perspective only, but rather was tantamount to

The Truth itself. This assumption expressed the components of one particular perspective (for example an ethnic community, social class, or lifestyle enclave), leaving them unexamined and unquestioned. It permitted Professor Mike to engage in his teaching with little critical reflection on or even identification of the perspective which, it was assumed, was The Truth; and without recognizing or valuing the varieties of perspectives represented by the students in the classroom.

Thus, for example, Mike could present an understanding of Christian love or justice without discussing with his students the fact that it was simply one understanding of love or justice in a given context, connected to a certain reading of the Bible and tradition by certain groups of people in certain historical and contextual moments. Further, Mike could teach in this way without ever stopping to explore with the students their own perspectives on love or justice and the connection of their perspectives with their own contexts, communities, classes, and so forth. In this way Mike's presentation of one perspective on love or justice could easily, if implicitly, be viewed as The Truth.

Once Mike realized that the teaching of ethics is concerned, at least in part, with the critical re-examination of such central assumptions, and concerned also with reflection from a variety of perspectives, the possibilities of the classroom experience were transformed for him. The diversity among the students and the variety and richness of their perspectives ceased to be obstacles to be overcome or ignored and became instead resources, indeed necessary resources for common ethical discernment.

Mike now began to attend to life experience as central to the learning process and central also to the discipline of ethics. Accordingly, he began to evoke from the students their own personal diverse experiences as well as the rich experiences of the social/ethnic/class/racial communities from which they came. He began to listen as well as to talk, to learn as well as to teach. In this process Mike's own identity as teacher began to change; the teacher as Truth-Teller receded as the teacher as resource person was born. The classroom became a space for engagement in mutual ethical discernment by persons with a variety of perspectives rather than a place in which Mike unilaterally set the agenda of learning from his one perspective — and did most of the talking.

B. The Question of Experience

The second and related epistemological question provoked by Mike's trip to South Africa focuses on the extent to which a pedagogy for ethics must be grounded in experience rather than disembodied, be concrete rather than abstract, be communally engaged rather than individualistic.

The trip to South Africa was a powerful learning experience for Mike, in part precisely because it was a different way to learn. Mike had earned a Ph.D. and had been teaching ethics for nine years before the trip. He had learned much in those years, but nothing compared with the transformed understanding that arose from his meeting with Seramane and the questioning of assumptions which ensued.

As Mike begins to attend to and engage human experience as a major medium of human transformative learning, he may begin to draw upon not only the past experiences of students, which have helped mold their perspectives, but their current experiences as well. Thus students (and faculty) can be encouraged to reflect on ethical dimensions and dilemmas posed by the intentional use of contemporary involvements and events. The classroom may be self-consciously linked to the community-based and/or parish-based local and global experiences of students and faculty in an ongoing dialogue of action and reflection. Consequently, the classroom may be organized so that the teacher as well as the course materials become resources to be drawn upon for reflection on, and in interaction with, current and diverse practical experiences. Ethics, with its practical and reflective components, lends itself particularly well to such learning.

Models for learning in theological institutions that bring together experience and reflection in this way are available both in the United States and from such places as the Philippines or Brazil, where innovative programs are a result not just of financial restraints, but more important, of a strong commitment to local and national contextual realities, and student experiences within them, which then are central in setting the educational agenda. I recall a priest in Brazil describing his seminary education in which after six intensive months in the field the students gathered for some months of study, first exploring with the professor what they thought they needed to study, based on their experiences in the field.

In sum, Mike's experience suggests common limitations of much of contemporary Christian ethics, at least as practiced in North America. His experience suggests the widespread failure of contemporary Christian ethics to be in conversation with Christian communities across the globe, even about ethical issues that are global in dimensions. But it also suggests the failure to teach students not as unattached individuals but as members of richly human communities, groups, and social classes which in turn have their own perspectives and historical experience to be drawn into the ongoing task of Christian ethical discernment. Related to this, Christian ethics must begin to confront the challenging task of creating new practices and experiences akin to Mike's in a globally shrinking world.

II. The Normative Center of Ethics

The other major question raised for Mike by his experience in South Africa focuses on the content of ethics itself. This question follows from the epistemological questions already considered. As Mike abandoned the universalist claims to Truth of his given ethical perspective, and recognized all thought, including Christian thought, as value laden and connected to interests, communities, and historical moments, he was enabled to respond positively to the plurality of truth perspectives and to teach his courses in ethics accordingly. Thus he was enabled to examine varieties of perspectives on the nature of Christian duty, obligation, character, and so forth, as well as on specific ethical dilemmas, thereby broadening the dialogue to include global dimensions. With this approach, Mike's pedagogy embodies his new insights into the importance of perspective and introduces students to the considered reflection of Christian communities from across the world.

By adopting a pluralistic model of pedagogy, Mike is liberated to utilize the resources his students bring to the classroom. He can celebrate that pluralism and introduce his students to an even greater plurality of voices and perspectives drawn from the global Christian community.

But this approach, as valuable as it is, only partially reflects the power of Mike's South African experience and the depth of the insight he gained from it. For while he learned that his truth is in a sense only one truth among many, and that in viewing it as The Truth he had little capacity to think critically about it (as well as losing the capacity to learn from the insights of other perspectives), he evidently has not abandoned the search for a broader truth in Christian ethics. He has not become an ethical relativist. It is not enough for Mike to include in his courses previously unattended voices from around the neighborhood and around the world. Rather he is convinced that he has now discovered the normative center for Christian ethics: "He now knew that the central focus of his teaching has to be justice. . . . It was the heart and soul of ethics."

How then does Mike avoid teaching one narrow perspective as The Truth, as he criticizes himself for having done for nine years, and still make justice the normative center of his courses?

Mike's commitment to critical re-examination of the formative although unexamined assumptions upon which his own study and teaching of ethics had been based suggests an approach that is both instructive to the student and a reflection of Mike's own ethical commitments. He can lead his students into their own inquiry into the normative center of Christian ethics. While he evokes and identifies both the varieties and sources of ethical perspectives in the course material and within the students in the classroom, Mike can also assume his own position in the dialogue. He can adopt a posture which is not itself disinterested or disembodied, but rather has a particular perspective openly identified and recognized as one perspective in a wide dialogue on Christian ethical truth. He thus can lead in the common effort of ethical discernment.

Finally, realizing that not every Christian will agree with Mike's new conviction that the normative center for Christian ethics must be justice, North American Christian ethicists must confront the ethical and theological plurality in the churches and in the seminaries while continuing the dialogue about the normative center of Christian ethical thought, since not every ethical perspective is equally expressive of Christian norms and values. As Mike now affirms, justice is indeed a central Christian ethical norm. Christians must accordingly confront the truth in the particular perspective of those Christians, such as Joe Seramane in South Africa, engaged in struggles for justice, and be challenged by it as truth relevant to their own particular contexts.

Notes

1. L. J. Sherrill. *The Gift of Power*. New York: Macmillan, 1955, p. 45.

2. W. B. Kennedy. "Integrating personal and social ideologies," in J. Mezirow (ed.), *Fostering Critical Reflection in Adulthood: A Guide to Transformative and Emancipatory Learning*. San Francisco: Jossey-Bass, 1990, pp. 99-115.

3. Professor Davies is working on this project for her dissertation in the joint Doctor of Education program at Union Theological Seminary and Teachers College Columbia University.

4. Laura Nash's chapter on "The Rhythms of the Semester" in M. M. Gullette, *The Art and Craft of Teaching* (Cambridge, Massachusetts: Harvard University Press, 1984) is a good example of helpful literature on planning and scheduling academic courses.

5. E. W. Eisner. "The three curricula that all schools teach," in *The Educational*

Imagination: On the Design and Evaluation of School Programs (2nd edition). New York: Macmillan, 1985, chap. 5.

6. P. Freire. *Pedagogy of the Oppressed*, trans. Myra Bergman Ramos. New York: Continuum, 1970, p. 85.

7. Ibid. p. 67.

8. D. A. Kolb. *Learning Style Inventory*. Boston: McBer and Company, 1976. A comprehensive review, "Learning styles: Interactions between culture and the individual," is found in C. I. Bennett, *Comprehensive Multicultural Education: Theory and Practice* (2nd edition). Boston: Allyn and Bacon, 1990, pp. 139-173. The chapter includes a "Selected bibliography of learning style assessment instruments."

9. W. B. Kennedy. *Encuentros: A New Ecumenical Learning Experience. Study/ Encounter* 8:2, 1972. Geneva: World Council of Churches, pp. 3-4.

10. D. H. Kelsey and B. G. Wheeler. "Thinking about theological education: The implications of 'Issues Research' for criteria of faculty excellence," *Theological Education* 28:1 (Autumn 1991); various chapters in B. G. Wheeler and E. Farley (eds.). *Shifting Boundaries: Contextual Approaches to the Structure of Theological Education.* Louisville: Westminster/John Knox, 1991; and many others.

11. I have found these to be helpful in my annual course for tutors: Gullette, *The Art and Craft of Teaching*; S. D. Brookfield. *The Skillful Teacher: On Technique, Trust, and Responsiveness in the Classroom.* San Francisco: Jossey-Bass, 1990; B. Joyce and B. Weil. *Models of Teaching* (3rd edition). Englewood Cliffs, New Jersey: Prentice-Hall, 1986; and W. B. Kennedy. "Highlander praxis: Learning with Myles Horton," *Teachers College Record* 83:1 (Fall 1981), pp. 105-19.

12. Copyright © 1993 by the Case Study Institute. The names of persons and places in this case have been disguised to protect the privacy of those involved in the situation.

13. The grid is based on the work of J. Mezirow, *Transforming Dimensions of Adult Learning*. San Francisco: Jossey-Bass, 1991.

[11]

INSTITUTIONAL CHANGE AND THE GLOBALIZATION OF THEOLOGICAL EDUCATION

ESSAY

DAVID A. ROOZEN

Thinking is easy; acting is difficult;
putting one's thoughts into action,
the most difficult thing in the world.
— Goethe

I. Introduction

Contributors to *Shifting Boundaries: Contextual Approaches to the Structure of Theological Education* report a remarkable change in thinking about theological education in the last decade. It is a shift, according to one of the book's editors, "from the long-standing focus on narrowly technical questions about how to be effective to theological ones about what goals should orient the practice of theological education and what shape the practice itself should take."[1] The quantity, quality and urgency of this "new" critical self-consciousness is, at the very least, indicative of wide-spread dissatisfaction "about both the *theology* and the *education* of theological education."[2] Yet from the perspective of the actual practice of theological education, the refrain of decades of educational reform remains: "Why—with all of our discontent and with all of the many proposals that people have made for innovation—why has so little changed?"[3]

Perhaps Goethe provides a clue. Like many of my academic colleagues I would like to believe that thinking is not as easy as Goethe implies, and that collective thought is especially problematic. Nevertheless, my experience is that putting one's thinking into action is, indeed, the greater challenge; and that is the challenge addressed in this essay.

300

A seminary president was beginning his response to preliminary drafts of papers that, in revised form, would be published as the Spring 1990 issue of *Theological Education* entitled "Fundamental Issues in Globalization." The president began by thanking the authors for their careful and thoughtful analyses. He appreciatively noted how the papers clarified and extended the increasingly nuanced understanding of the pedagogical and theological issues at stake in the globalization of theological education. "But," he continued:

I'm at a slightly different place. Where I really need help is on how to translate all this into the praxis of my institution; how to embody it within our program and core commitments. *What do we know about this?*

Silence.[4]

It is not uncommon, of course, for theological scholars to hesitate when asked "practical" questions; nor for theological administrators to be quietly skeptical — perhaps even disillusioned — about the possibility of genuine re-creation. It also is true that both the scholarly and applied literature on planned change in seminaries hover somewhere between the scarce and non-existent. Nevertheless, the fact is that more is known than the silence greeting the president's question would indicate. There is a considerable secular literature about institutional change in general and about institutional change in higher education in particular;[5] there is an increasingly sophisticated and rigorous literature on institutional change in and for local churches;[6] and there is a growing experimentation with "globalization" programs within theological education that provides an expanding base for systematizing anecdotal wisdom.[7] The purpose of this essay is to bring the latter three into dialogue toward the beginnings of a direct answer to the president's question.

Two of the few things that organizational theorists and practitioners readily agree upon are 1) that organizations are changing all the time — some changes intended, some just happening; and 2) that organizations have a stubborn core structure and identity that manage to absorb little changes while resisting fundamental change. Within these two givens, the primary focus of this essay is on *planned, transformational change.*[8] There are two reasons for this focus, both elaborated in other essays in this volume. First, globalization is most fundamentally the *context*, rather than the content, of theological education. The world situation has become more interdependent (and more self-conscious about this interdependence and the diversity and disparity that undergird it), and the forces driving the change are largely beyond the control of seminaries. The change, therefore, is a given that will affect theological education — for better or worse — regardless of how purposefully responsive North American schools are to it. The only real issue is how intentional theological institutions are in their response. (The implications of ignoring the changes are not addressed in this essay.)

Second, there is a virtual consensus among the contributors to this volume that an appropriate response to the changed and changing context of theological education demands a conversion in the thinking of most theological educators and a pervasive change in the ethos of the schools in which they serve. Whatever else the envisioned *content* change in response to the globalizing *context*, there is common agreement that the content change cannot be but one more dish added to the intellectual potluck table of our formal and informal curriculums. Whether the transformation comes quickly or patiently may be a strategic option, but the goal is fundamental change.

In developing a perspective on institutional change I draw heavily on organizational theory. Since the study of organizations is not the natural home of most theological educators (nor a field that seems overly concerned with developing a common vocabulary), I begin by presenting an elementary framework for viewing the varied dimensions that intertwine in the messy wholeness of any institution. I then turn to a brief consideration of the unique characteristics of seminaries as a sub-type of organizations, and of the unique implications of "globalization" as the intent of a planned change effort. With this as background I present two planned change models, discuss their relationship to each other and to my initial framework for understanding organizations. I then conclude by using the models to systematize the emerging anecdotal wisdom about bridges and barriers to change in the globalization of theological education.

II. Framing Organizational Change

In this essay I advocate a systemic, non-reductionist, conceptual pluralism for guiding one's thinking about enacting institutional change. My primary focusing lenses or "frames" are taken from Bolman and Deal's *Reframing Organizations: Artistry, Choice and Leadership*.[9] Frames are, as described by Bolman and Deal,

> both windows on the world and lenses that bring the world into focus. Frames filter out some things while allowing others to pass through easily. Frames help us to order experience and decide what action to take. Every manager, consultant or policy maker uses a personal frame or image of organizations to get information, make judgements, and determine how best to get things done. The more artistic among them are able to frame and reframe experience, sorting through the tangled underbrush to find solutions to problems. . . .
>
> Frames are also tools for action, and every tool has its strengths and limitations. With the wrong tool, it may be impossible to finish a job, while the right tool can make it easy. One or two tools may suffice for very simple jobs but not for more complex ones. Managers who master the hammer and expect all problems to be nails will find organizational life confusing and frustrating.[10]

The four frames suggested by Bolman and Deal include the *structural* frame, the *human resource* frame, the *political* frame, and the *symbolic* frame. To their four I add a fifth, the *environmental* frame.

A. The Structural Frame

The organizational images of the structural frame are rational and mechanistic. The frame directs our attention to organizational goals; technology and program; division of labor (i.e., roles); and coordinating mechanisms (i.e., communication and control). The frame's primary interest, however, is less with the individual pieces and more with their interacting configuration (i.e., structure) and its fit with an organization's external environment. From the structural perspective it is assumed that:

- Organizations exist to accomplish established goals;
- Organizations work most effectively when external influences and personal preferences are constrained by rationality;
- Specialization brings greater individual expertise into the organization and this leads to enhanced performance;
- Coordination and control of differentiated roles are essential to effectiveness.[11]

Within this set of assumptions organizational change is primarily a matter of establishing new goals, choosing or creating the appropriate technology/program, and adjusting roles and their coordination. That is, organizational change is primarily a matter of "restructuring."

From the structural perspective most institutions of higher education are what Bolman and Deal, borrowing from Mintzberg, call *professional bureaucracies*.[12] Professional bureaucracies are relatively "flat" in the sense of having a very large production sector (i.e., professors) relative to other sectors (primarily strategic and support administration), with few organizational layers between professors and strategic administrators.

Decision making in professional bureaucracies tends to be decentralized, with a great deal of responsibility residing within the functional groupings of the program sector (e.g., departments). Accordingly, overall organizational coordination and control tends to be more lateral — meetings, task forces, cross-departmental committees — than vertical. Additionally, the primary control mechanism for most professional bureaucracies resides "outside" the organization and "inside" of the professional guilds through which professors receive their "professional" training and enculturation.

From the structural perspective, professional bureaucracies are intended to insulate their key players (professors) from formal interference, allowing them to concentrate on using their expertise. While this has obvious benefits, it comes with some costs in regard to coordination and quality control, particularly in tenured systems in which tenured professors are largely immune to formal sanctions. The departmental structure of most educational, professional bureaucracies further complicates concerns with overall organizational coordination and control, perhaps most evident in the almost stereotypical tension between administrators (tending toward more unified missions, more centralized structures and more formalized, vertical control) and professors (tending toward a protection of their divisional interests and related lateral means of coordination). The autonomy of the professional (reinforced by a strong external orientation to his or her professional guild), and the decentralized structure within which they are embedded are major contributing factors in the often noted, stubborn resistance of professional bureaucracies to systemic, transformational changes. The two factors also contribute to the goal diffuseness found in many seminaries which in turn further complicates rational movement toward systemic changes.

B. The Human Resource Frame

The primary currency of the human resource frame are the needs, feelings, commitments, energy, ideas and skills of the individuals who inhabit an organization. The focus is on the interplay between organizations and people, and on the interplay of people with people. The frame's key to effectiveness is tailoring organizations to employees. The human resource perspective assumes that:

- Organizations exist to serve the human needs of their employees;
- Organizations and employees need each other;
- When the fit between the individual and the organization is poor, one or both will suffer;
- A good fit between individual and organization benefits both.[13]

Within this set of assumptions, organizational change is primarily a matter of changing people, either through training or replacement, or through various motivational enhancements.

The concept of *need* is essential to the frame's application, and at least in the organizational literature derivatives of Maslow's "hierarchy" provide the dominant conceptual base. Maslow's hierarchy not only recognizes that humans have different needs (and therefore different motivators), but also suggests that these needs become operational in a specific order. "Lower" needs dominate behavior when they are not satisfied. "Higher" needs become salient when lower needs are satisfied. From lower to higher, Maslow's hierarchy of human needs includes physiological, security, love, esteem, and self-actualization.

Given such a conceptualization of need it is hardly surprising that the two dominant themes within the human resource frame related to increasing organizational effectiveness are: (1) the movement from external control to self-control and self-direction with respect to individual job performance; and (2) the movement from hierarchical to participatory decision making with respect to organizational structure.

It is perhaps equally evident that the human resource frame is of particular salience within institutions of theological education. From a purely organizational perspective, people are both a school's primary technology and a school's primary product. But perhaps more importantly, a concern for persons is typically a foundational theological value and only secondarily a matter of organizational efficiency. Additionally, the human resource frame's emphasis on self-direction and participatory decision making is not only consistent with the autonomy of professionals and the decentralized structures within which they work, but also represent consistent (although not totally unproblematic) themes in much of modern American theology. Still further, because (1) most seminaries abdicate the training of their professionals to external agencies, (2) the tenure system tends to make the replacement of professionals a long-term project (typically through retirement rather than dismissal), and (3) the use of financial motivations tends to be severely constrained, more psychologically driven motivations are the primary means available for "changing people."

If the human resource frame and its accompanying emphasis on self-direction and participatory decision making were all there was to the story, seminaries arguably should be among the most efficient and effective types of organization. I am aware of few, however, who would so argue, which points to several typical weaknesses that critics ascribe to the human resource frame. Perhaps the most serious (and certainly the most seriously theological) critique is that human resource theorists hold a mistaken conception of human nature and seek to impose an academic, middle class value system on everyone. The human resource perspective is also found by many to be: (1) too optimistic about the possibility of integrating individual and organizational needs, and (2) too indifferent to issues of power, conflict and scarcity.

C. The Political Frame

The political frame views organizations as *arenas* in which different interest groups compete for power and scarce resources. Conflict is intrinsic because differences in needs and perspectives are intrinsic. Coalitions, bargaining, negotiation, coercion and compromise are the standard currency. Problems arise because power is concentrated in the wrong places or because it is so broadly dispersed that nothing gets done. Solutions are developed and change initiated through political skill. Bolman and Deal point to five assumptions that summarize the political perspective:

- Organizations are *coalitions* composed of varied individuals and interest groups;
- There are *enduring* differences among individuals and groups that are slow to change and seldom entirely reconcilable;
- Most of the important decisions in organizations involve the *allocation of scarce resources*;
- The combination of scarce resources and enduring differences makes *conflict* central to organizational dynamics, and *power* the most important resource;
- Organizational goals and decisions emerge from the competition of the political process.[14]

It is important to note that the political frame does not attribute politics to individual selfishness or incompetence. Rather, it attributes it to the fundamental organizational properties of interdependence, enduring differences and scarcity; that is, politics will be present in any and every organization regardless of the individuals involved. Within such a set of assumptions interest driven political process replaces both the structural frame's goal driven rationality and the human resource frame's organization/person win/win as the means of or to organizational change. Not atypically, given the presumption of enduring differences, different parties often even disagree on how to reach agreement.

Several important implications for organizational change flow from this perspective. The assumption of enduring differences suggests that "politics" will be more visible and dominant under conditions of diversity than of homogeneity. The focus on scarcity suggests that politics will be more salient and intense when resources are tight or contracting than when they are expanding. The two foci further suggest that the politics of any decision-making process should escalate over time as the implications of what is at stake become more concrete, and relatedly as more people (and therefore more different interests) stake their claims.

The frame's focus on power provides an interesting twist. Politics tends to be more visible and operative in organizations in which power is diffuse (decentralized, professional bureaucracies typically being organizations in which power is diffuse). The same tends to be true for organizations with diffuse goals because there is no clear rational basis for regulation. Where power is concentrated or goals are narrow and sharp, politics tends to be tightly regulated and highly constrained. However, this does not mean politics is not present, only that it has been forced underground.

Given the centrality of power in the political frame, it is instructive to compare this frame's view of power with that typical of the previous frames. In analyzing power the structural frame tends to emphasize *authority* — role legitimated power that provides system coordination and control. The human resource frame tends not to talk of "power," but rather of "empowerment" in the sense of giving individuals voice or enhancing self-actualization. From the latter perspective, authority in the traditional sense of one-way influence is perceived as a negative that impedes the integration of organizational and individual needs. The human resource frame therefore prefers forms of influence that enhance mutuality and collaboration.

The political frame views authority as one among many forms of power. Other types of power include information and expertise; control of rewards; coercive power; alliances and networks; access and control of agenda; control of symbolic meanings; personal charisma; and trust and/or indifference. The political frame shares with the human resource frame an appreciation for different individual and group needs and interests. But because of a greater emphasis on scarcity and the enduring nature of differences, the political frame does not share the human resource frame's faith that an incompatibility of preferences can be significantly reduced. The structural frame seeks solutions through rational exploration. The human resource frame seeks integration through open dialogue. The political frame seeks wins through the mobilization of power.

Within the political frame neither power nor politics is necessarily "bad," although both can be used for exploitation and personal dominance. Nevertheless, both can also be a means of creating vision and collective goals, and channeling human action in cooperative and socially valuable directions.

The key skills of the political process include agenda setting; networking and coalition building; and bargaining and negotiation. The weaknesses of the political frame are the flip side of its strengths. It tends to underestimate the significance of both rational and collaborative processes; and it tends to be normatively cynical and pessimistic. It also tends to share with the human resource frame the problematic assumption that individuals and groups really know their needs and interests.

D. The Symbolic Frame

The shift in thinking required in moving to the symbolic frame is dramatic. Indeed, the organizational image changes from the machine of the structural, the organism of the human resource and the arena of politics to organization as *theater*. In the symbolic frame organizations are cultures that are propelled more by rituals, ceremonies, stories, heroes and myths than by rules, power or mutuality. Problems arise when actors forget their story lines, symbols lose their meaning, and ceremonies and rituals lose their potency. Change requires the use of myth and drama to re-create and express a shared meaning. The symbolic frame is grounded in the following assumptions:

- What is most important about any event is not what happened but what it *means*;
- Events and meanings are loosely related; the same event can have very different meaning for different people;
- Many of the most significant events and processes in organizations are *ambiguous or uncertain* — it is often difficult or impossible to know what happened, why it happened or what will happen next;
- The greater the ambiguity and uncertainty, the harder it is to use rational approaches;
- Faced with uncertainty and ambiguity, human beings create *symbols* to resolve confusion, increase predictability and provide direction;
- Many organizational events and processes are more important for what they express than for what they produce.[15]

Symbolic phenomena are particularly salient in organizations with unclear goals, uncertain technologies and unstable environments — all being conditions which arguably characterize seminaries today. Symbolic phenomena are also highly salient in organizations that place a premium on "meaning." For both organizational and essentialist reasons, therefore, this frame is of particular importance for theological education.

The currency of the symbolic frame includes all of those "things" that reflect and express an organization's culture — the pattern of beliefs, values, practices and artifacts that define for its members who they are and how they do things. Culture is both product and process. Its symbolic nature is particularly well suited for bringing meaning out of chaos, clarity out of confusion and predictability out of mystery (or at least in making chaos, confusion and mystery seem other than they may be). Myths and other narrative forms provide explanations, reconcile contradictions and resolve dilemmas. Metaphors make complexity or confusion comprehensible. Rituals provide direction for action in uncharted or unchartable terrain.

Of the five organizational frames proposed in this essay, the symbolic is the newest, least developed and mapped out. With appropriate tentativeness, Bolman and Deal nevertheless suggest several important tenets, including:

- How someone becomes a group member is important. It is always more than a rational decision, and always enriched by some form of formal or informal ritual;
- Within limits, diversity gives a group a competitive advantage. Not only does it allow a group to draw on a wider pool of skills and perspectives, but it also makes the group more self-conscious about its culture;

- Example and informal process are as important as command for holding a group together;
- A specialized language fosters cohesion and commitment (although it comes at some cost of exclusion);
- Stories carry a group's history and values, and reinforce group identity. Stories are the touchstone guides of everyday behavior.
- Humor and play reduce tension and encourage creativity;
- Ritual and ceremony lift spirits and reinforce values;
- Informal cultural players make contributions disproportionate to their formal roles;
- Transformation is as much a matter of the soul as it is a matter of mechanics. In a sense, the soul (i.e., culture) must give permission for the mechanics to transform, and then must transform itself to sustain the new mechanics.[16]

The symbolic frame can become a basis for optimism about the possibilities of organizational change. But as is the case for power and politics, symbols have two faces. One is the affirming, hopeful, directive pull toward the future. The other is mask, distortion and resistance, in which symbols serve dishonest, cynical, repressive and/or conserving purposes.

E. The Environmental Frame

The previous four frames point to an organization's inner life. The environmental frame directs our attention outward to the local-to-global setting within which the internal is embedded. Adaptation and response are the two sides of the internal/external interaction—the former focusing on organizational inputs, the latter on outputs. The environmental frame views the world as a segmented (e.g., multi-cultural), layered (local to global) and constantly changing constellation of constituents, markets, resource flows and interdependent populations. Primary concerns are an organization's openness to and fit with this changing world. The environmental frame can be summarized in terms of two foundational assumptions:

- The boundaries between an organization and its environment are permeable, and organizations are continually engaged in importing, transforming and exporting matter, energy, information and people;
- Organizations are capable of negative entropy. That is, they can survive and grow, rather than decay and die, if they are able to work out a mutually beneficial relationship with their environment.[17]

From this perspective organizations are dependent upon their environment both as a source of resources and as a recipient of products, with exports having at least some effect on inputs and inputs having at least some effect on exports. Organizations, however, are not totally constrained by their environments because the organization can exercise some selectivity over both inputs and outputs. Organizational change, within such a frame, is primarily a matter of adaptive response toward attaining an organizationally desirable balance between inputs and outputs.

The frame takes on particular salience when: (1) internal dynamics push for a change in either inputs or outputs; and (2) environmental changes alter the flow of inputs or the receptivity for outputs.

Environments are multi-dimensional. Hall suggests the following six categories as a helpful way for organizational analysis to conceptualize the nearly endless possibilities: technological; political; economic; demographic; inter-organizational relationships; and cultural.[18] Pedagogy, research methodology and practical theology are arguably the three most essential technologies for institutions of theological education. From the perspective of the environmental frame the key question in their regard is: How do they get "into" the organization? Research by and the professional development of existing personnel is certainly a major option. It does require, however, the expenditure of organizational resources — faculty time probably being the most precious of these, especially in seminary settings. Perhaps for this reason, anecdotal evidence suggests that the dominant mechanism for bringing new technology into religious institutions is new personnel (e.g., faculty "turnover") or new clients (e.g., students) who have had contact with alternative technologies and advocate their use.

The connection of politics to constituencies, demographics to markets, and economics to institutional finances are sufficiently visible in seminary life today that their importance needs little amplification here. They represent obvious examples of organizational dependence on the environment. They also provide examples of an organization's strategic control over inputs and outputs: M.Div. enrollments are down so an M.A. in lay ministry is added; more expertise in congregational studies is desired so a D.Min. program is started; denominational subsidies decline so a grant officer and director of development are hired; cultural diversity is a market or curriculum issue so racial/ethnic advocates are added to the board of trustees.

Implicit in these examples are two central principles of the interrelationship between organization and environment. First, adaptive organizations in uncertain or turbulent environments tend to develop more specialized, diversified and decentralized structures, which in turn require more elaborate and flexible approaches to coordination and control. Second, since both restructuring and the addition of new expertise typically require a significant initial investment of institutional resources (dollars, time, willingness to change, etc.) organizations with few or no slack resources are at a competitive disadvantage when confronted with environmental change. On the other extreme, an overabundance of resources (particularly financial and reputational resources) tends to insulate an organization from environmental changes and thereby reduce its adaptability.

The number and variety of other organizations with which most theological schools have relationships is immense. It is, therefore, an important aspect of their environmental scan, but is beyond the scope of much elaboration here. Three elementary reminders must suffice. First, relationships demand time and expertise to develop and maintain; some selectivity — either strategic or otherwise — is therefore inevitably operative in an organization's "choice" of partners.

Second, most significant organizational partnerships — whether formal or informal — come with a combination of constraints and access to resources. Church structures, for example, provide seminaries money and markets on the one hand; and theological, curriculum, polity and market (e.g., geographic, gender, racial/

ethnic) constraints on the other. The legitimacy and other resources gained from accrediting agencies and associations come with the constraint of adhering to standards. Government scholarships come at the cost of government regulation.

Third, while multiple relationships are ripe with opportunity and their diversity can provide strategic advantages in changing environments, they are typically the source of significant cross-pressures. The inherent tension in most seminaries' twin loyalties—to the church and to the academy—is a classic case in point. Serving multiple denominations, or even multiple judicatories within a single denomination, is another.

Given that the primary content of theological education focuses on values and belief, most theological educators have a built-in sensitivity to the cultural dimensions of their institution's broader environment. Indeed, a good bit of seminary education is devoted to how culture influences theological expression (e.g., historical-critical approaches to scripture), how to make theological expression relevant to a given cultural setting (e.g., contextualization), and how to defend one's inherited faith tradition against cultural competitors (e.g., apologetics).

Cultural sensitivity per se, therefore, is less an issue for theological education than it is for many other kinds of organizational forms. However, precisely because the world of theological education is so strongly oriented to the cultural dimension, its institutions often lack the skills and predispositions necessary for understanding and acting upon the implications of external cultural dynamics for their own organizational life. Indeed, theological education's symbolic and ideational bias often becomes the proverbial hammer with which it turns all problems (or choices) into nails.

F. Conceptual Pluralism and Organizational Change

Although most of us have an intuitive sense that social systems are multidimensional, there are four reasons in particular why it is helpful for those persons leading institutions through change to have some explicit map of these dimensions. The first two of these reasons are grounded in the fact that all the dimensions are active or potentially active in every situation, and are so in a double sense. First, they are active (or potentially active) as the different interpretive frames that different participants bring to a situation, and therefore which differently define different participants' expectations for or behavior in the same situation. Indeed, we often characterize (hopefully with as much love as frustration) our colleagues in terms of differences in the orientation they bring to organizational situations. "There goes Sue again. Just the tasks and facts for her." "Watch out for Milgros. Best to be on her side; she's so political." "That's Hank. You never know what he's really thinking because he doesn't want to offend anyone. But he's a great story teller and a wonderful friend."

Second, the same situation can be used to accomplish different organizational purposes. Figure 1 lists a variety of typical organizational events and processes, and the purposes they can serve within each of Bolman's and Deal's four frames. I trust that everyone will readily identify with the reality pointed to in the table, and that I need not elaborate with specific examples of organizations struggling with which purpose should be primary in their enactment of a given event or process (but if you need one, think about performance evaluation), or examples

FIGURE 1
Conceptual Pluralism: All the Frames Are Operative All the Time

	Structural Frame	Human Resource Frame	Political Frame	Symbolic Frame
Meetings	Formal occasions for making decisions	Informal occasions for involvement, sharing feelings	Competitive occasions to win points	Sacred occasions to celebrate and transform the culture
Decision making	Rational sequence to produce right decision	Open process to produce commitment	Opportunity to gain or exercise power	Ritual to provide comfort and support until decision happens
Planning	Strategies to set objectives and coordinate resources	Gatherings to promote participation	Arenas to air conflicts and realign power	Ritual to signal responsibility, produce symbols, negotiate meanings
Goal setting	Keep organization headed in the right direction	Keep people involved and communication open	Provide opportunity for individuals and groups to make interests known	Develop symbols and shared values
Reorganization	Realign roles and responsibilities to fit tasks and environment	Maintain a balance between human needs and formal roles	Redistribute power and form new coalitions	Maintain an image of accountability and responsiveness; negotiate new social order
Evaluating	Way to distribute rewards or penalties and control performance	Process for helping individuals grow and improve	Opportunity to exercise power	Occasion to play roles in shared ritual
Motivation	Economic incentives	Growth and self-actualization	Coercion, manipulation and seduction	Symbols and celebrations
Communication	Transmit facts and information	Exchange information, needs and feelings	Vehicles for influencing or manipulating others	Telling stories
Approaching conflict	Maintain organizational goals by having authorities resolve conflict	Develop relationships by having individuals confront conflict	Develop power by bargaining, forcing or manipulating others to win	Develop symbols and shared values

Adapted from Bolman and Deal, p. 323

of participant or organizational frustration because a given event or process didn't seem to be accomplishing its ostensive purpose ("How come we do so much planning but seldom ever have a plan?").

Third, and most important for present purposes, different frames take on greater importance in different conditions. As Bolman and Deal note, each perspective "has a unique, comparative advantage. Each of the ... frames describes a set of phenomena that are present in any human system, but each is likely to be more salient and illuminating in some circumstances than in others."[19] The different circumstances could be different schools, different historical periods, or different stages in a change process. Figure 2 outlines the conditions of salience for our four internal frames. I have already noted that the environmental frame takes on special significance when internal dynamics push for a change in either inputs or outputs or environmental changes alter the flow of inputs or the receptivity for outputs.

The fourth reason that some explicit map of the multi-dimensional nature of organizations is important is that most changes, but especially transformation changes, have effects in all dimensions and therefore require not only awareness, but also compensatory action in and out of each frame. Figure 3 summarizes the implications of change for each of our four internal organizational frames. A fundamental premise of the environmental frame is that organizational effectiveness is contingent upon how well an organization's internal structure and process matches or can deal with the demands of the environment.

III. Of Seminaries and Globalization

The preceding discussion of organizational frames notes several characteristics of seminaries relevant to the change process. For example: the natural empathy of theological education to the symbolic and human resource frames; the prob-

FIGURE 2
Conditions in Which Frames Have Special Salience

Frame	Conditions for Salience
Structural	Goals and information clear; cause-effect relations well understood; strong technologies and information systems; low conflict, low ambiguity, and low uncertainty; stable legitimate authority.
Human resource	Employee leverage high or increasing; employee morale and motivation low or declining; resources relatively abundant or increasing; low or moderate conflict and uncertainty; diversity low or moderate.
Political	Resources scarce or declining; goal and value conflict; diversity high or increasing; distribution of power diffuse or unstable.
Symbolic	Goals and information unclear and ambiguous; cause-effect relations poorly understood; weak technologies and information systems; cultural diversity.

Adapted from Bolman and Deal, p. 315.

lematic nature of integration in professional bureaucracies; and the paradoxical adaptiveness of decentralized structures in a changing environment on the one hand, but their resistance to organization-wide transformation on the other. In this section I highlight several other characteristics of seminaries and their engagement with globalization that impinge upon the processes of change.

A. Seminaries and Change

Most seminary administrators encountering Newman's and Wallender's "Managing Not-for-Profit Enterprises" as background reading for the Institute for Theological Education Management (ITEM) are struck by how well the article's generalized description of the unique characteristics of not-for-profit organizations fits the seminary situation.[20] Specifically, Newman and Wallender point to the following: (1) most not-for-profit organizations deal with intangible services that are hard to measure; (2) most have multiple service objectives; (3) customer influence is weak; (4) there is strong employee commitment to the professions; (5) resource contributors often intrude into internal management; (6) there are restraints on the use of explicit rewards and punishments—this reinforced by 1 and 4; and (7) charismatic leaders and/or an organization's "mystique" are often the principal means of resolving conflicts and providing organizational direction. The implications of several of these for organizational change have already been discussed (e.g., 2, 5 and 6); others deserve attention here.

Proliferation of programs is common in theological education today, with obvious constituent and financial benefits. But it often comes with "hidden" costs as suggested in the following value laden phrases from Robert Wood Lynn's introductory essay to The Good Steward: A Guide to Theological School Trusteeship:

FIGURE 3
The Implications of Change within Different Frames

Human Resource:
Change causes people to feel incompetent, needy and powerless. Developing new skills, creating opportunities for involvement and providing psychological support are essential.

Structural:
Change alters the clarity and stability of roles and relationships. This requires attention to realigning and renegotiating formal patterns and policies.

Political:
Change generates conflict and creates winners and losers. Avoiding such issues drives conflict underground. Managing change effectively requires the creation of arenas where issues can be negotiated.

Symbolic:
Change creates loss of meaning and purpose. People form attachments to symbols and symbolic activity. When the attachments are severed, people experience difficulty in letting go. Existential wounds require symbolic healing.

Adapted from Bolman and Deal, p. 377.

"jerry-built educational structures with add-on programs jutting out in different directions," " 'functional sprawl,' a condition in which no one asks questions so long as there is continued growth," "Mission Madness," and settling "for 'vague and vapid goals' instead of holding out for 'precise aims that force choices and provoke serious disagreements.' "[21]

The status of a seminary's primary customers (i.e., students) is often a point of organizational self-reflection. But even within those schools with strong commitments to involving students in organizational decision making, there are three pervasive and general dynamics that perpetuate the comparatively weak influence that students have. These include: (1) a lingering presumption that the service provider knows best what the customer should receive; (2) most seminaries have some combination of a geographic and/or denominational monopoly; and (3) student turnover is considerably greater than for other organizational players (faculty, administrators, trustees, etc.).

Diffuse goals, weak customer influence and contributor intrusion all serve to confound rational approaches to planning and decision making — diffuse goals and contributor intrusion through complexity and ambiguity; weak customer influence through the absence of a market check. This is not because rationality is not valued (although within certain interest groups that is an added point of tension), but rather that the unique characteristics of seminaries make it exceptionally difficult to achieve. The confounding of rational approaches enhances the salience of the political and the cultural frames. Nevertheless, because the intellectual ethos of theological education gives priority to explicit cognition, at some point in any change process attention must be given to the rationale for, if not the rationality of, a new direction.

The provision of services whose results are hard to measure further complicates rational approaches to planning. When "results" are obscure, planning tends to deal with the performance of activities. Doing becomes the goal, and it is assumed that if we perform the function (e.g., teach), we will accomplish our mission (e.g., learning). In organizations with diverse, decentralized structures, centralized planning tends to retreat at least one step further from a focus on results to a focus on resource inputs. That is, dollar budgets or personnel allocation become the primary focus, with the implicit assumption that allocated resources will be used for proper activities which in turn will produce desired results.

David S. Schuller notes two additional barriers to change typically confronted by seminaries.[22] First, as *religious* organizations seminaries share in the "conserving" predisposition of being a "community of memory." Indeed, one of the most significant purposes of theological education is to convey the "tradition." Additionally, as religious *organizations* seminaries share in the intrinsically conservative nature of any organization. Given that most seminaries in North America are long-standing, the naturally "conserving" forces of any organization are particularly strong. Organizationally speaking, re-creation is more difficult than new creation.

Second, Schuller notes the pervasively individualistic ethos of most North American seminaries. This has roots in the intrusion of both professional and general cultural values into seminary life; and it is strongly reinforced by the individualistic pedagogy that dominates theological education. To the extent that seminary professors understand themselves as change agents, they tend to see themselves as facilitators of "growth" in their individual students. When brought to issues of organizational change, such an ethos enhances the salience of our human resource frame and neglects the importance of others.

All of the above lead to the experientially obvious conclusion that decision making and planned change in theological education (as indeed is true of all organizations) is always less than rational in the value/goal driven sense. At the least, the very question of values/goals is "whose?" But even beyond this there are the inevitable "compromises" among multiple goals and needs — of different constituents, different internal functional specializations, and the different dynamics of the different dimensions that frame organizational life.

Compromise and choice (even if implicit) are always difficult, particularly in contexts of fixed or scarce resources. But compromise and choice are especially difficult in religious organizations because of their strong emphasis on truth, their strong concern with integrity, the affect laden character of their cognition, and their ideal of total commitment. The difficulty is made even more problematic by the fact that the dominant theological models to which religious organizations turn for guidance (or justification) tend to be, in order of their dominance: (1) theologies of individuals, communities or social cultures, but not theologies of organizations; (2) theologies of the "church" (i.e., denomination, congregation or "church universal") into which the potential organizational uniqueness of seminaries are squeezed; or (3) theologies of seminary mission(s) or purposes, which have yet to be integrated with the "earthenness" within which the "treasure" is carried.

B. *Globalization and Institutional Change*

The two most significant implications of a globalizing context for organizational change are increasing complexity and diversity. These twin realities put extreme pressure on all relationships between the particulars and the whole. They also make an organization increasingly aware that many things once taken for granted as givens were really choices, and that within a world of options, choices rather than givens increasingly define an organization's future. Indeed, since few North American seminaries are under strong, immediate, external pressure to respond to the globalizing environment, even the question of whether or not to respond is a choice.

From the perspective of the environmental frame, perhaps the three most critical questions posed for the globalization of theological education are: (1) which culture(s) should be taken as primary? (2) what kinds of students should be targeted? and, (3) what do the answers to 1 and 2 imply for theological education's external resource base, that is, its suppliers of students, professors, curriculum materials, funding and legitimacy? All of the latter are important; the last often least understood by organizational leaders. But there is a growing body of both theory and research that indicates that long-range ideological change is not possible without the continued support of an external reference group.[23]

At least some increase in multi-culturalism is required of an empathetic response to globalization. From the perspective of the structural/technological frame this means that specialized skills in increasing numbers of cultures will be needed, as will an increasing emphasis on both contextualized, distance education (e.g., immersions, student exchanges, semesters "abroad") and cross-cultural pedagogies "at home." All push toward a proliferation of functional groupings and thereby increase structural decentralization with its related problematic for communication, coordination and control.

Within the human resource frame, an increase in multi-culturalism will inevitably require some re-training of existing personnel and psychological support for their adjustment to a more diversified organization structure. It will also require the addition of new specialists (and perhaps new kinds of students and inter-organizational relationships), who will widen the differences in attitudes and needs with which the organization must deal. Additionally, to the extent that an organization's cultural system increasingly emphasizes notions of mutuality, cooperation and reciprocity—which are dominant themes in the current theological literature on globalization—there will be added pressures on and tensions with the individualistic ethos of western society, professionalism and educational pedagogy.

Change is always a challenge within an organization's cultural frame. But the frame is essential to transformative change. People and purposes form attachments to symbols and symbolic activity. Change requires letting go ("unfreezing" in the language of organizational development), and passing through a stage of lost meaning. The perpetuation of an organizational change ("re-freezing") requires the reformation of symbolic attachments, just as the personal internalization of an innovation requires a new cognitive structure. Theological education is rich in the cultural frame skills required for change. Nevertheless, the intrinsically symbolic nature of the seminary world compounds the problems of "letting go."

One of the unique realities of the current state of exploration regarding the "globalization of theological education" is that the phrase has no self-evident or singular meaning. Rather, multiple theological options have been advanced, including at least seven approaches to "engaging the other"[24] and a twenty-cell grid combining theological priority and mode of social analysis.[25] Some would point to this as a healthy arena for the participatory search for common ground. But it is an arena, nevertheless, and one within which the potential salience of the cultural frame as a resource for change has itself become contested. Coupled with all of the other uncertainties and required "choices" of the globalization of theological education, the contested nature of current theological symbolism implies that politics and power will be particularly strong currents in the change process.

IV. Models of Organizational Change

There are three general types of literature on organizational change. The more research oriented literature tends to elaborate the correlates of change. The practitioner literature tends toward specific recipes for different kinds of organizational interventions. Moving between these two types is what I call the "model" literature. It tends to present relatively holistic but general road maps to the tasks and steps of the change process. For present purposes I turn to the latter.[26]

Figure 4 presents the basic tasks identified in Herriott's and Gross's "Expanded Leadership Obstacle Course" model of change.[27] It is built on a relatively standard organizational development base, but with several adaptations derived from intense study of large-scale change efforts in public education. The model highlights several important aspects of change. Perhaps the most fundamental of these is that change is a process that moves through many distinct phases. In our exam-

FIGURE 4
Basic Tasks in Change Efforts under the Expanded Leadership Obstacle Course

Exploration/Goal Setting

1. Identify the major current problems of the school system.

2. Identify the priority in which these problems need to be addressed.

3. Identify the range of possible solutions to priority problems in view of the "political" situation.

4. Identify the obstacles within the school system that can block particular solutions to priority problems.

5. Identify the strengths within the school system that may facilitate particular solutions to priority problems.

6. Identify the resources from beyond the school's system that may be available to implement particular solutions to priority problems.

7. Identify the most promising solution(s), i.e., the innovation(s) to be attempted and goal(s) to be pursued.

Adapted from Herriott and Gross, p. 360.

Strategic Planning Given Goals

1. Identify potential obstacles to the implementation of the goal.

2. Identify potential facilitators to the implementation of the goal.

3. Develop a realistic strategy for minimizing each obstacle and maximizing each facilitator.

4. Obtain financial and other resources necessary to implement the goal.

5. Specify internal and external political considerations that can have a major bearing on the implementation and develop strategies to cope with them.

Initiation

Overcoming obstacles identified during the strategic emergent obstacles such as:

a. Faculty/staff lacks the necessary motivation

b. Faculty/staff lacks the necessary technical knowledge

c. Faculty/staff lacks the necessary interpersonal skills

d. Faculty/staff lacks the necessary instructional resources

e. Dysfunctional organizational arrangements within the school

f. Conflicts between different groups within the school

g. Conflicts between the school system and its external constituents

h. Conflicts between the school and its external funding sources

i. Cultural values within the community in conflict with the idea of change

j. Lack of consensus about or support for the change effort.

Attempted Implementation

Overcoming previously identified obstacles and ongoing activity of the school by:

a. Misunderstandings about the objectives of the school

b. Misunderstandings about the procedures of the innovation

c. Change in key school personnel

d. Turnover in the membership of the board

e. Turnover in the staff of the external funding agencies

f. Role overload on the part of faculty or administrators

g. Delays in receipt of necessary instructional resources

h. Serious political problems confronting the change effort.

Incorporation/Rejection

Ensuring that the innovation remains a viable part of the school by:

a. Obtaining views about the innovation from faculty

b. Obtaining views about the innovation from students

c. Obtaining views about the innovation from external constituents

d. Obtaining objective evidence on the degree to which the innovation is achieving its intended objectives

e. Obtaining objective evidence of the financial costs of continuing the innovation

f. Considering the desirability of continuing the innovation without modification

g. Considering the desirability of continuing the innovation with modification

h. Considering the desirability of abandoning the innovation altogether.

ple, it begins with diagnosis and goal setting and moves through to "re-freezing." In terms of our organizational frames, the general movement is from the structural to the human resource then back to the structural, with a constant alertness to both organizational and environmental politics. As typical of organizational development models, it gives scant explicit attention to the cultural frame. However, when one teases out the special functions of the CEO across Herriott's and Gross's stages as I have done in Figure 5, one of the CEO's primary roles is symbolic. Figure 5 also reinforces the need for organizational leaders to be conceptual pluralists.

The model also highlights the importance of building on organizational strengths as resources to the change process, as well as the importance of the more typical inclination toward identifying problems that need fixing. It further highlights that both the *what* and the *how* of earlier stages have implications for the later stages; and that those things thought resolved in an early stage often resurface. Not only does the latter happen because of poor communication or repressed opposition. It often happens because the implications of early choices are not fully understood or appreciated until one has to live with them, and/or because those directly affected didn't give the early choices their full attention.

Most organizational development models of change are linear; building on rationalistic assumptions, they tend to view goal definition as relatively unproblematic. They also tend to be more oriented to incremental innovations than to

FIGURE 5
Special Functions of the CEO across Stages of Institutional Change

Exploration/Goal Setting	Strategic Planning Given Goals	Initiation	Attempted Implementation	Incorporation/Rejection
Articulating sense of need ———————— > >		Articulating vision ————————————————————— > >		
Attending to external constituencies —————————————————————————————————— > >				
Supporting internal leaders —————————————————————————————————— > >				
Attending to overall fit/integration of envisioned innovation —————————————————————————————————— > > with existing structure				
	Obtaining, reallocating necessary resources — staff and —————————————————— > > financial			
		Building motivation: affirmation/recognition; incentives/ —————————— > > rewards		
		managing conflict ————————————————— > >		
		monitoring and holding institution accountable ————————————————— > >		

organizational transformation. The model of organization change operative in the Pilot Immersion Project for the Globalization of Theological Education (PIP/GTE) incorporates several alternatives.

The PIP/GTE is a five year project working with twelve seminaries, clustered in groups of four. Its purpose is to help each participant institution articulate its own understanding of globalization, and then make the institutional changes necessary for making this vision integral to the program and ethos of the institution. The components of the PIP/GTE change model are presented in Figure 6. The flow of the components over time is presented in Figure 7, from the perspective of an individual school.

Project interventions include a mix of external and internal catalysts, all relatively standard fare when taken by themselves, including an internal planning process. Even the project's "systems" assumption is not particularly unusual, except perhaps as operationalized in the PIP/GTE's co-mingling of faculty, administrators, trustees and students in the immersion, with a disproportionate emphasis on faculty, deans, presidents and board chairs. The immersions are the least ordinary of the individual components, incorporating transformational approaches to education as described in, for example, *Pedagogies for the Non-Poor*.[28]

The model's most distinguishing feature is not in its individual components, but rather in its "wave" process. As indicated in Figures 6 and 7, the wave dynamic is intended to: (1) provide four interactive, reinforcing cycles of reflection/plan-

FIGURE 6
Pilot Immersion Project Model of Institutional Change: Components

Systems — Wave — Catalytic Intervention

Systems: Involvement of faculty, administration, trustees and students because of the assumption of a diffuse decision-making structure in most seminaries.

Wave: Three international immersions, plus a local immersion over a four year period to:
- Build a critical mass of persons involved in the common experience of the project;
- Provide for interactive, reinforcing cycles of reflection, planning, experience, reflection ... ;
- Maintain globalization as a visible priority over the extended time period necessary for "discovery," clarification, planning and implementation.

Catalytic Interventions:
- Pro-active advocacy of national staff;
- International immersions led by national staff;
- External consultant;
- Reporting requirements including planning goals and ongoing assessment;
- External, formative evaluator;
- Faculty research and student scholarship money for each school;
- Required financial commitment from each school;
- Required internal project coordinator and core committee at each school;
- Requirement of a local immersion designed by each school;
- Cluster sharing.

ning, immersion/experience, reflection/planning; (2) build a critical mass of persons involved in the common experience of the project; and (3) maintain globalization as a visible priority over the extended time period necessary for "discovery," clarification, planning and implementation. (In Figure 7, the major timing of internal reflection/planning is represented in the timing of the consultant visits.)

The immersion experiences serve three important change functions. First, they model a type of cross-cultural pedagogy. Second, they provide an extended (typically three week) communal experience. Few participants ever spend so much face-to-face time with their colleagues, or share with colleagues such an intense, common experience. But not only do the immersions provide an opportunity for community building à la our human resource frame, but also a neutral arena for the engagement of differences. Third, the immersions provide what March and Olsen call a "technology of foolishness"[29]; that is, a means of leading participants through experiences inconsistent with their pre-existing perspectives and behavior in order to develop new perspectives. In regard to "thinking" and goal discovery, technologies of foolishness reverse the typical intentions/goals-to-action paradigm. They are absolutely necessary, March and Olsen argue, for the discovery of truly new goals. They help both the "unfreezing" of old perspectives and the imagining of new possibilities. DiMaggio and Powell reinforce the significance of this for organizational change, especially in organizations with a strong cognitive orientation. They argue that one of the most important reasons that institutionalized arrangements are intrinsically conservative is because the individuals who inhabit them "cannot even conceive of appropriate alternatives (or because they regard as unrealistic the alternatives they imagine). Institutions do not just constrain options; they establish the very criteria by which people discover their preferences. In other words, some of the most important sunk costs are cognitive."[30]

Although the PIP/GTE gives some attention to technological/structural planning and to the arena of politics and power, neither has yet become a dominant focus in practice. Rather, the most significant focus of the project's attention is on the human resource and symbolic/cultural dynamics of the immersions. The project is still in progress and a complete evaluation has yet to be completed; nevertheless it currently appears that these will be the project's respective strengths and weaknesses toward the accomplishment of project purposes.

V. Bridges and Barriers to Change

Observations from the author's vantage point as an external evaluator for the PIP/GTE and from the Association of Theological School's publication of six developmental case histories of seminary-based globalization programs[31] provide a growing base of systematically gathered, yet still relatively anecdotal wisdom concerning bridges and barriers to organizational change. In the following I provide a list of emerging insights, ordered in terms of our five organizational frames, and indicate whether a given factor has thus far served as a typical bridge or typical barrier across institutions, or if its effect has been highly institutional specific.

A. General Bridges

1. Environmental:
  • Conscious awareness of need. Typically this is related to location within a setting that makes cultural diversity an unavoidable reality, although it can

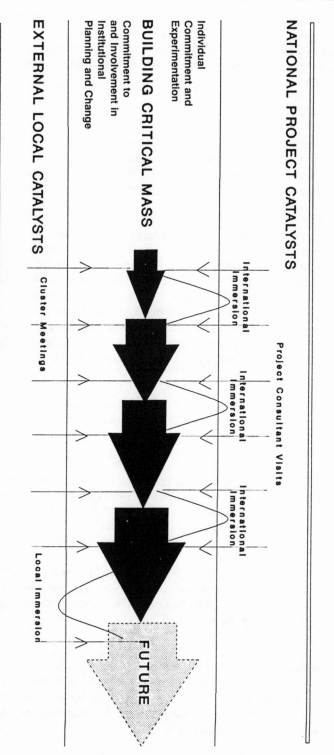

FIGURE 7
Systems-Wave Catalytic Intervention Model of Change:
Time Flow

also be fostered by an organizational or constituent relationship in which one has a strong investment.

- Involvement of a high profile, external consultant. Not only does this provide a source of expertise, but also legitimation of the organization's involvement in globalization efforts.
- Accountability to an external source.

2. *Symbolic/Cultural:*

- Strong pre-existing emphases within an institution's history which can be drawn upon to legitimate current efforts toward globalization.
- Support of strategic administrators, especially deans and presidents.
- Conscious engagement of a new vision or paradigm.

3. *Human Resources:*

- Faculty involvement in immersion experiences or other supervised cross-cultural experiences. Cross-cultural immersions are an almost universal component of seminary-based globalization programs and, although most are geared to students, even these typically involve some faculty leadership which can be rotated to broaden faculty participation. Such involvement can be an important source of re-training and community building. And for program skeptics, it can also serve as an important source of attitudinal change. Innovation research demonstrates that adoption of a new idea is more likely to take place when a partial behavioral change precedes attitudinal change.

4. *Structural:*

- Pre-existing program elements and skills relevant to globalization.
- Clarity of the strategic implications of a new vision.

B. *General Barriers*

In addition to the more specific factors listed below it should be noted that change efforts tend to put pressure on any and all pre-existing, unresolved sources of tension, conflict, division or fragmentation. Change efforts also frequently provide a new arena for "losers" or zealots to re-contest "old" issues.

1. *Environmental:*

- Students and the church, i.e., external constituencies. Most seminaries receive little consistent pressure for globalization from students, trustees and church instrumentalities, and in fact "globalization" ranks relatively low among the many pressures for change from external constituencies.

2. *Symbolic/Cultural:*

- Diffuse organizational identity. Most seminaries are highly diverse in regard to the theological/value affirmations of faculty, trustees and administrators, except at the most abstract levels. Higher levels of abstraction can serve an integrative function during periods of stability, but during periods of "choice" masked differences inevitably come into play.

3. Human Resource:
- Faculty predispositions. Faculty persons have a peculiar set of predispositions which seem to inoculate against institutional change, especially change efforts grounded in "experiential" pedagogies. Faculty are strongly cognitive, strongly invested in and articulate about one or more theological frameworks, accustomed to being in control of their situations, and accustomed to engaging their colleagues in competitive ways (e.g., academic critical and/or departmental turf).
- Time pressure. Most faculty and administrators are, or at least feel, overloaded with their current work load. Most change efforts involve work that is piled on top of this.
- The relative social and cultural homogeneity of most seminary faculties, student bodies and boards of trustees.

4. Structural:
- The disciplinary structures of theological education. Decentralized structures always present challenges for integrative efforts because they diffuse decision making, power and accountability. Within theological education this is further complicated by the fact that the different professional guilds to which different disciplines are oriented have different approaches to and/or investments in globalization.
- Diffuse decision making, power and accountability, to which the disciplinary structure of theological education is only one contributing factor. Other contributors include the multiple external constituencies to which most seminaries are related, and the relatively weak influence of students (i.e., a market check), a deep concern with persons and diffuse organizational identities.

5. Political:
- The internal processes of most seminaries either repress conflict or so highly ritualize it that it precludes serious engagement of differences.

C. Bridge or Barrier, Depending on Situation Circumstances

1. Human Resource:
- Pre-existing "globalization" skills/experience of the faculty and strategic administrators.

2. Structural:
- Size. As already noted, large, decentralized organizations tend to change through incremental innovations segmented off in various functional units, which combines with a typically diffuse organizational identity to mitigate against organization-wide transformation. Smaller organizations with less decentralized structures and less diffuse cultures tend to resist small innovations, but their organizational rigidity is conducive to a large scale conversion because any given individual or set of circumstances can exert considerable influence over the entire organization.
- The link of task groups to an institution's formal planning and decision-making structure. Most change efforts are assigned to a specialized task group to

develop and manage. When and how the work of this group is linked to the "habitual," organization-wide planning and decision-making processes is a critical strategic consideration.

• An accurate and empathetic understanding of an organization's existing situation, through which clarity concerning the implications of change can be articulated and discussed.

3. Political:
   • The balance of power between, especially, faculty and strategic administrators. At some schools, faculty push globalization harder than administrators, but appear to lack power (especially concerning the allocation of resources). At other schools, top administrators appear deeply committed to globalization, but lack the will, skill or power to engage divided faculties or skeptical trustees. Both the status and the style of the academic dean tend to be critical to the negotiation between faculties and presidents/trustees.

VI. Conclusion

The increasing experience of seminaries intentionally responding to the globalizing context of theological education provides a solid base of lessons concerning organizational change. This body of experience also provides an optimistic assessment of the possibility for adaptive innovation in regard to the globalization of theological education and a deepening reservoir of pilot projects and programmatic resources. However, it provides a much more sobering assessment concerning the possibility for organizational transformation through anything other than a very long-term accumulation of incremental change.

Of the nearly twenty schools available to the author for systematic assessment,[32] only two currently come close to meeting our initial definition of a transformed institution:

> qualitative discontinuous shifts in organizational members' shared understandings of the organization, accompanied by changes in the organization's mission, strategy, and formal and informal structures. In contrast to carrying out comparatively simple incremental changes, organizations undergoing transformation come to understand themselves and their mission very differently than they originally had.

And both of these two institutions combine two relatively peculiar characteristics. First, they are located in strongly multi-cultural regional settings—one in the province of Quebec and the other in southern California; and their historical roots are in what is or is rapidly becoming a minority culture in this setting. Second, their organizational structure concentrates power in a single person—one being a diocesan seminary whose bishop mandated change (and who visibly and skillfully managed the change); the other being extremely small internally, which enhanced the president's strong advocacy (which he combined with skillful political engagement of critical external organizational relationships).

In all other cases the movement from segmented innovation to organizational transformation became captive to, or is currently trying to work its way through, the uncertainties and struggles of the political arena. A particular irony in this is that the symbolic/cultural frame, which both organizational theory and the unique heritage of theological education suggest should be a primary vehicle for resolution, is itself a contested arena.

CASE STUDY[33]

Globalization Gone Wild

President Robert Lyman sat in his office wondering about globalization and its ramifications for Fort Worth Seminary (FWS). In moments like this, he felt as though globalization had gone wild! Everyone at the seminary talked about "globalization" but meant different things by it. Each group that returned from an immersion trip had a new project or issue to push. On his desk lay a written request from the recently returned faculty/trustee/student group from South Africa asking that the administration assist them in raising funds to endow an annual Nelson Mandela Lecture at Fort Worth Seminary.

His thoughts were interrupted by a phone call from Martha Wilson, director of the Urban Educational Resource Center. The Center was in serious financial trouble. Martha wanted him to lead a fund raising drive in his denomination and among local churches in the city. Otherwise the Urban Educational Resource Center staff might be unable to host the Fort Worth faculty and trustees on an inner city week-long immersion next spring, as part of the globalization project's local immersion intended to implement "thinking globally and acting locally." Having just announced a multimillion dollar campaign for the Seminary, President Lyman wondered: "Is there no end to globalization? Will its continuing demands and its potentially divisive character sink the ship or at least divide the crew so that it tries to sail off in all directions at once?"

Background

Eight years earlier, in his inaugural address, President Lyman had raised globalization of theological education at Fort Worth Seminary as one of his top priorities. He wanted FWS to educate persons to become aware of new global realities and the interconnected nature of the world, to prepare persons to proclaim the gospel with power and relevance in that world, and to move the church to work for peace and justice in that world. The Association of Theological Schools was just beginning seriously to explore globalization. In the early years of his administration, Lyman had to concentrate on a number of other issues such as finances, fund raising, deferred maintenance and low morale among faculty and staff. He formed a small faculty committee on globalization but received few results.

Lyman had traveled abroad to conduct research in his academic field and led a number of groups on international educational trips. He was also a strong participant in his denomination's Committee on Global Theological Education. Still, little happened at Fort Worth. He wanted something that would significantly affect the Seminary, its self-awareness, make-up and how it carried out its educational program.

The Globalization of Theological Education (GTE) Project sponsored by the Plowshares Institute seemed to be an answer to his prayers. Fort Worth was selected as one of the twelve seminaries in the Pilot Immersion Project. Through its three immersion trips to Africa, Asia and Latin America, plus an additional one to the Middle East that Lyman arranged on his own, almost a quarter of the trustees and three quarters of the faculty and senior administrative staff were exposed to intensive educational experiences in critical areas of the world.

Faculty Ownership

The GTE project assumed from the outset that the critical groups to effect long-term institutional change were faculty, administrators and trustees. Lyman concurred with the thesis that faculty, with the greatest longevity, could block most anything they chose. To reorder a seminary around a globalization perspective would require faculty "conversion" and commitment to a new way of perceiving and implementing its educational task.

From the beginning the overwhelming majority of the Fort Worth faculty were enthusiastic about the GTE project, although Lyman felt that almost no one understood what the project involved, much less the potential implications for institutional change. Early in the project, while urging a prospective faculty person who was being interviewed, one of the Fort Worth faculty remarked, "Do you like to travel? Join Fort Worth; that is what we shall be doing for the next three years!"

Each group returned from an immersion experience not only with tales of its intensity but with a commitment and a project "to change" things. Many significant results emerged. Some faculty incorporated new materials and bibliography in their courses. New courses dealing with the issue of globalization were developed. Faculty even agreed to institute a year-long faculty study and discussion on the meaning of globalization and its implications for theological education. The compulsion "to change" also resulted in projects to share information, raise others' consciousness and focus the seminary on some social change efforts. The Middle East group wanted to form a lobbying group for Palestinian rights and pressed the seminary to take an institutional stand. The Latin American group wanted each course to include Latin American materials, particularly since there was a large group of Hispanic students in the seminary.

President Lyman found himself applauding each initiative publicly while privately dreading the implications for his work load and the pressure of priorities.

The Nelson Mandela Lectureship felt right, but it was one thing too much. Ronald Johnson, a bright young African American faculty member, whom Fort Worth had just fought hard to keep, wanted to raise the Fort Worth Seminary community's consciousness about the plight of African Americans in the United States, particularly the inner city African American community in Fort Worth. Ron pushed hard for the Southern Africa immersion group to choose that inner city community as the focus of its project as a way to lead the whole faculty in that direction. The Nelson Mandela Lectureship was a central component in that strategy.

Many of Ron's faculty colleagues supported the inner city initiative. As Phil Blake, an ethicist on the faculty wrote in a paper to his colleagues, "Globalization made local requires doing theology that is good news to more than the comfortable, dominating, white minority of the global sphere. Indeed, relevant theology is called and sent to break decisively the back of the destructive domineering dogmas of the major Christian faith traditions. Adequate theologizing points and moves in the direction of liberation of people from various bondages to the building of just and equitable community."

Bob Stevens, a local pastor who was a member of the FWS Board of trustees and a participant in the Southern Africa immersion, announced that the travel seminar group was committed to raising $30,000 to endow the lectureship. The trustees had given significant support to the GTE program, and immersion seminar participants from the Board, like Bob, were advocates of the global perspective vision. President Lyman, hearing this proclamation in the Board of Trustees meeting, thought: "Wonderful! If they can raise it, I will support the idea." He also knew how much effort was involved in gearing up and carrying through such a fund raising effort and the cost of not fully cooperating with a trustee-supported project like this lectureship.

The vice president for Development reacted even more dramatically in the privacy of Lyman's office after the meeting. "We need another lectureship like a hole in the head. We have enough difficulty rounding up a respectable crowd for the lectures we already have. They will want my office to raise the money, conduct public relations and ensure an audience for each lecture. We already have enough on our plate."

Charles Jackson, the academic dean, had been a member of one of the immersion trips and was committed to globalization, but he had deep concerns about the direction globalization was moving among the faculty. Follow-up projects were fine, but he shared with Lyman his apprehension that engaging in social action projects could divert the faculty from its real task of theological education. He also worried that globalization had brought to the surface deep theological, ideological and social differences in the faculty. The year-long study and debate on globalization issues through which he led the faculty made these differences evident and in some cases may even have exacerbated them. Jackson was convinced that to conduct solid theological education a faculty must have a common core of theological understanding, commitment and method. In Jackson's words, a Nelson Mandela Lectureship and focus on the plight of inner city African Americans was "not a substantial or appropriate basis on which to build such a core. If globalization requires radically new analyses of the world context of theological education, it also requires a steady focus on the gospel, without which it has no theological content and direction."

Stan Ripley, professor of New Testament, who was on the Southern Africa trip, whole-heartedly agreed. "We must refocus on Christ and spiritual formation as our core, not on social action or liberation theology," he said.

President Lyman reflected that GTE had indeed begun to transform FWS. Many of his globalization goals of a decade earlier were being achieved. The ringing of his office phone called him back from his reflections. It was his secretary. "Ron Johnson is here wanting to see you for a minute. He says it is urgent!" President Lyman wondered what to say and do. He was basically pleased and excited with where FWS was going but felt himself and the seminary sinking deeper into the quicksand of globalization.

TEACHING NOTE

Globalization Gone Wild

I. Goals

If the case is used with seminary administrators, faculty, trustees or students, the goals could be:

1. To illustrate the complexity, challenge and stress involved in institutional change.

2. To sensitize those involved in institutional change to some of the critical issues with which they will be confronted.

3. To help develop alternative responses to the challenges of institutional change.

If the case is used with a group of lay leaders in a local church, the goals could be:

1. To explore the primary tasks of theological education and how persons are best prepared for ministry.

2. To consider the effects of globalization on major institutions in North American society including local churches.

3. To discuss what globalization would mean in their congregations and how they would implement strategies to effect such change.

Following are several questions around which a case leader could structure a discussion to meet these goals.

II. Analysis of Central Issues

A. In this case what would you identify as the *change agents* at work in Fort Worth Seminary (FWS) toward the goal of globalization? How does the identified agent effect change? (Visually place FWS at the center of a chalk board or newsprint. "Surround" the seminary with the change agents as they are raised.)

Possible suggestions:

1. *Persons*:

Administrators: President Lyman (e.g., stated globalization goals in inaugural address, traveled abroad, formed faculty committee, supported joining GTE, etc.)

Dean Charles Jackson, Vice President for Development

Faculty: Ron Johnson, Stan Ripley

Board: Bob Stevens

2. *Events*: e.g., changes in the world situation, such as entering a post–Cold War period; immersion experiences; faculty forums, etc.

3. *Actions*: e.g., new courses, course material, programs, lectures, budgeting commitments — all affect institutional structures as they become permanent.

4. *Outside agents*: GTE program, Plowshares staff, The Urban Educational Resource Center.

B. If one considers the change agents discussed above as *potential bridges* to change, which persons or factors do you see as *potential barriers* to change at FWS?

Possible responses: competing institutional and presidential priorities (budget, endowment, new programs, faculty development, outside agencies, etc.); unclear decision-making process; individual faculty agenda; conflicting understandings of globalization; conflicting images of preparation for ministry.

III. Focus on President Lyman

What *alternatives* does he have to "tame" the globalization process so that it does not "sink the ship" or energize a "divided crew" to "sail off in all directions at once"?

How does he sustain the energy raised in the international immersions without encouraging this energy to push the institution in narrow directions? How would you advise him, for example, to respond to the request to raise funds for the Nelson Mandela Lectureship?

How does he respond to the obvious divisions in his faculty, which have emerged during this period of increased dialogue on the purpose of theological education?

This part of the discussion could be conducted within the framework of a role play with one participant or the case leader playing the role of President Lyman, who asks the participants to advise him. Be sure to allow enough time to "de-role" the participants.

Whatever course of action he takes, what *resources* are available to President Lyman? How can the faculty be a resource? How could the trustees help? What outside resources could be tapped?

IV. Optional Questions (for use in a congregational setting)

A. If a church-based group uses the basic design above, conclude with additional time devoted to discussing how a particular congregation can be a resource to the seminary.

B. Other questions for congregations:

How do issues of globalization affect all institutions in North American society, including churches?

What would globalization mean in your congregation? How would you develop strategies to effect such change?

Contrast the understandings of theological education held by Stan Ripley and Charles Jackson. What other understandings do faculty, students and congregations have that are not represented in the case?

Which skills, knowledge and formation do students need to minister effectively in contemporary congregations? How can seminaries best help students acquire these skills and abilities?

COMMENTARY

Globalization Gone Wild

ELEANOR SCOTT MEYERS

President Lyman and FWS are caught in a common problem. Across theological education, not only at FWS, there is a difficulty defining "globalization." This difficulty is due to the fact that definitions are political in nature. In this instance, we have organizations—institutions of graduate education (seminaries) and the church—that were and continue to be structured by leaders from the politically dominant culture. Check out the attendance at the Association of Theological Schools Biennial meetings (almost 100 percent white and male) or national/regional/local clergy (overwhelmingly white males). Globalization is at its core about changing such institutional arrangements.

Definitional problems lead to organizational dilemmas. Many involved in theological education *would* like to have our curriculum more responsive to the changing needs of society and church because we understand and care about what is happening. We *would* like to have greater diversity among our faculty, students and trustees, because we know it would enrich our planning, our teaching and our learning. We *would* like to know that our educating institutions are making a difference on issues related to justice in a time when there seems to be so little for so many. We *would* like to think that the leaders we educate will help society change for the better for that is part of our mission in theological education.

But we want the organizational dilemma resolved without changing our understanding of what constitutes good scholarship or what the appropriate disciplines are and how they should be constructed into a curriculum for theological education. Theological educators want to continue to be in charge of the institutional processes of decision making and the allocation of resources as we have been in the past. Leaders at Fort Worth Seminary are no different. Their hopes are real; so are the institutional constraints.

Why do FWS faculty seem to be taking globalization in the "wrong" direction? If their definition of globalization was too weak to give guidance throughout the development of the project and the immersions, the follow-through will be "off the mark." A weak definition of globalization cannot adequately address the deep ideological and structural apparatus of theological education.

Critical Issues in the Case Study

President Lyman faces many of the critical issues that are also before those of us involved in theological education. From my reading of the case seven issues seem immediately definable, ones around which we need to enlarge our understanding. The seven include several organizational practices, such as (1) a tendency

toward individualization in institutional analysis and problem solving, (2) an avoidance of conflict, (3) failure to set priorities, and (4) the tendency toward politicization of issues and processes within the institutions. The final three issues the
case raises for me include (5) the importance of the leadership task of creating a
vision, (6) how institutional realities often work against the vision, and (7) the
need for a program of contextualized learning in a diverse society.

*Individualization: "Globalized" individuals come home with their "own" new
project.*

Institutions are a collection of individuals. We all come from different experiences, but never before have our educational institutions tried to function with
the degree of diversity present in them today. As President Lyman said, immersion
returnees urged that issues be addressed as they saw them. Leaders need to
develop processes for listening and building programs collectively to meet an institution's mission. Individual self-interest, if allowed to direct program development,
can stalemate institutional mission.

*Institutional Conflict: "Globalization's demands and divisive nature" are
killing the institution.*

The management of higher education has become a contested terrain. Organizational conflict has increased as diversity has increased. A white male colleague
leaned over in a faculty meeting and whispered to me, "I don't understand why
everything [emphasis added] is so difficult these days. Why, I can remember when
we [members of the faculty] used to gather around a table over lunch and decide
what to do and how to proceed without any difficulty at all."

Things have changed. And not only among the faculty. Students gather in advocacy groups: women *vs.* men, various ethnic/racial groups *vs.* one another, com-
muters *vs.* residents, part-time students *vs.* full-time students, and vice versa!
Program initiatives come to the administration from all directions, and decisions
about the allocation of resources are controversial.

The shape given to conflict over change has real consequences for an organization. Avoidance is a short-term strategy at best. Organizational leaders need to
do all they can to be engaged in ongoing decision-making processes that are carefully constructed and carried out with an openness to input from various institutional stakeholders. However, there is a fine line to be followed. Organizations
can become paralyzed — and organizational mission defeated — in overly processed
managerial efforts.

It is important to put conflicting issues on the table and for organizational
leaders to learn to live with the creative chaos that can result. We often fear so-
called "potential" conflict when, in reality, it already exists. Seminary leaders need
to learn to identify and use conflicting opinions with sensitivity. A practical objective such as an institutional decision can help to focus a faculty dialogue on differences and similarities. Such a strategy aims to lessen the pain conflict causes
while developing more useful internal strategies for enabling institutional mission.

Need to Set Priorities: A new lectureship? When the seminary has too many already!

Individualized approaches escalate the problems of competing values without a plan for institutional priorities. When a process is in place for planning and program development, it is easier to let go of one program when another is added. Institutional leaders cannot afford the "just add it" strategy. Options must be placed on the table and choices/priorities made. The institution-wide understanding of the mission is the primary guide in this selection process.

The issues before us are often interrelated. It appears that if President Lyman does not help to keep the Resource Center alive (perhaps at the expense of his own multimillion dollar campaign), he will jeopardize local immersion plans. All organizations face competing interests among a set of interrelated goals. Trustees, along with members of a faculty, are directly responsible for the establishment of the mission and long-range goals of the institution. If trustee responsibilities are carried out appropriately, institutional leaders will have a basis for adjudicating claims for organizational attention and resources. President Lyman might do well to work directly with the trustees to establish priorities based on FWS's long-range plans.

Politicization of Issues: The president found himself "applauding each separate initiative publicly" while dreading organizational implications involved.

The politicization of institutional processes creates an "us vs. them" and "win or lose" organizational ethos. This kind of polarization presents great difficulty in many institutional arenas, but especially in the identification, selection and exercising of organizational leadership. Different groups within the organization look for leaders—presidents, trustees, faculty members or students—who will promise to deliver on each group's political agenda. What organizations need instead are leaders who will engender an overall spirit of openness to a process of decision making within the framework of complex issues related to the organizational mission. Organizational processes must be carried out within a context wherein each group views other groups and acts toward others out of a sense of integrity for the diversity of the whole. It is easier to describe such a process than it is to carry it out in a time of competing organizational claims.

Institutional Vision and the Program to Make It Happen

The case points out the importance of the leadership task of creating a vision and how institutional realities often work against the vision. President Lyman has had to concentrate on "finances, fund raising, deferred maintenance and low morale among faculty and staff." Such concerns and the need to find and address the basic issues in such a way that organizational needs are met is a big challenge that can put organizational change on the back burner.

However, the FWS president is committed to a process of globalization. He knows about the important interconnectedness of education and successful ministerial leadership, the necessity for contextualized education for ministry in light of new global realities. For him, the proclamation of the gospel depends upon such a program. But "it" is taking over, challenging every issue that sits on his desk. His organizational plan, the faculty (including the way faculty members were trained), budgetary commitments, and the understanding of the nature of the church and its ministry among the faith communities the seminary serves are all difficult to shake loose from old patterns.

He agonizes over the faculty member's description of the globalization project: "We're going to travel!" Such a moment clarifies the difficulty of thinking new thoughts and seeing new visions within an institutionalized context.

Barriers are everywhere. The academic dean is concerned that a faculty must have "a common core of theological understanding, commitment and method." A "common core" does sometimes make it easier to get things done. However, globalization suggests that a faculty with a variety of theological understandings, commitments and methods is more helpful to the process of deciding how to meet the changing needs of the church. The call for unanimity in traditional institutions suggests that dominant voices continue to define institutional ways of being and doing. Unity is a word of the colonizers, those holding institutional power. Theological education needs common agreements *concerning our diversity* as we approach the development and maintenance of the educational program necessary to fulfill our mission.

If theological education does not require a "common core," leaders do not need to set critical issues such as the impact of the situation in urban areas and racism against the critical issues of careful study of the gospel and the engendering of new forms of spirituality for this era in the life of the churches and society. In fact, when we value multiple issues, we begin the important integration of the various realities and needs that ministers must face daily in the churches.

Faculty members are not in agreement about the institutional mission and how they will contribute. They need to work their agreement out together, but they need not all follow the same methods. And the criteria for faculty recruitment, assessment, promotion and tenure must also allow for the diversity of educational method and research strategies. Unless these criteria accompany the agreement to follow different avenues in the serving of the institutional mission, processes will likely be politicized, and important institutional change will be extremely difficult to accomplish.

Contextualized Learning

Finally, President Lyman's reflections point to the need for contextualized education. Contextualized learning is powerful: "Each group returned from the immersion . . . with a commitment to change." Courses changed. Trustees asked new questions. The GTE project has proven the importance of getting outside our own agendas and arenas of familiarity. We learn to see, think and act in new ways and learn to risk change.

Institutional Change

The invitation to globalization is the call for institutional change. Globalization raises critical issues because it challenges the root causes of institutional and societal failure in the current era. The case study underscores the importance of personal experience and commitment in the leadership of an institution. President Lyman was looking for significant change as he worked on a vision for his own institution.

The globalization of theological education begins at home with a self-awareness of who we are, how we got (and remain) that way and why. Globalization is about understanding how who we are and what we do helps and hinders the future of the church that must teach and preach and lead in a highly diverse cultural context. Globalization calls those of us in theological education to prayerful resting and wrestling with very real turmoil while holding onto a sense of openness and faith in the future, knowing that the future is God's and not our own.

I believe the only way into needed organizational change is "conversion," as hoped for by President Lyman. In theological education we should celebrate and lean on the conceptual tools of the religious context within which we labor. The language of conversion is the language that calls us toward the mutuality of globalization.

Notes

1. Barbara G. Wheeler, "Introduction." In Barbara G. Wheeler and Edward Farley (eds.), *Shifting Boundaries: Contextual Approaches to the Structure of Theological Education* (Louisville: Westminster/John Knox Press, 1991), p 9.

2. Ibid., p 7.

3. Barry W. Holtz, "Making Change Happen: Prospects for Innovation in Jewish Education." *The Melton Journal* (Spring, 1992), p 21.

4. David A. Roozen, "Editorial Introduction." *Theological Education*: Patterns of Globalization: Six Studies (Spring, 1991), p 5.

5. Four excellent overviews of organizational theory include, in the order I would recommend them to theological educators: Lee G. Bolman and Terrence E. Deal, *Reframing Organizations: Artistry, Choice and Leadership* (San Francisco: Jossey-Bass Publishers, 1991); Gareth Morgan, *Images of Organization* (Newbury Park, CA: Sage Publications, 1986); Richard H. Hall, *Organizations: Structures, Processes and Outcomes*, Fifth Edition (Englewood Cliffs, NJ: Prentice Hall, 1991); and Charles Perrow, *Complex Organizations: A Critical Essay*, Third Edition (New York: McGraw-Hill, 1986). For the more cognitively oriented, see Michael D. Cohen and Less S. Sproull (eds.), "Organizational Learning," *Organization Science* 2 (February, 1991) and 3 (February, 1992); and, Peter M. Senge, *The Fifth Discipline: The Art and Practice of the Learning Organization* (New York: Doubleday/Currency, 1990).

6. See, for example, Jackson W. Carroll, Carl S. Dudley and William McKinney (eds.), *Handbook for Congregational Studies* (Nashville: Abingdon Press, 1986); Carl S. Dudley, Jackson W. Carroll and James P. Wind (eds.), *Carriers of Faith: Lessons from Congregational Studies* (Louisville: Westminster/John Knox Press, 1991); and Joseph C. Hough and Barbara G. Wheeler (eds.), *Beyond Clericalism: The Congregation as a Focus for Theological Education* (Atlanta: Scholars Press, 1989).

7. See, for example, *Theological Education*: Patterns of Globalization: Six Studies, (Spring, 1991).

8. As helpfully summarized in "Research Executive Summary: Future of Religious Orders in the United States," in the organizational literature *transformation* refers to "qualitative discontinuous shifts in organizational members' shared understandings of the organization, accompanied by changes in the organization's mission, strategy, and

formal and informal structures. In contrast to carrying out comparatively simple incremental changes, organizations undergoing transformation come to understand themselves and their mission very differently than they originally had" (*Origins: CNS documentary service*, vol. 22: no. 15 [September 24, 1992], p. 259).

9. For a direct application of "conceptual pluralism" to the study of religious organizations, see Jackson W. Carroll, Carl S. Dudley and William McKinney, (eds.), *Handbook for Congregational Studies*. The *Handbook* presents a variety of tools for understanding four dimensions of a congregation's life: Identity, Social Context, Process and Program. Although there is considerable overlap and continuity between Bolman's and Deal's "frames" and the *Handbook*'s dimensions, I opt for the former for several reasons, including: (1) congregations and seminaries tend to have different basic forms partially captured in the distinction between voluntary organizations (congregations) and professional bureaucracies (seminaries); (2) Bolman and Deal are more explicitly oriented to organizational change; (3) my longstanding sense that, intentions notwithstanding, "people" tend to get lost when looking through the *Handbook*'s lenses — to which I find Bolman's and Deal's "human resource" frame a helpful corrective; and (4) Bolman and Deal more explicitly tie their frames to organizational theory and, perhaps as a consequence, give greater attention both to the interaction between frames and to "when" certain frames are more salient than others. I remain mystified, however, by Bolman's and Deal's general — although not total — lack of attention to an organization's broader "social context." Not only is a consideration of "social context" a major topic in organizational theory, but it strikes me as an absolute necessity within current organizational practice. I therefore add it as a fifth frame.

10. *Reframing Organizations*, p 11.

11. *Reframing Organizations*, p 48.

12. *Reframing Organizations*, p 88.

13. *Reframing Organizations*, p 121.

14. *Reframing Organizations*, p 186.

15. *Reframing Organizations*, p 244.

16. *Reframing Organizations*, pp 293-303.

17. *Reframing Organizations*, p 317.

18. *Organizations: Structures, Processes and Outcomes*, pp 204-10.

19. *Reframing Organizations*, p 314.

20. *Academy of Management Review* (January, 1978), pp 24-31. For a discussion of ITEM and emerging directions in executive leadership in theological education see *Theological Education*, vol. 29, no. 1 (Autumn, 1992).

21. Robert Wood Lynn, "The Responsibilities of Stewardship." In *The Good Steward: A Guide to Theological School Trusteeship* (Washington, DC: The Association of Governing Boards of Universities and Colleges, 1983), pp 1-9.

22. David S. Schuller, "Globalization: A Study of Institutional Change in Theological Education." *Theological Education*, vol. 27, no. 2 (Spring, 1991), pp 136-57.

23. See, for example, Gene W. Dalton, Paul R. Lawrence and Larry E. Greiner, *Organizational Change and Development* (Homewood, IL: The Dorsey Press, 1973).

24. Mark Kline Taylor and Gary J. Bekker, "Engaging the Other in a Global Village." *Theological Education*, vol. 26, supplement 1 (Spring, 1990), pp 52-85.

25. S. Mark Heim, "Mapping Globalization for Theological Education." *Theological Education*, vol. 26, supplement 1 (Spring, 1990), pp 7-34.

26. Robert R. Blake and Jane Srygley Mounton's *Consultation: A Handbook for Individual and Organizational Development* (Reading, MA: Addison-Wesley, 1986) is an excellent "cookbook" of organizational interventions. Not only does it present a

wide range of specific intervention techniques, but it also discusses their strengths and weaknesses and uses a grid compatible with our organizational frames to identify when they are especially appropriate. Gerald Zaltman, Robert Duncan and Jonny Holbek's *Innovations and Organizations* (New York: Wiley-Interscience, 1973) provides an extensive review of predisposing correlates of organizational change. Merton P. Strommen and Shelby Andre's *Five Shaping Forces: Using Organizational Dynamics to Do More With Less* (Minneapolis: Search Institute, n.d.) identifies numerous factors related to an organization's "readiness to change" based on a large study of not-for-profit organizations including several schools and religious organizations.

27. Robert E. Herriott and Neal Gross (eds.), *Dynamics of Planned Educational Change* (Berkeley, CA: McCutchan Publishing, 1979).

28. Alice F. Evans, Robert A. Evans and William Bean Kennedy (eds.), *Pedagogies for the Non-Poor* (Maryknoll, NY: Orbis Books, 1987).

29. James G. March and Johan P. Olsen, *Ambiguity and Choice in Organizations* (Bergan: Universitetsforlaget, 1979), pp 69-81.

30. Paul J. DiMaggio and Walter W. Powell, "Introduction." In DiMaggio and Powell (eds.), *The New Institutionalism in Organizational Analysis* (Chicago: University of Chicago Press, 1991), pp 1-40.

31. *Theological Education*, vol. 27, no. 2 (Spring, 1991).

32. Including participants in the PIP/GTE and cases appearing in *Theological Education*, vol. 27, no. 2 (Spring, 1991).

33. Copyright © 1993 by the Case Study Institute. The names of persons and places in this case have been disguised to protect the privacy of those involved in the situation.

[12]

MUTUALITY IN GLOBAL EDUCATION

ESSAY

MORTIMER ARIAS

Any global perspective has to be mutual; otherwise it is not global.

Theological education cannot be global unless mutuality is intertwined in the curriculum, at the heart of pedagogical praxis, part of the administration of resources, inherent in the faculty formation and plurality, reflected in the student body, effective in the seminary-community and seminary-church interactions, and workable in the international partnership and relationships of theological institutions.

The case "Apart from His People," which is included in this chapter, illustrates the problems of mutual understanding and the challenge of interaction between churches and seminaries in the North and in the South. The case focuses on the local congregation where the theologically-trained pastor works. Henry S. Wilson spells out some of the emerging issues for the ministry and theological education in this "post-colonial era." We would not be surprised if we discover that in every chapter of this book issues and implications emerge which call for mutuality in theological education.

Mutuality in Koinonia

Mutuality is a fundamental biblical idea. Paul calls mutuality "koinonia." It is a profound theological concept and leads to the most concrete actions of all. This is why koinonia is translated as "communion," "fellowship," "offering," and "collection."

This koinonia was Paul's special project. It took him a couple of years of planning, promotion, organization, and . . . theologizing. We have some traces of it in his letters: I Corinthians 16:1-4, II Corinthians 8-9, Romans 15:25-26, and in the Book of Acts 11:27-30.

The problem Paul faced was the hunger of the community of believers in Judea, which other communities were trying to help (Acts 11:29-30). Paul made a point in engaging the gentile churches under his leadership (Galatia, Achaia, Macedonia) in a massive effort which he called "a ministry to the saints," "an offering for the poor" (Rom. 15:25-26), a koinonia.

Paul wrote letters to the churches with specific instructions, such as saving each week for the final collection (I Cor. 16:2). He selected the most able and reliable administrators for this enterprise (II Cor. 8:17-24); he invited the communities to appoint appropriate people for it (I Cor. 16:3-4); and he committed himself to it even to the point of risking his own life (Rom. 15:28).

For Paul this was not just a matter of good service and good administration. This koinonia was the deepest spiritual act, an act of praise, calling for gratitude and mutual intercession among the Christian communities in the "oikoumene" (II Cor. 9:11-14). It was a ministry of total dedication to God and to others (II Cor. 8:5). It was framed in the highest theological vision, "God's grace" and "inexpressible gift" (II Cor. 9:15) and undergirded by a solid Christological foundation: "For you know the grace of our Lord Jesus Christ, that though he was rich, yet for the sake of the poor became poor, so that by his poverty you might become rich" (II Cor. 8:9).

Paul's rationale for this ministry of sharing is mutuality between the gentile and the Jewish churches, the rich and the poor, the older and the younger, the mother and the daughter churches. It is only proper to share what we have materially or spiritually:

I do not mean that others should be eased and you burdened, but that as a matter of equality [mutuality!] your abundance at the present time should supply their want so that their abundance may supply your want, that there may be equality. As it is written, "He who gathered much had nothing over, and he who gathered little had no lack" (II Cor. 8:13-15).

So here we have the golden text of mutuality. Let's spell out the meaning of mutuality in terms of concrete challenges and opportunities for globalization in theological education.

Mutuality in the Curriculum

The classical curriculum of our seminaries was born out of the global intention to include what was considered "universally" necessary for the professional ministry in the church: systematic theology, biblical studies, history, and practical theology. But this universality was the projection of the European ideology about culture, theology, education, and ministry, which was adopted and somehow adapted to the educational requirements for the ministry in North America and later in the rest of the world. In spite of its universalizing intention, the classical curriculum was and is local and unilateral rather than global.[1]

This sort of Western "globalization" does not respond either to the global context in the world today or to those Western societies which are increasingly multi-ethnic, multi-racial, and multi-cultural. On the other hand, North Atlantic theological and pedagogical assumptions have been radically questioned by contemporary,[2] liberation,[3] and local theologies.[4] Furthermore, this kind of "globalization" leaves no room for mutuality. It is not global enough.

The classical model, which is still the norm for seminary curriculum revisions and accreditations, is already subject to self-criticism from inside.[5] Suggestions on the curriculum and new experiences in multi-cultural situations are beginning to emerge.[6] There are indications that the initial explorations on "globalization" by ATS are uncovering attempts to move beyond the classical model and toward globality with mutuality.[7]

From Feudalism to Mutuality

Meanwhile there is an increasing trend for curricula in our seminaries to be more inclusive, making room for inputs from ethnic, gender, and political types of theology. Subjectwise, mutuality is beginning, but it remains to be seen how far mutuality goes in terms of true globalization in curricular structure and methodology. Most of the time, however, new inputs or emphases are marginalized as elective courses, lectures by international visitors, or temporary visits to a given course.[8] Nothing yet suggests a radical revision of the classical curriculum perspective. Even with some encouraging developments of "new curriculum," business goes on as usual when decisions are made about time distribution and allocation in required courses. Finally, in the negotiations with faculty to implement the "new curriculum," some of the resources for renewal and globalization are sub-utilized.

And yet there are challenges and opportunities for mutuality inside the traditional curriculum. One of the permanent risks of specialization and separate development of the curriculum disciplines has been a sort of "academic feudalism," the lack of mutual communication, coordination, and integration between what is taught in one course and what is taught in other courses. Instead of mutuality, we often have fence-building. It is *verboten* — the unforgiven academic sin — to touch on anything that is our colleagues' private turf. It seems natural to have more collegiality with our peers in a given secular discipline than with the faculty team in our theological institution. Ironically, we expect that somehow a miracle will happen and our students will be able to integrate the pieces that we jealously kept separate! This is no good for the formation of our theologians and ministers, and this is not globalization by any means.

Even though this academic tradition and the specialization trends have been ingrained in our theological schools, in the last decade or so seminaries have been moving toward a more integrated curriculum and using faculty retreats and academic council meetings for mutual sharing, mutual responsibility, and mutual support instead of competition and mutual defensiveness.

Mutuality in the Faculty Lounge

Globality and mutuality are already present in the faculty of our seminaries! I have had the rare privilege of being part of several faculty bodies as a visiting professor in the United States, and I have been the beneficiary of this kind of mutuality in more ways than I can account for.

In the areas of mission and evangelization, I have been given the freedom to experiment with mutuality in content and method. In my courses on evangelization from a holistic perspective, I have contended that any discipline in the seminary has something to contribute: New Testament deals with the original source of our message (the good news of Jesus Christ); church history and ecumenics show how the good news has been communicated and incarnated in an ongoing community of faith; Christian theology is nothing but the articulation of the good news and Christian faith in terms of our cultural world; Christian education is the solidifying of the good news in each stage of life and in each context; all the practical theology or arts of ministry courses are the natural instruments for sharing the good news and making faith real and relevant through pastoring, serving, communicating, and organizing; and worship is the central experience of God in community and the richest and most profound means of communication of the good news through proclamation, celebration, and fellowship (Is there a more meaningful evangelistic invitation than the Eucharist, calling to come to the Table to "receive the Lord," "to be in communion with Christ and the community?").

My first course on evangelism at Perkins School of Theology benefited from the input by professors of other disciplines who came to our class to tell what the good news means from their subject's perspective. And we, both students and instructor, were deeply enriched and stimulated to embrace a global vision and holistic understanding of mission and evangelization.

Globalization as Mutual Learning

Mutuality in education is, of course, not new. After all, education is about mutual learning and mutual sharing. Paulo Freire, the great Brazilian pedagogue of our times, has challenged "the banking approach to education," the assumption that to educate is to put ideas from the teacher to the learner as in a bank deposit. Mutuality is at the heart of pedagogy in Freire's dictum: "We teach while learning, and we learn while teaching."

This mutuality is also at the heart of the future pedagogy for a globalization approach to theological education. This is precisely the thesis of Fumitaka Matsuoka, who believes that globalization in the pluralistic world of North America demands no less than a *counterparadigm* which is transformative rather than developmental, inductive rather than deductive, which begins with the painful assumption of our particularity in the midst of plurality,[9] and which implies a mutuality paradigm.

Here I have to witness again to what I have been learning in the process of teaching in the United States. Claremont School of Theology is one of the schools that has been trying to implement the global perspective in the curriculum and in methodology. I had the joy of co-teaching with Dr. Joseph C. Hough, Jr., in his course on theology of ministry for D.Min. candidates, and I had the chance to bring a Latin American perspective and my own ministerial experience to the course. But I must say that in the process I was learning much more than the students, in terms of content, method, and perspective!

Of course, mutually at the faculty level as well as the student level depends on our openness to learn from others. Education in a global perspective is mutuality.

A similar experience of mutual learning and enrichment has been the teaching and co-teaching at Iliff School of Theology, where the global concerns are high in the priorities of the institution's polity and program. There I experienced in a unique way the mutuality of the faculty that made possible the continuity of my courses under the dramatic circumstances of my cancer diagnosis, surgery, and treatment. With input in the course "Biblical Paradigms for Mission" (already planned in the syllabus) from colleagues in the fields of Old Testament, New Testament, preaching, and history, my forced absence during surgery was covered, and the students had the chance to assume the continuity of the course themselves. What might have been an academic disaster became a learning experience and an opportunity for growing in the community, that is in mutuality.

The above is an illustration of an emergency situation, but the point is that mutuality is there, at the doorstep of the faculty lounge or the classroom. Perspective and direct contributions from other disciplines should not be the exception but the rule in the curriculum.

Mutuality with the Marginalized Minorities

Mutuality does not imply simply an interdisciplinary exercise with each discipline enriching and being enriched by other disciplines. It is a matter of bringing global perspectives into each discipline, particularly those perspectives that have been ignored, marginalized, or submerged in our inherited and assumed models of theological education.

Today we realize that if we want to be really global or inclusive, we cannot do without incorporating into our syllabi the African-American, the Native American, the feminist, the Third World, the living religions, the ecological,[10] and other perspectives present in our pluralistic world.

For example, how can we speak of mission and the history of the church in the Americas without the perspective of Native Americans, the earlier inhabitants of these lands who were the object of the European "discoveries," conquest, colonization, and evangelization? This was the burning question of the so-called "celebration" or "commemoration" of the Columbus Quincentenary.[11] It is imperative that our courses on church history and missiology look critically at the record, not occasionally but regularly, from the Native American's perspective and in terms of the theological, ideological, and missiological assumptions of the transplanted and developed churches in the American continent and their missionary outreach.[12] Meanwhile, the recognition of the ecological witness of Native American religions and cultures and the introduction of Native American values and practices in the context of Christian worship are a beginning of mutuality.[13]

For a long time, the agenda of globality and mutuality for African-Americans has been part of the political, social, cultural, and economic struggles in the United States. Mutuality has also reached the fields of religion, church, theology, and theological education.[14] In spite of so many shortcomings in the process, we are already gathering the first-fruits of learning from each other. After the indispensable start with self-identity and confrontation, we are moving to a multi-racial mutuality that can bring us closer to the global dimensions of the kingdom of God.[15]

In the same way, it is time for North American theological educators to be mutual about the Hispanic component in church history, mission, worship, and theology. Hispanics are not only newcomers and migrants; they were in North America before the Pilgrims or the British colonies as Spanish names from Florida to California and Colorado testify: Spanish-speaking colonies "included more than half of what used to be Mexico and more than double the territory of the United States."[16] Hispanics are in North America to stay as part of our global context and as mutual partners in mission. Church historian Justo González notes:

The roots of Hispanics in this country are old and deep. . . . Hispanic Americans have been here for so long and yet they keep their identity, that it is rather doubtful that they will follow the same process of assimilation by which the Swedes, Irish, and Italians have joined the mainstream of American society. Especially now that there is an increasing awareness of the values of one's culture and traditions, it seems safe to predict that Hispanic Americans will be around *mañana* and for as many *mañanas* as it pleases God to grant this country.[17]

To be mutual with the Hispanic-Americans as well as with Native Americans, African-Americans, and other ethnic-Americans means to be inclusive in our seminaries not only in the curriculum, but also in student and faculty recruitment and training where Hispanics and other minorities are part of the "under-represented constituencies."[18] Issues of under-representation have emerged in the early explorations of globalization in theological education.

Mutuality with the Submerged Majority

Mutuality holds great potential for the present trend to incorporate feminist or womanist perspectives in our courses and other educational events. Women are not a marginalized minority either in society or the church but a submerged majority. There is an amazing increase in the number of women in seminary student bodies; with not a few strains the number in faculties is increasing gradually.

For mutuality to be effective, however, increasing numbers or imposing quotas is not enough. What we need is the women's perspective at all levels. In this case, the obstacle to mutuality is androcentrism, the "mind-set or attitude in which the male is understood as the human norm and the female is generally rendered invisible behind the human (male) norm."[19]

I have always invited women teachers to my courses to bring their views on our subject and to introduce the class to the growing feminist perspective. As a Christian male, I continue to be re-educated by a process of their sharing and my reading. And yet, beyond the personal benefits of sharing with women, it is essential for the globalization of theological education to incorporate women's perspectives in the curriculum and in the methodology of theological education. I believe, for instance, that we cannot do without women's perspectives in such a crucial area as hermeneutics.[20] I must confess that after being enlightened by feminist hermeneutics I can no longer read the Bible without realizing the explicit or submerged implications of women's perspectives in the Scripture. The same is true with theology.[21]

Mutuality with the submerged majority is not a matter of an input here or there from a colleague, a student, or a book. Mutuality means incorporating the world view of women in our own global view.

Mutuality with the Excluded Majority

At a deeper level, mutuality in globalization demands that we take seriously the perspective of the poor. The poor are the true majority on a global scale. Their numbers are increasing with the "new order" under the powerful grip of the materially, industrially, technologically, and financially rich of the world. The poor are the vast majority in the so-called Third World or Two-Thirds World, but their numbers are increasing in affluent countries such as the United States.

They are the "excluded ones." They are excluded from the projections of expanding industry, technology, and banking profits; from the politics of neo-liberal regimes; and from the global strategy of the transnationalization of the markets. And it may be that they are also "the excluded ones" from our own missionary visions, our global theologizing, and our globalization schemes for theological education.

Inside that huge mass of those excluded from the banquet of life are some of the fastest growing Christian churches in the world and the multi-millions who profess the living religions of India, Southeast Asia, and the Moslem world. What is their place in our global perspective? What is God's purpose with the six billion on our planet? What is their place in the kingdom of God? What is God doing among the poor of the earth? What is the church supposed to do? What would be the meaning of mutuality in relation to "the excluded ones"?

Fumitaka Matsuoka gives a blunt answer to this last question in relation to the globalization of theological education in North America when he says:

> The dynamics of theological pluralism would not become a driving force of theological education unless a *partisan treatment of the marginalized* is intentionally realized *in curriculum as well as in the make up of faculty, staff, students, and board.* Unless the objects of signification, women, people of color, and other disadvantaged people of North American societies become the primary signifiers in theological education, the tenacity of our accustomed way of education would most likely remain intact. Globalization will not reach the foundation of theological education (emphasis added).[22]

We are beginning to realize that this counterparadigm of solidarity in particularity that we are calling mutuality will not be easy. Mark Kline Taylor and Gary J. Bekker point to the particular captivity of theological educators:

> In short, theological educators who use the vocabulary of "globalization" occupy a social location that (1) is politically privileged both in respect to the world context and within North American society, (2) is economically affluent to the point of having the wealth that gives access to world travel and comparative analysis, (3) is steeped in an accompanying socio-psychological tension constituted by the contradiction between an awareness of global need and interdependence and an inability by themselves to address the needs of the global context, and (4) is theologically troubled by the demands to rethink the relationship between universality and particularity.[23]

Mutuality Is Humility in Hermeneutics

Captivity by social location has been particularly present in the interpretation of the Scriptures in the hands of the non-poor of the world, as Norman K. Gottwald fully recognizes.[24] Mutuality in hermeneutics means to read the Bible in dialogue with those who are different and on the other side of the world. As Robert McAfee

Brown puts it, "We must be in dialogue not only with the Bible, but also with Christians in other parts of the world who read the Bible in a very different way."[25] This posture and exercise may appear threatening, but they can lead to a trip of discovery in mutuality.[26]

Max Stackhouse sees the need for a "humble confidence" as the basic posture of theological education today.

> Humility also means subjecting one's faith, one's scholarly work, one's teaching and preaching, one's hermeneutical principles, and one's most precious loyalties to tests that one cannot control — to the judgment and evaluations not only of peers, but of peoples who share little or nothing of one's religious commitments, gender, class, race, culture, or civilizational history.[27]

Can we find a better description of mutuality than this "humble confidence" and this humility as we subject our theological education to the test of the "peoples who share little or nothing" of what we have?

Elsa Tamez, a Mexican theologian who teaches at the Seminario Biblico Latinoamericano in Costa Rica, highlights this "humble confidence" of the majority of the "excluded ones" in her doctoral dissertation, "Justification by Faith Today in Latin America." She has come to the conclusion that to understand Paul's gospel of justification by faith we have to see it in relationship to the "excluded ones." Taking this hermeneutical key, she looks at the excluded ones in the Latin American world and discovers that for them justification by faith means no less than the "affirmation of life." And in this mutuality with the "excluded ones" she finds the basis for her theological reconstruction.[28]

Mutuality in the Classroom

Mutuality in the search for globality necessitates including in the classroom students not only from different parts of the world and ethnic and gender groups, but also from different sectors of our surrounding society. In this microcosm of the pluralistic world, students can learn from each other. We had an example of student inclusiveness in a truly pioneer course entitled "Ministry in the Global Context" at the School of Theology at Claremont, California, under the leadership of Dr. Dean Freudenberger. The purpose of the course was the preparation of future ministers to work in the global (multi-racial, multi-ethnic, multi-cultural) context of California and similar places in the United States. I was invited as one of the co-teachers to bring a Hispanic perspective and component in the course; the director of Black Studies was to do the same from his black perspective; a rabbi was invited to contribute from his Jewish tradition.

I believe that the experience was very good for all of those involved in this learning process. But I have the feeling that this type of experience was not mutual enough. Maybe what I am going to say is unfair because the course and the spirit were truly global-oriented, but my impression is that we (the Hispanic, the Black, the Jew) were there to account for our particularity (or peculiarity?) in a way that the others (the WASPS?) were not called to do. When I asked one of the students about her cultural identity, she answered, "I am a Southern Californian." I was left asking myself, "Is this all there is to one's cultural identity?"

Is it possible that in courses such as this, with input from different cultural or ethnic groups, the assumption is that those belonging to the dominant culture are the norm and the rest are the exceptions who need to explain and justify themselves? When we are trying to be global in our theological education, in intercultural courses, why don't we ask the members of the Anglo-Saxon culture or tradition why they are ethnically and culturally different from others?

Fumitaka Matsuoka has a prophetic word to say about the need for solidarity and mutuality in the midst of our particularities:

> Those who feel the pain of their own particularities in the plurality of our societies are the ones who will have the courage to enter into the realm of the unknown. . . . The liberation necessarily involves becoming particular, one component in the full mosaic that is humankind—becoming particular in such a way that this particularity cannot be what it is unless others are equally present in the historical space that is human liberation.[29]

This is the way we are—naturally ethnocentric. And this is the reason why to become global we need a conversion. We are not different from the Jews, calling all the others "gentiles," or the Greeks, calling all the others "barbarians." It takes conversion to enter into the global world of Christ in whom "there is neither Jew nor Greek, neither slave nor free, neither male nor female; for you are all one in Christ" (Gal. 3:28). Ethno-theology may be necessary and unavoidable, but it must be conscious, through mutuality, as a genuine component of a global church, a global gospel, and a global humanity.

Mutual Self-Discovery by Immersion

Our natural ethnocentricity is part of the rationale behind the immersion method, exposing groups to new contexts and moving them beyond their usual location and perspective to enter "the world of the other." The discovery of our cultural identity is one of the most meaningful experiences in traveling seminars or immersion trips abroad. We discover who we are in the process of trying to understand who the others are and why they are the way they are.

Often discovery of our cultural identity or theological perspective comes by contrast with the host culture and with the hosts' contextual theology. People have different color, different language, different priorities and styles of life, different forms of living their faith. We are surrounded by unfamiliar sights, sounds, and smells. And our hosts' difference helps us (the guests) to realize our difference. In that environment, the hosts are the norm and we (the visitors) are the exception called to explain our particularity!

Sometimes this experience provokes shock and confusion to those sincerely trying to be responsive to the exposure. Members of a Pilot Immersion Project seminar to Brazil visited a very poor waterfront area in Rio de Janeiro. During a group evaluation session which followed the visit, a North American student blurted out, "Why is it so shocking? What am I going to do? How to respond? I feel like disintegrating"—and she then broke into tears. At times an immersion experience is traumatic, but most of the time it leads to a process of learning and self-discovery.

Self-discovery also comes by affinity, through the realization of our common humanity. In that same evaluation session in Rio de Janeiro, another student from the United States, the daughter of a migrant worker, referred to the sight of a rat swimming on the waterfront. She said, "Migrant workers, going from one place to the other, in provisional homes, know about rats visiting you during the night. You have to cover your face with the blanket in order to keep them from walking on your face while you sleep. I know about that, and I know what God has done for me — the divine pull to life in Christ."

Mutual Epiphany!

This immersion seminar took place in Brazil during Epiphany season. Epiphany is God's manifestation to humanity in the human Jesus. I reminded the group of the experience of the Magi as a paradigm of what we were going through. The wise men (and the affluent ones) from the East were also in a global pursuit to find, following the stars, the Savior of humanity for whom they were taking gifts out of their riches and wisdom. They had to find their way through other countries and other cultures and descend to the humble conditions of the manger in Bethlehem in that out-of-the-route "Third World" country. Their expectations were fulfilled, but not in the way they expected: *they had to find God in common humanity*. The Magi might have thought this was condescension on their part, but the story in the gospel stresses God's condescension to them: the free gift of Epiphany!

So, globalization in education also means self-discovery through mutuality. We are simultaneously at the giving and at the receiving end. We meet God in others' human hands and faces, and they meet God in us. We become epiphanies to each other!

The seminaries involved in the Pilot Immersion Project agreed to plan "local immersions" to follow the immersions abroad with an expectation of self-discovery through affinity and contrast and conversion through the change of location. And there at home, those engaged in this venture will discover the same challenge to learn, to share, to avoid paternalism, and to resist the temptation to use others for their own growth in experience and wisdom. Here again is the challenge to mutuality.[30]

Mutuality in Student Exchange

In the light of what has been said and done, it may be a truism to say that the exchange of students from the North to the South, from the South to the North, and between different cultures is of paramount importance. Receiving students from the whole world and sending researchers and candidates to other countries has a long tradition in North America. To come to the United States as a student in theological education or any other area has been the dream of hundreds of thousands who apply for visas at USA consulates around the globe.

Today, education is and is going to be global: the world is the university. But student exchange is available only for a few.[31] It is expensive to travel and study in another country. Theological institutions are always short of endowments and scholarships for students in their own country, and mutuality demands thoughtful provisions and sharing.

There is also the risk of de-contextualized education, taking the students "apart from their people," as in the case study, as well as the risk of students or teachers being co-opted by the host country, church, or institution. But in a global approach risk is inevitable. It has to be calculated and carefully handled. Seminaries and scholarship commissions have discovered, for instance, that it is better to postpone study abroad until students have finished the first degree in their own country. It is then important for students to keep links with their home countries, their families, and church, and reduce to a minimum the time spent abroad. This consideration is especially true if the international standard of living is out of proportion to the student's home environment.

Mutuality between Institutions

One of the most encouraging developments in theological education at the international level is the growing exchange between seminaries and schools through traveling study groups and a regular exchange of students. A problem arises, however, with reaching mutuality when the economic and academic resources are so disparate.

As a former president of the Seminario Biblico Latinoamericano in Costa Rica, I had the opportunity to participate in the development of student exchange with some of the leading seminaries in the United States. One important item was the recognition of subjects and grades by the sending and receiving institutions. Another agreement was that the receiving institution would provide tuition, room, and board for the guest student in reciprocity for the same provisions in the sending institution. Because of the difference in the economic situation of persons and institutions in the United States and Costa Rica, this reciprocity was not precisely mutual.

It was an honor and privilege for the seminary in Costa Rica to receive students from Europe, who came with scholarships to pay for all their expenses, and from North America. However, we had to limit the number of visiting students because in our small classes a sizable group of students from the First World would change the dynamics of the course in terms of language, lifestyle, and so on. In addition, we did not have enough accommodations for both First World students and those coming from other Latin American countries.

Similar limitations apply to receiving study and immersion groups from the North. Central American seminaries cannot possibly receive all the groups wanting to have an experience in Central America because of limited premises, personnel, and the structures necessary to provide lodging, food, teachers, groups with which to interact, and arrangements for visits with authorities, churches, and to cultural places. A whole year would not be enough just for that kind of service. However, even with these problems, reciprocal exchange is essential.

While some seminaries in the North are already taking serious steps to include a period abroad as part of theological education for all their students, they may find that there are not enough partner seminaries for all! Mutuality requires seminaries in the North to be specifically careful not to use the rest of the world (so to say) for the sake of their global education![32] Seminaries in the North and South need to be sensible and imaginative from the very beginning as they develop potential partnerships in *mutual consultation*.

It has been suggested to the ATS Task Force on Globalization that an issue of *Theological Education* be dedicated to feed-back from the seminaries abroad that have been partners in exchange experiences with North American seminaries. These contributions could provide important hints for the next steps in mutuality.

Mutuality in Faculty Exchange

Since early missionary times, the West has shared with the rest of the world its human resources, not only for ministry in the church but also and especially in theological education. Most of the Third World seminaries were started with Western faculty from the sending churches and boards.

In the last few decades we have witnessed an increased interest in North Atlantic seminaries, especially in North America, in having resident faculty from the Third World not only for specialization programs or additional degrees, but also for teaching in those seminaries. Many of the visiting faculty members have become permanent faculty in the North—a mixed blessing. While contributing to "globalization" in North American seminaries, these faculty are in fact depriving seminaries in their own countries from benefiting from their own specialty or global vision. Here again we see the effect of the asymmetry between the First World and Two-Thirds World. Theological faculty become part of the "brain drain" toward the First World, which can offer economic compensation, social recognition, and other gratifications, including freedom to teach that may be lacking at home, which many Two-Thirds World countries cannot match.

This disparity is not the fault of the inviting institutions or the accepting faculty; it is part of the disparity in our world, a global phenomenon. Additional dimensions to be considered by Third World faculty are personal vocational and/or family options. Seminaries in the North face real challenges as they try to be mutual in the process of globalization of faculty.

One way to compensate for a permanent "drain" from the Third World is for seminaries in the North to continue to share their faculty resources with the rest of the world in the new terms and conditions of a "post-colonial," global world. There continue to be places for missionary faculty to serve under churches and seminaries abroad for long or short terms.

The sabbatical period, a blessing not very common in the Southern hemisphere, may be a very creative area for mutuality in globalization. Surely there is room in the Two-Thirds World for sabbatical periods of faculty from the First World! At first sight a "Southern sabbatical" may not appear to be as academically attractive as a sabbatical in the traditional academic centers of Europe. But it can be very rewarding in terms of a global experience and a global perspective which will enrich teaching at home.

A significant problem for many in the North is the language barrier. Students and faculty going to North America must work in English, but English-speaking faculty who have worked with other modern languages useful for the trade such as German or French and who are willing to teach abroad for a period are not always willing nor do they always have the time to learn the language of a country in the South. They must often limit their teaching to countries where English is used at least at the university level. It takes real determination and political will to do what some seminaries in the United States are doing: they are engaging the faculty in the study of Spanish, which will be an asset at home as well as abroad. To learn another language is a concrete form of incarnation and solidarity – a first step in mutuality.

May God give us as students, faculty, and administrators the spiritual depth, the theological vision, and the concreteness in action in Paul's koinonia paradigm!

CASE STUDY[33]

Apart from His People

The Reverend Anthony Robinson slowly stood up from the conference table, gathered the papers before him, and put these into his briefcase as he once again addressed the two other men in the room. "Gentlemen, my coming to you today should not in any way be seen as a threat to leave the ordained ministry. I simply want to apprise you of the issues at hand and ask that you help me struggle creatively with the most responsible alternatives to this dilemma."

After Tony Robinson left, George Howard, leader of a Protestant denomination in Jamaica and member of the seminary board of trustees, and Edward Aimes, senior pastor of a large church in Kingston, talked for over two hours. Anthony's dilemma was complex. The three-year contract with his first parish would be up in just four months. According to Anthony, his middle class congregation seemed only concerned with the "pomp and ceremony of worship and with maintaining the status quo." Tony had said, "The preaching and the verbal approach don't seem to affect the lives of my members."

It was largely for this reason, as well as his deep social concern, that Tony tried first to be an example to his congregation. He had told the two men, "I have worked diligently in the poverty areas of Kingston to declare Christ's love for these people, and yet my church doesn't really seem to care. I continue to work alone. I have brought some of the boys from the slums into the church only to be told by the officers, 'We don't want that type around here.' I have to go through the church board for everything I do, and now the members have voted that I am not to use any of my church hours in the slums. I am failing in the areas of Christian witness that I think are the most important."

In addition to being committed to the ministry of the church, Anthony Robinson was a gifted pianist. The extension masters degree course he was taking with the Royal College of Music in London had gone exceptionally well, and he had been encouraged by a faculty member to pursue music as a full-time vocation. However, Tony stated that it would be "immoral" to renounce his vows of ordination to the ministry. He continued to feel a definite call to alleviate the crying social needs of those Jamaicans in the slums of Kingston. Yet this calling was the area of his greatest pain and frustration.

Tony had concluded by saying, "There are simply no viable government or social agencies that can give these people a sense of personal dignity and worth. The church is the best vehicle to bring about change. Yet it is extremely difficult for me to continue in a ministry with this sense of failure. The church board has also expressed displeasure with my second job. But I must support myself in some way, and my music seems to be the only option."

After Anthony had left, George Howard and Edward Aimes began to discuss the situation. Rev. Aimes was noticeably upset. "George, if I've said it once, I've said it a thousand times. It's a mistake to allow these young men to study abroad with our support and blessings. Needless to say, I appreciate the kind of academic education they receive there. But once they have been exposed to the stimulation of highly technical cultures and the creature comforts that our churches simply can't afford, we've lost them for any effective ministry here on the island.

"Our membership is predominantly from a struggling middle class. The poverty of thousands in our midst is downright threatening to those who have just begun to 'make it.' Anthony has been exposed to the social conscience and liberation theology of professors from the North and South American middle class who are secure enough to risk reaching out to those who need help. Well, our church members aren't there now, and the role of a responsible pastor is to serve the needs of his congregation, not impose alien theology on them. Our churches have a hard enough time supporting a pastor, and the denomination does not have enough funds to support a ministry in the slum areas.

"Anthony is one of the brightest and most capable young men to enter the ministry in a number of years. But after five years and two advanced degrees, one in the United States and another in Brazil, he's simply over-educated and can no longer relate to the needs of his own people. I think we ought seriously to consider not letting any more of our young men study abroad."

"Now hold on a minute, Ed," George Howard cut in. "Some of your points are valid, but you're getting carried away. We have to see Tony's situation and that of each young pastor on an individual basis. I feel Tony's frustration with his position is related to the expectations he developed abroad, but that is only part of the issue. I fully agree that a painful number of our church people admit no social consciousness at all, but I see that as a challenge rather than an accepted fact. On top of that, by standards of comparison, especially to the United States, our ministers are paupers, and yet our living costs are relatively high. You and I both know that a good number of our pastors have second jobs to supplement their incomes, as do many of the Protestant pastors in Brazil. Tony is one of the few to be criticized for doing that."

Ed intervened, "That criticism is justified. Most of the pastors have taken on very quiet jobs in tutoring or other work at home. But Anthony had been playing the piano three nights a week in one of those exclusive tourist clubs. I know his deacons are divided on the issue. Some said it was necessary even though Tony didn't have a family to support. But there are just as many who feel that it is openly sinful for him to go into those dens of iniquity and profit from them. He has spoken to us about being an 'example,' and that's a very poor one for him to set for his congregation.

"I realize that he supported himself overseas quite well with his piano, but both the United States and Brazil have freer cultures than ours. Many of the parishioners and church officers who have been disturbed about his second job are the same ones who are upset about Anthony's programs in the ghetto. These people don't understand what Anthony means when he says that we should be 'in the world, but not of it.' For the most part, our church people are conservative, both theologically and socially. But that is who we are, and we as pastors must minister to those people."

George Howard sighed. "Edward, I know that's who we are, and I for one am a bit disturbed by that fact. I think Tony is young; he may be expecting too much too soon. But it is just this kind of infusion of theological ideas, an enthusiasm to apply the gospel to our daily lives, that Tony brings to us through his experiences abroad. We must help protect those visions rather than chastise him for them.

"I realize that since our independence, an increasing sense of national pride dictates that we train all our young men in our own seminaries. You and I both received some training abroad, and we both know our seminaries have some inadequacies. I don't think our pride should get in the way of wanting our clergy to be as well prepared for the ministry as possible. I realize that Tony Robinson's case is not an exception, but a good number of those pastors trained abroad do return and readjust to fruitful and innovative ministries."

"Our pride is not the point," Edward Aimes responded. "It's the possibility of losing a good man like Anthony. It doesn't matter how well a scholar can parse a Hebrew verb. If he grows so culturally apart from his people that he can't relate the gospel to them in the area of their understanding, that kind of training is useless."

"Well, Ed," George broke in, "I don't see how we can solve that one today. What we have to work on now is what concrete suggestions we can give to Anthony about his future ministry in the church."

TEACHING NOTE

Apart from His People

I. Goals

This case works well in both academic and parish situations. The teaching note is designed for either.

1. Explore the mutual benefits and obligations of seminary education in North/ South or South/South exchanges. Consider appropriate candidate selection, preparation for study abroad, and re-entry processes for international exchange students.

2. Examine approaches for denominational and seminary leaders to best equip students for faithful and effective ministries that cross class and cultural lines.

II. Opening

Ask participants to consider privately their own class or social location. Ask what factors they considered to distinguish their class (e.g., education, speech, finances, profession, etc.). How can one's social location affect his or her role in North American society? In the church? Should the church be concerned with issues of class? Why or why not?

III. Identify the Persons in the Case

George Howard
Edward Aimes
Leaders of Tony's congregation
Anthony (Tony) Robinson
Boys "from the slum areas"

1. What is each person's major concern about Tony's ministry in the congregation and slum areas?

2. What are their views about theological education for future candidates?

3. Give special attention to the feelings of each as well as to what he or she thinks should be done.

IV. Consideration of Changes for More Faithful and Effective Ministry

A. Jamaican Theological Education

1. What are the advantages and disadvantages of a North/South versus a South/South exchange experience?

2. What responsibilities do host seminaries in the North or South have when inviting candidates from developing countries? What specific guidelines would be helpful for the Jamaican, North American, and Brazilian seminaries Tony attended?

3. What kind of socio-cultural and economic analysis should be provided by seminaries?

4. What kind of training across class lines or in multi-cultural ministry would be helpful for ministerial candidates?

5. How would you respond to Edward Aimes's concerns about sending ministerial candidates overseas to study?

B. Congregations

1. What were the probable expectations Tony's congregation had for him before he arrived? How can pastors and congregations develop realistic expectations of one another? What role can the seminary play in the process?

2. Consider why a middle class congregation resists mission to slum areas. What models of education for social justice ministry might be helpful for this congregation? Explore indirect as well as direct, experiential means of introducing congregations to ministry in the inner city.

C. Pastoral Leadership

1. What skills in and approaches to conflict management might help Tony in the leadership of his congregation?

2. A significant number of clergy in the Two-Thirds World and an increasing number in North America are in tent-making ministries or hold second jobs to support their ministries. Examine the implications of this factor for clergy and congregations. What advice would you give Tony about his night club job?

V. Identify Resources of Grace

What resources can Tony, the congregation, and seminary and church leaders draw on as they respond to Tony and develop a long-term mission strategy for the congregation?

Consider as illustrative resources:

1. Experience of Jamaican pastors who have successfully made a cross-cultural transfer from overseas to home;

2. Biblical study by congregation and conference on issues of church and society;

3. A consultant to work with the congregation, Tony, and the denomination on expectations and strategies for ministry;

4. Models of field education that bridge the distances between middle-class congregations and poor communities;
5. Children from the slum areas;
6. Prayer, Eucharist, and biblical reflection in situations which cross class lines.

COMMENTARY

Apart from His People

HENRY S. WILSON

Introduction

In today's world people's consciousness about their self-dignity and self-worth has been raised through various programs of empowerment. This empowerment in turn has led to the search for living and being in a way which is more authentic to one's self both individually and collectively. In other words, we are increasingly becoming conscious of the plurality in our world and are creating a space for the same. Simultaneously, through the massive commercialized network of communication and the operation of multi-national corporations, people from different parts of the world are drawn closer to an environment of a "global village" dominated by the cultural manifestation of the industrialized/computerized North.

The Christian community, being part of the larger human community, is affected by such developments. The Christian community has begun to look critically into its own doctrinal formulations, ecclesiastical practices, and training for young people through theological seminaries/colleges. The case, "Apart from His People," touches the issue of theological education and ministerial practices appropriate to the changing environment. One will not be in a position to deal fully with theological education without also looking into the prevailing doctrine of ministry and the rite of ordination as well as ecclesiastical structures. However, since our concern here is about a particular incident of theological education and ministerial practice, we will limit ourselves to the focus of the case.

A Glimpse at the Pattern of the Post-Colonial Era

In many of the so-called "younger" churches in the Southern hemisphere, a shift in leadership in theological education took place about a generation ago along with the dismantling of colonial systems and other types of local/national government interventions. Such changes in several nations came unexpectedly, and there was not time for serious thinking about ministerial training and the development of patterns appropriate to each context. For example, it is said that in 1964 when the overseas missionaries were to leave Sudan, there were only four trained local pastors in the Presbyterian Church of the Sudan. In a case such as this, it is natural for a church to try to keep the available personnel and financial infrastructure for ministerial training, that is, residential seminaries, under missionary patronage and support. These theological institutions were so dependent on missionary leadership and management that various deteriorations took place.

To offset such difficulties national church bodies in the North sent qualified individuals to seminaries overseas in the hope that once there were enough qualified local persons, the training could be organized locally. In countries where national movements had a firm grip on people, training national leadership locally was strongly advocated. Therefore, one could easily understand George Howard's statement in the case study: "I realize that since our independence, an increasing sense of national pride dictates that we train all our young men in our own seminaries. You and I both received some training abroad, and we both know our seminaries have some inadequacies. I don't think our pride should get in the way of wanting our young men to be as well prepared for ministry as possible."

This arrangement was also welcomed by the churches overseas, especially in the North, who had bilateral relationships with churches in the South. Some of the missionary societies/boards were taken by surprise by the rapid political changes in the South. These groups were confronted by the fact of missionary domination which prevented adequate leadership development. Churches in the North were challenged to help in the leadership training of Christians in the South. Consequently, many church leaders from the South were trained in the North and then called to give leadership in the seminaries and theological faculties of their respective countries. These leaders, having consciously or unconsciously appropriated the models for theological education of the North, began introducing such models in their own national context. In several cases, that meant rejuvenating the models introduced by missionaries in the past. But in the context of newly independent churches in the South, the needed financial resources could not be raised to maintain programs of theological training comparable to those in the North. These financial limitations forced a rethinking of the theological education model.

The financial dependency of many Christian bodies had a long history and a negative effect on the churches in the South. The late Dr. S. L. Parmar of India explained it as follows:

We have inherited a tradition of being cared for and provided for by mission organizations. Over the years the form has changed, structures have been reshaped, but an attitude of dependence persists. Our thinking is affected by this welfare-trap legacy. We continue to expect others to do what we should be doing for ourselves. This has weakened considerably the movement towards genuine autonomy and indigenization.[34]

In some countries the residential model must be replaced by the extension model. Extension education was developed in order to cut down the enormous financial cost, as well as to equip persons theologically without dislocating them from their usual living environment.

Even when attempts were made to develop new models of theological education, the training that persons received in the North constrained their thinking about new models. I recall an incident of debating appropriate models for a doctor of theology program for South Asia. The debate among the church leaders and the theological educators soon demonstrated how individuals' positions were firmly based on the theological education model under which they had received their training, that is, either North American, British, or European (mainly German). At certain points the debate centered around bringing together these three models with some South Asian flavor. Of course, there is no such thing as a South Asian model of theological education. Even the secular education in South Asia is very much a continuation of what the British introduced during the colonial period, although it has undergone some revision in the course of years. Through different experiments which are taking place now, we have to develop our own model in the South. It is at this stage of experimentation, however, that one gets into certain difficulties with local church leadership. Because of their training or formation, many church leaders may be familiar and comfortable with the model inherited from the missionary past. In this context one has to raise the question whether theological education overseas, especially in the North, is helpful.

South to South exchange is another channel for strengthening ministerial formation in our time. Since there are many commonalities among countries in the South which are seeking an appropriate theological education model, should not the ever-shrinking financial resources available for theological education be used for enhancing South to South exchange? Even though such attempts are encouraged by ecumenical organizations, a few missionary societies/boards, and churches, as far as I know such exchanges are far too few compared to the South-North exchange of theological students and faculties. The comparable proximity in socioeconomic situations of the countries in the South will certainly facilitate more authentic mutual learning and development of a sense of solidarity for transforation of the present general situation in the South. In this context of South-South exchange, if there is participation by the North, the quest for globalization of theological education in the North may find more challenge than just from the South-North exchange.

Since theological training in the North is shaped according to the needs in the North, the candidates from the South will have certain disadvantages unless careful planning is done to rearrange their program of study. This is especially true if the candidate travels to the North for basic theological training. To that extent Edward Aimes's statement is relevant: "It doesn't matter how well a scholar can parse a Hebrew verb. If he grows so culturally apart from his people that he can't relate the gospel to them in the area of their understanding, that kind of training is useless." That is one of the reasons why many ecumenical scholarship agencies follow the policy of sponsoring theological students at the postgraduate level only. Seminaries in the North should be guided by this concern in their recruitment and admission of both students and faculty from institutions of the South.

However, having basic theological education in the South is not a guarantee that the candidates will be more culturally/contextually oriented. Their orientation very much depends on the type of theological institution where the candidate receives the training as well as the orientation of the candidate selected for theological training. One can categorize theological seminaries/schools in the South into two groups. In the first group are seminaries belonging to the mainline Protestant denominations. In recent years those seminaries have tried to move in the path of ecumenism, either creating united theological seminaries or forming regional associations of theological seminaries for mutual interaction and cooperation. In such united seminaries and/or associations of theological seminaries attempts are also made to relate students to their contextual situation: religious, cultural, socio-political, and economic. In the second group are seminaries belonging to conservative-evangelical churches. Since the 1970s, these churches or groups which did not seriously consider formally training candidates in the past started theological seminaries to prepare leadership in their own churches. Theological orientation in such seminaries tends to reflect the orientation of their Northern partners located in Europe, North America, Australia, New Zealand, and even in some economically rich Asian countries. Since these two broad groupings reflect a global division, this issue of cultural/contextual orientation cannot easily be solved by churches in the South alone.

In spite of several studies that have already been undertaken on the subject "Gospel and Culture," church leaders gathered for the Assembly of the World Council of Churches at Canberra in February 1992 discussed the issue of gospel and culture very vehemently and authorized further reflection on this subject leading to the next Assembly. The prospects and limits of relating faith to one's culture will remain with us as they were with the early Christians. Since culture is in constant evolution, theological education has not only to address it, but also to equip candidates to cope with it. Therefore contextualization which will include even globalization will remain a challenge in the foreseeable future.

Appropriate Theological Education

President George Howard and senior pastor Edward Aimes are concerned about whether the theological education Reverend Anthony Robinson received overseas was in itself a hindrance. They do not completely write off the usefulness of the education Tony had in the United States and Brazil, where he spent five years and earned two advanced degrees. But their concern is about the way in which Tony involved himself in the ministry and his impatience or frustration with his middle class congregation. The matter which does not seem to bother them is whether theological education is intended for "domestication" or "transformation" of an individual. If a candidate is in some ways transformed through his theological studies at home or abroad, such transformation is bound to be reflected in the ministry he or she is going to do.

Serious reflection on ministerial training has brought several changes in theological education, even when carried out as a residential program. The focus of theological training was meant not only to meet the spiritual needs of the people, but also to work toward transformation of socio-political, economic structures which reduce millions of people, Christians and others, to a dehumanized situation. M. M. Thomas's book, *Salvation and Humanisation*,[35] is an example of the thinking in mission and ministry which has influenced theological education since the 1960s. The theological education I underwent in the late 1960s included not only participating in church activities such as conducting worship, Christian education, youth work, and so on, but also participating for a period in organizations committed to socio-political change, development, and programs of empowering oppressed and marginalized persons. Even though two decades ago such involvements were introduced as part of ministerial training, when such insights gained through theological training are put into practice, there is usually a confrontation between leadership in the church and daring individuals such as Tony.

The issue in the case may not be so much that Tony is alienated from his culture, but that Tony is unwilling to compromise with middle class values. Tony feels uncomfortable with the status quo nature of the congregation he is serving.

The middle class congregation, especially those members who, as Rev. Aimes expresses it, "have just begun to 'make it,' " may be holding to a success-oriented theology which interprets poverty as a kind of divine retribution to those who are not favored by God. Such a theology prevails in many quarters and is one of the serious heretical teachings which "well-to-do" Christians find very difficult to overcome. Tony, like several other pastors in different contexts who challenge such a theology, is doing good rather than damage to Christian theology.

In many situations one observes the tendency to separate pastoral ministry from a ministry to meet the social needs of the people, Christians and others. Expecting the pastor to serve only the needs of the congregation indicates a limited understanding of pastoral ministry. Pastoral ministry is there to equip the whole congregation for its mission in the world, of which social justice is very much a part. The Christians in Kingston can't be blind to the social needs of the people in the slums of Kingston. Tony's way of thinking is very much part of the theological reflection in some institutions of the developing countries in the South. Much of the impetus for such thinking has come from liberation theologies of Latin America and other Third World theologies and is increasingly becoming an element in the curriculum of seminaries in the North. So the impression of Rev. Howard and Rev. Aimes that Tony's involvement in social issues is because he was exposed overseas to social consciousness and liberation theology only exposes their provincialism.

They seem to be out of touch with the emerging understanding of ministry in different parts of the world. Such emerging understanding tries to see pastoral ministry as equipping each of the local congregations for evangelistic and social involvement mission in a given context. One can say that this exchange exposes the generation gap between the leaders of Tony's church and Tony. This generation gap might have also contributed to the theological gap. One is reminded of the in-service training and continuing education for pastors which attempt to bridge this theological gap.

Some Emerging Issues in Ministry

Tony's conclusion that there are no viable government or social agencies that can perform the function of bettering the quality of life in the slums and that the church is the best vehicle to bring about change should be taken with some caution. In the recent past the churches in many Third World countries have taken responsibility for social development. But when such developments are undertaken primarily through financial and program thrusts from the donor countries in the North, the churches in the South fall victims to the process of Non-Governmental Organizations (NGOs). Many development projects are supported by finances channeled through special departments of the churches and bar congregations from getting involved in social ministry. In some cases, managing the money, personnel, and projects so occupies the church departments for development that they hardly have time to engage congregations in social programs. This process only perpetuates the dichotomy between pastoral and social ministry.

The church board is displeased about Tony's second job. The reality of many pastors having a second job to supplement their incomes is an important emerging issue. A pastor's supplementary income is no longer a problem just for Third World churches. As the active membership of churches drops in Northern countries, this issue is also emerging there. An important consideration is whether the present model of one pastor–one congregation is the only or even the best way to organize the life of a congregation. There was a time when education was not universally available, and a trained clergy person was needed for each congregation to equip the Christians theologically. Until recently the church was also a central institution to which people turned for numerous individual and social needs. But the privileged status which institutional churches have enjoyed is fast withering away. New models of leadership and financial supports for church leadership are important issues, and Third World churches need to find their own answers. These new developments also influence the way ministers are trained and the type of curriculum which they should follow.

The inability of many denominations to provide a pastor for each single congregation has led churches to experiment with different models of pastoral care. For example, in the Church of South India, honorary presbyters and licensed preachers greatly assist full-time paid presbyters to meet pastoral needs. Part-time presbyters, who hold secular jobs for their livelihood, are theologically equipped through a series of study sessions and practical training under senior presbyters before they are ordained or commissioned by the local bishop for exercising pastoral ministry in their respective congregations or in congregations in their neighborhoods. In another experiment to supplement paid ministry, the Church of England makes use of non-stipendiary clergy who are ordained after a non-residential course of theological training.

Even when churches of the South have a full-time paid male pastor, many congregational functions such as diaconal services and Christian education programs are carried out by women. Now that the discrimination against women is being challenged in many Protestant churches, due recognition and greater involvement of women in ministry will significantly strengthen both the content and quality of pastoral care of congregations.

For centuries churches neglected to make use of the skills of women for ministry. Another area of neglect is the utilization of the talent of the laity. While churches rethink suitable ministerial training and care in the present time of social change, churches must also look into appropriate space and training for valuable lay contributions to ministry.

Conclusion

Individuals such as Tony, with or without official sponsorship, will continue to make use of opportunities available abroad for ministerial training. But that does not mean that they will all end up holding what appears to be radical theology and practice. The presence of Third World students and faculty in the seminaries of the North and increasingly in some institutions of the South committed to cross-cultural exchange will certainly have an impact on the seminary community in general and in North/South or South/South partner institutions in particular depending on the scope for interaction that is available in each context.

Changes in the South, especially in the realm of international economics, will not come about unless there are also changes in the North. Candidates from the South studying in the North may well become unsung missionaries or agents of transformation. The very fact that they ventured to study in institutions outside their cultural context speaks for a certain amount of daring independence. Further, their willingness to cope in different environments indicates that they are willing to risk and to experiment. Can ministry result in anything concrete if the element of risk is avoided? As it is sometimes said, too much preoccupation with security and status quo may be one's mortal enemy, especially for pastors. Tony is trying to resist this preoccupation, and he needs support as do many other daring younger pastors in different situations.

As with many individuals, the enthusiasm and the radical spirit one exercises while one is still young gives way to more manageable engagement as one grows older. Most mortals are subject to a natural domestication. So it is appropriate that Howard and Aimes encourage and guide Tony to achieve his Christian calling as an ordained minister since Tony is not planning to leave the ordained ministry. Howard is a realist in this case when he responds to Aimes, saying, "Tony is young; he may be expecting too much too soon. . . . We must protect those visions rather than chastise him for them."

I hope Howard will succeed in convincing Aimes and Tony's church board that pastoral and social ministries are inseparably linked. Tony and his congregation can grow together in understanding the variety of gifts each can bring to the church.

Notes

1. European theology is recognized as "situational and contextual" by Dïrk Döring and Erghard Kamphausen in their paper "EATWOT and Its Significance: A European Perspective," in Virginia Fabella and Sergio Torres, eds., *Irruption of the Third World: Challenge to Theology* (Maryknoll, NY: Orbis Books, 1983), p. 265. For a contemporary attempt on global theology, see Tissa Balasuriya, *Planetary Theology* (Maryknoll, NY: Orbis Books, 1983).

2. See the growing body of creative and challenging new theologies coming from the Ecumenical Association of Third World Theologians, edited by Sergio Torres, Virginia Fabella, and John Eagleson (Maryknoll, NY: Orbis Books): *The Emergent Gospel: Theology from the Underside of History* (1976); *African Theology en Route* (1977); *Asia's Struggle for Full Humanity* (1979); *The Challenge of Basic Christian Communities* (1980); *Irruption of the Third World: Challenge to Theology* (first overall evaluation after five years, 1981); *Doing Theology in a Divided World* (a dialogue between Third World and First World theologians in Geneva, 1983).

3. Among the mass of literature on and around the theology of liberation, two volumes provide insights, experiments, and questions from this contemporary stream of theology which are relevant for our concern with the globalization of theological education: Deane William Ferm, *Third World Liberation Theologies: An Introductory Survey* and *Third World Liberation Theologies: A Reader* (Maryknoll, NY: Orbis Books, 1986).

4. See Robert J. Schreiter, *Constructing Local Theologies* (Maryknoll, NY: Orbis Books, 1985). A sort of mutuality between "local" and "global" theologies emerges as a conclusion.

5. See, for instance, Edward Farley, *Theologia: Fragmentation and Unity of Theological Education* (Philadelphia: Fortress, 1983), and the discussion of Farley's ideas in *Theological Education* 20 (Spring 1984). See also Max Stackhouse, *Apologia: Con-*

textualization, Globalization, and Mission in Theological Education (Grand Rapids: Eerdmans, 1988).

6. For example, in Joseph C. Hough, Jr., and John B. Cobb, Jr., *Christian Identity and Theological Education* (Chico, CA: Scholars Press, 1985), and the articles on "Curriculum Development in Multicultural Theological Education" in *Theological Education* 26 (Autumn 1989).

7. See "Fundamental Issues on Globalization," *Theological Education* 26 (Spring 1990), Supplement I; and "Patterns of Globalization: Six Studies," *Theological Education* 27 (Spring 1991).

8. See José Míguez Bonino, "Global Solidarity and the Theological Curriculum," in *Global Solidarity in Theological Education: Report on the U.S./Canadian Consultation* (Geneva: World Council of Churches, 1981).

9. Fumitaka Matsuoka, "Pluralism at Home: Globalization within North America," *Theological Education* (Spring 1990), Supplement I, pp. 35-51.

10. For an example of an ecological type of theology, see John B. Cobb, Jr., and Charles T. Birch, *The Liberation of Life* (Cambridge, MA: Cambridge University Press, 1982). This type of theology includes all of life, not only the human, and stresses both globality and mutuality as suggested by the expression now in circulation, "interconnectedness."

11. See the special issue of *Concilium* on the subject, no. 26:232 (November, 1990). Cf. the National Council of Churches Governing/General Board declaration of May 16-18 from its meeting in Pittsburgh, Pennsylvania.

12. The emerging ecological conscience may help us hear the strong message from Van Deloria, Jr., in his early work *God Is Red* (New York: Dell, 1973) and his criticism of Christian missions in later works.

13. An experiment in Native American focus on theological education at the Vancouver School of Theology is described in James N. Pankratz, "Globalization Begins at Home," *Theological Education* (Spring 1991), pp. 68-86.

14. For an exciting story of theological self-identity and beginning of mutuality with other theologians, see Gayraud S. Wilmore and James H. Cone, eds., *Black Theology: A Documentary History, 1966-1979* (Maryknoll, NY: Orbis Books, 1979).

15. James Cone has given witness to his pilgrimage starting from a heavy dependence on white or Western theology to a distinctive theologizing from the black experience and then enlarging his theological reflection with the contribution of Latin American, African, and feminist liberation theologies. See James Cone, "Black Theology: Its Origin, Methodology, and Relationship to Third World Theologies," in *Doing Theology in a Divided World*, pp. 93-105.

16. Justo L. González, *Mañana: Christian Theology from a Hispanic Perspective* (Nashville, TN: Abingdon, 1990), p. 32.

17. Ibid., p. 33. For an exposure to mutuality with the "Hispanic margin," see also Virgilio P. Elizondo, *Galilean Journey: The Mexican-American Promise* (Maryknoll, NY: Orbis Books, 1983); Orlando Costas, *Christ Outside the Gate: Mission Beyond Christendom* (Maryknoll, NY: Orbis Books, 1982); Luis Rivera-Pagán, *Evangelización y Violencia: La Conquista de America* (San Juan, Puerto Rico: Ed. Cenu, 1990); and the journal *Apuntes: Reflexiones Teologicas desde el Margen Hispano* (Dallas, TX: Mexican-American Program, Perkins School of Theology, Southern Methodist University).

18. The Association of Theological Schools has created an Under-represented Constituencies Committee.

19. Joanna Dewey, "Teaching the New Testament from a Feminist Perspective," *Theological Education* (Autumn 1989), p. 87.

20. The flow of feminist literature, particularly in hermeneutics, is running "like a mighty river" these days. For the sake of space, we have to refrain from offering even an indicative list, but look for some of the names: Elsa Tamez, Elisabeth Schüssler Fiorenza, Phyllis Tribble, and some anthologies such as Wendy S. Robins, ed., *Through the Eyes of a Woman: Bible Studies on the Experience of Women* (London: World YWCA, 1986); John S. Pobee and Bárbel Von Wartenberg-Potter, eds., *New Eyes for Reading: Biblical and Theological Reflections by Women from the Third World* (Geneva: World Council of Churches, 1986).

21. There is also a growing body of feminist theological literature. Letty M. Russell and Rosemary Radford Ruether are some of the most productive writers in this area.

22. Matsuoka, p. 47

23. Mark Kline Taylor and Gary J. Bekker, "Engaging the Other in a Global Village," *Theological Education*, Supplement I, p. 56.

24. N. K. Gottwald, *The Tribes of Yahweh: A Sociology of the Religion of Liberated Israel, 1250-1050 B.C.E.* (Maryknoll, NY: Orbis Books, 1979), p. 11.

25. Robert McAfee Brown, *Unexpected News: Reading the Bible with Third World Eyes* (Philadelphia, PA: Westminster, 1984), p. 13. For a full-length reading of the Scripture through the lectionary by the poor people of an island in Nicaragua with the poet-priest Ernesto Cardenal, see his four volumes, *The Gospel from Solentiname* (Maryknoll, NY: Orbis Books, 1978-82).

26. Carlos Mesters summarizes his feelings in Bible studies with Christian Basic Communities in Brazil, "reading the Bible with the eyes of life and reading life with the eyes of the Bible," in his delightful book, *Defenseless Flower* (Maryknoll, NY: Orbis Books, 1989).

27. Stackhouse, pp. 214-15.

28. Elsa Tamez, *Contra Toda Condena: La Justificación por la Fe desde Los Excluidos* (San José, Costa Rica: DEI/SEBILA, 1991, 1a ed).

29. Matsuoka, pp. 43f.

30. For experiences of immersion and globalization at home, see "Patterns of Globalization: Six Studies," in *Theological Education* 26 (Spring 1991).

31. S. Mark Heim also recognizes this as a major question for globalization at "a global scale" in "Mapping Globalization for Theological Education," *Theological Education* (1990), Supplement I, pp. 11f.

32. "We need to be clear that the agenda of globalization that we are discussing is a very specifically Western one, addressing the contexts of theological schools in North America and their needs to attend to the whole church and the whole world. It is not something that can be franchised to other parts of the world as the model for theological education. It is not a way of escaping or minimizing our particularity. The process aims at understanding our own particularities in true relation to the wider context" (ibid., p. 12).

33. Originally published as "A Matter of Pride." Copyright © 1985 by the Case Study Institute. The names of persons and places in this case have been disguised to protect the privacy of those involved in the situation.

34. S. L. Parmar, *Towards a Creative Instability* (1968).

35. M. M. Thomas, *Salvation and Humanisation* (Madras: India: Christian Institute on the study of Religion and Society by the C.L.S., 1971).

CONTRIBUTORS

Mortimer Arias, Professor of Biblical Studies, Uruguay; former Methodist Bishop of Columbia and President of Seminario Biblico Latinoamericano, Costa Rica.

Craig L. Blomberg, Associate Professor of New Testament, Denver Baptist Seminary.

Walter Brueggemann, Professor of Old Testament, Columbia Theological Seminary.

Erskine Clarke, Professor of American Religious History; Director of International Programs, Columbia Theological Seminary.

M. Shawn Copeland, Assistant Professor of Theology and Black Studies, Yale Divinity School.

Gordon Dicker, Principal, United Theological Seminary, N.S.W., Australia.

Toinette M. Eugene, Associate Professor of Social Ethics, Garrett-Evangelical Theological Seminary.

Alice Frazer Evans, Director of Writing and Research, Plowshares Institute.

Robert A. Evans, Executive Director, Plowshares Institute.

Pierre Goldberger, Principal/Director, United Theological Seminary, Montral, Canada.

Catherine G. González, Professor of Church History, Columbia Theological Seminary.

Justo L. González, Fund for Theological Education.

Daniel J. Harrington, Professor of New Testament, Weston School of Theology.

Paul G. Hiebert, Professor and Chair of Department in Anthropology and Missions, Trinity Evangelical Divinity School.

W. L. Herzfeld, Director for Global Community, Evangelical Lutheran Church of America.

Liso Jafta, Department of Theology, Rhodes University, South Africa.

L. Shannon Jung, Director, Center for Theology and Land, Wartburg Theological Seminary and University of Dubuque Theological Seminary.

William Bean Kennedy, Skinner and McAlpin Professor of Practical Theology, Union Theological Seminary, New York.

William E. Lesher, President, Lutheran School of Theology at Chicago.

G. Douglass Lewis, President, Wesley Theological Seminary.

M. Douglas Meeks, Academic Dean, Professor of Systematic Theology and Philosophy, Wesley Theological Seminary.

365

Eleanor Scott Meyers, President, Pacific School of Religion.

Itumeleng J. Mosala, Professor of Biblical Studies, University of Cape Town, South Africa.

Heidi Hadsell, Professor of Ethics, McCormick Theological Seminary.

James N. Pankratz, President, Concord College, Winnipeg, Canada.

Harold J. Recinos, Associate Professor of Theology, Culture and Urban Ministry, Wesley Theological Seminary.

Anne Reissner, Academic Dean, Maryknoll School of Theology.

David A. Roozen, Director, Center for Social and Religious Research, Hartford Seminary.

Garth M. Rosell, Professor of Church History and Director of the Ockenga Institute, Gordon-Conwell Theological Seminary.

Robert J. Schreiter, Professor of Theology, Catholic Theological Union.

Jane I. Smith, Vice President, Dean of Academic Affairs, Iliff School of Theology.

Daniel Spencer, Assistant Professor of Theology and Ethics, Drake University.

Robert L. Stivers, Professor of Religion, Pacific Lutheran University.

Elsa Tamez, Professor of Biblical Studies and Theology, Seminario Biblico Latinoamericano, Costa Rica.

Susan Brooks Thistlethwaite, Associate Professor of Theology, Chicago Theological Seminary.

Richard F. Vieth, Professor of Systematic Theology, Lancaster Theological Seminary.

Ronald C. White, Jr., Research Scholar, The Huntington Library; Visiting Professor of History, University of Southern California.

Henry S. Wilson, Secretary of Theology, World Alliance of Reformed Churches; former Professor of Church History and Director, Board of Theological Education, India.

Barbara Brown Zikmund, President, Hartford Seminary.

Translations by

Karen Sue Hernandez, Master of Divinity Student, McCormick Theological Seminary.

F. Ross Kinsler, New Testament and Theological Education, Seminario Biblico Latinoamericano, Costa Rica.